Nicht Anlassen,
solange Motor oder Anlasser sich bewegen.
Sobald der Motor anspringt
Druckknopf loslassen.
Abblendlicht links
Abblendlicht rechts
Turm-Sicherungen
Schaltbrett-leuchte
Kraftstoff-pumpe
Steckdosen
Kraftstoffpumpe
km/h
COOLANT
Oel

MACHINES OF WAR

BW
XXX
ZK308

DK

MACHINES OF WAR

THE DEFINITIVE VISUAL HISTORY OF MILITARY HARDWARE

DK DELHI
Project editor Deeksha Saikia
Project art editor Pooja Pipil
Editorial team Smita Mathur, Charvi Arora
Art editors Amit Verma, Nidhi Rastogi, Rohit Bhardwaj
Jacket designer Dhirendra Singh
Jackets editorial coordinator Priyanka Sharma
Senior DTP designers Jagtar Singh, Rakesh Kumar, Shanker Prasad
DTP designers Rajesh Singh Adhikari
Picture researcher Surya Sankash Sarangi
Managing jackets editor Sreshtha Bhattacharya
Picture research manager Taiyaba Khatoon
Pre-production manager Balwant Singh
Production manager Pankaj Sharma
Managing editor Kingshuk Ghoshal
Managing art editor Govind Mittal

DK LONDON
Senior editor Hugo Wilkinson
Editorial assistant Amelia Collins
Jacket editor Claire Gell
Jacket design development manager Sophia MTT
Producer, pre-production David Almond
Senior producer Edward Kneafsey
Managing editor Gareth Jones
Senior managing art editor Lee Griffiths
Special sales and custom publishing manager Michelle Baxter
Art director Karen Self
Associate publishing director Liz Wheeler
Publishing director Jonathan Metcalf
Special sales and custom publishing manager Michelle Baxter

DYNAMO
Project manager Judy Caley

Historical consultant Simon Adams

Includes content previously published in *The Military History Book* in 2012, *The Motorbike Book* in 2012, *The Aircraft Book* in 2013, *Firearms* in 2014, *The Tractor Book* in 2015, *The Bicycle Book* in 2016, *Weapon* in 2016, *The Tank Book* in 2017, and *Flight* in 2017

This edition published in 2019
First published in Great Britain in 2017 by
Dorling Kindersley Limited
80 Strand, London, WC2R 0RL

10 9 8 7 6 5 4 3 2 1
001–307200–August/2019

A CIP catalogue record for this book is available from the British Library.
ISBN: 978-0-2414-2047-8

Printed in China

A WORLD OF IDEAS:
SEE ALL THERE IS TO KNOW

www.dk.com

Endpaper images: *Front:* **Dorling Kindersley:** Gary Ombler / The Tank Museum, Bovington

Contents

PRE-INDUSTRIAL WEAPONS

From the first primitive weapons fashioned out of wood and flint through to the introduction of bronze and iron weaponry and on to the first cannon.

THE INDUSTRIAL ERA: 1815–1914

The gradual replacement of swords, bayonets, and knives with pistols, rifles, and later, machine-guns, as well as the development of field artillery.

WORLD WAR I: 1914-18

A highly mechanized war of rifles, machine-guns, field guns, and howitzers, alongside the new technology of aircraft, tanks, and armoured, motorized vehicles.

BETWEEN THE WARS: 1918-39

How the lessons of World War I were applied to the development of improved rifles, machine-guns, and personal weapons, and in tanks, aircraft, and armoured cars.

WORLD WAR II: 1939-45

A global war that saw advances in the design of tractors, tanks, fighter and bomber aircraft, submarines, and artillery; the development of new bombs and missiles.

THE COLD WAR: 1945-91

The stand-off between the two superpowers, resulting in the introduction of long-range nuclear bombers and submarines, new helicopters, fighter aircraft, tanks, and other combat vehicles.

THE MODERN WORLD: 1991-PRESENT

In a period of insurgency and terrorism, how modern warfare has become increasingly technological, with unmanned drones watching from the skies and new classes of submarines patrolling the seas.

Evolution of Weapons

THE DEVELOPMENT OF ARMS and armaments is central to the story of military history. While the aims and intentions of humans at war have remained essentially the same since the dawn of civilization, the history of weaponry has been a process of near constant adaptation, reinvention, and progression, with the result that battlefield technology has grown increasingly effective, and ever more deadly.

The earliest weapons took the form of stone axes, and clubs, but, with the adoption of bronze, and then iron, these were improved, developed, and then superseded. Swords, spears, and bows dominated the field of battle from the era of Ancient Egypt and Assyria to the late Middle Ages, until the introduction of gunpowder weapons in Europe in the 14th century. This invention heralded a step-change in warfare, as human strength was aided and then all but replaced by chemical and mechanical power.

This process accelerated during the Industrial Revolution, with an exponential growth in the range and accuracy of weapon systems, both on land and at sea. In the early years of the 20th century, war became motorized with the development of the tank, and reached the skies with the invention of the aircraft, expanding the reach of military might across the globe.

The advent of the nuclear bomb, in 1945, made the prospect of full-scale conflict almost too terrible to contemplate, but it did not stop the pace of technological change in conventional arms throughout the rest of the century.

In the modern age, the increasing sophistication of smart weapons has heralded a revolution in warfare. We have now reached an era in which human combatants are slowly being replaced by computer-controlled machines.

“Whatever happens, we have **got The Maxim gun**, and they have **not.”**

HILAIRE BELLOC, IN HIS POEM, *THE MODERN TRAVELLER*, 1898

A constant theme in this book is the development of firearms. Throughout their history, firearms have had a profound effect on human activity. Created to wage war, guns soon provided a means for hunting as well as self-defence. They also helped sustain the tradition of target shooting that began with bows and arrows. From their first appearance, as simple metal tubes firing spherical balls of lead or stone propelled by burning gunpowder, to the technologically advanced weapons of today, firearms have always played a central role in warfare.

The following pages offer a beautifully illustrated account of this long, historical process, showcasing significant armaments and other military pieces across 5,000 years and a vast geographical range. However, this book - a fruitful collaboration between leading military history writers and expert consultants from specialist institutions in the US and the UK - is much more than simply a catalogue of weaponry. Seventeen of the most important and innovative weapons and vehicles are examined in detail, while accounts are presented of some of the key events in military history. To examine these pages is to understand the important role military development has played in human history.

SIMON ADAMS
HISTORICAL CONSULTANT

UP TO 1815
PRE-INDUSTRIAL WEAPONS

Early humans developed weapons from wood and stone, such as clubs, axes, and spears, for hunting and fighting. The growth of civilizations from around 3000 BCE onwards led to advances in technology and organization. New military developments slowly emerged – stone weapons were replaced by copper and bronze, then iron and steel. Meanwhile, missile weapons increased in range and penetrative power with the advent of the composite bow, the crossbow, and, with the invention of gunpowder, the cannon and guns.

3000 BCE–1000 CE

The ability of human beings to manufacture tools was an early step toward gaining mastery over their environment. Among the first tools to appear were simple hand blades and axes made from hard rock. These would have been used to kill and dismember animals, but they also had the potential to be employed against other humans. The distinction between hunting and military weaponry remained blurred for many millennia. With the invention of the handle or shaft, and the development of projectile weapons – such as the spear and, above all, the bow and arrow – a revolution in hunting and fighting was underway.

▷ Flint Arrowheads

Date c.2700–1800 BCE
Origin Unknown
Length 5 cm (2 in)

The invention of the bow during the Paleolithic period made it possible to shoot projectiles at great range and with accuracy. Because these flint arrowheads were barbed, they embedded themselves deep in the victim's flesh.

△ Flint Hand Dagger

Date c.2000 BCE
Origin Unknown
Length 30 cm (12 in)

The addition of wooden shafts to flint blades, bound with sinew or leather strips, created stabbing spears, and allowed the bearer to use the full force of his arm to strike blows.

△ Germanic Bronze Sword

Date 1000 BCE
Origin Germany
Length 66.5 cm ($25\frac{3}{4}$ in)

Bronze-Age one-piece, leaf-shaped swords were designed for slashing and were often more effective than a spear or longer thrusting sword. This suited the method of fighting the Celts preferred.

△ **Flint Dagger Head**

Date c.2000 BCE

Origin Unknown

Length 15 cm (6 in)

By the Neolithic period, sophisticated blades such as this dagger head were being made by striking off flakes from a hard flint core, producing a sharp, flat blade.

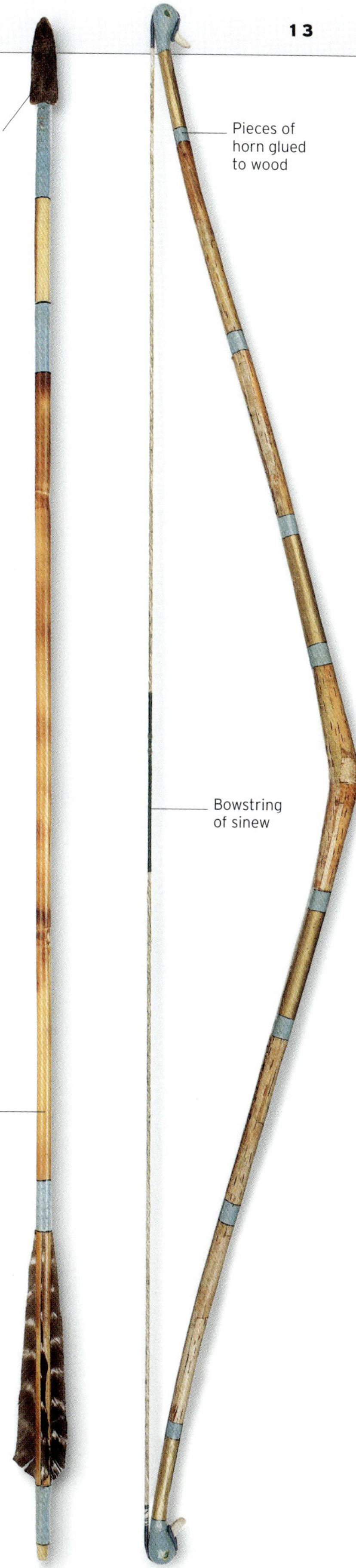

▷ **Assyrian Bow and Arrow**

Date c.750 BCE

Origin Assyria

Length (Bow) 1.42 m (4¾ ft)

Archers formed the main part of the Assyrian infantry. They operated in pairs – one man acting as a shield-bearer, while the other used a bow, such as this one, a replica made from horn, sinew, and wood.

3000 BCE–1000 CE (cont.)

◁ ***Scutum***

Date 1st century CE
Origin Roman Empire
Weight 6.8–9 kg (15–20 lb)
Width 73 cm (29 in)

The *scutum* (legionary shield) was a long rectangle that curved inward to form a part cylinder, giving greater protection to its wearer. As depicted on this modern replica, it was adorned with legionary insignia. When not in use, it was protected by a leather cover.

△ ***Hasta* and *Pilum***

Date	Late 1st century CE
Origin	Roman Empire
Length	2 m (6½ ft)

The Roman military *pilum* (javelin) was a throwing weapon, designed so that its pointed head would break off on hitting a target, making it impossible to hurl back. The *hasta* (thrusting spear) was a more substantial spear, used to thrust in close-quarter combat. The versions shown here are modern replicas.

FULL VIEW

◁ **Painted Wooden Shield**

Date	900–1000 CE
Origin	Northern Europe
Weight	5 kg (11 lb)
Diameter	70–100 cm (28–39 in)

Viking shields were made from wood and covered with leather. They had an iron boss in the centre, which could be used for striking opponents. This example is a modern replica.

1000-1500

European warfare repeatedly demonstrated the effectiveness of disciplined foot soldiers, from Genoese crossbowmen to the longbowmen of the English kings. The use of gunpowder also crept into warfare during this period, initially valued more for its element of surprise – the flashes and bangs – than for its practical impact. Improvements in the construction of metal cannon and in the quality of gunpowder created the potential for a transformation in siege warfare and fortifications, although it would take considerably longer for the armoured knight to disappear from the battlefield.

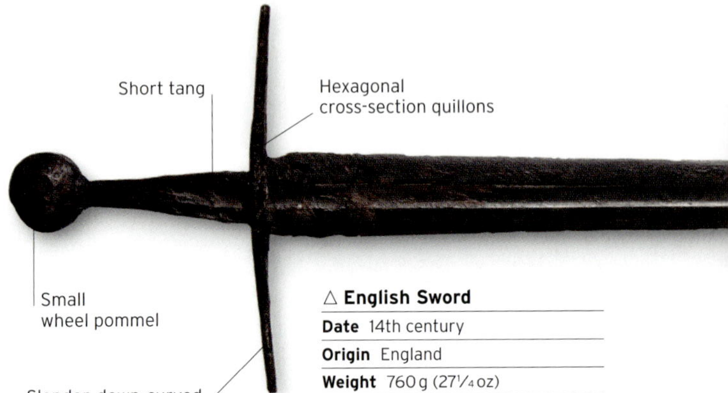

△ English Sword

Date	14th century
Origin	England
Weight	760 g (27¼ oz)
Length	1.04 m (3½ ft)

The long, double-edged, tapering blade of this sword incorporated a shallow fuller for two-thirds of its length. It has a notably short tang, a small wheel-shaped pommel, and slightly down-curved quillons.

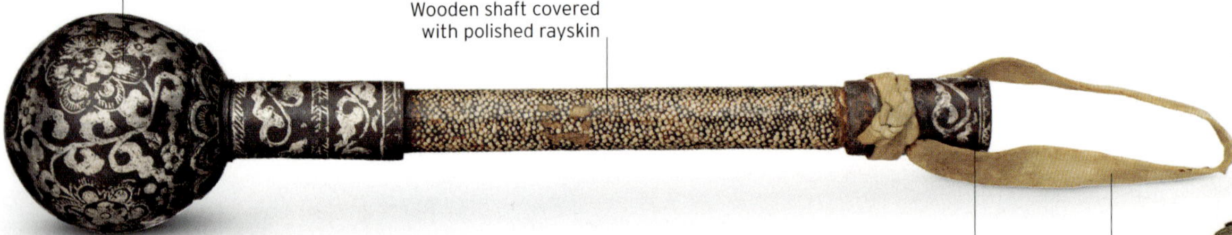

△ Iron Mace

Date	14th century
Origin	China or Mongolia
Weight	1.17 kg (2½ lb)
Length	40 cm (15¾ in)

This iron mace dates from the period when the Mongols, under Kublai Khan, overthrew the native ruling dynasty of China and took power. The intricate decoration suggests that it belonged to a warrior of high status.

△ 15th-century Bombard

Date	15th century
Origin	Europe
Length	198 cm (78 in)
Calibre	3½ in

Although a rather primitive-looking weapon, this lightweight bombard represented the future of artillery in the late 15th century. Rather than being used solely for siege operations, its greater mobility meant it could travel with an army and be used on battlefields.

Fuller: a groove running down the blade to make it lighter while maintaining its strength
Iron straps to hold bombard onto carriage
Wooden wheel

1000–1500 (cont.)

◁ Rondel Dagger

Date	15th century
Origin	England
Weight	230 g (8 oz)
Length	35 cm (13¾ in)

The rondel was the main military dagger during the early 15th century, distinguished by the round disks that formed the guard and the pommel. It was also known as the *dague à rouelles*, and was a popular dagger among those of high social status.

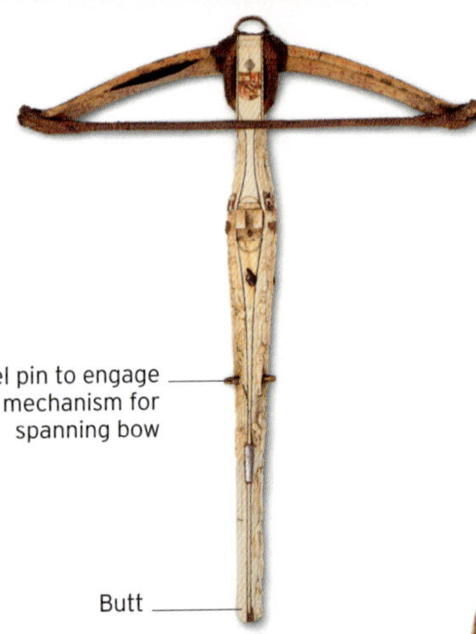

FULL VIEW

▽ Crossbow

Date	c.1460
Origin	Europe
Weight	4.4 kg (9¾ lb)
Length	72 cm (28¼ in)

Widely used in Europe from the 12th century, the crossbow, when fired from the shoulder, was very effective against armoured knights. Although the bolt was released with great power, crossbows were slow to reload, so their rate of fire was far lower than longbows.

◁ Crossbow Bolts

Date	c.1500
Origin	Germany
Weight	35 g (1¼ oz)
Length	37 cm (14½ in)

Shorter and heavier than longbow arrows, bolts (or quarrels) had different tips depending on the effect required. Barbed broadhead bolts were used primarily for hunting, whereas chisel-headed arrowheads were used against armoured soldiers. The tip of the bolt served as a sight when aiming.

△ Chinese Iron Cannon

Date	c.1500
Origin	China
Weight	Unknown
Length	100 mm (4 in)

This small cannon was fired from a trestlelike stand. It was cast with a bulbous breech region to resist pressure. Rather than firing a single projectile, it was loaded with a number of smaller missiles.

Battle of White Mountain
Fought on 8 November 1620, between the Imperial Army, led by Count Tilly, and the Bohemian Army, led by Christian of Anhalt, the Battle of the White Mountain saw the use of both traditional pikes and mounted cavalry, as well as more modern rifles and cannon. The battle was a decisive victory for the Imperial Army, and ended the possibility of Bohemian independence.

△ ***Khanjar***	
Date	c.1520
Origin	Turkey
Weight	376 g (13¼ oz)
Length	39 cm (15¼ in)

The sturdy cross section of the blade is designed for piercing mail. An area of unsharpened blade below the quillons allowed the soldier to grip closer to the quillons for greater control.

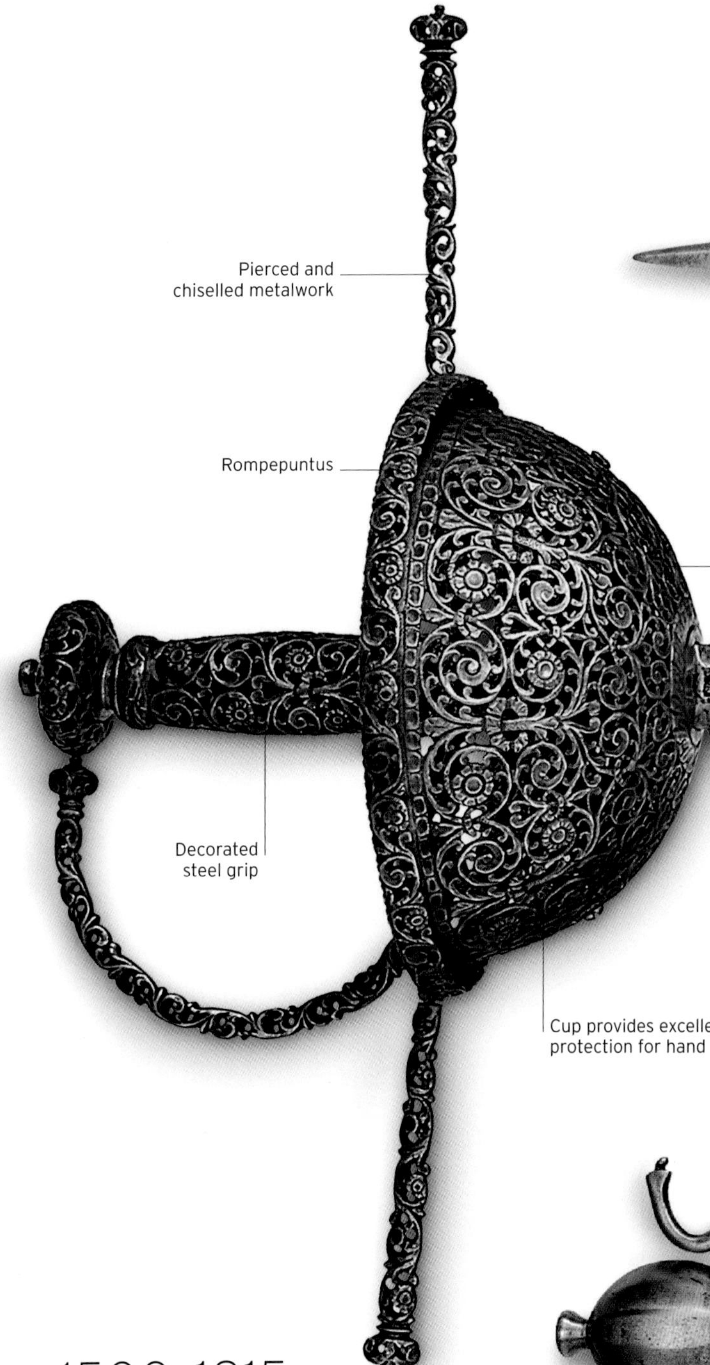

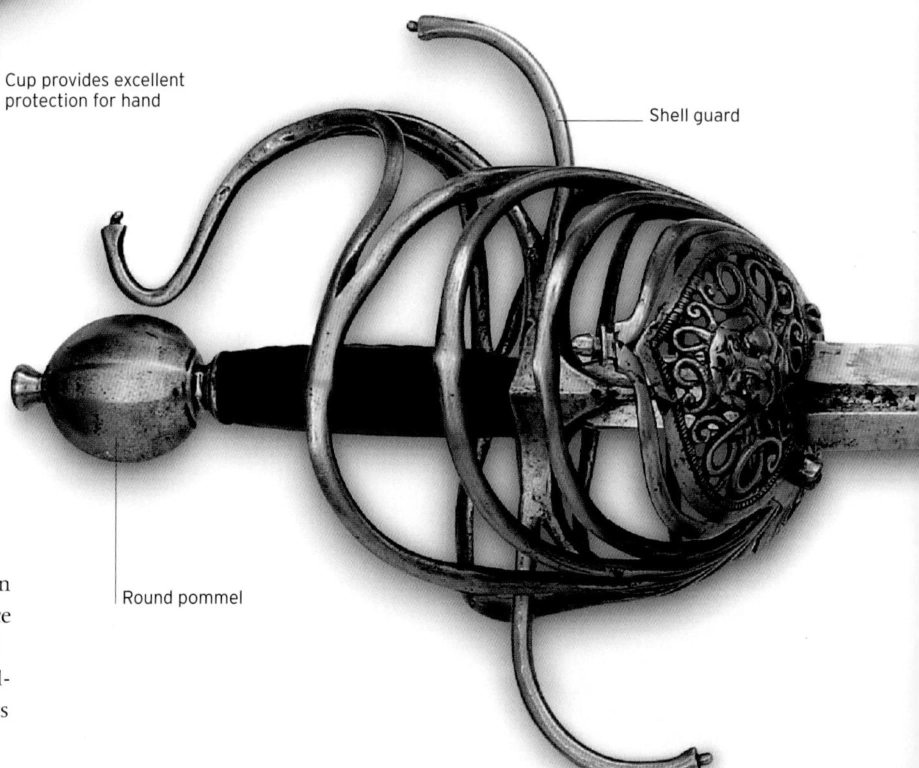

1500-1815

After 1500, the sword became less important as an infantry weapon, although it was still valued by the heavy and light cavalry and also often fulfilled a ceremonial role. Artillery was now established as an effective battlefield weapon, leading to the appearance of a wide range of ordnance, including practical field artillery and lighter pieces for naval use. By the mid-1600s, artillery was firmly established, with gun units integrated into infantry regiments.

FULL VIEW

△ **Cup-hilt Rapier**

Date	c.1650
Origin	Spain
Weight	1.02 kg (2¼ lb)
Length	96 cm (37¾ in)

In Spain, and those parts of Italy under Spanish influence, the guard of the rapier became fully enclosed, producing the "cup-hilt" guard form shown here. The Romepuntus is used to trap opponents' blades.

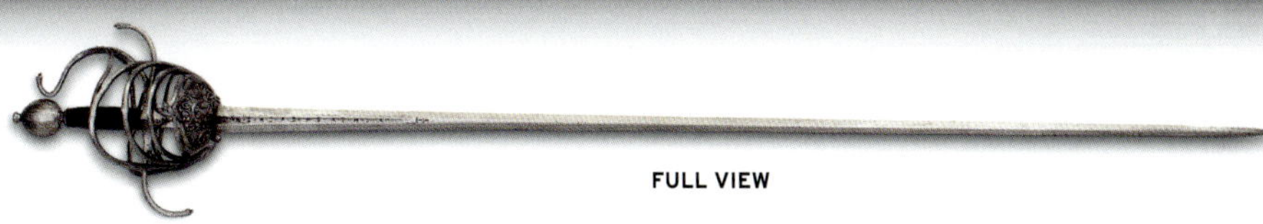

FULL VIEW

△ **Pappenheimer Sword**

Date	1625-50
Origin	Northern Europe
Weight	1.17 kg (2½ lb)
Length	1.28 m (4¼ ft)

This style of sword was popularized by Count Pappenheim, a Bavarian field marshal in the Thirty Years' War. It is characterized by the pommel, the complex side bars, and the pierced plate or shell guard on either side of the blade.

1500–1815 (cont.)

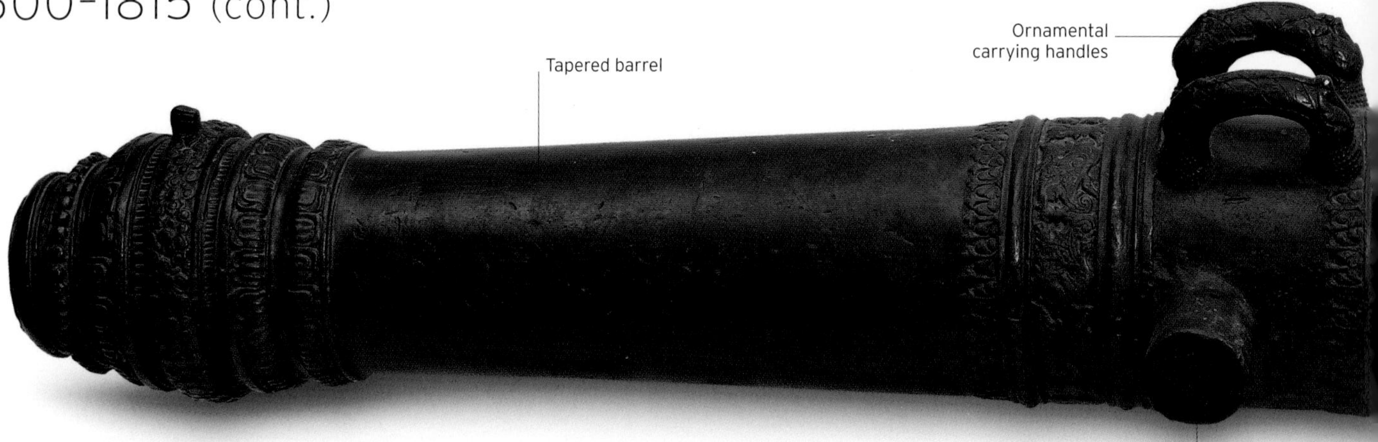

△ Malaysian Bronze Saker

Date c.1650
Origin Malaysia
Length 2.29 m (7½ ft)
Calibre 89 mm (3.5 in)

Sakers were light cannon designed for long-range attack. This ornate model was cast in Malacca, Malaysia, by local craftsmen who probably followed a Dutch model.

△ Bronze Breech-loading Swivel Gun

Date c.1670
Origin Netherlands
Length 1.22 m (4 ft)
Calibre 7.4 cm

This swivel gun was owned by the Dutch East India Company and was used to protects its ships from pirate attacks on the long sea voyages from the East Indies to the Netherlands. The swivel gun was most effective when engaging close-range targets.

Decoration depicting arms of Prince Maurice of the Netherlands
Ornamentation for display purposes only

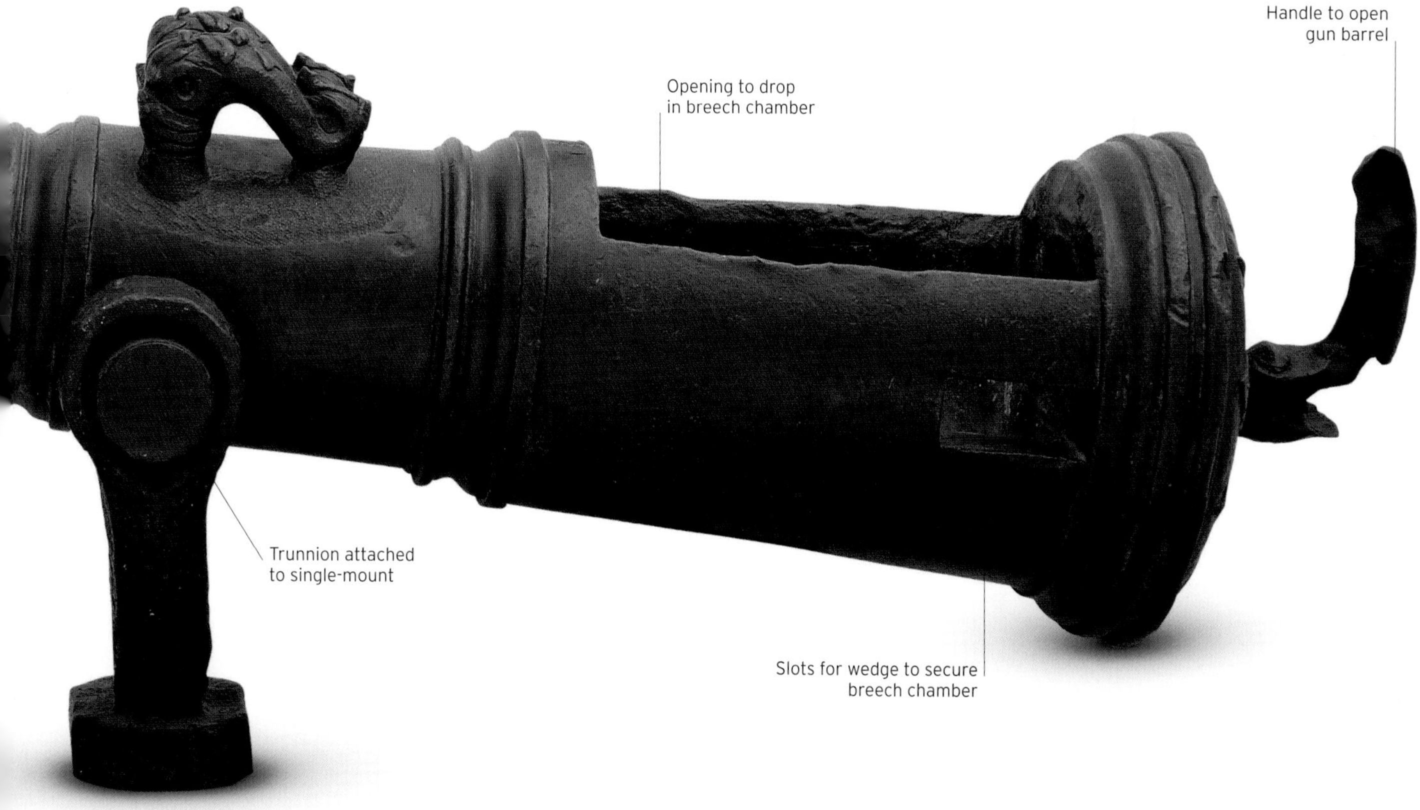
Handle to open gun barrel
Opening to drop in breech chamber
Trunnion attached to single-mount
Slots for wedge to secure breech chamber

1500-1815 (cont.)

▷ Cast-iron 3-pounder

Date Late 17th century
Origin England
Length 2 m (6½ ft)
Calibre 3 in
Shot 1.36 kg (3 lb)

Cast-iron guns were much cheaper to make than bronze guns and gradually replaced them during the 17th and 18th centuries. They were cast solid and bored out. The rear-chock carriage lessened recoil when the gun was fired.

▽ *Tanto*

Date 1792
Origin Japan
Length 28.5 cm (11¼ in)

A *tanto* was a sword or dagger with a blade less than 31 cm (12 in) in length. It was often worn as an alternative to a *wakizashi*. This example is black-lacquered, with the scabbard housing a *kogai* on the outer face and a *kozuka* at the rear.

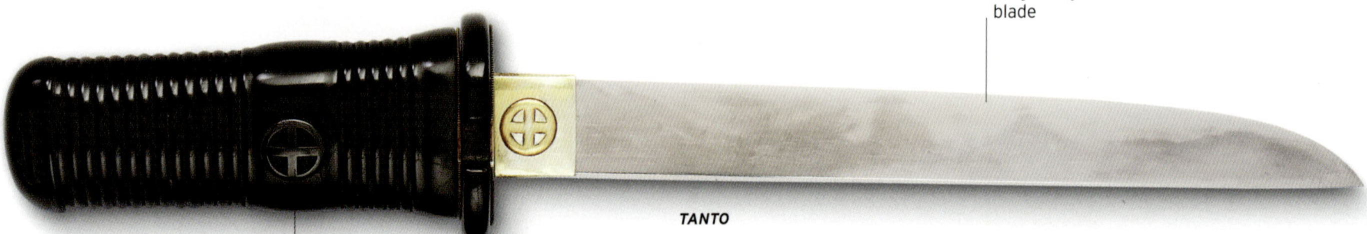

TANTO

SCABBARD

KOGAI

KOZUKA

Cast iron treated with antirust protection
Main weight of gun supported by wooden carriage
Supporting bolt
Sturdy, solid wooden wheel

1815–1914 THE INDUSTRIAL ERA

Between 1815 and 1914, technological progress transformed combat. High-explosive and rapid-fire mechanisms made weaponry more effective. The long reign of the flintlock musket ended with the development of the rifle, pistol, and revolver. The pace of change increased from the 1870s as smokeless propellants and high explosives in shells replaced gunpowder. New naval fleets were built, with steel ships equipped with breech-loading rifled turret guns, while bolt-action repeater rifles became standard infantry equipment.

Flintlock and Percussion-cap Long Guns

Percussion ignition, whether using caps or other devices, was a major improvement over the cumbersome flintlock. Not only was the percussion mechanism easier to use and maintain, it was also more weatherproof. In another key development, most European and American infantry had their smoothbore muskets replaced with muzzle-loading rifles, which had an accurate range several times greater than that of the musket. As a result, much of this new generation of muskets and rifles saw long service in various national armies.

▷ **Baker Rifle**

Date	1800-37	**Origin**	UK
Weight	4 kg (8¾ lb)		
Barrel	76 cm (30 in)		
Calibre	.625 in		

The rifle designed by English gunsmith Ezekiel Baker was chosen for riflemen in the British Army. Accurate to around 140 m (460 ft), it was a great improvement over smoothbore muskets.

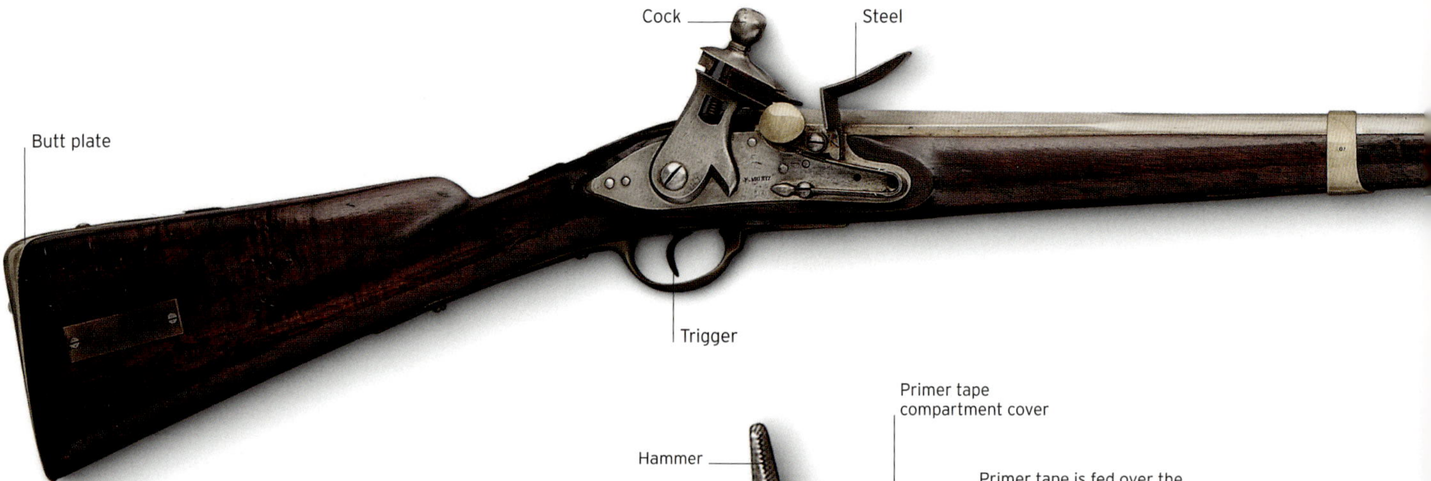

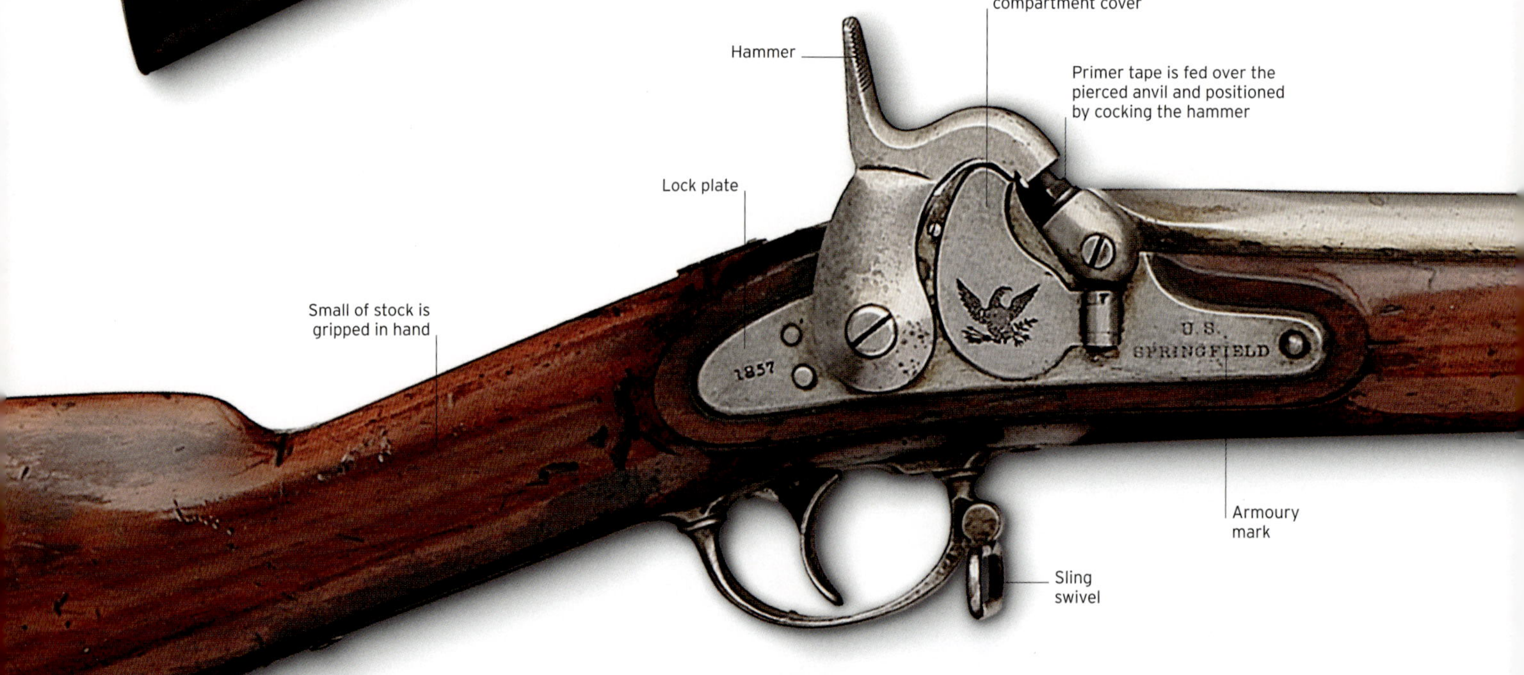

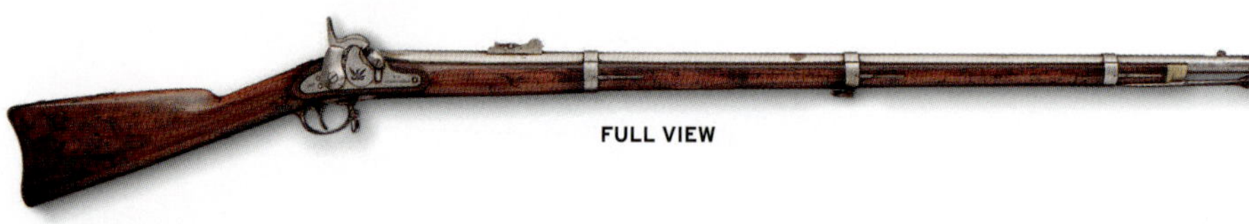

FULL VIEW

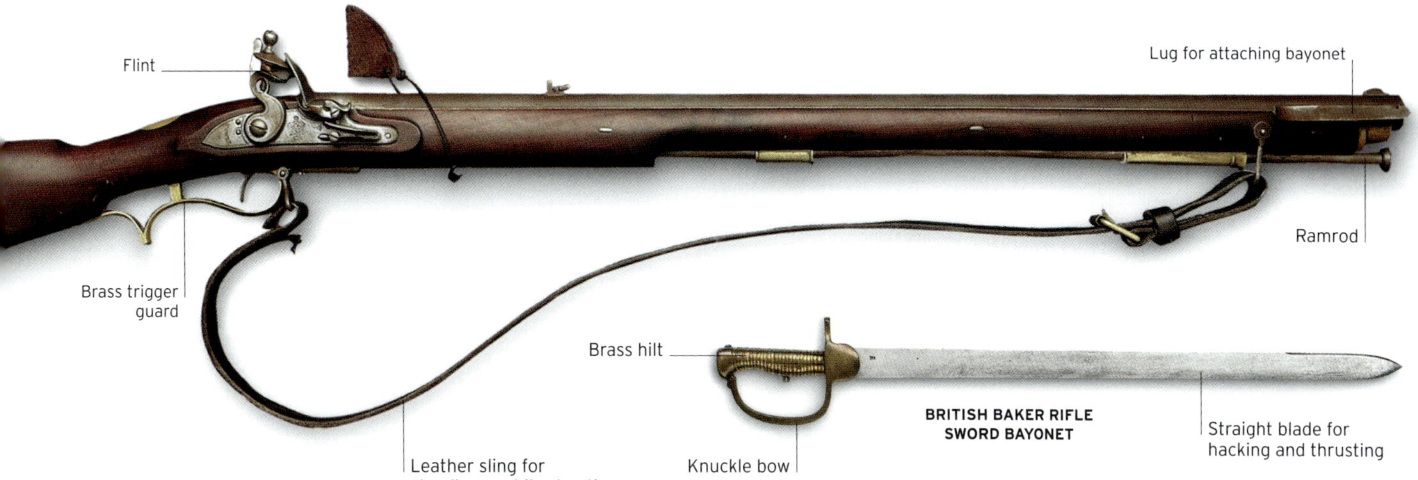

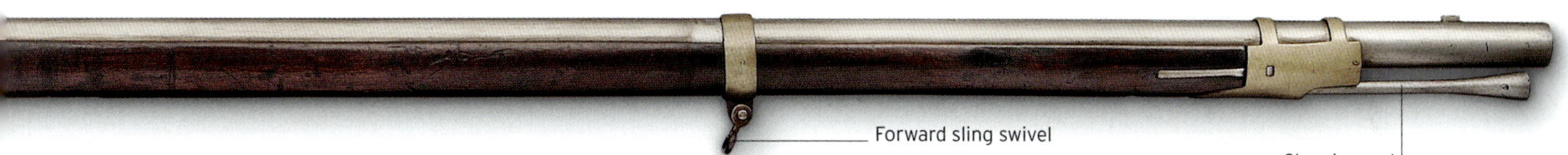

△ Prussian 1809 Pattern Musket

Date 1809	**Origin** Germany
Weight 4 kg (8¾ lb)	
Barrel 1.04 m (3½ ft)	
Calibre .75 in	

The 1809 Pattern musket was the Prussian equivalent of the British Brown Bess and the French Charleville. Unlike its competitors, it had a brass flash guard around the pan as standard. Most of these flintlocks were later converted to percussion.

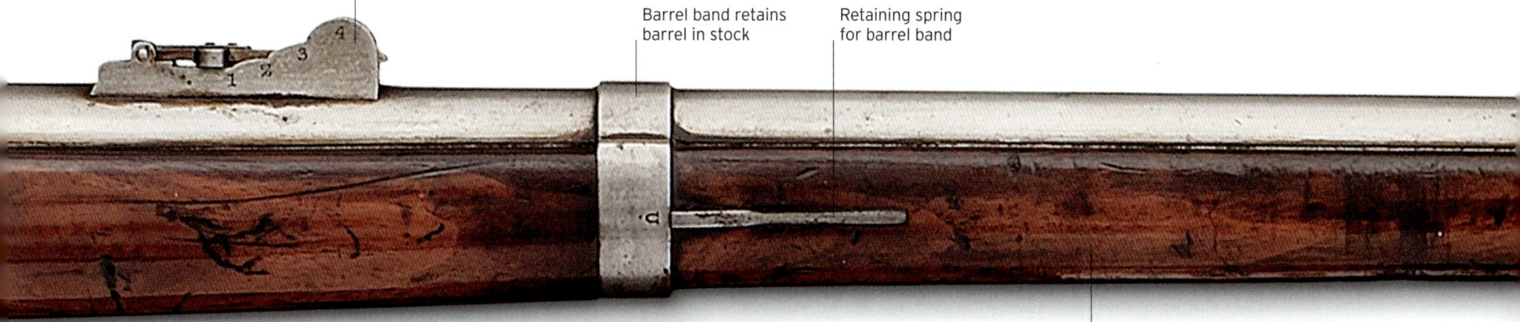

△ Springfield Model 1855

Date 1855	**Origin** US
Weight 4.1 kg (9 lb)	
Barrel 101.5 cm (40 in)	
Calibre 14.7 mm (.58 in)	

The first regulation American percussion rifle was the Model 1841 Mississippi Rifle, with a 83.8-cm (.33-in) barrel. It was later given a longer barrel and modified to use Maynard's tape primer, fed from a roll housed inside the lock (instead of individual copper caps placed over the nipple) becoming the Model 1855 rifle.

Swords and Bayonets

During the 1800s, edged cavalry weapons evolved into the long, straight, thrusting sword of the heavy cavalry and the light cavalry's curved sabre designed for cutting and slicing. For the infantry, swords were already well on their way to becoming ceremonial weapons and were increasingly decorative. Despite the development of long-range firepower, armies continued to place great emphasis on the bayonet, not least because it was believed to encourage an aggressive, offensive spirit among the infantry.

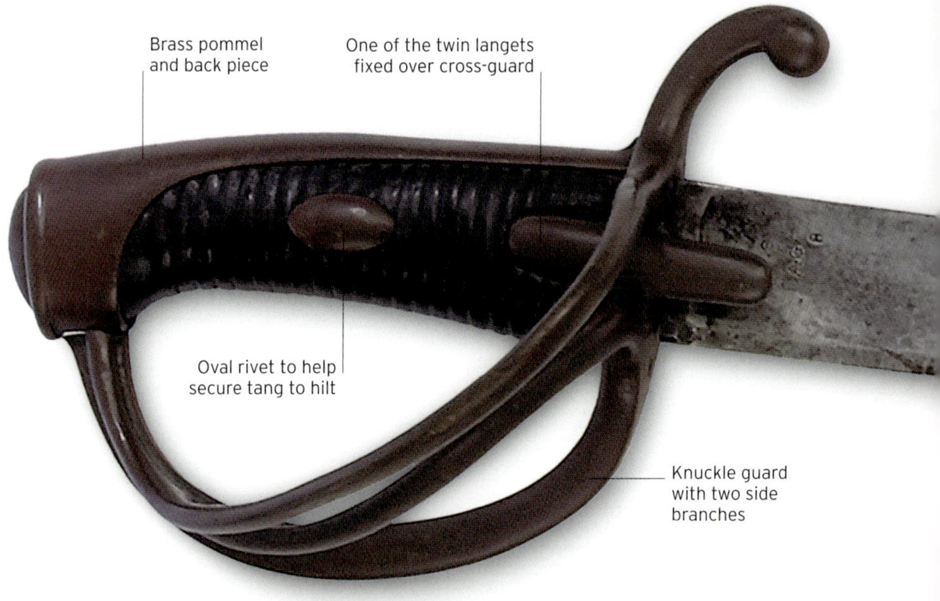

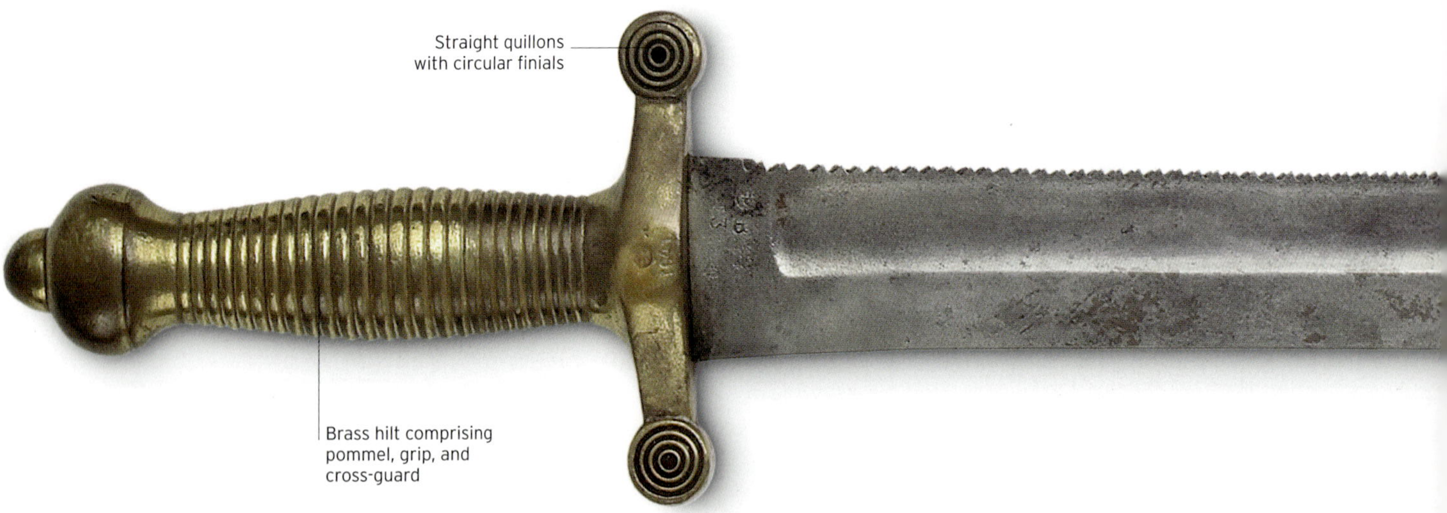

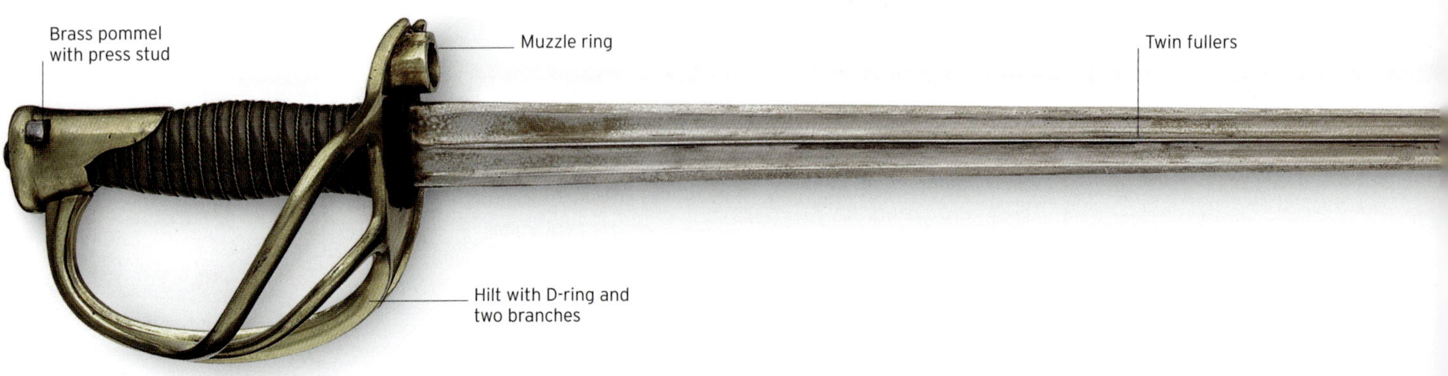

FULL VIEW

Single-edged blade

△ **Model 1827 Cavalry Trooper's Sword**

Date c.1827
Origin Russia
Weight 1.22 kg (2¾ lb)
Length 1.02 m (3½ ft)

The Russian Model 1827 cavalry trooper's sword had a curved, single-edged blade with a single, wide fuller and a brass hilt. Twin langets could be used to trap an enemy's sword.

Serrated edge for sawing wood

△ **Pioneer Sword Model 1847**

Date 1847
Origin Russia
Weight 1.18 kg (2½ lb)
Length 63.5 cm (25 in)

The hilt of this Russian sword is based on the French Model 1831 infantry sword. Both reflect the influence of the Roman gladius short sword.

△ **Sword Bayonet**

Date Mid-19th century
Origin France
Weight 790 g (27¾ oz)
Length 1.15 m (3¾ ft)

This French sword bayonet, with a long, narrow blade, is unusual in having a basket hilt – a feature usually associated with a cavalry sword.

Swords and Bayonets (cont.)

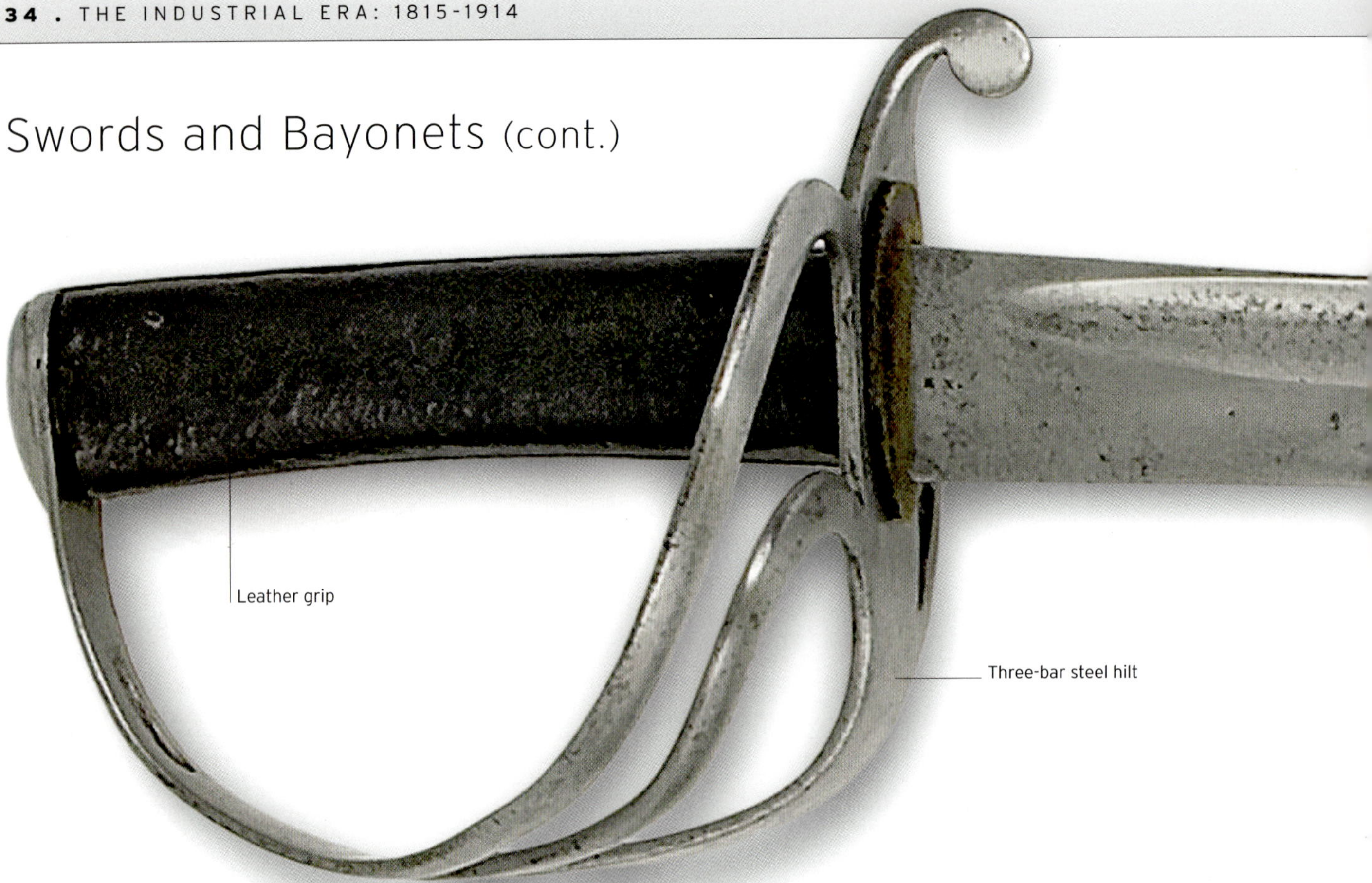

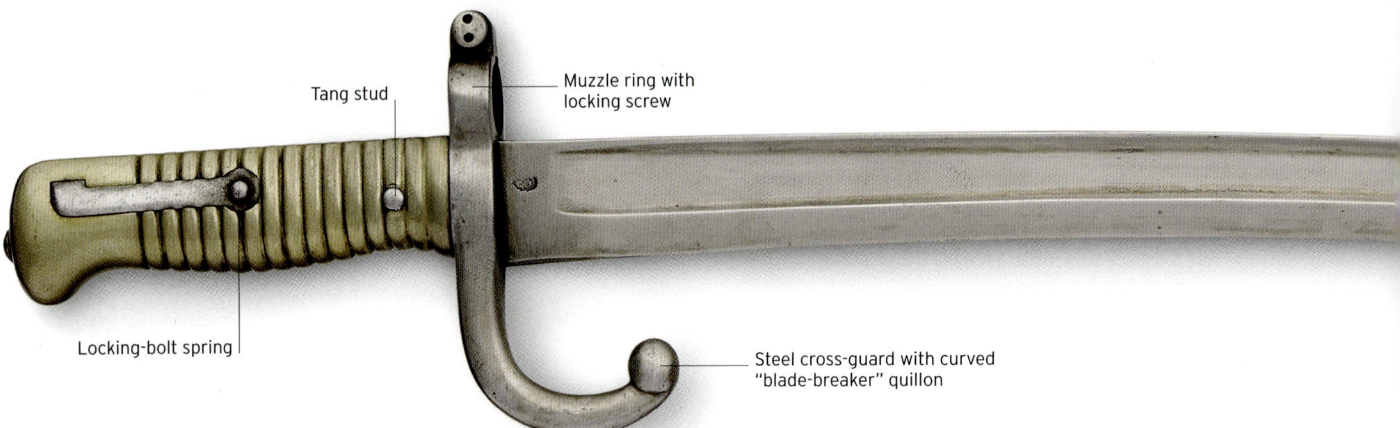

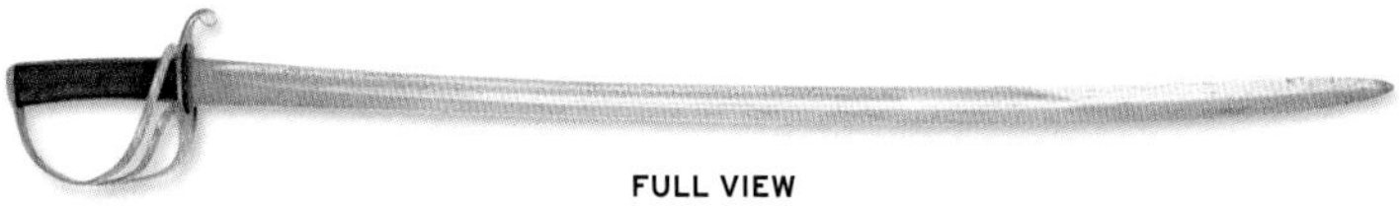

FULL VIEW

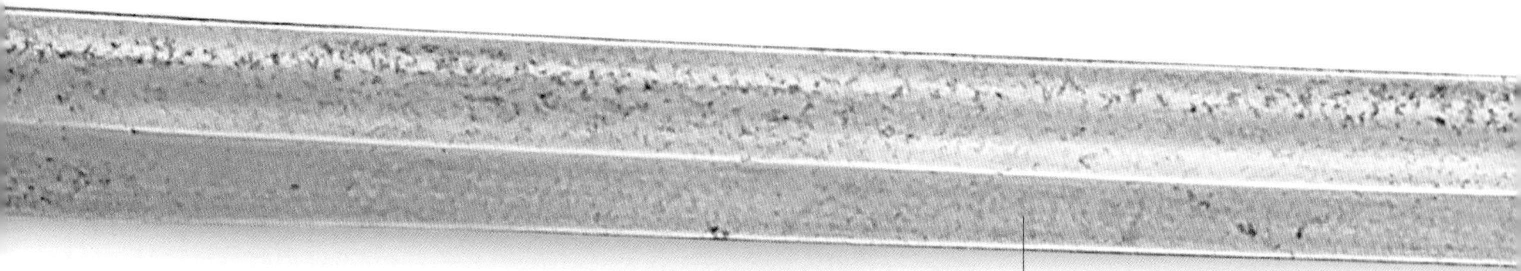

△ **Cavalry Trooper's Sword Pattern 1853**

Date 1853
Origin UK
Weight 1.13 kg (2½ lb)
Length 1 m (3½ ft)

Of fairly conventional construction, the 1853 Pattern cavalry trooper's sword equipped British heavy cavalry in the Crimean War and during some of Britain's subsequent colonial campaigns.

▽ **MLE 1866 Chassepot Bayonet**

Date 1866
Origin France
Weight 760 g (27¾ oz)
Length 70 cm (27½ in)

This bayonet is from the Chassepot breech-loading rifle that armed the French during the Franco-Prussian War of 1870–71. The recurved *yataghan*-style blade influenced many European and American designs.

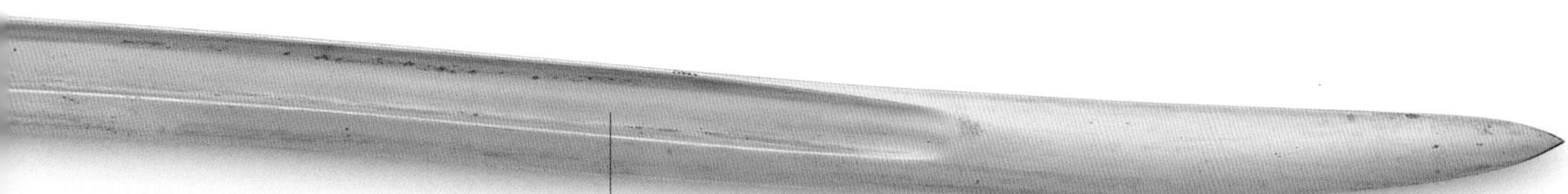

▽ **Martini-Henry Socket Bayonet**

Date c.1876
Origin UK
Weight 0.45 kg (1 lb)
Length 64 cm (25¼ in)

Lighter, cheaper, and as efficient as a sword bayonet, socket bayonets were issued for use with the Martini-Henry rifle (although senior NCOs were allowed their more prestigious sword bayonets). They were attached to the barrel muzzle and held in place with a mortise slot and locking ring.

Flintlock Pistols and Early Revolvers

During the 1800s, pistols and revolvers evolved from the flintlock mechanisms of the previous two centuries to the percussion-cap models developed by Samuel Colt and others. With each shot, a fresh chamber was brought into line with the barrel and its percussion cap under the hammer. By the early 1900s, the design of both pistol and revolver had evolved so that little could be done to improve their reliability.

△ Spanish Cavalry Pistol

Date 1841	**Origin** Spain
Weight 1.3 kg (2³/₄ lb)	
Barrel 19.6 cm (7³/₄ in)	
Calibre .71 in	

The Spanish Army introduced a bridled flintlock closely modelled on those in French service. A small boss on the barrel's surface held the ramrod in place, rather than the swivel mount found on other martial pistols of this period.

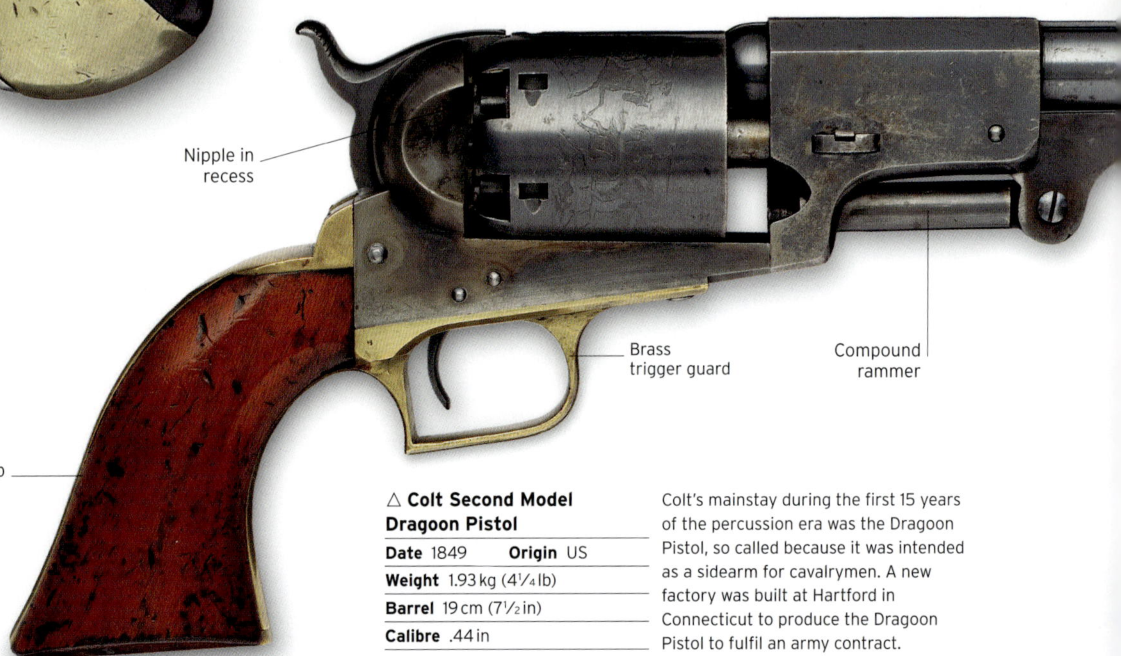

△ Colt Second Model Dragoon Pistol

Date 1849	**Origin** US
Weight 1.93 kg (4¹/₄ lb)	
Barrel 19 cm (7¹/₂ in)	
Calibre .44 in	

Colt's mainstay during the first 15 years of the percussion era was the Dragoon Pistol, so called because it was intended as a sidearm for cavalrymen. A new factory was built at Hartford in Connecticut to produce the Dragoon Pistol to fulfil an army contract.

△ **Smith & Wesson Military and Police**

Date 1900	**Origin** US
Weight 0.85 kg (1 lb)	
Barrel 12.7 cm (5 in)	
Calibre .38 in Special	

Having championed the hinged-frame revolver, Smith & Wesson, with the advent of more powerful ammunition, was obliged to switch to a solid frame with a swing-out cylinder for its Military and Police pistol. This was chambered for the long .38 in Special round.

Rear sight
Prawl prevents pistol from slipping through hand under recoil
Grip panels attach to frame
Frame hinge
Butt-retaining screw
Trigger guard with steadying spur
Notched hammer acts as rear sight
Hard rubber-composition grip
Trigger

△ **Smith & Wesson No. 3 Russian Model**

Date 1871	**Origin** US
Weight 1.25 kg ($2\frac{3}{4}$ lb)	
Barrel 20.3 cm (8 in)	
Calibre .44 in S&W Russian	

Smith & Wesson won a contract to supply the Russian Army with 20,000 of their No. 3 pistol, chambered for a special cartridge. These were the most accurate revolvers of the day.

△ **Colt Single-action Army Model 1873**

Date 1873	**Origin** US
Weight 1.1 kg ($2\frac{1}{2}$ lb)	
Barrel 19 cm ($7\frac{1}{2}$ in)	
Calibre .45 in	

The Colt SAA ("Peacemaker") married the single-action lock of the old Dragoon model to a bored-through cylinder in a solid frame, into which the barrel was screwed.

Metallic Cartridge Revolvers

Smith & Wesson acquired the patent for a revolver with a bored-through cylinder to accept brass cartridges in 1856 from Rollin White. By the time their patent protection expired in 1869, the centre-fire cartridge (with the primer located in the centre, rather than in the rim, as in earlier examples) had been devised, and the world's gunmakers were ready to begin manufacturing what would prove to be the cylinder revolver in its final form. Later refinements made it possible to charge and empty the chambers more rapidly.

△ **Remington Army Model 1875**

Date 1875	**Origin** US
Weight 1.1 kg (2½ lb)	
Barrel 19 cm (7½ in)	
Calibre .45 in	

This gun was similar in build to the Colt Single-action Army Model of 1873. It had a web beneath the barrel to help guide it while being stored in its holster. It was also adapted for .40 in and .44 in cartridges.

Metallic Cartridge Revolvers (cont.)

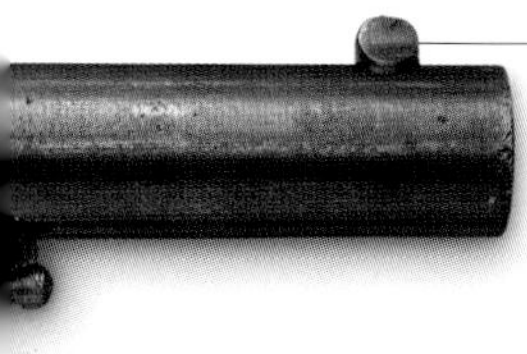

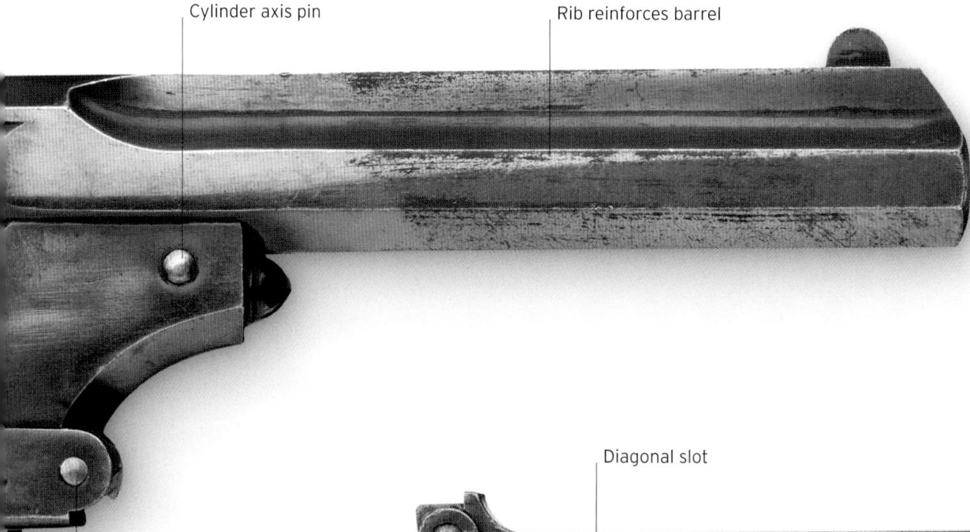

◁ Webley-Pryse No. 4 Revolver

Date 1877	**Origin** UK
Weight 1.3 kg (2¾ lb)	
Barrel 16 cm (6¼ in)	
Calibre .45 in	

In 1876, Charles Pryse designed a tip-down, break-open revolver with a rebounding-hammer action and simultaneous extraction of spent cartridges. This Fourth Model Webley-Pryse, recognizable by its fluted cylinder, was made in calibres ranging from .32 in to .577 in.

△ Mauser M1878 "Zig-Zag"

Date 1878	**Origin** Germany
Weight 1.2 kg (2½ lb)	
Barrel 16.5 cm (6½ in)	
Calibre .43 in	

The "Zig-Zag" was a six-shot revolver with a top-hinged frame. Diagonal slots cut into the cylinder face were used with a corresponding arm link to rotate the cylinder.

Battle of Omdurman
The short but mismatched Battle of Omdurman, fought on 2 September 1898, saw the heavily armed British Army led by General Sir Herbert Kitchener, equipped with Maxim guns, modern rifles, and artillery, fight against a Sudanese Mahdist army led by Khalifa al-Taashi, armed only with spears and some old muskets. More than 12,000 Sudanese were killed, in stark contrast to the 47 British fatalities.

Weapons of Africa and Oceania

Throughout the 19th century, Europeans had only had an impact on the coastal regions of Africa. Despite European colonization, most Africans were still largely unaffected by European ideas and technology. African states and tribal societies used traditional forms of warfare, despite the presence of imported firearms. The same was true of Oceania, where traditional weaponry was being made well into the 20th century. However, here too, their effectiveness was thwarted by superior European technology and weaponry.

△ **Finger Knife**

Date	c.1890–1950
Origin	Uganda
Weight	50 g (1³⁄₄ oz)
Length	9.5 cm (3³⁄₄ in)

This small, broad-bladed knife probably comes from the Labwor people of northeastern Uganda. Made of iron, it was worn on a finger, and could be used for everyday purposes such as cutting meat, as well as for fighting. Its advantage as a weapon was that, because of its diminutive size, it could be concealed in the hand.

▷ West African Fighting Pick

Date	19th century
Origin	Ghana
Weight	0.65 kg (1½ lb)
Length	51 cm (20 in)

This unusual fighting pick from West Africa has a barbed metal point with a tang inserted into a wooden shaft. The roughened skin of a monitor lizard has been used to improve the grip on the handle.

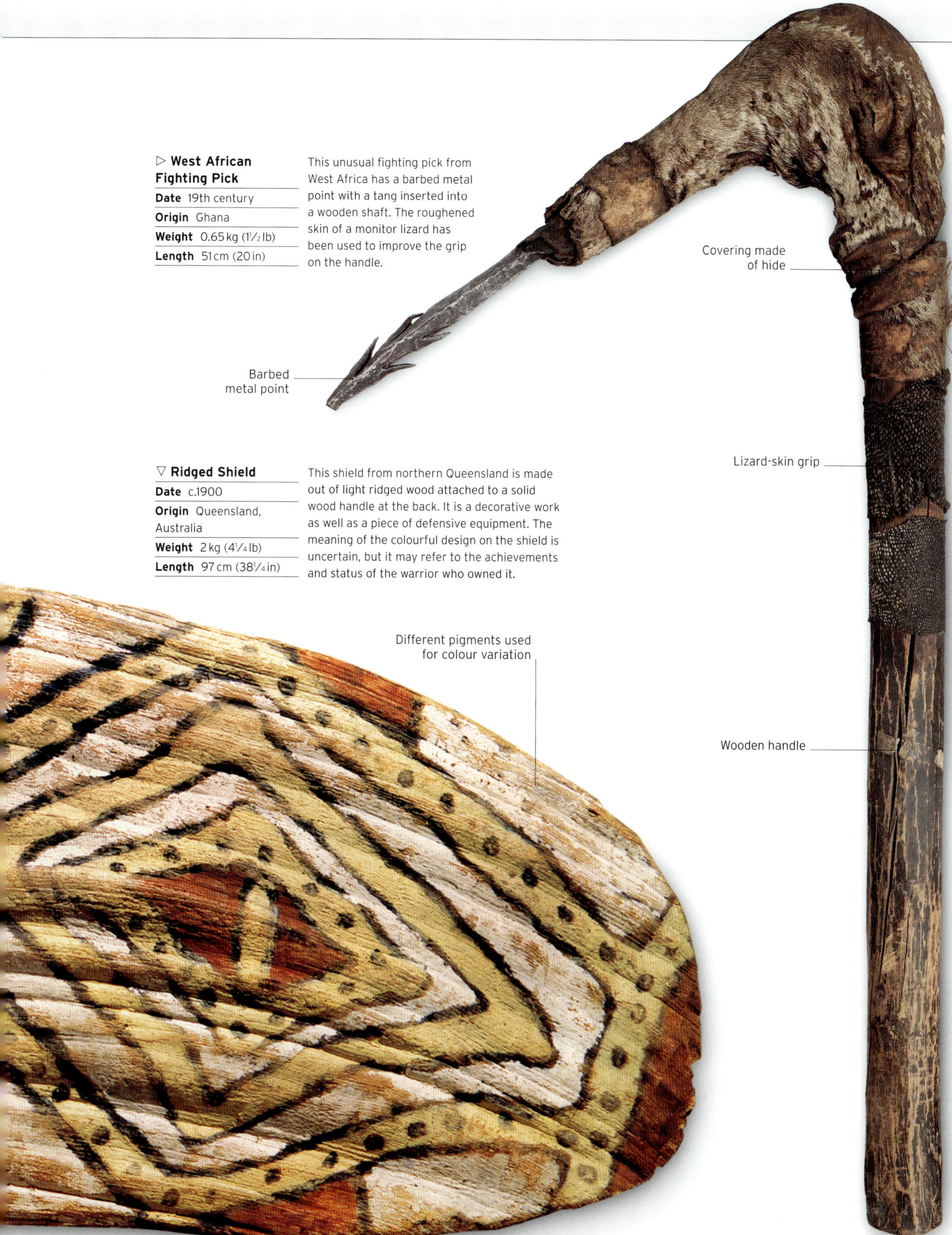

▽ Ridged Shield

Date	c.1900
Origin	Queensland, Australia
Weight	2 kg (4¼ lb)
Length	97 cm (38¼ in)

This shield from northern Queensland is made out of light ridged wood attached to a solid wood handle at the back. It is a decorative work as well as a piece of defensive equipment. The meaning of the colourful design on the shield is uncertain, but it may refer to the achievements and status of the warrior who owned it.

Asian Weapons

The fine decorative tradition of Asian weaponry continued into the 19th and early 20th centuries. Both Indian *dhals* or shields and Chinese swords were elaborate in design, as were the *kukri* daggers of Nepal. Although firearms were widely used throughout Asia, armour, shields, daggers, and knives remained in use for much longer than in Europe. In line with the samurai tradition in Japan, the blades of swords and daggers were made from the highest grade steel honed to a fine cutting edge.

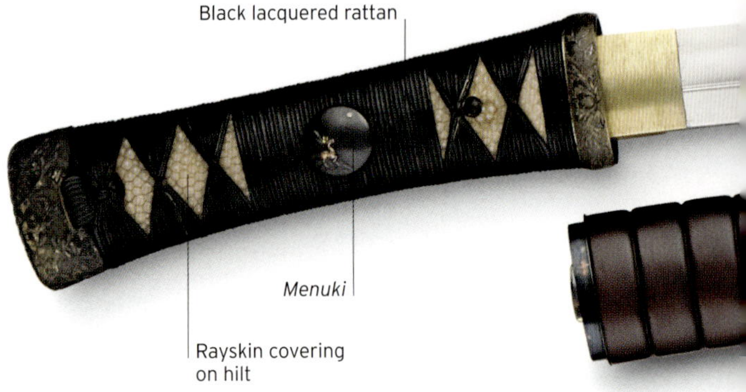

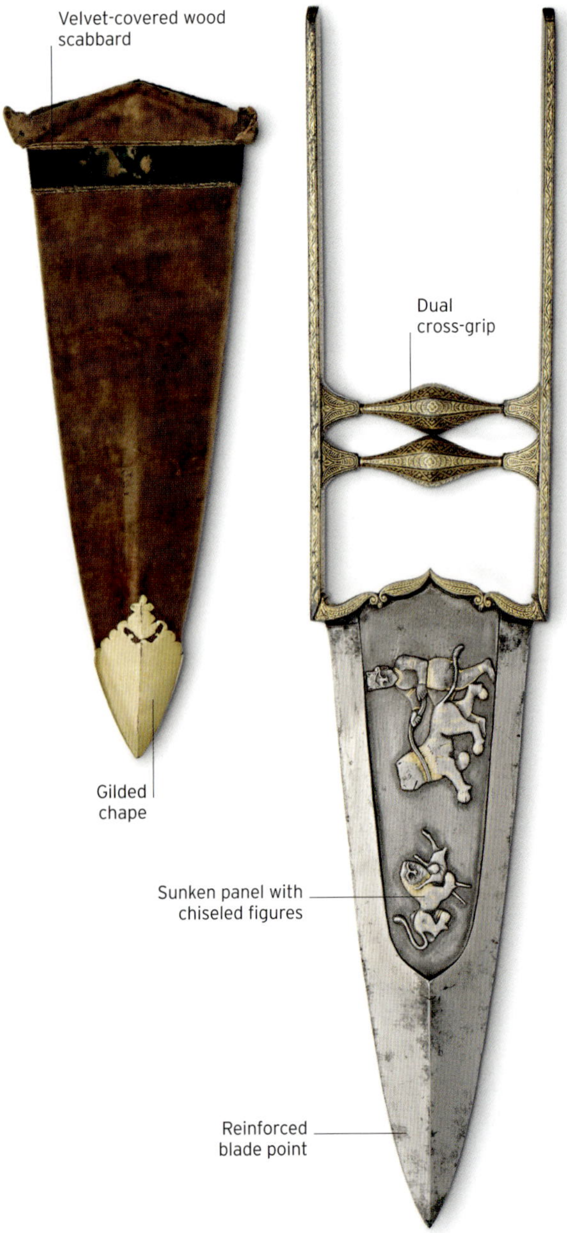

◁ **Indian *Katar***

Date Early 19th century
Origin India
Weight 0.57 kg (1¼ lb)
Length 42.1 cm (16¾ in)

To use this north Indian dagger, the warrior grasped the cross-grips, making a fist, so that the sidebars of the hilt lay on either side of his hand and forearm. With the blade horizontal, he then stabbed with a punching motion. The *katar*'s form changed little over hundreds of years; this example is from the 19th century.

▷ **Sikh *Dhal***

Date 1847
Origin India
Weight 3.8 kg (8½ lb)
Length 59 cm (22¼ in)

This round shield, or *dhal*, dates from the wars between the Sikhs and the British East India Company. The intricate decoration in gold damascene includes Persian inscriptions, so perhaps the shield was not the work of an Indian craftsman.

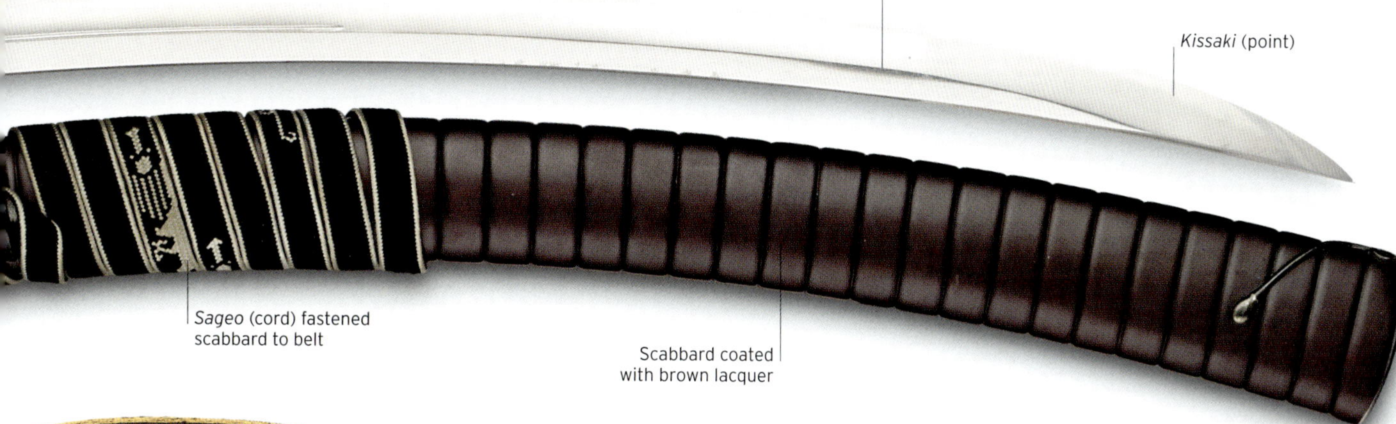

△ *Aikuchi*

Date	19th century
Origin	Japan
Weight	0.28 kg (1/4 lb)
Length	55.8 cm (22 in)

The *aikuchi* was one of the many types of Japanese dagger, distinguished by having no hand guard (*tsuba*). It was often carried by ageing samurai in semi-retirement. This *aikuchi*, shown with its scabbard, is a 19th-century reproduction of a medieval weapon.

FULL VIEW

Asian weapons (cont.)

◁ **Indian Parrying Weapon**

Date	c.1900
Origin	India
Weight	0.82 kg (1¾ lb)
Length	47 cm (18½ in)

This weapon combines a steel parrying stick for defence and a fist dagger for attack. Holding the grip with knuckles toward the dagger, a man could fend off blows, using the stick as a shield, and deliver punching stabs with the dagger.

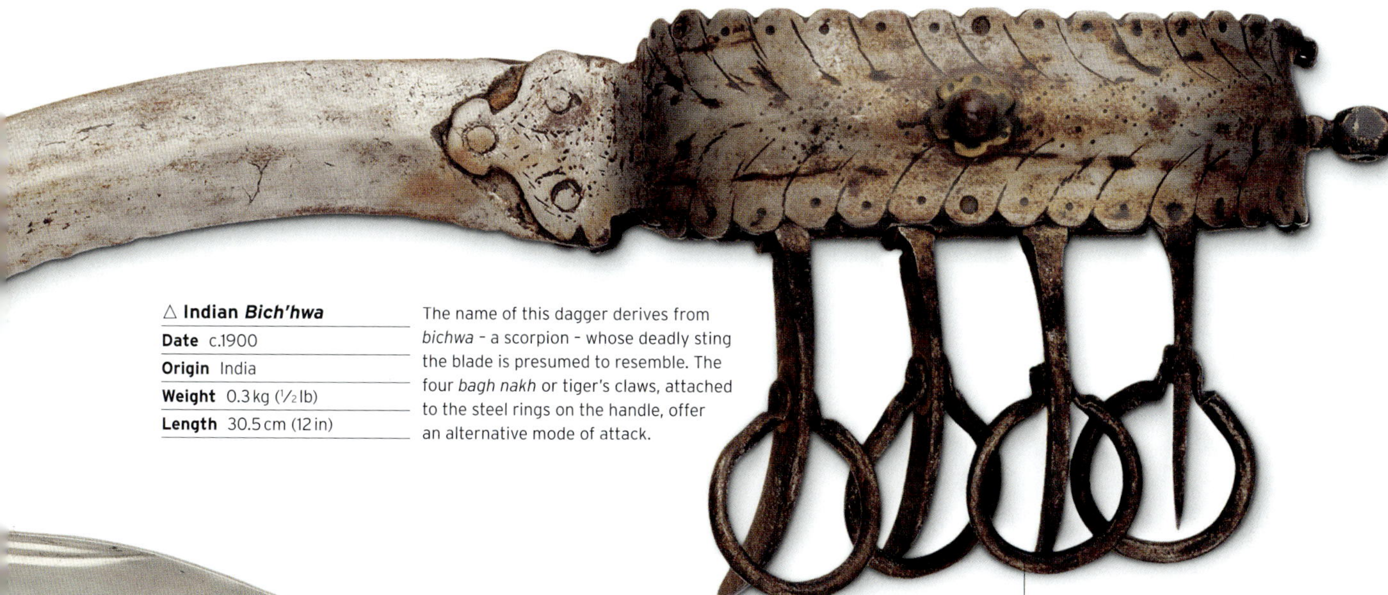

△ **Indian *Bich'hwa***

Date	c.1900
Origin	India
Weight	0.3 kg (½ lb)
Length	30.5 cm (12 in)

The name of this dagger derives from *bichwa* - a scorpion - whose deadly sting the blade is presumed to resemble. The four *bagh nakh* or tiger's claws, attached to the steel rings on the handle, offer an alternative mode of attack.

◁ **Nepalese *Kukri***

Date	c.1900
Origin	Nepal
Weight	0.48 kg (1 lb)
Length	44.5 cm (17½ in)

With its wooden handle, broad, angled blade, and notch or *cho*, this is a typical example of the Nepalese Gurkhas' *kukri*. The *cho* has religious significance as the symbol of the destructive Hindu god Shiva. The quality of the sheath suggests this was the property of a wealthy man.

Manually Loaded Repeater Rifles

There had been attempts to produce repeater rifles and muskets as early as the 16th century. Notwithstanding the success enjoyed by the "cap-and-ball" revolvers of Colt and others, it took the unitary cartridge containing primer, charge, and projectile in one package to make the repeater rifle a feasible machine. The breakthrough came midway through the 19th century, and within a decade repeating rifles had become commonplace. Contained in magazines, their ammunition was fed to the breech as part of the single action that cleared the chamber of a spent cartridge case, cocked the action, and readied the gun for firing.

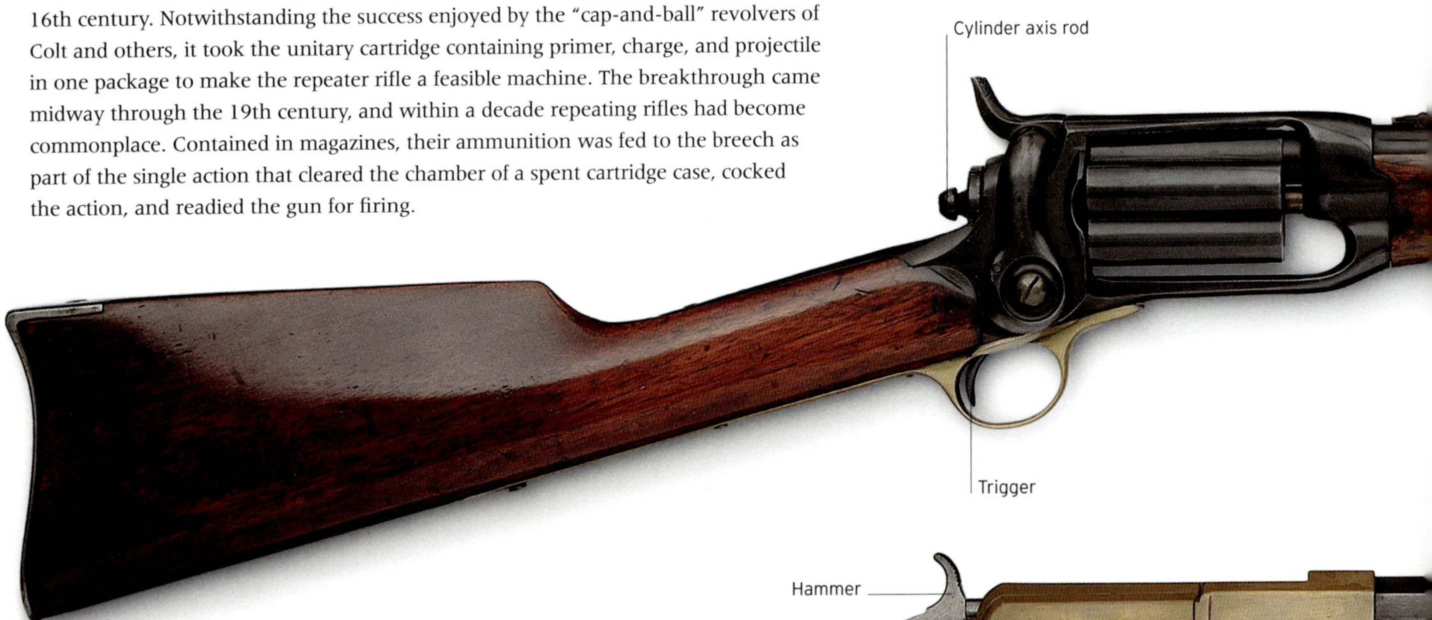

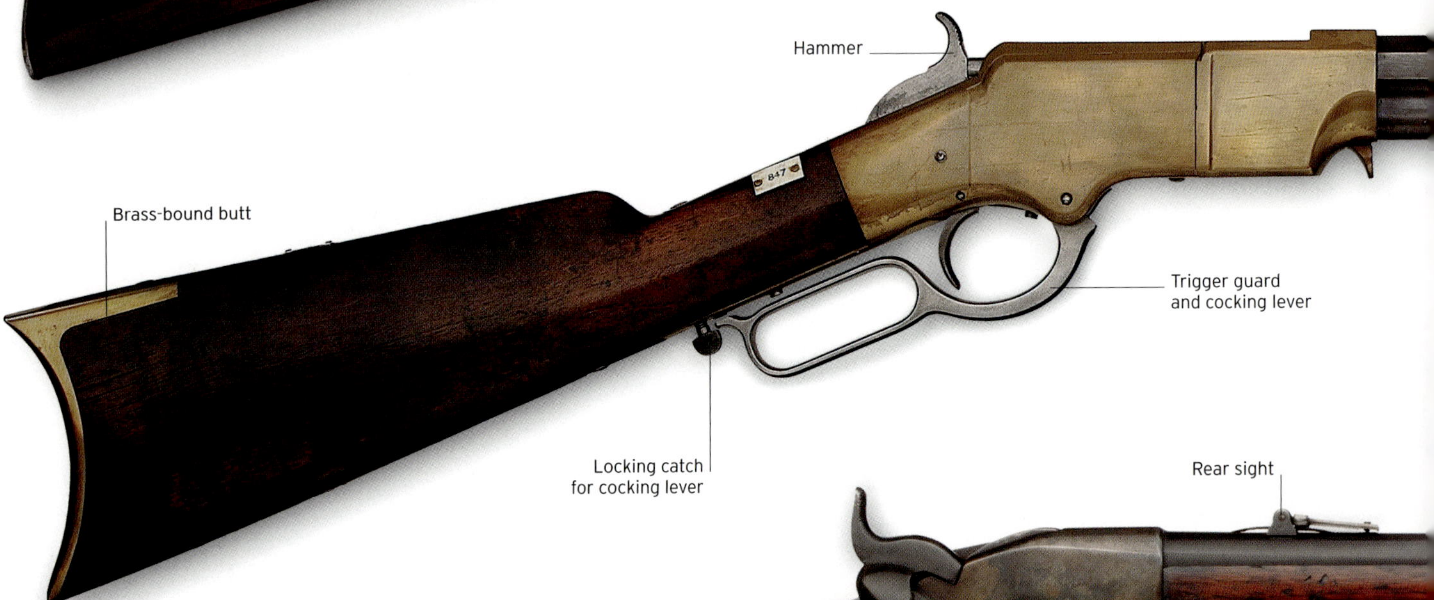

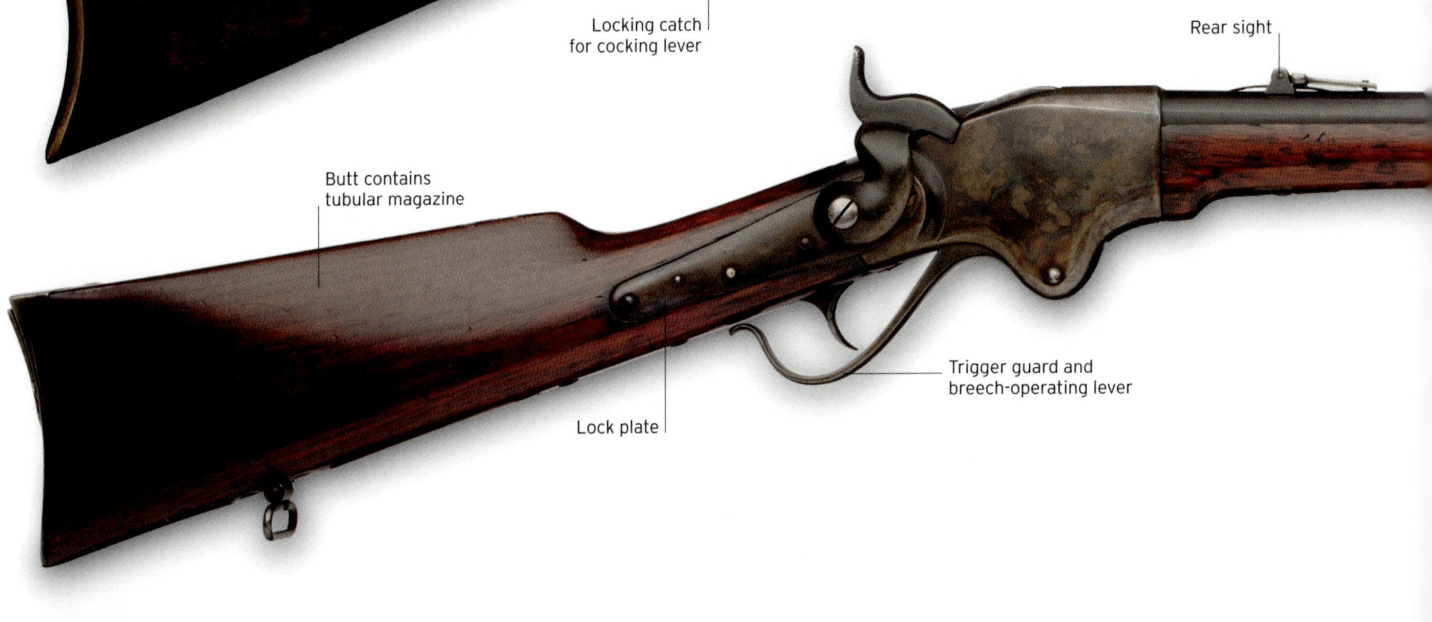

△ Colt Revolving Rifle Model 1855

Date 1855	**Origin** US
Weight 3.45kg (7½lb)	
Barrel 68.2cm (26¾in)	
Calibre .56in	

The 1855 was the third model of the Colt Manufacturing Company's 1838 revolving rifle. It made a considerable impact, even though the loading procedure of the five-chambered cylinder was cumbersome.

△ Henry Model 1860

Date 1860	**Origin** US
Weight 4kg (8¾lb)	
Barrel 51cm (20in)	
Calibre .44in Rim-fire	

In Tyler Henry's repeating rifle, an under-lever ejected a spent round, chambered a new one, and left the action cocked. A two-piece bolt joined by a toggle-joint locked the action.

△ Spencer Rifle

Date 1863	**Origin** US
Weight 4.55kg (10lb)	
Barrel 72cm (28¼in)	
Calibre .52in	

The Spencer, which had a tubular seven-round magazine in the butt stock, was the world's first practical military repeater. It was adopted by the Union Army in the American Civil War.

Manually Loaded Repeater Rifles (cont.)

△ Mosin-Nagant M91

Date	1891
Origin	Imperial Russia
Weight	4.43 kg ($9\frac{3}{4}$ lb)
Barrel	80.2 cm ($31\frac{1}{2}$ in)
Calibre	7.62 mm x 54R

The "3-line," as it was called, was Imperial Russia's first repeater rifle and its first in a modern calibre. The "line" was a measure approximating one-tenth of an inch and refers to its calibre.

△ Lebel MLE 1886/93

Date	1893
Origin	France
Weight	4.3 kg ($9\frac{1}{2}$ lb)
Barrel	80 cm (32 in)
Calibre	8 mm x 50R

In 1885, Georges Boulanger was appointed to the ministry of war in Paris. One of his first priorities was to introduce a modern rifle. The result was the first rifle firing a small-calibre, jacketed bullet propelled by smokeless powder (invented by Meille in 1884). Despite being mechanically unsophisticated, it rendered every other rifle in the world obsolete. This modified version followed in 1893.

△ Springfield Model 1903

Date	1903
Origin	US
Weight	4 kg ($8\frac{1}{2}$ lb)
Barrel	61 cm (24 in)
Calibre	.30 in-03

Impressed by the Mauser rifles US troops encountered during the war against Spain, the United States Ordnance Department looked to replace its Krag rifles. Negotiating a license to build a Mauser design of its own, the result was the .30in Rifle, Magazine, M1903. The example shown here has an experimental 25-round magazine.

Self-loading Pistols

The German gun maker Hugo Borchardt emigrated to the US in 1860, where he worked for Colt and Winchester. When he returned to Germany in 1892 to work for Waffenfabrik Loewe, the company was already producing Maxim guns. This motivated him to experiment with the development of a self-loading pistol. By 1893 he had produced a satisfactory, if somewhat cumbersome, design. His work inspired other gun manufacturers and by the end of the century there were a dozen self-loading pistols on the market, all designed and produced in Europe.

△ Mauser C96

Date	1896–1930s
Origin	Germany
Weight	1.15 kg (2½ lb)
Barrel	14 cm (5½ in)
Calibre	7.63 mm Mauser

Despite shortcomings, chief among which was its complexity, the Mauser C96, chambered for a particularly effective and popular round, was one of the most successful designs of its day.

▽ Borchardt C93

Date	1894
Origin	Germany
Weight	1.66 kg (3¾ lb)
Barrel	16.5 cm (6½ in)
Calibre	7.65 mm

The C93 was the first successful self-loading pistol. For its locking mechanism, it drew on the design of Maxim's machine-guns, which Borchardt's employer, Loewe, was producing under license in Berlin.

▷ **Browning Model 1900**	
Date	1900
Origin	Belgium
Weight	0.63 kg (1½ lb)
Barrel	10.2 cm (4 in)
Calibre	7.65 mm

John Browning, probably the most prolific gun designer ever, moved to Belgium from his native US in 1895. There he produced an improved version of his first semi-automatic pistol, which became known as the Model 1900. It used a breech of the blowback type. Small and light, the Model 1900 was hugely popular, and over 700,000 units were sold before production ceased in 1911.

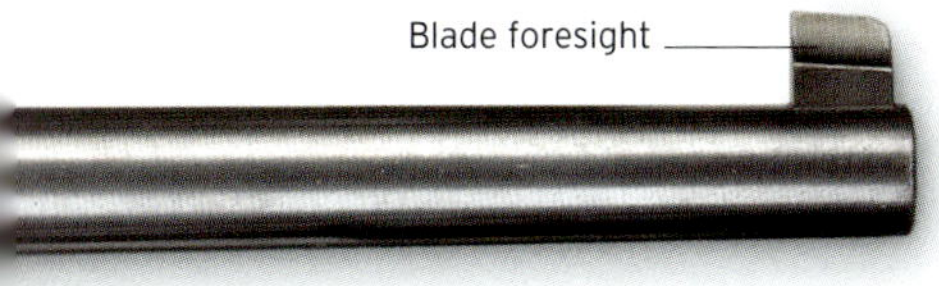

FULL VIEW

Muzzle-loading Artillery

In the 19th century, infantrymen firing rifled small arms achieved greater range than smoothbore cannon, so attempts were made to apply rifling to field artillery. The first rifled cannons were developed in the 1840s but some – such as the Whitworth 12-pounder, which saw service in the American Civil War – were breech- rather than muzzle-loaders. Breech-loaders permitted a higher rate of fire and were generally safer to use, but muzzle-loaders were cheaper to manufacture and used cheaper ammunition. As a result, muzzle-loaders continued to be popular for military use.

▷ British 9-pounder Field Gun

Date 1876	**Origin** UK
Weight 1.04 tonnes (1.14 tons)	
Length 1.79 m (5¾ ft)	
Calibre 3 in	

Field guns like this muzzle-loading rifled British 9-pounder played an important role in both sieges and field battles in the British Army's overseas engagements of this period.

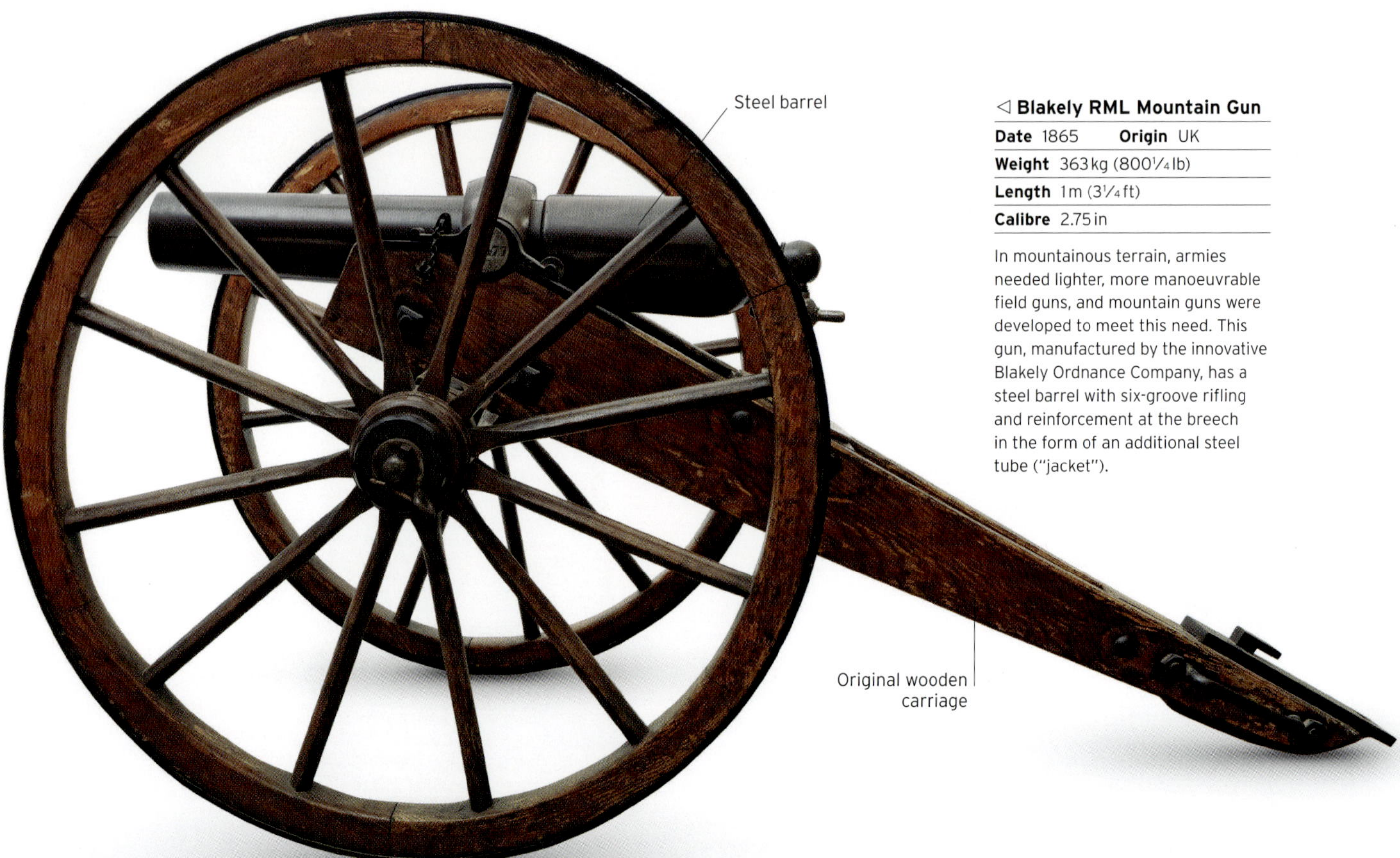

◁ Blakely RML Mountain Gun

Date 1865	**Origin** UK
Weight 363 kg (800¼ lb)	
Length 1 m (3¼ ft)	
Calibre 2.75 in	

In mountainous terrain, armies needed lighter, more manoeuvrable field guns, and mountain guns were developed to meet this need. This gun, manufactured by the innovative Blakely Ordnance Company, has a steel barrel with six-groove rifling and reinforcement at the breech in the form of an additional steel tube ("jacket").

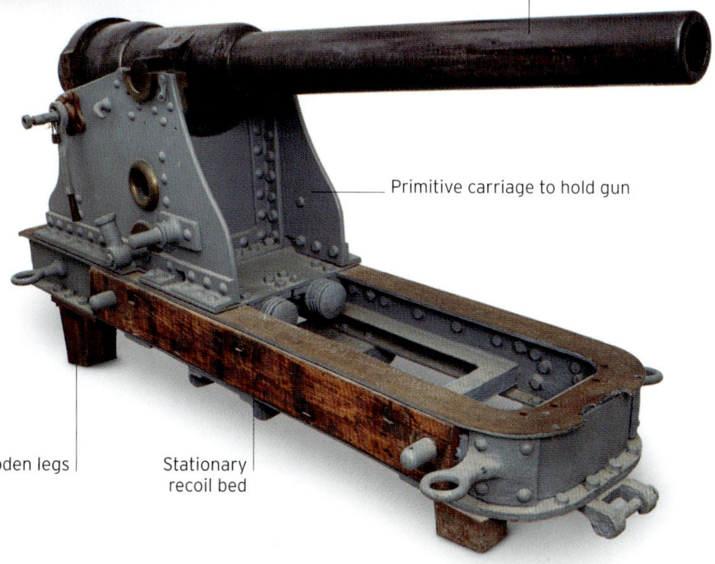

▷ Armstrong RML 12-pounder

Date 1878	**Origin** UK
Weight 415 kg (915 lb)	
Length 2.23 m (7¼ ft)	
Calibre 3 in	

The initials RML in the gun title stand for "rifled muzzle-loader". This steel 12-pounder was manufactured by Armstrong in Newcastle, northern England, for merchant marine use.

▷ **Armstrong RBL 12-pounder**

Date 1859	**Origin** UK
Length 2.13 m (7 ft)	
Calibre 7.62 cm	
Range 3.1 km (1.92 miles)	

The Armstrong rifled 12-pounder gun required a crew of nine men to operate it. The gun that entered British Army service in 1859 had a 2.13 m (7 ft) barrel, while the British Royal Navy used a 1.83 m (6 ft) barrel version. In 1863, the shorter version became standard.

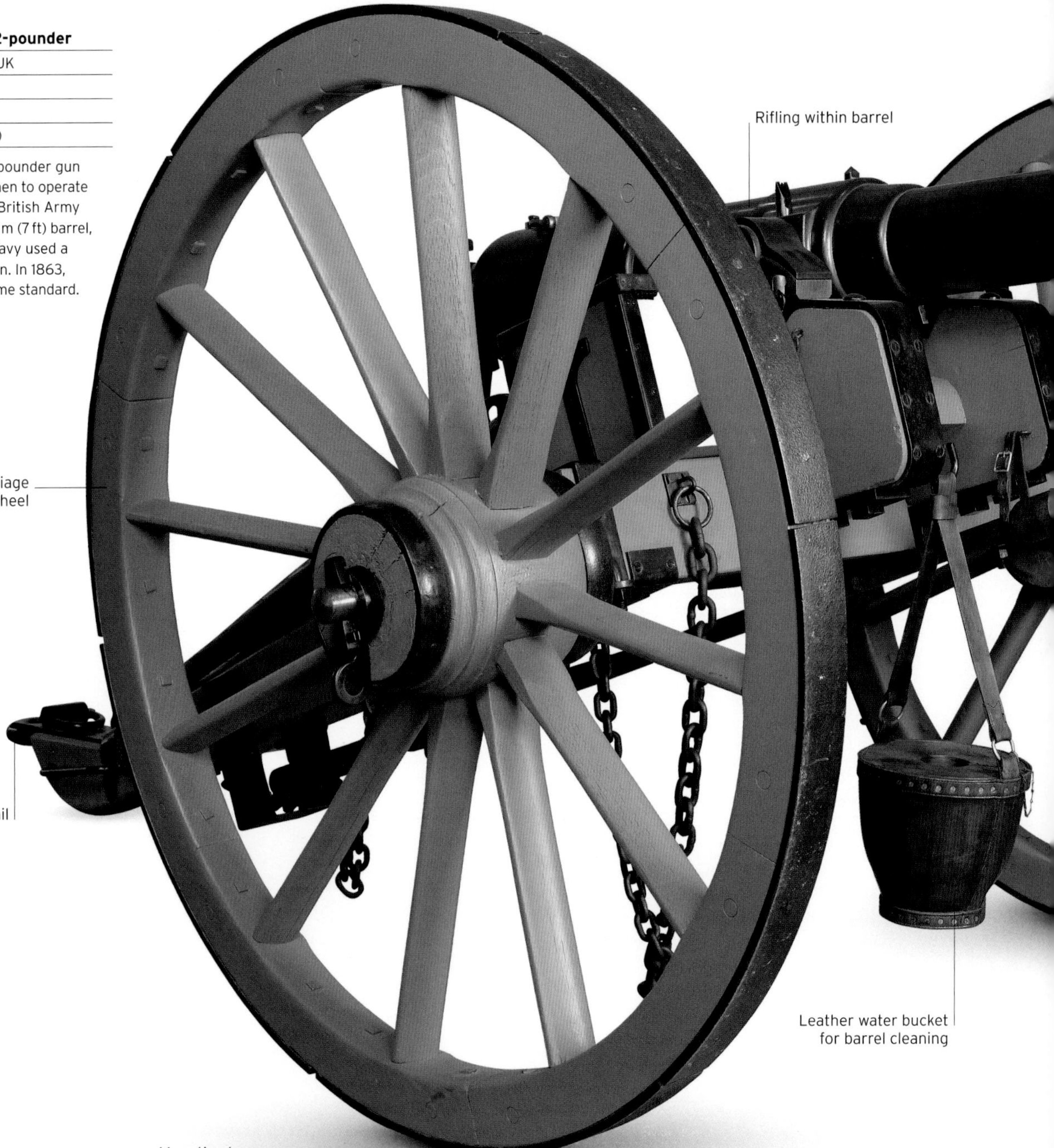

▷ **Armstrong RBL 40-pound Gun**

Date 1861	**Origin** UK
Length 3 m (9³⁄₄ ft)	
Calibre 12 cm	
Range 2.56 km (1.59 miles)	

The Armstrong rifled breech-loading 40-pounder was used by the British Royal Navy as a broadside gun, and by the army as a defensive gun in military forts. It saw action in the Royal Navy's bombardment of Kagoshima, Japan, in August 1863.

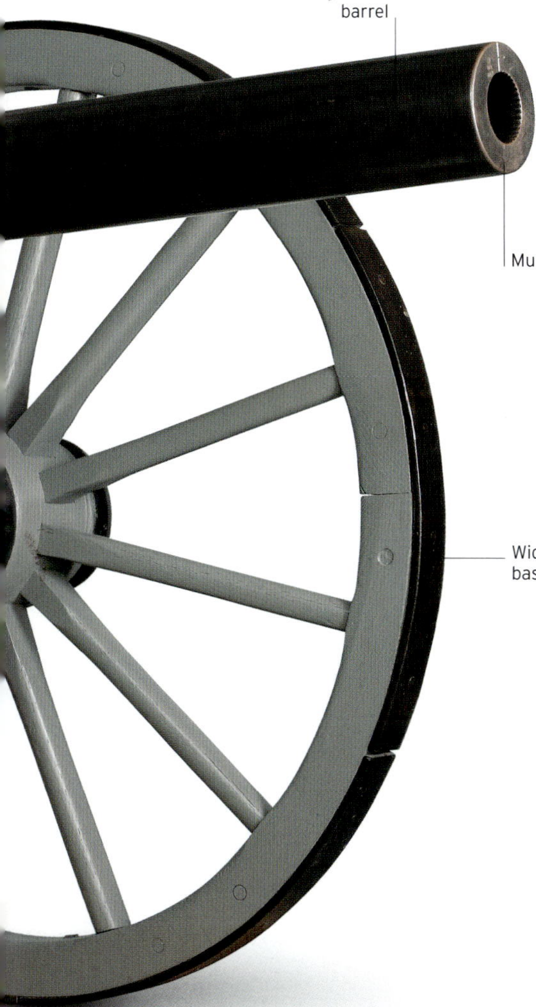

▷ **Whitworth 45 mm Breech-loading Boat Gun**

Date 1875	**Origin** UK
Length 94 cm (37 in)	
Calibre 45 mm	
Range 360 m ($393\frac{3}{4}$ yards)	

This boat gun had hexagonal rifling with a Whitworth sliding-lock breech-loading mechanism. It was set on a cone mounting mostly used for small naval guns. This example was mounted on an armed yacht.

Breech-loading Artillery

British engineer William Armstrong designed the first efficient breech-loading rifled field gun in 1855. The shell and gunpowder propellant were loaded at the breech, which was closed with a "vent-piece" secured in a slot with a hollow screw. Armstrong's 12-pounder gun of 1859 was the first rifled breech-loading field gun to enter British Army service, and the Armstrong RBL 40-pounder was an adaptation of this gun used as a medium artillery piece both by the British Army and Navy.

Breech-loading Artillery (cont.)

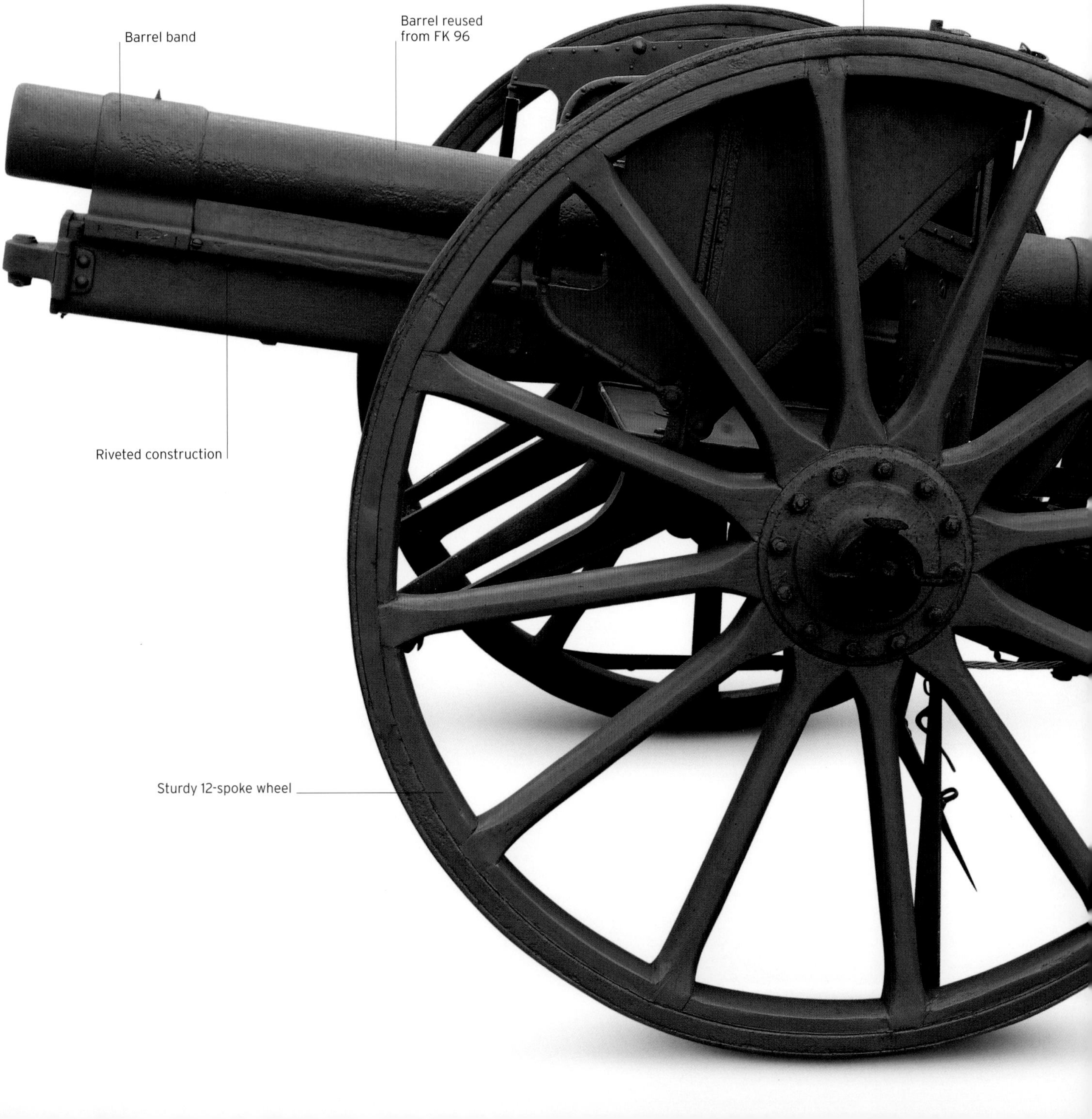

▷ **Krupp 8.9 cm Field Gun**

Date 1895	**Origin** Germany
Length 2.6 m (8½ ft)	
Calibre 8.9 cm	
Range 2.3 km (1 mile)	

This rifled breech-loading field gun was fitted with high brackets to make it sit in an elevated position in the carriage, and enable it to fire over the parapet of a fortified site. It is thought to have been captured by British forces from Boers at Pietersburg (modern-day Polokwanè), South Africa, in 1901.

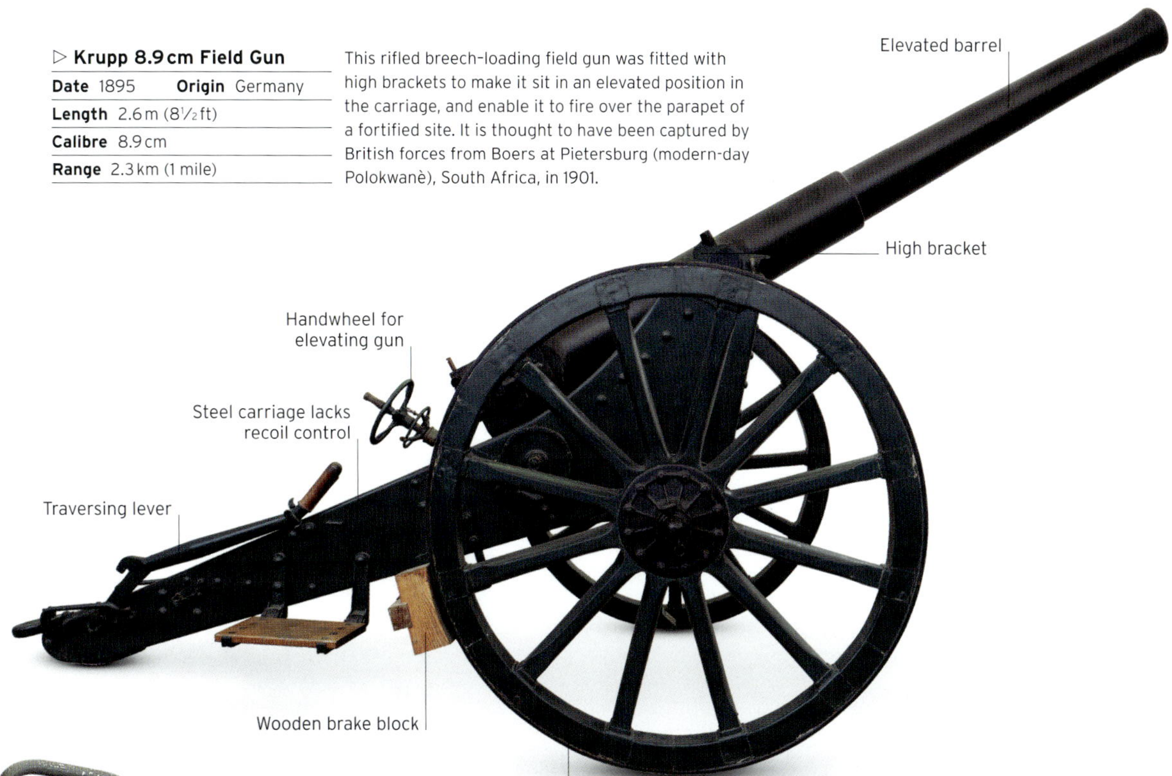

△ **7.7 cm FK 96 NA**

Date 1905	**Origin** Germany
Length (Barrel) 2.1 m (6¾ ft)	
Calibre 77 mm	
Range 7.8 km (4.84 miles)	

The 7.7 cm Feldkanone 96 Neuer Art was an upgraded version of the FK 96, featuring improvements to the carriage and the breech, and the addition of a recoil system. It was the standard German field gun at the start of World War I, and although reliable, its elevation was limited. A crew of five could fire ten rounds per minute.

Foresight
Magazine slot
Antirotation pawl
Barrels
Pivot for revolving mechanism
Wheel hub
Cotter

Gatling Gun

By the second half of the 19th century, improvements in engineering had made it possible to manufacture reliable rapid-fire weapons. This gun, patented by Richard Gatling in 1862, employed multiple barrels, as would all early machine-guns. It was first developed during the American Civil War and was deemed a success.

SPECIFICATIONS	
Model	Gatling Gun
Date	1865
Origin	US
Barrel	67.3 cm ($26\frac{1}{2}$ in)
Calibre	.45 in, .65 in, or 1 in
Maximum weight of gun	27.2 kg (60 lb)
Length	107.9 cm ($42\frac{1}{2}$ in)
Rate of fire	Up to 400 rounds per minute
Crew	Four

THE GATLING GUN went through many changes in its 49-year production history, its calibres varying from .30 and .42 to .58 and 1 in as new and more powerful cartridges were introduced. As the calibre of its ammunition changed, so did the number of barrels, with some models increasing the number from the initial six to ten.

In 1893, the Gatling was adapted to take the smaller new .30 Army cartridge, by which time its maximum initial rate of fire had increased from 200 to between 800–900 rounds per minute. This new M1893 version was later powered by an electric motor and belt to drive the crank. Under test, this electric Gatling could fire up to 1,500 rounds per minute.

FRONT VIEW

Riveted iron trail was placed on ground for stability during combat, and at other times could be attached to a horse-drawn limber containing ammunition

How Gatling gun worked
The gun's barrels - at first six, later 10 (as shown in this prototype) - were arranged around a cylindrical shaft. A hand-operated crank made the barrels revolve, and cartridges dropped into place from above as each barrel came around. A firing pin then struck and fired the bullet; the barrel turned and the process was repeated. As each barrel descended, its spent case was ejected.

1

2

READYING THE GUN

The Gatling gun was required to be both manoeuvrable and, once in position, stable. The carriage on which it stood was easily towed into place, the towing rings were secured to each wheel hub by a cotter (wedge-shaped fastener), while a traversing handspike fixed on the right side of the trail was used for additional grip when manoeuvring the carriage. The wide wheelbase increased the carriage's stability. Once in place, the riveted iron trail was placed firmly on the ground for stability. The barrel was then elevated to the right firing height using the foresight. A hand-operated crank rotated the barrels prior to firing, with the ammunition already loaded into the magazine.

1. Foresight and barrels **2.** Antirotation pawl **3.** Magazine slot **4.** Elevating gear **5.** Wheel hub **6.** Hand-operated crank **7.** Traversing handspike

3

4

5

6

7

Machine-guns

By the time of the American Civil War (1861–65), there was widespread interest in the potential benefit offered by rapid-fire weapons during combat. Two designers in particular, Wilson Ager and Richard Gatling, developed guns that showed potential. Their early machine-guns used a primitive type of cartridge in the form of reloadable steel tubes fitted with percussion caps, and consequently suffered from problems. However, the development of reliable unitary, metal-encased centre-fire cartridges, carrying propellant, projectile, and primer in one package, enabled these guns to achieve high rates of fire.

▽ Early Gatling Converted to Metallic Cartridge

Date c.1862	**Origin** US
Weight Unknown	
Barrel 1.4 m (4½ ft)	
Calibre .50 in	

Richard Jordan Gatling patented his hand-cranked, multi-barrelled gun in 1862, and first used reloadable steel cartridges fired by percussion caps. Problems with misfires were common. In order to solve these issues, this early machine-gun was eventually modified to utilize the improved unitary cartridges.

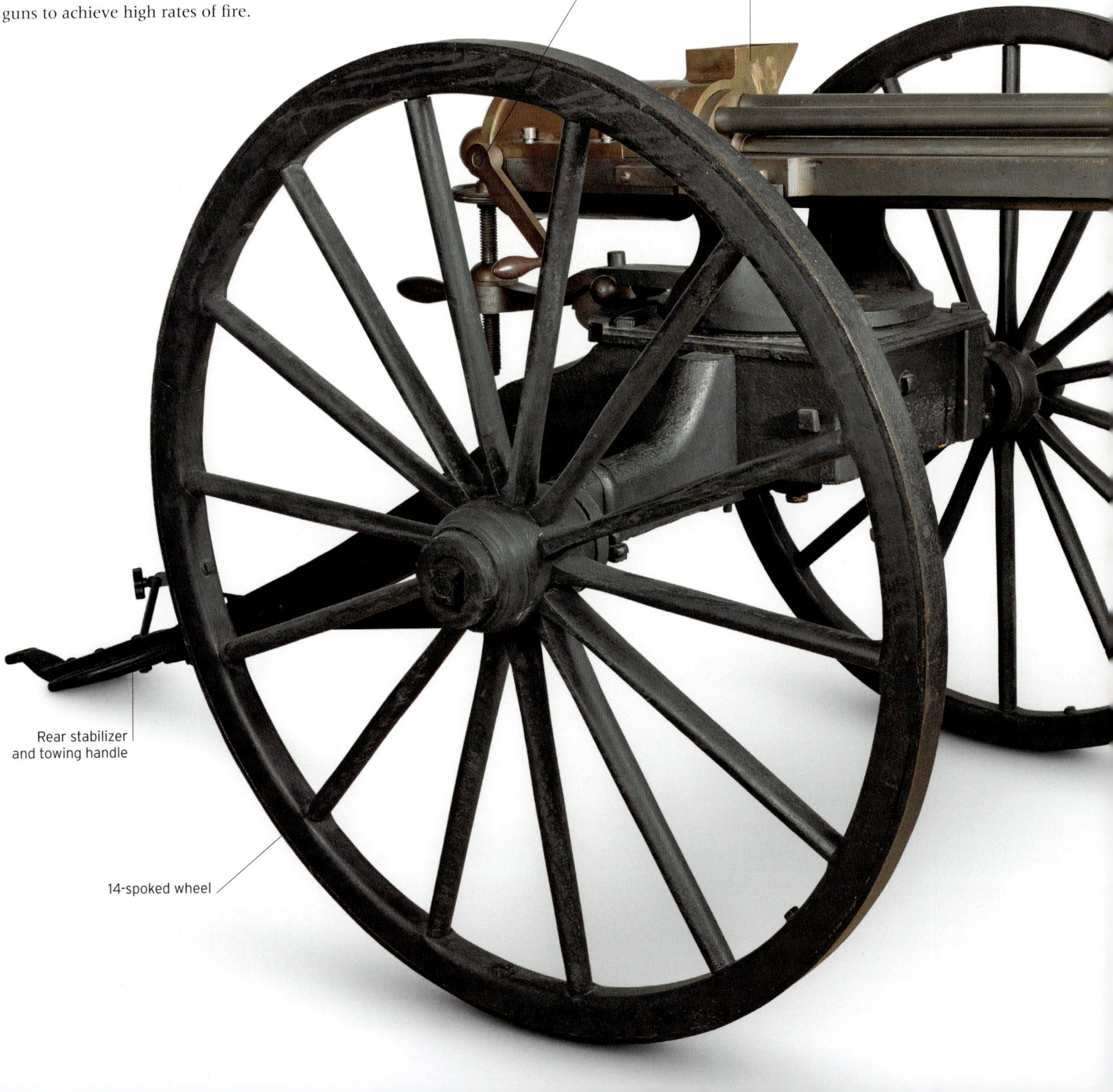

▷ Vickers "Light Pattern" Model 1908

Date 1908	**Origin** UK
Weight 18.1kg (40lb)	
Barrel 72.3cm (28½in)	
Calibre 7.7mm	

Designed to resolve shortcomings in the Vickers-Maxim "New Light" model, the locking toggle was modified in this gun: it now broke upward, reducing the size of the receiver. The "disappearing" tripod mount allowed the gun to be fired from the cover of a parapet.

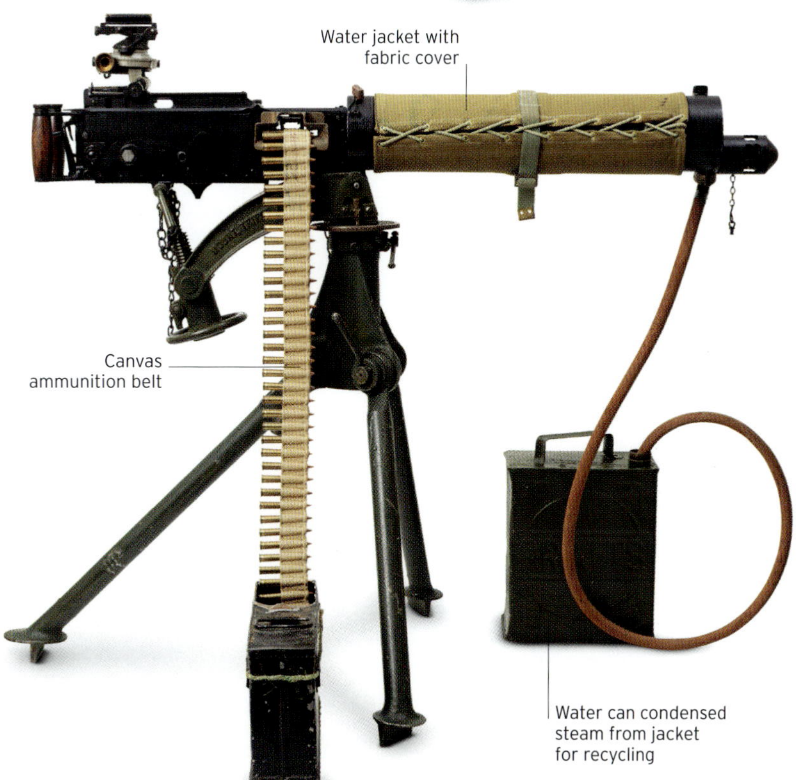

◁ Vickers MK I

Date 1912	**Origin** UK
Weight 18.1kg (40lb)	
Barrel 72.1cm (28½in)	
Calibre .303in	

Employed in both world wars, the water-cooled Vickers was an extremely reliable medium machine-gun, and, when firing the Mk 8Z bullet, was capable of a range of up to 4.1km (2.54 miles).

Battle of Tsushima
Having sailed halfway round the world from the Baltic, the Russian fleet encountered a smaller Japanese fleet in the Tsushima Straits between Korea and Japan. The battle on 27–28 May 1905 was the first between modern steel battleship fleets and the first in which wireless telegraphy played a major role. Two-thirds of the Russian fleet was destroyed, and the subsequent peace treaty with Japan resulted in revolution in Russia.

Mikasa

The only remaining example of a pre-dreadnought battleship, the *Mikasa* was the Japanese flagship at the Battle of Tsushima in 1905, which saw the Imperial Russian fleet virtually annihilated.

BASED ON the Royal Navy's *Majestic* class, the *Mikasa* was the last of four similar battleships built in British yards for the Imperial Japanese Navy. Constructed by Vickers at Barrow-in-Furness, the *Mikasa* entered service on 1 March 1902.

The ship's main armament consisted of four 12 in guns, 40 calibres long, mounted in twin centre-line turrets fore and aft. These could be fired at a rate of three shots every two minutes. The *Mikasa*'s secondary armament included fourteen 6 in quick-firing guns, lighter guns for defence against destroyers and torpedo-boats, and four submerged torpedo tubes.

The *Mikasa* was one of the first ships to have "Krupp Cemented" steel armour. In addition to forming the main deck, this armour was fitted in belts around the waterline up to 23 cm (9 in) thick, and in 356 mm- (14 in-) thick "barbettes" around the 12 in gun installations. The armour proved effective at Tsushima, when some 30 hits from Russian guns failed to put the *Mikasa* out of action. Ironically, the ship sank in the harbour four months later after an accidental explosion in a magazine. Although raised in 1906 and repaired, the *Mikasa* never saw combat again and was decommissioned in 1923. It is now a museum ship at Yokosuka.

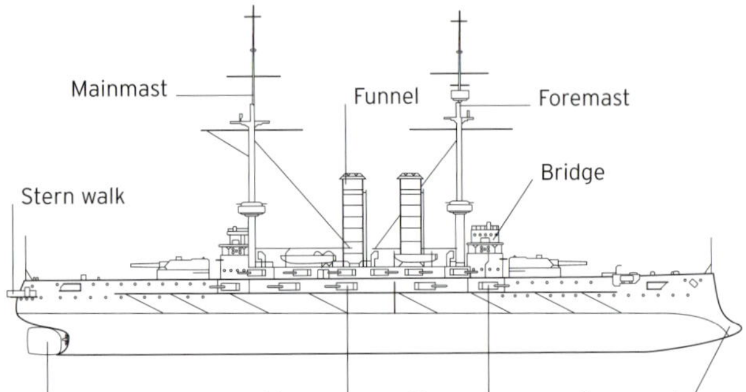

SIDE VIEW

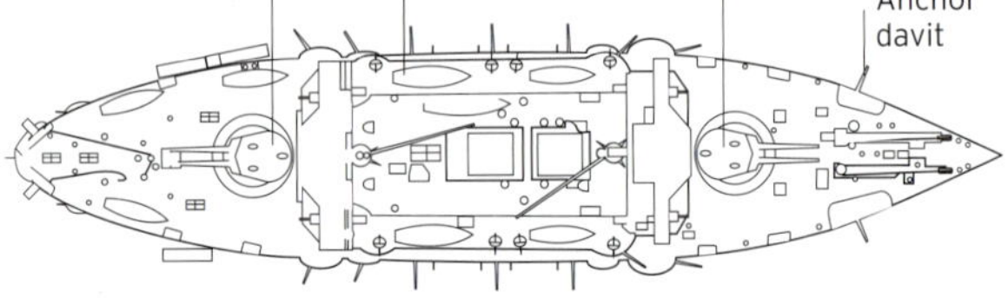

PLAN VIEW

Decorative golden imperial seal on bow

Mikasa
About 132 m (432 ft) long and displacing 15,140 tons, the *Mikasa* was powered by two triple-expanding steam engines that gave a top speed of 18 knots.

SPECIFICATIONS	
Class	Modified *Majestic*-class battleship
Commissioned	1902
Origin	Japan
Displacement	15,140 tons
Length	132 m (432 ft)
Beam	23.2 m (76 ft)
Engines	2 x vertical triple-expansion steam engines
Top Speed	33.4 km/h (18 knots)
Range	17,000 km (9,000 nautical miles)
Complement	836
Armament	4 x 12 in main guns, 14 x 6 in quick-firing guns, 20 QF 12-pounder 12 cwt guns, 8 x 3-pounder 47 mm, 8 x 2.5-pounder 47 mm, 4 submerged 18-in torpedo tubes
Armour	10-23 cm (4-9 in) around belt; 50-76 mm (2-3 in) on deck; 20.3-35.6 cm (8-14 in) around guns

ON DECK

Situated in front of the foremast, the bridge gave an uninterrupted view forwards and to each side. The long wings of the bridge, on which two 90 cm (35 in) searchlights were mounted, extended the full width of the ship. The pilothouse and chartroom were topped by an open platform bearing a compass and rangefinder. Orders were given to the pilothouse via speaking tubes beside the compass.

1. Bridge **2.** Funnels **3.** Command post **4.** Stern walkway **5.** 6 in guns **6.** Rangefinder **7.** 3 in gun casemate **8.** Port to 3 in battery **9.** 6 in gun breech **10.** Officers' wardroom **11.** Admiral's cabin **12.** Pilothouse

1

2

3

4

5

6

7

8

9

10

11

ARMAMENTS AND QUARTERS

To supplement its main armament, the *Mikasa* mounted a variety of smaller-calibre guns, from 6 in ones for use against cruisers and destroyers to 12-, 3-, and 1-pounders. There were also rifle-calibre machine-guns. Living conditions were almost unchanged from the days of sail, with the men sleeping in hammocks and eating at fold-up tables.

12

3

1914–18 WORLD WAR I

The war that broke out in August 1914 revolutionized military technology. Rapid-fire machine-guns dominated the battlefields, while increasingly powerful artillery hurled huge shells across enemy lines. As stalemate descended along the Western Front, new weaponry emerged. Poison gas was first used by the Germans in April 1915 and tanks were first used by the British in September 1916. Aircraft, at first used just for reconnaissance, became fighters and bombers, while submarines took the war under the waves.

Manually Loaded Repeater Rifles

The main difference between the rifles used during the Boer War and those used in World War I lay in the length of their barrels. At the turn of the century, the barrels of infantry rifles were 75 cm (29 in) long. By 1914, some had been shortened by 10 cm (4 in), and the rest were soon to follow. The exception was France, where the barrel of the Berthier rifle, introduced into service in 1916, had actually increased in length.

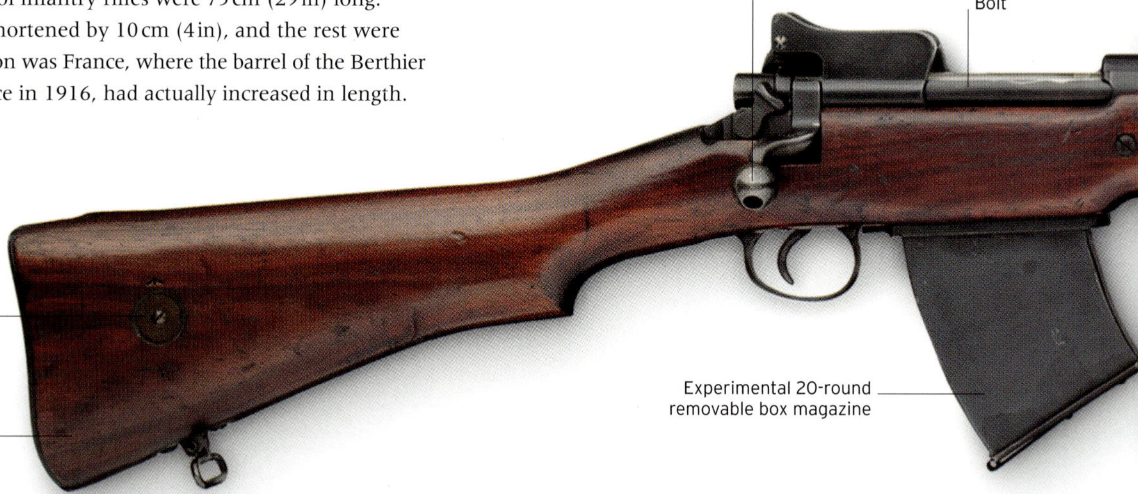

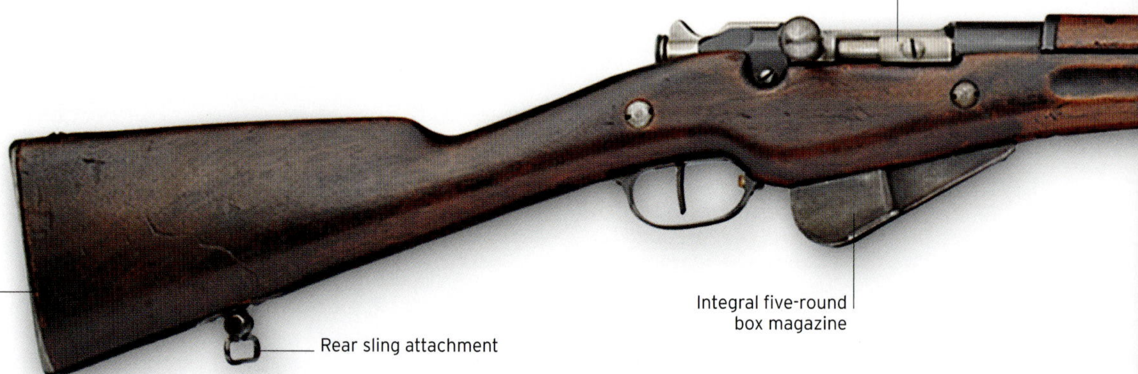

▽ Enfield Pattern 1914

Date 1914 **Origin** UK

Weight 4 kg (8½ lb)

Barrel 66 cm (26 in)

Calibre .303 in Mauser

Around the onset of World War I, the Pattern 1913 rifle was modified to use the .303 in chambering, and the weapon was redesignated as the Pattern 1914. The Model 1917, a .30 in-calibre version of the Pattern 1914, was later adopted by the US Army.

▽ Short Magazine Lee-Enfield with Mills Bomb Launcher

Date 1915 **Origin** UK

Weight Unknown

Barrel 64 cm (25¼ in)

Calibre .303 in

The Mills Bomb was adapted for rifle-use by the addition of a rod to the base cap. The rifle itself was fitted with a ring or cup, mounted at the bayonet lug, to retain the grenade's arming lever. To fire the grenade, a specially formulated blank cartridge was used.

△ Berthier MLE 1916

Date 1916 **Origin** France

Weight 4.15 kg (9 lb)

Barrel 79.8 cm (31¼ in)

Calibre 8 mm x 50R

A modified version of the 1902 model Berthier rifle, this gun had a five-round magazine in place of the original's three-round magazine. The piling hook below the foresight was used to stack the rifles "teepee-style" when troops were encamped.

Machine-guns of World War I

The first generation of machine-guns were too cumbersome to be used in anything but fixed positions, so there was a need for a lighter, portable weapon, capable of sustained fire. Despite its success, with more than 130,000 produced, Germany's Maxim MG08/15 was still too heavy. The barrels of the first light machine-guns tended to overheat. This problem was solved by the development of systems that enabled the barrels to be changed quickly and easily, even under combat conditions.

▽ Hotchkiss Modèle 1914

Date 1914	**Origin** France
Weight 23.58 kg (52 lb)	
Barrel 77.5 cm (30½ in)	
Calibre 8 mm Lebel	

The Modèle 1914 was a slight improvement on earlier designs, but was still prone to overheating. It had a problematic feed system that used 24-round metallic strips, rather than fabric belts. However, it was still reliable when used correctly, and saw service until the early 1940s.

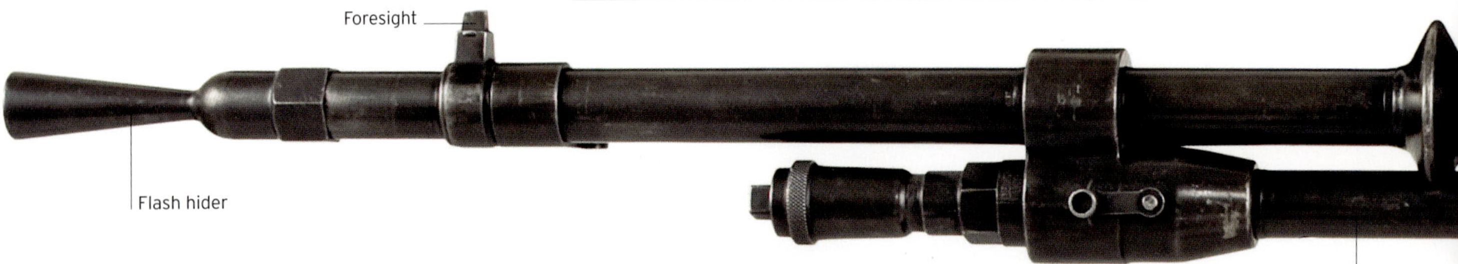

▽ Maxim MG08/15

Date 1915	**Origin** Germany
Weight 14 kg (30¾ lb)	
Barrel 71.9 cm (28½ in)	
Calibre 7.92 mm Mauser	

Germany's first, hurried attempt to produce a light machine-gun saw the DWM MG08 fitted with a butt, a pistol grip, and a conventional trigger, resulting in the Maxim 08/15. This improved version of the MG08 had a recontoured receiver to reduce the gun's weight and an integral bipod with a shortened ammunition belt contained in a drum-like container. Weighing 14 kg (30¾ lb), it was still far too heavy.

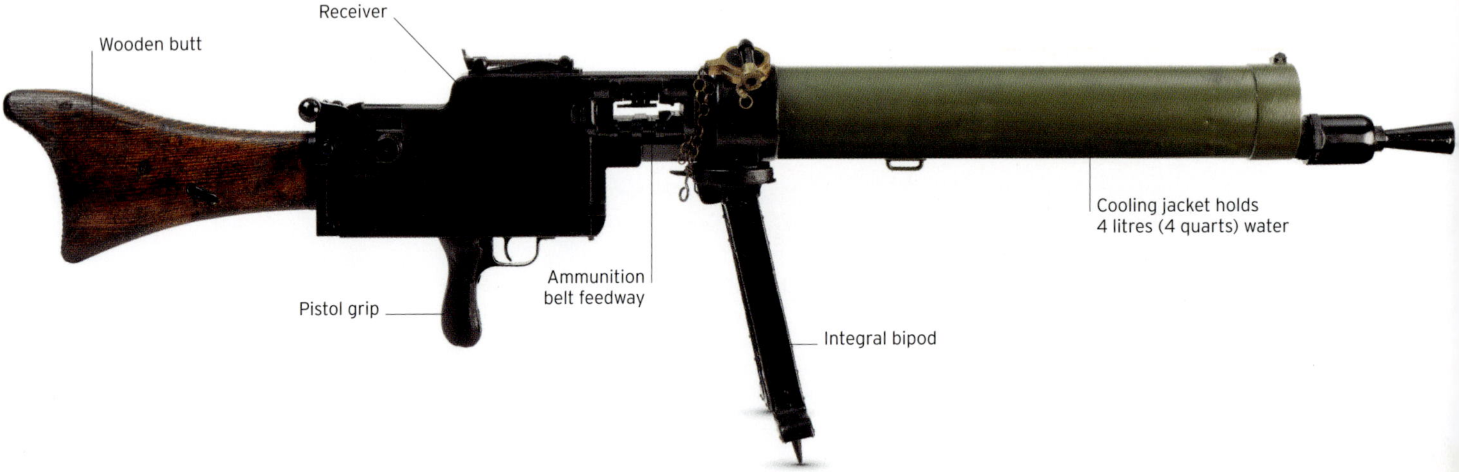

△ **Browning Automatic Rifle (BAR) M1918**

Date 1918	**Origin** US
Weight 7.28 kg (16 lb)	
Barrel 61 cm (24 in)	
Calibre .30-06 Springfield	

John Browning responded to pleas to provide infantrymen with a weapon they could fire in bursts from the hip while advancing. The gas-operated BAR was too heavy and cumbersome ever to be a success in that role, but it survived as the US Army's stock LMG until the 1950s.

FULL VIEW

Trench Weapons

Throughout World War I, assaults on enemy positions almost inevitably ended in hand-to-hand combat in the confined spaces of trenches and dugouts. Pistols came into their own in such circumstances, but were mainly only issued to officers. Individual soldiers armed themselves with the rifle-and-bayonet as well as expedient weapons, such as knives and axes, which were chosen for their ability to disable or kill at a single stroke. The first grenades were not quite fit for purpose but soon improved dramatically.

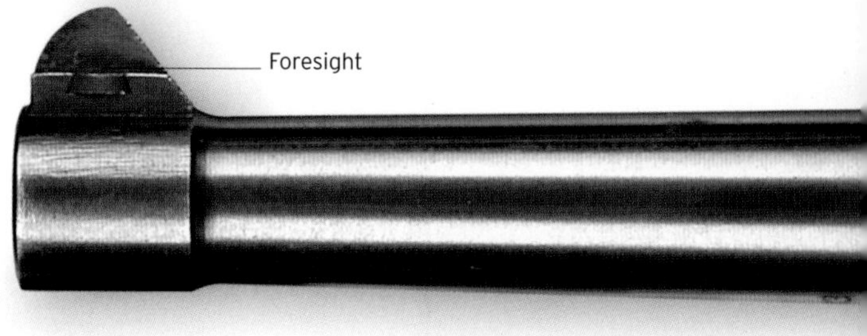

△ Luger P08

Date 1908–42 **Origin** Germany

Weight 880 g (31 oz)

Barrel 10 cm (4 in)

Calibre 9 mm Parabellum

Georg Luger's Pistole '08 – the P08 or "Parabellum" – was the German officer's handgun of choice during World War I. Its 9 mm Parabellum round (9x19 mm) was more powerful than others of similar dimensions, and became a world standard.

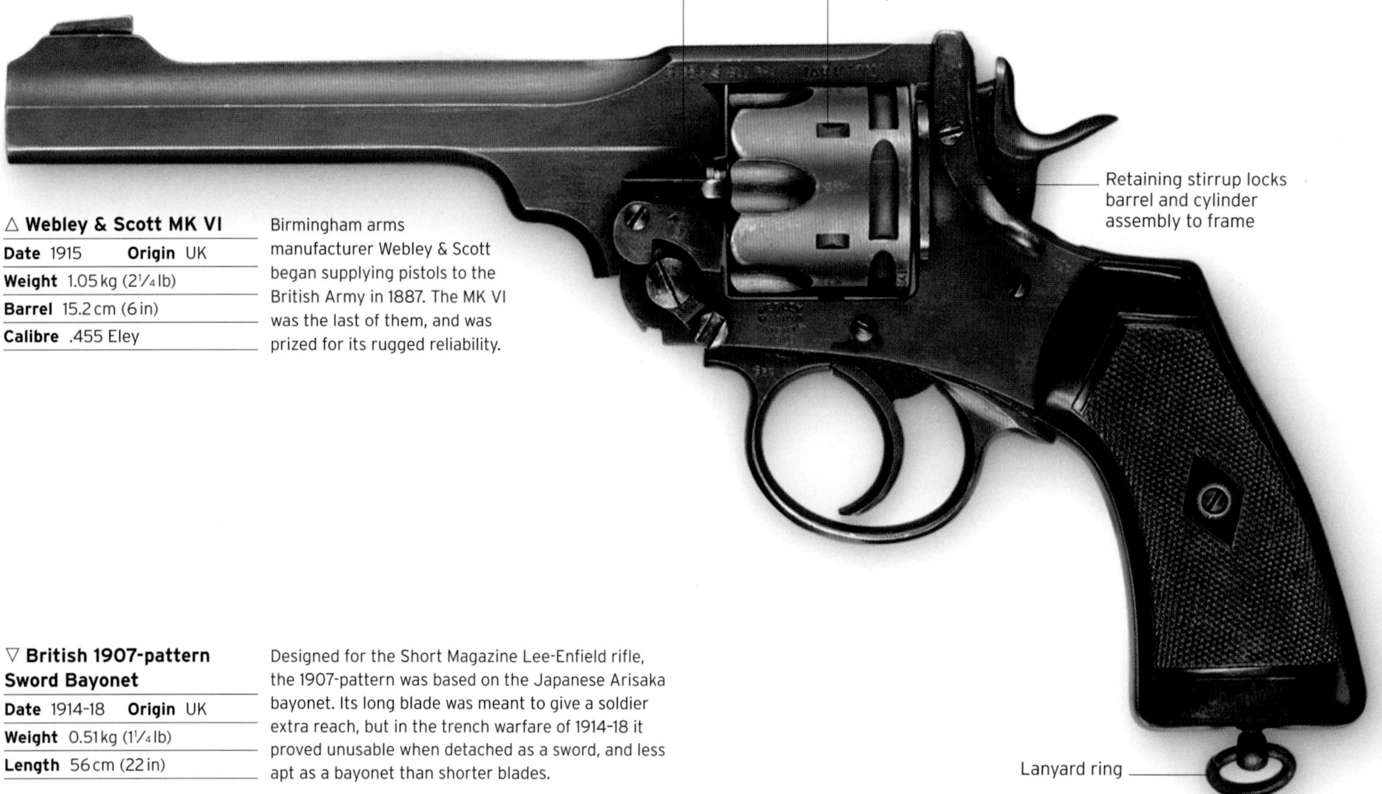

△ Webley & Scott MK VI

Date 1915 **Origin** UK

Weight 1.05 kg (2¼ lb)

Barrel 15.2 cm (6 in)

Calibre .455 Eley

Birmingham arms manufacturer Webley & Scott began supplying pistols to the British Army in 1887. The MK VI was the last of them, and was prized for its rugged reliability.

▽ British 1907-pattern Sword Bayonet

Date 1914–18 **Origin** UK

Weight 0.51 kg (1¼ lb)

Length 56 cm (22 in)

Designed for the Short Magazine Lee-Enfield rifle, the 1907-pattern was based on the Japanese Arisaka bayonet. Its long blade was meant to give a soldier extra reach, but in the trench warfare of 1914–18 it proved unusable when detached as a sword, and less apt as a bayonet than shorter blades.

◁ **No. 36 Mills Bomb**

Date	1915	**Origin**	UK
Weight	765 g (27 oz)		
Length	95.2 mm (3¾ in)		

Grenades became more effective when reliable time-fuses became available. The British Mills Bomb, with its "pineapple" casing filled with a TNT-based explosive called Baratol, was the first of its type, and was widely copied.

Trench Weapons (cont.)

△ **Nailed Cosh**

Date 1916

Origin UK

The simplest trench-fighting weapons were clubs and truncheons, often - as in this example - with nails or spikes added to increase their lethality, and usually with a retaining loop.

FULL VIEW

△ **British Spiked Club**

Date c.1916

Origin UK

This club, hand-whittled from hardwood, incorporates both horseshoe nails and a stabbing spike in its enlarged head. It also has serrations to improve the grip, and a wrist strap for security.

▷ **Trench Axe**

Date 1916

Origin UK

Issued to British troops as a general-purpose tool, the trench axe was widely employed as a weapon in close-quarter fighting during raids and assaults on enemy positions.

▽ 15 cm Heavy Field Howitzer M1914/16

Date 1916	**Origin** Austria-Hungary
Weight 2.77 tonnes (3.05 tons)	
Length 2.12 m (7 ft)	
Calibre 149 mm	
Range 8.75 km (5.43 miles)	

The M1914/16 was manufactured by Skoda for the Austro-Hungarian army. A skilled crew could fire two 41 kg (90¼ lb) shells a minute for a limited period of action. Large numbers of the gun were handed over to the Italian army in World War II.

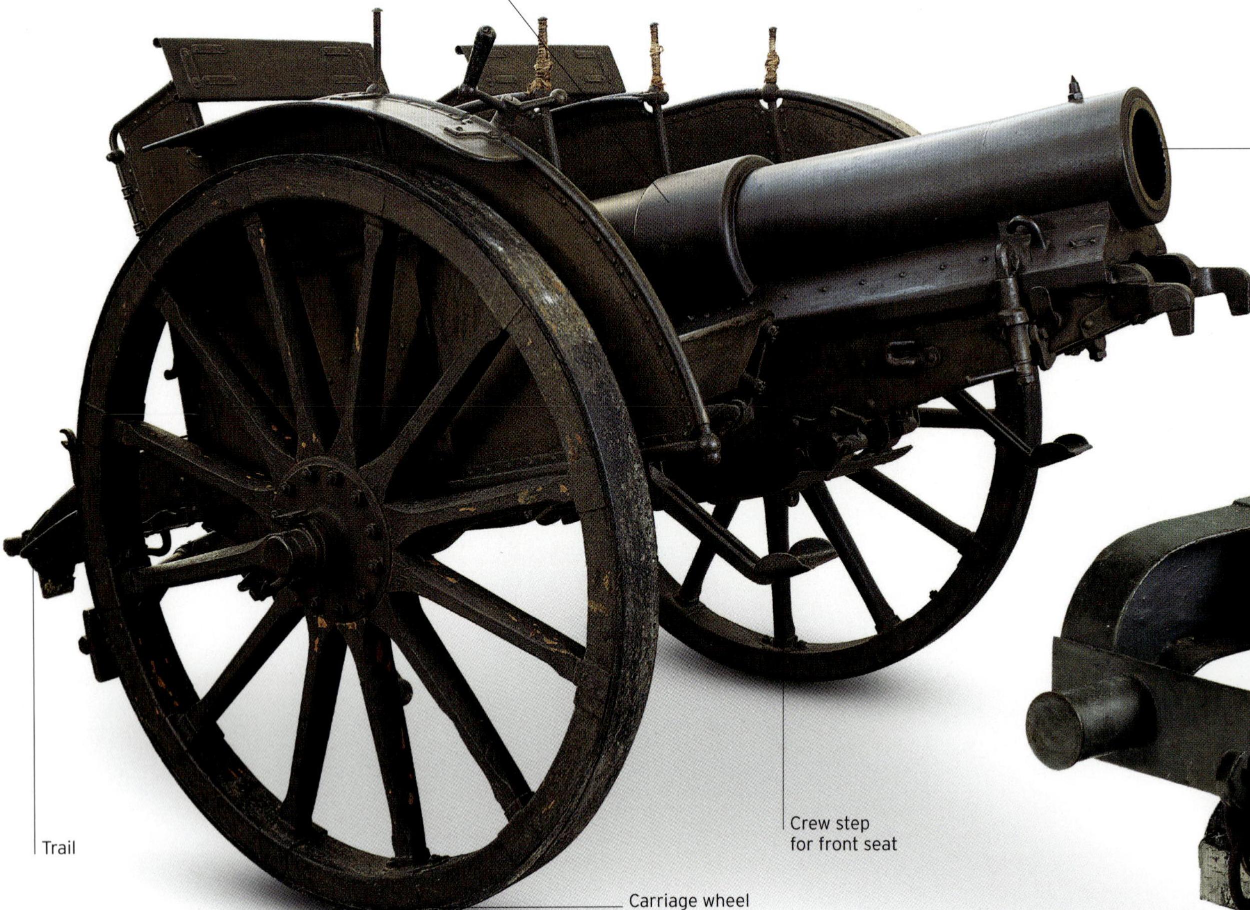

Howitzers

The artillery pieces in use after 1914 were capable of inflicting casualties on an industrial scale. They ranged from mountain guns that could be broken down quickly and carried by mules, and light guns such as the 18-pounder quick-firer – which were used on the battlefield rather than fired from a dug-in position – to howitzers. Guns mounted on railway tracks that could reach a target more than 40 km (25 miles) away were used for long-range bombardment.

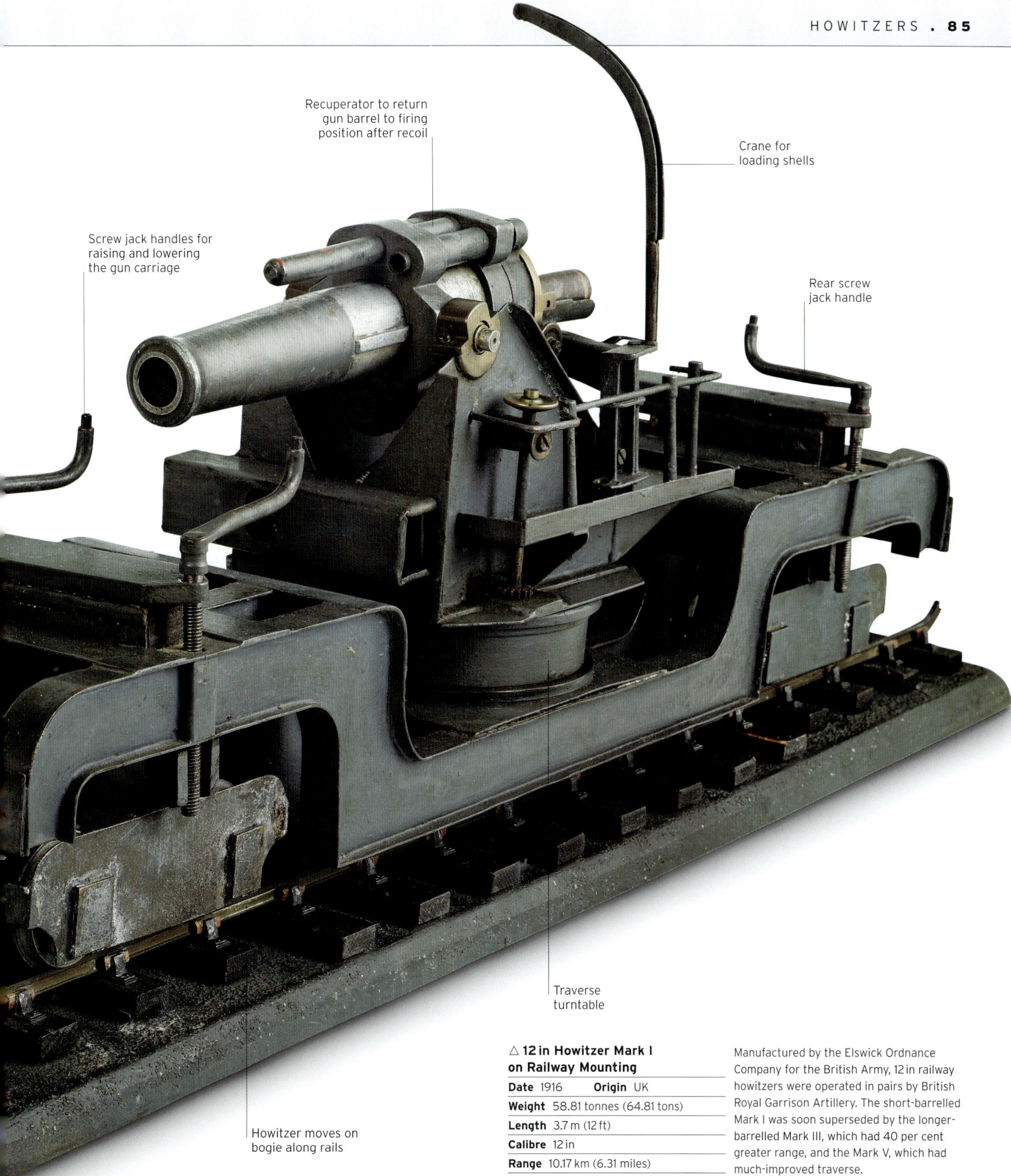

△ 12 in Howitzer Mark I on Railway Mounting

Date 1916	**Origin** UK
Weight 58.81 tonnes (64.81 tons)	
Length 3.7 m (12 ft)	
Calibre 12 in	
Range 10.17 km (6.31 miles)	

Manufactured by the Elswick Ordnance Company for the British Army, 12 in railway howitzers were operated in pairs by British Royal Garrison Artillery. The short-barrelled Mark I was soon superseded by the longer-barrelled Mark III, which had 40 per cent greater range, and the Mark V, which had much-improved traverse.

Heavy artillery
Both sides in World War I used heavy artillery to soften up enemy lines before an attack. Here a British howitzer fires at German lines during the bloody Battle of the Somme, in 1916.

Armoured Cars

The first armoured vehicles to see action in World War I were used by the British and Belgians around Antwerp in 1914. They engaged the German forces as they advanced and acted as rescuers for pilots forced down behind enemy lines. These early cars often had improvised armour and weapons, but specially designed vehicles were soon in service. The stalemate on the Western Front limited the use of armoured cars, but they still had value in places where the fighting remained mobile.

▽ Peugeot Modèle 1914 AC

Date 1914	**Origin** France
Weight 5 tonnes (5.5 tons)	
Engine Peugeot petrol, 40 hp	
Main armament 37 mm Mle 1897 gun	

There were two versions of the Peugeot armoured car: the AC (autocannon) and the AM (automitrailleuse, or machine-gun). Like most armoured cars, it was of limited use during the stalemate on the Western Front, and by the time mobile warfare returned in 1918 there were very few left.

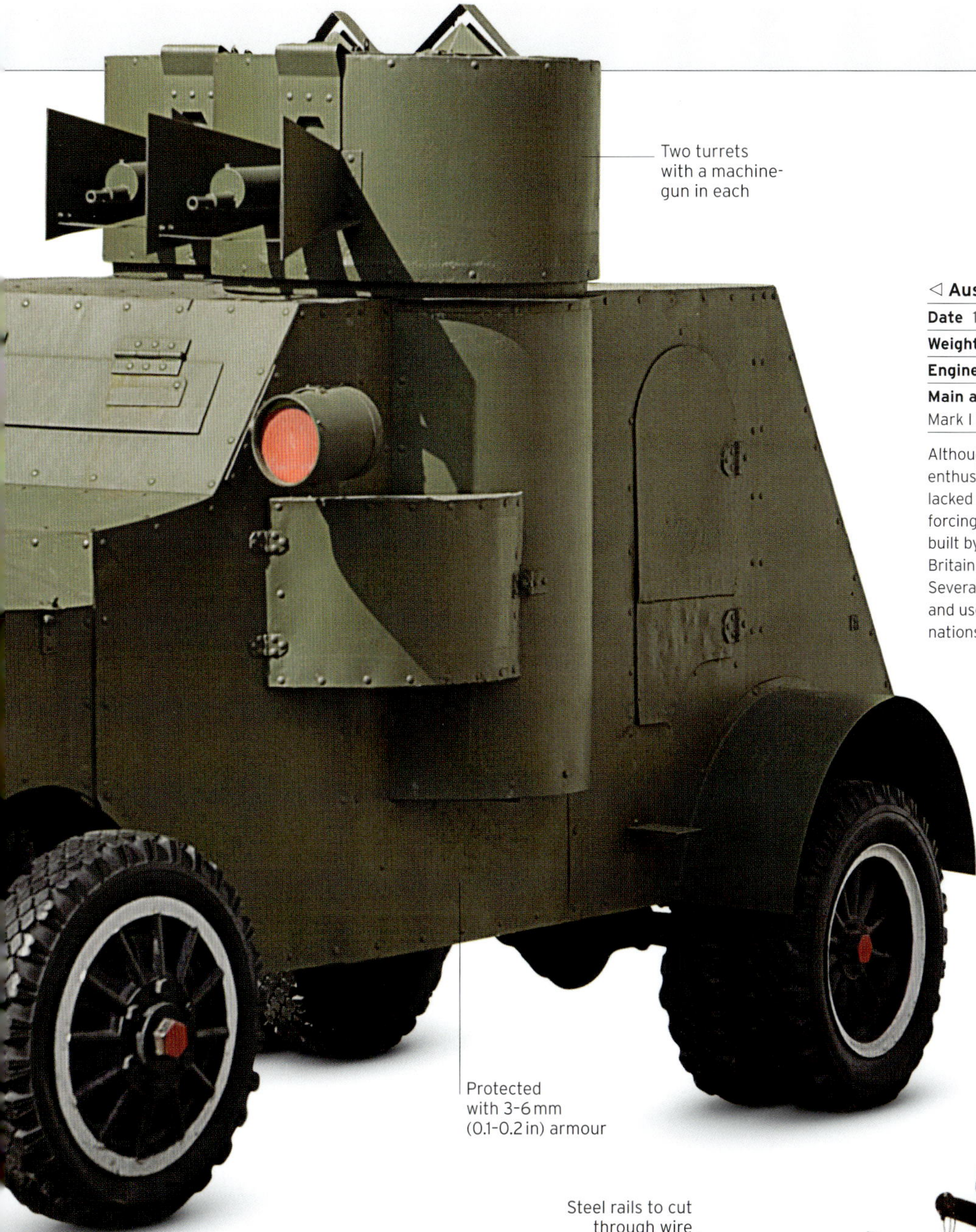

◁ **Austin Armoured Car**

Date 1914	**Origin** UK
Weight 4.2 tonnes (4.6 tons)	
Engine Austin petrol, 50 hp	
Main armament 2 x .303 Hotchkiss Mark I machine-guns	

Although the Russian Army was enthusiastic about armoured cars, Russia lacked the industrial capacity to build them, forcing it to look overseas. This vehicle was built by the British Austin Company, and Britain subsequently adopted it in 1918. Several Russian versions were captured and used by the new Eastern European nations after the war.

▷ **Lancia Ansaldo IZ**

Date 1916	**Origin** Italy
Weight 3.8 tonnes (4.1 tons)	
Engine Lancia V6 petrol, 40 hp	
Main armament 3 x 6.5 mm FIAT-Revelli M1914 machine-guns	

The mountainous Italian Front was not suited to armoured cars, but the Lancia Ansaldo played an important role in protecting the Italians retreating after the disaster at Caporetto in 1917. A total of 120 were built, only 10 of which were double-turreted. A few remained in use in Italy's African colonies until World War II.

Mark IV

More Mark IVs were made than any other British tank during World War I. Although it looked similar to the earlier Mark I, it featured improvements including an armoured fuel tank at the rear, and thicker 12 mm (0.5 in) frontal armour to protect against armour-piercing bullets. The sponsons housing the guns on each side could be pushed inside the tank to allow transportation by train, unlike those on the Mark I, which had to be removed.

SPECIFICATIONS	
Name	Tank, Mark IV
Date	1917
Origin	UK
Production	Approx 1,220
Engine	Daimler/Knight straight six, 105 hp
Weight	28.4 tonnes (31.4 tons)
Armament (male)	2 x 6-pounder QF guns; 3 x .303 Lewis machine-guns
Armament (female)	5 x .303 Lewis machine-guns
Crew	8
Armour thickness	12 mm (0.5 in)

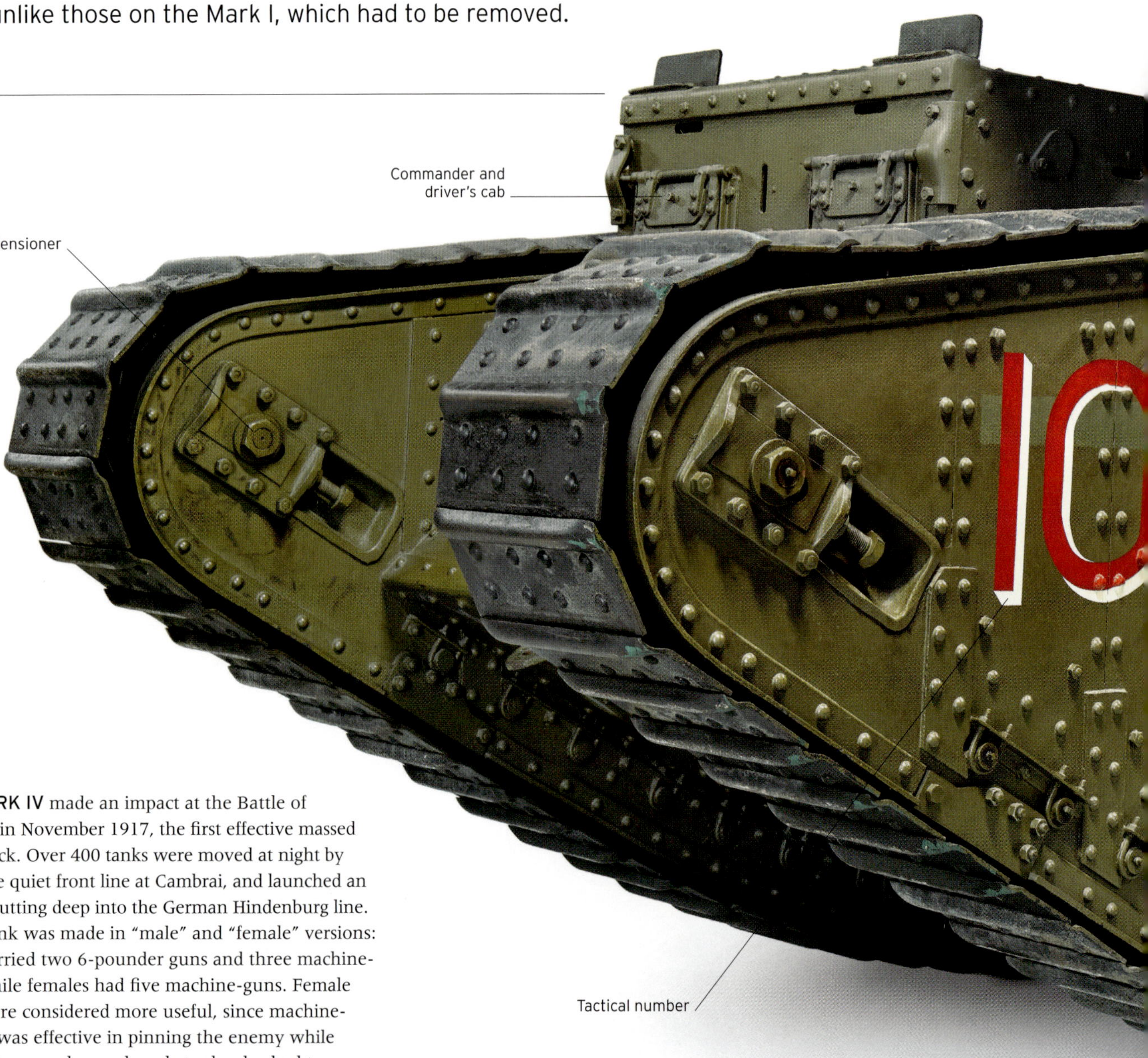

THE MARK IV made an impact at the Battle of Cambrai in November 1917, the first effective massed tank attack. Over 400 tanks were moved at night by rail to the quiet front line at Cambrai, and launched an assault, cutting deep into the German Hindenburg line.

The tank was made in "male" and "female" versions: males carried two 6-pounder guns and three machine-guns, while females had five machine-guns. Female tanks were considered more useful, since machine-gun fire was effective in pinning the enemy while friendly troops advanced; male tanks also had to stop to allow the 6-pounder gunner to aim. After April 1918, "hermaphrodites" with one male and one female sponson were built.

REAR VIEW

FRONT VIEW

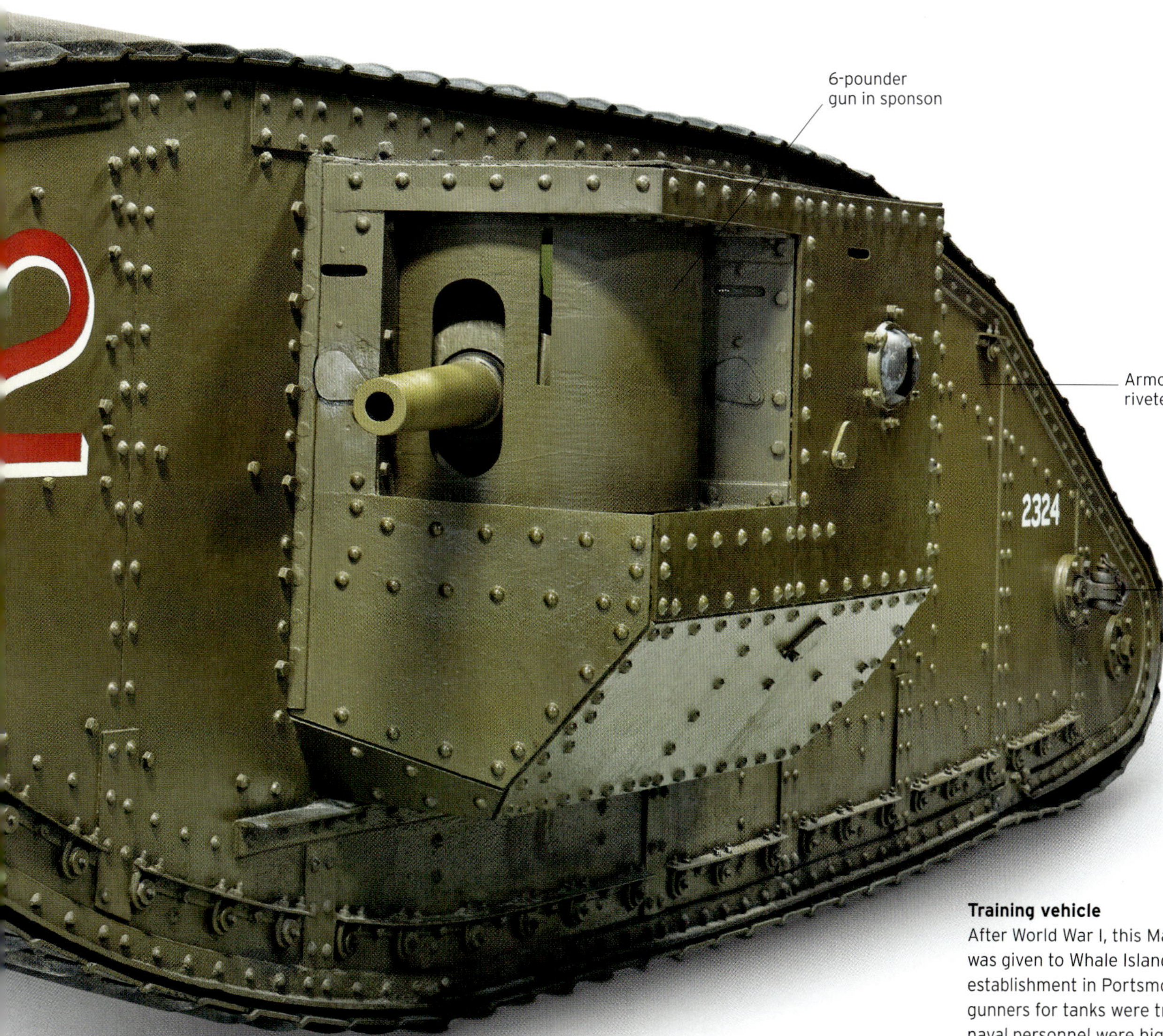

6-pounder gun in sponson

Armour plates riveted together

Towing handle

Training vehicle
After World War I, this Mark IV male tank was given to Whale Island, a Royal Navy establishment in Portsmouth, UK. Many gunners for tanks were trained here, since naval personnel were highly experienced at firing weapons from moving platforms.

EXTERIOR

The Mark IV clearly shows the riveted construction of the early tanks – the armour plates were hot-riveted or bolted to a metal framework. The construction meant there were numerous small gaps that allowed bullet "splash" to enter. Crews were issued with masks to protect their faces from hot metal splinters.

1. Male sponson with 6-pounder gun **2.** Sponson ball machine-gun mount (without gun) **3.** Ventilation louvres **4.** Track plates **5.** Starboard side 6-pounder gun breech **6.** 6-pounder ammunition stowage **7.** Oil tank to lubricate secondary gears **8.** Secondary gear levers **9.** Engine **10.** Differential housing **11.** Front commander and driver's positions **12.** Steering lever **13.** Differential lock lever

1

2

3

4

5

6
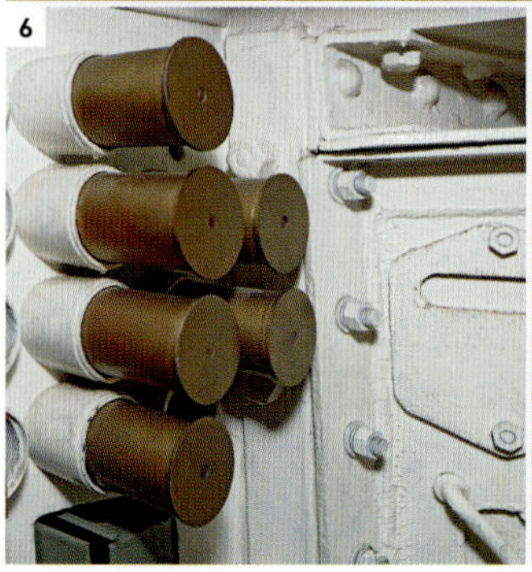

7

10

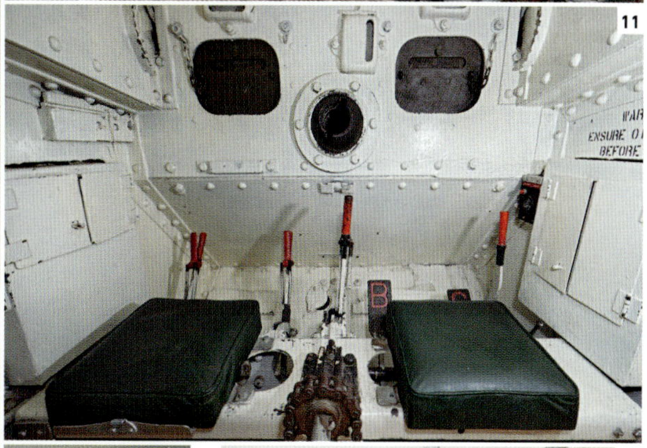

11

12

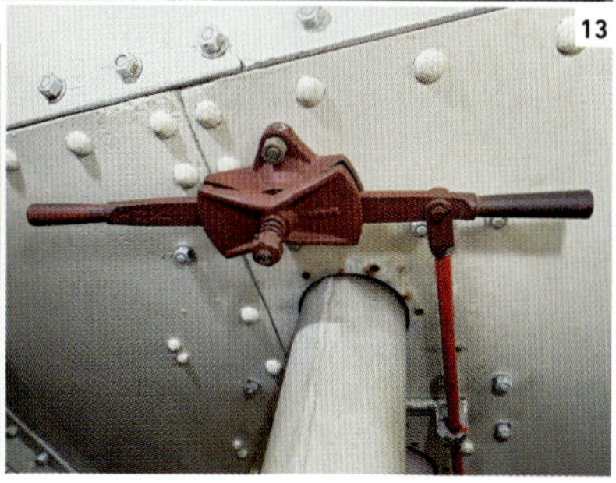

13

8

9

INTERIOR

The Mark IV's Daimler 105 hp engine was positioned in the middle of the same compartment as the crew, creating a great deal of heat, fumes, and noise. The tank's lack of suspension and seating meant that the crew also had a rough ride – when not in action, the gunners would often ride on top or walk beside the tank.

Tanks of World War I

Tanks were first used on 15 September 1916. Between then and 11 November 1918, Britain, France, and Germany all invested in their development. Britain's heavy tanks, which had tracks around their entire bodies, were adapted for crossing trenches in support of infantry. The faster Medium Whippet was developed to support cavalry in more open country. As well as a small number of heavier vehicles, the French used masses of light FT tanks. Germany built only a small number of A7Vs, relying more on captured British Mark IVs instead.

△ **Mark IV**

Date 1917 **Origin** UK

Weight 28.4 tonnes (31.4 tons)

Engine Daimler petrol, 105 hp

Main armament 2 x QF 6-pounder 6 cwt Hotchkiss L/23 guns

The Mark IV was an improvement on Britain's earlier tanks. It was better armoured and its guns and sponsons were modified to improve mobility. Also, its petrol tanks were larger, armoured, and were vacuum- rather than gravity-fed. Over 1,200 were built, seeing action from June 1917 until the end of the war.

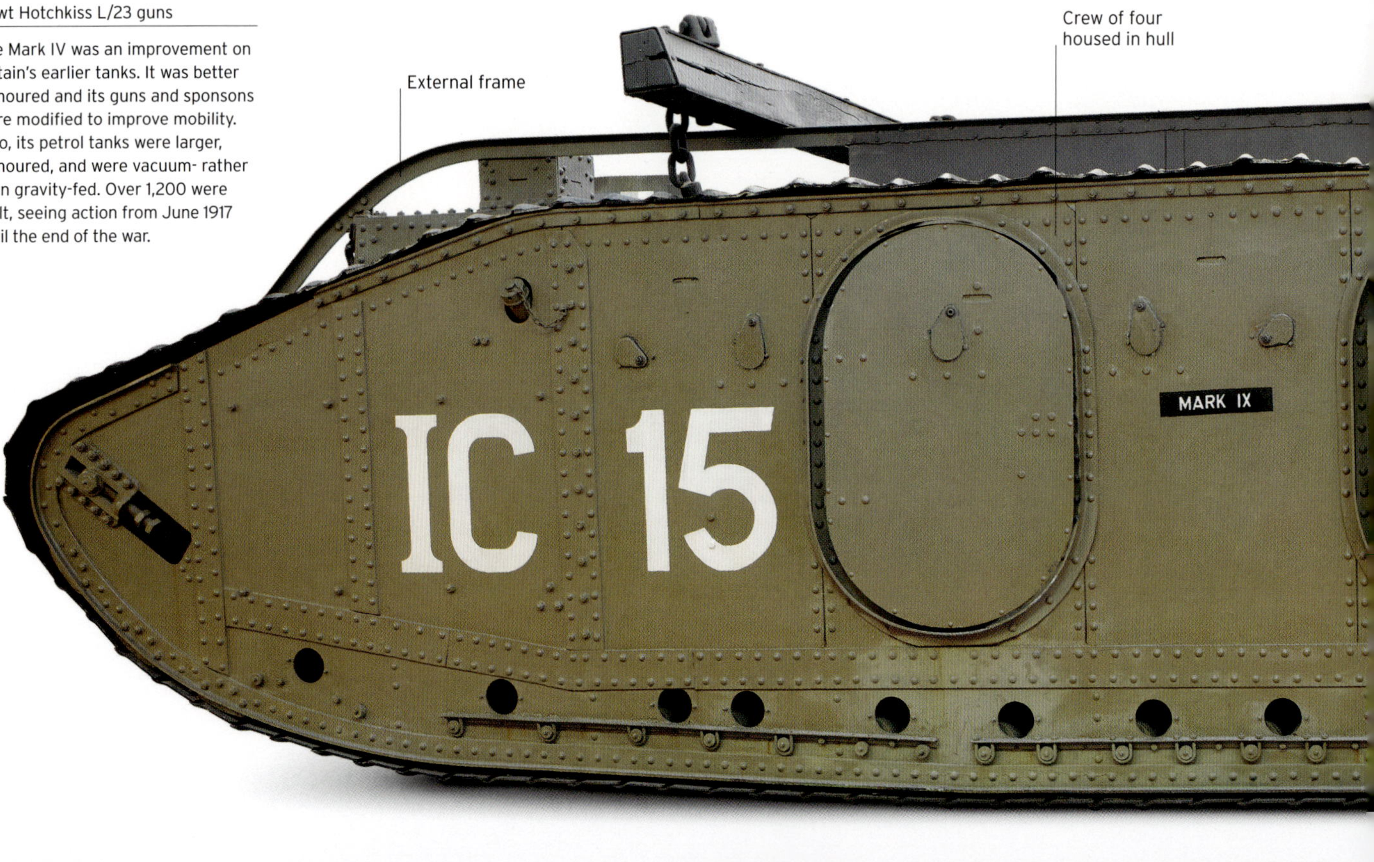

▽ **Schneider CA-1**

Date 1917	**Origin** France
Weight 13.5 tonnes (14.9 tons)	
Engine Schneider 4-cylinder petrol, 60 hp	
Main armament 75 mm Schneider Blockhaus gun	

The first French tank to see service, the six-man Schneider was based on the Holt tractor. Its 75 mm gun was offset to the right, limiting its field of fire. Four hundred were built, but took heavy losses when they first saw action on 14 April 1917. They struggled to cross trenches, but fared better in the advances of 1918.

◁ **Mark IX**

Date 1918	**Origin** UK
Weight 37.6 tonnes (41.4 tons)	
Engine Ricardo petrol, 150 hp	
Main armament 2 x .303 Hotchkiss Mark I* machine-guns	

Officially called a tank, the Mark IX was in fact the first Armoured Personnel Carrier (APC), carrying 30 infantrymen. It was underpowered as it used the same engine as the Mark V, but weighed 9 tonnes (10 tons) more. One Mark IX was used for trials as an amphibious tank, with large floats attached to the side.

Tanks of World War I (cont.)

▷ **Medium Mark A Whippet**

Date 1918 **Origin** UK

Weight 14.2 tonnes (15.7 tons)

Engine 2 x Tylor petrol, 45 hp each

Main armament 3 x .303 Hotchkiss Mark I machine-guns

Intended as a fast tank, the three-man Whippet could reach 13 km/h (8 mph). Each track had its own engine, and steering was controlled by adjusting the two throttles. Whippets were first used in March 1918 and played a significant role in the open warfare of the final months of the war.

▷ **Mark VIII**

Date 1918 **Origin** UK, US

Weight 37.6 tonnes (41.4 tons)

Engine Ricardo petrol, 300 hp

Main armament 2 x QF 6-pounder 6 cwt Hotchkiss L/23 guns

The Mark VIII "International" was an Anglo-American design intended to be built in France and used by the Allies. It was the first British-designed tank to separate the engine from the crew, improving conditions. After the war, 100 were built in the US, serving until 1930.

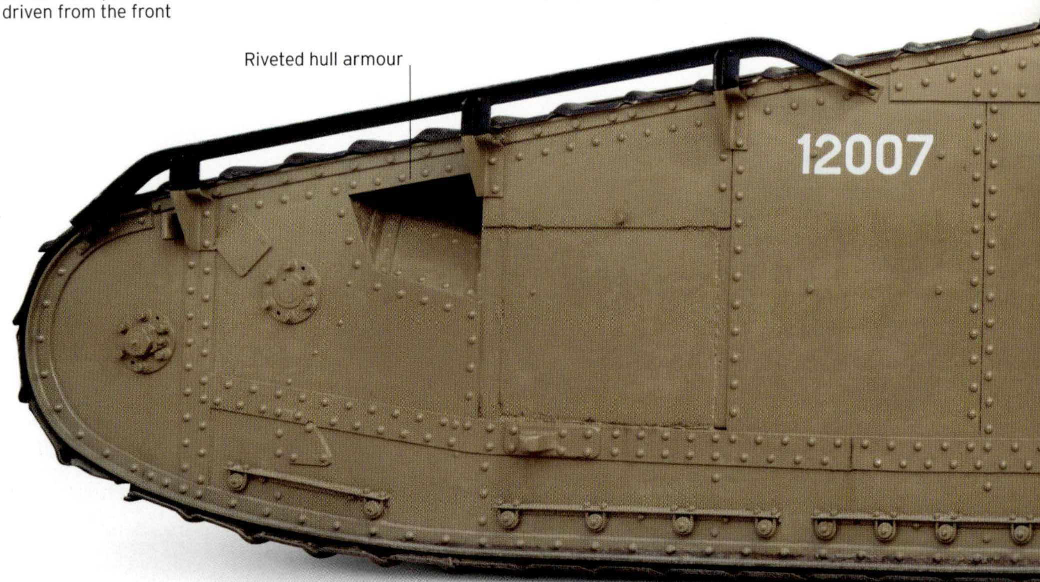

△ **Mark V**

Date 1918 **Origin** UK

Weight 29.5 tonnes (32.5 tons)

Engine Ricardo petrol, 150 hp

Main armament 2 x QF 6-pounder 6 cwt Hotchkiss L/23 guns

The Mark Vs were similar in armament and speed to their predecessors, but they had a new epicyclic gearbox that enabled them to be driven by one man. They played a key role in the Allied victory in 1918, and saw postwar service in Ireland, Germany, and Russia. Four hundred were produced.

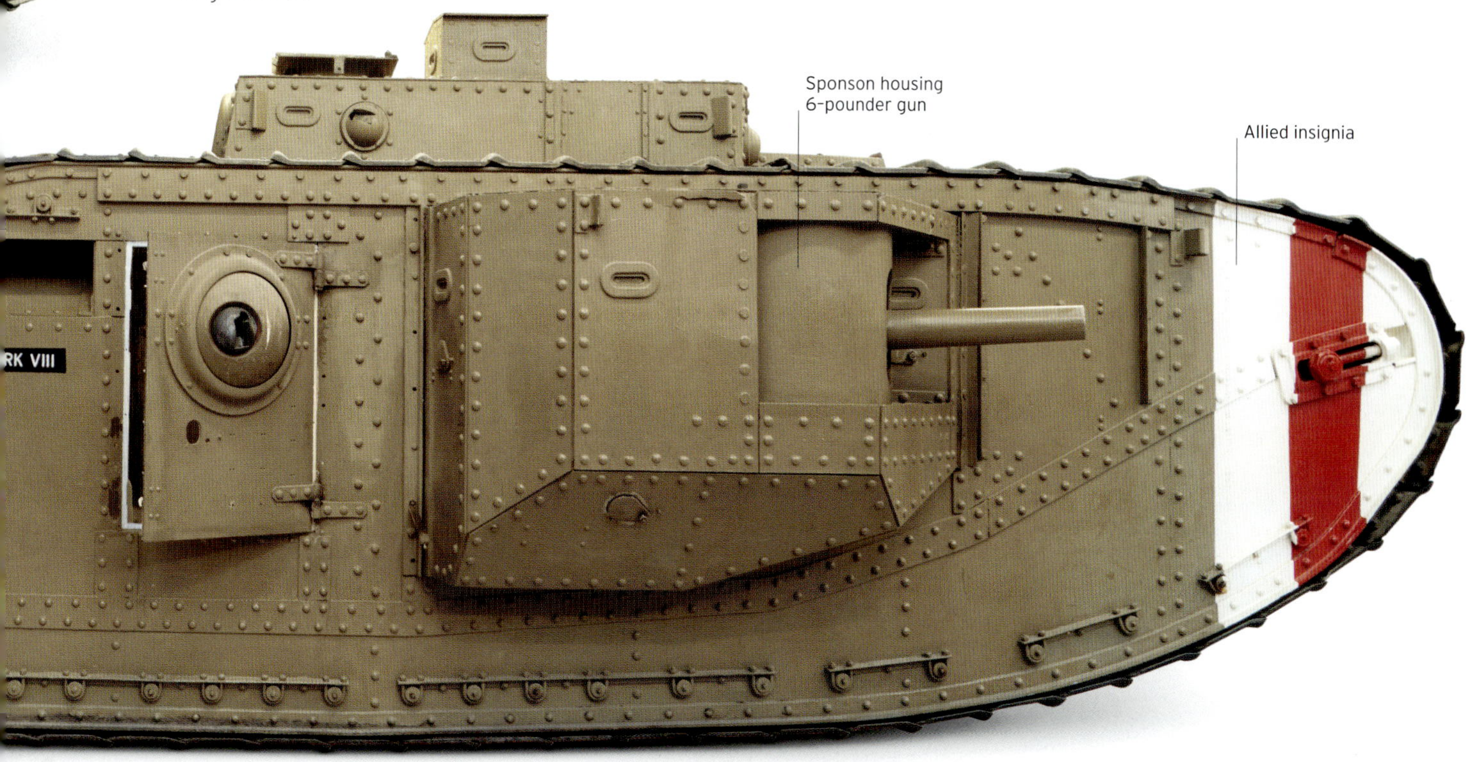

Renault FT-17

The Renault light tank was developed when General Estienne, father of the French tank force in World War I, asked Louis Renault to design a light two-man tank that could support infantry in mass attacks. Renault at first declined since he thought his company lacked experience in such matters, but when asked again in the summer of 1916, he changed his mind and took on the project.

SPECIFICATIONS	
Name	Renault FT-17
Date	1917
Origin	France
Production	3,950
Engine	Renault 4-cylinder petrol, 35 hp
Weight	6.5 tonnes (7.2 tons)
Main armament	37 mm Puteaux SA 18 (shown here) or 8 mm Hotchkiss Mle 1914
Secondary armament	None
Crew	2
Armour thickness	8-16 mm (0.3-0.6 in)

THE RENAULT was essentially a tapered metal box with an engine at the rear and a crew (commander and driver) at the front. It had the very first fully rotating turret, which also had a small dome that could be opened and tilted to ventilate the turret. The armour-plated hull acted as its chassis, and the Renault 35 hp engine and gearbox provided five gears (four forward and one reverse). The tank could reach speeds of just under 8 km/h (5 mph) on the road and had a range of 34 km (22 miles). Its small size and weight of just over 6 tonnes (7 tons) meant the tank was easily transportable by truck.

The tank first saw action in May 1918, and two months later 408 broke through the German front at Soissons, although the French cavalry failed to capitalize on their success. It then evolved into a number of variants, and saw service with the US Army in World War I before being sold to many other nations after the war. France still had ten battalions of Renaults in service in September 1939.

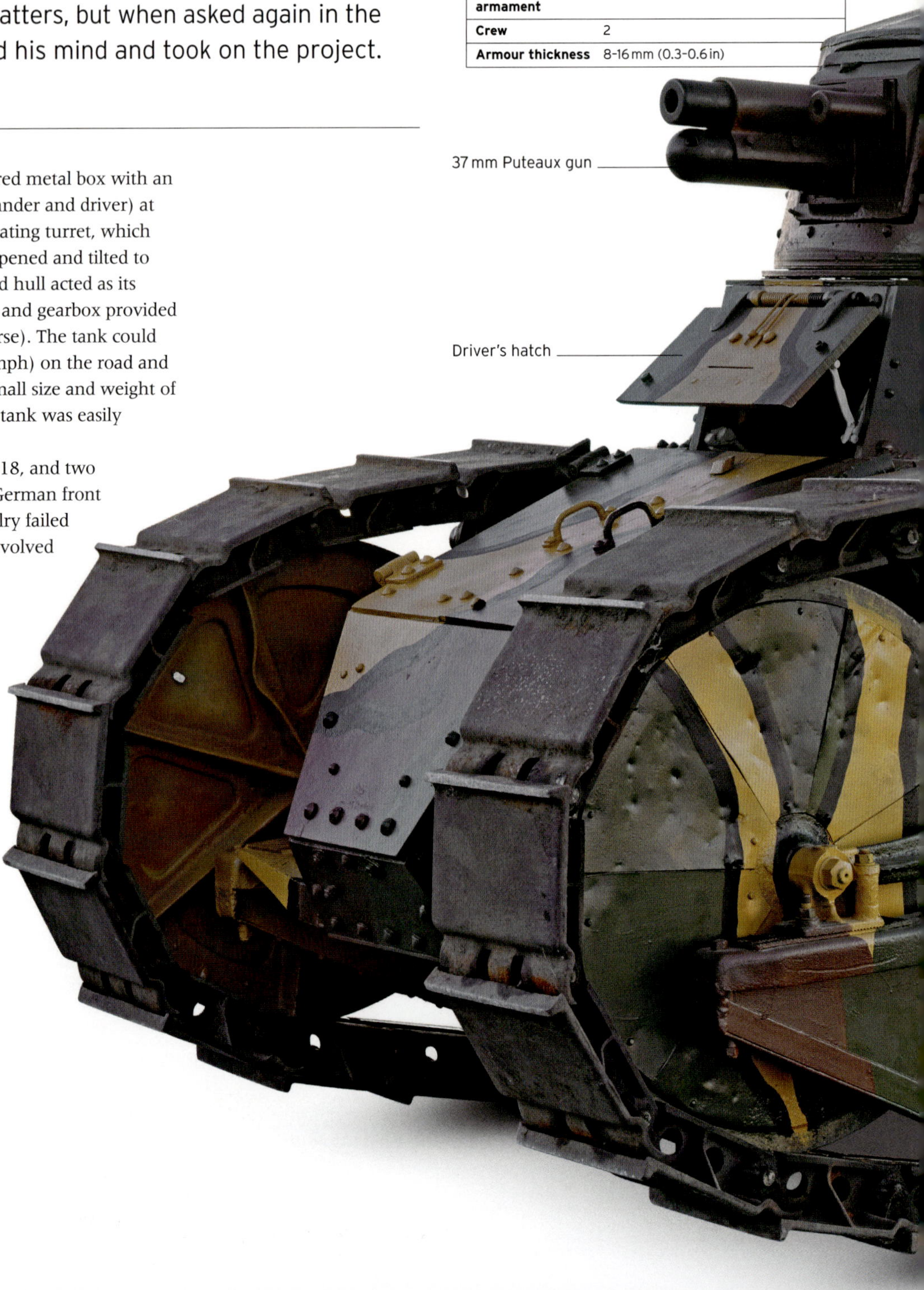

The first modern tank
With its engine in the rear and crew positioned in the front beneath a fully-rotating turret containing the tank's main weapon, the FT-17's configuration was highly influential. It remains the standard layout for tanks today.

FRONT VIEW

REAR VIEW

EXTERIOR

The Renault improved many of the shortcomings of the first French tanks that went into combat. The large front wheel with wooden inserts enabled it to climb in and out of shell holes, and the detachable "tail" extended its trench-crossing ability. Also, the turret had a small dome that served as a cupola and could be opened for ventilation.

1. Idler wheel **2.** Driver's hatch **3.** Paired suspension wheels **4.** 37 mm Puteaux gun and recuperator **5.** Exhaust silencer **6.** Rear drive sprocket and top roller rail support **7.** Starting handle **8.** Turret interior, showing ammunition stowage racks **9.** Commander's hatch **10.** Engine control pedals **11.** Driver's position looking down to engine

1

2

3

4

5

6

7

8

9

10
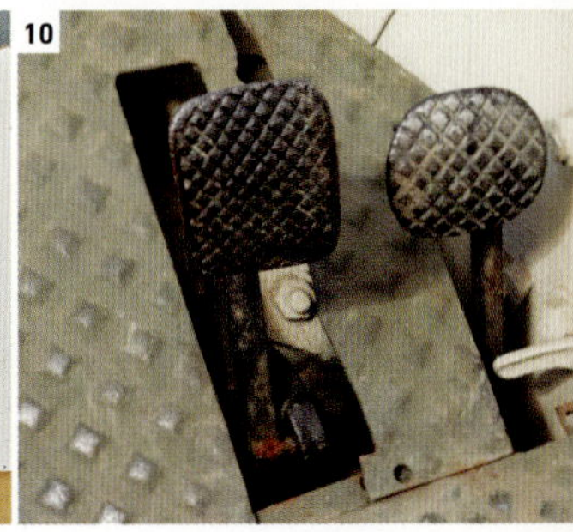

INTERIOR

As a light tank, the FT-17 had to keep weight down, and it did so partly by being extremely compact. This meant that the crew had to endure unusually cramped conditions; the commander sat on a canvas sling or folding seat, and the driver made do with a floor cushion. The entire crew was surrounded by ammunition stowage and had very poor vision when the hatches were closed; the view ports were simply slits in the armour. The tank's armour was also minimized, being 16 mm (0.6 in) on the front, but only 8 mm (0.3 in) on the sides.

11

Reconnaissance and Fighter Aircraft

Initially, military aircraft were employed to observe the battlefield, but it soon became imperative to control the airspace over it. The first dogfights involving pistols and rifles were inconclusive. Machine-guns, which could be fired in bursts while the pilot corrected his aim, were the answer. However, it was not until a method was developed that allowed weapons to follow the pilot's sightline and fire through the propeller's arc that the fighter came into its own. Interrupter mechanisms were developed, which shut off the gun while the blade passed through the line of fire.

▽ Royal Aircraft Factory B.E.2c

Date 1912 **Origin** UK

Engine 90 hp Royal Aircraft Factory 1a air-cooled V8

Top speed 120 km/h (75 mph)

Some 3,500 of this slow but stable reconnaissance and light bombing machine were built. In 1914, the observer gained a machine-gun, but by 1916, the aircraft was dangerously outdated.

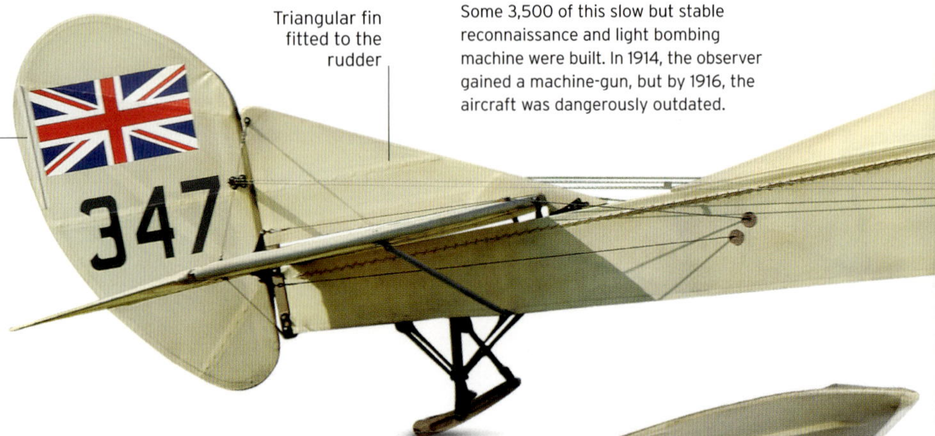

▽ Caudron G.3

Date 1914 **Origin** France

Engine 80 hp Le Rhône 9C air-cooled 9-cylinder rotary

Top speed 106 km/h (68 mph)

Although of primitive design, using wing warping, the Caudron had a good rate of climb and was useful for reconnaissance. It was later used for training purposes.

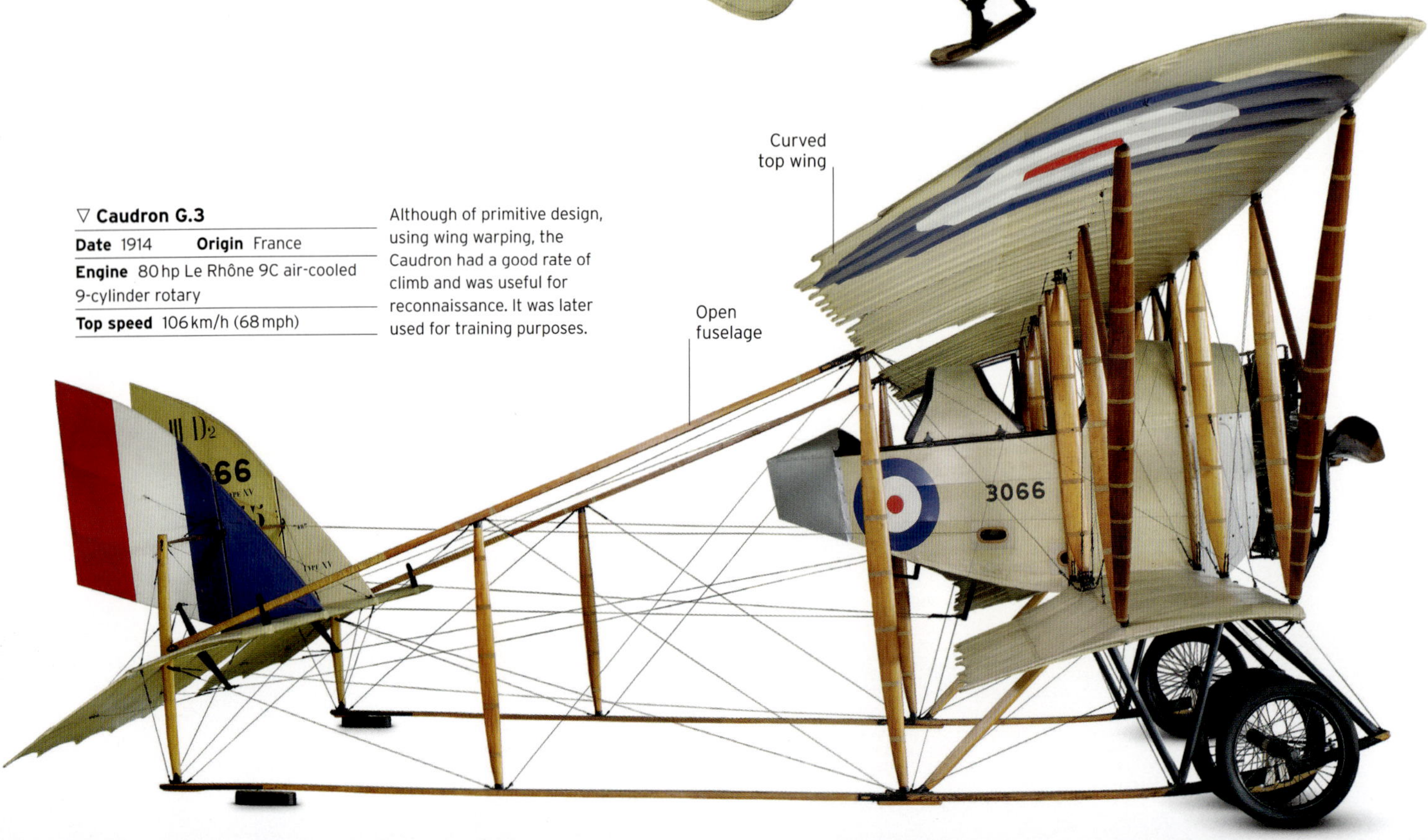

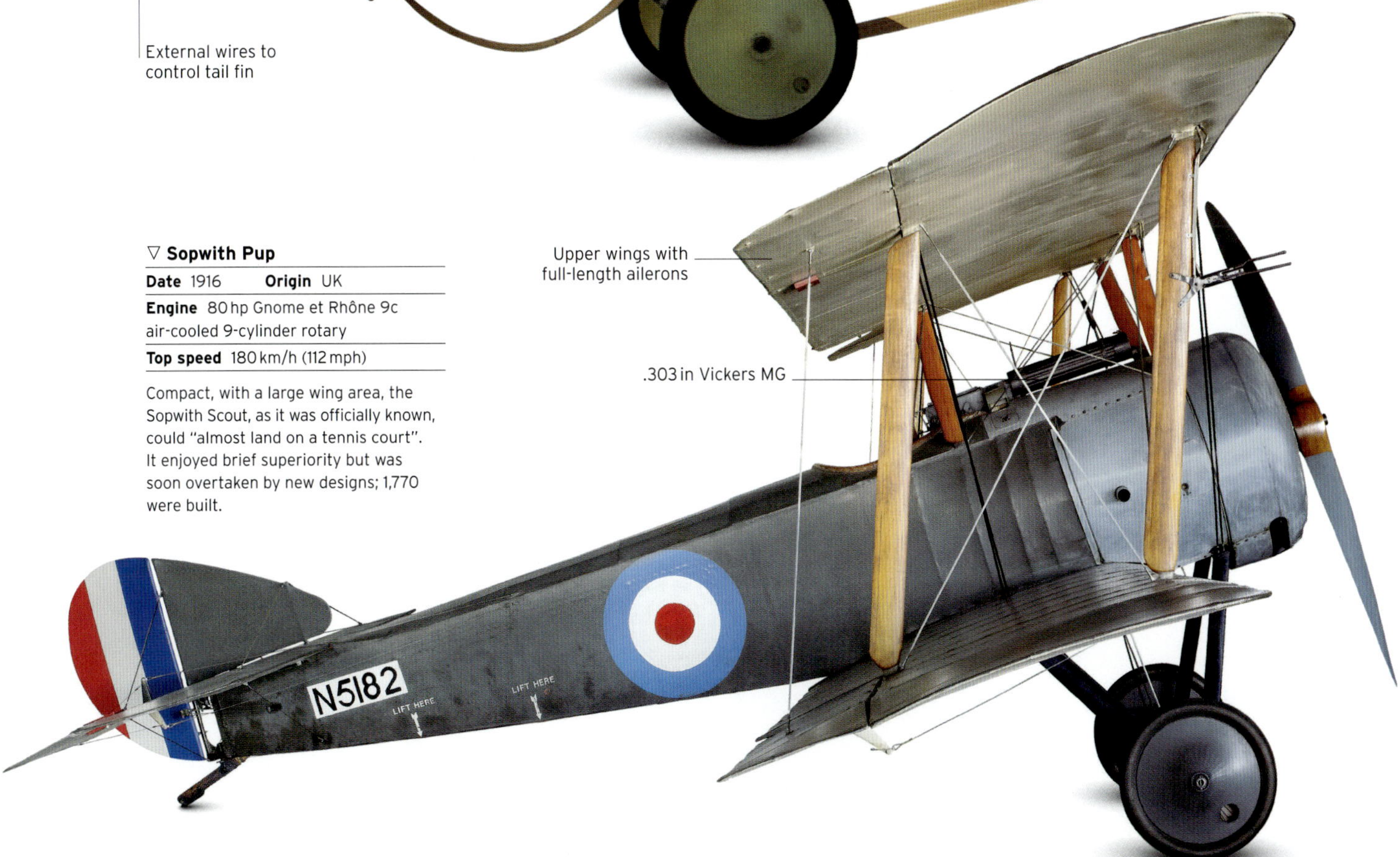

▽ **Sopwith Pup**

Date 1916 **Origin** UK

Engine 80 hp Gnome et Rhône 9c air-cooled 9-cylinder rotary

Top speed 180 km/h (112 mph)

Compact, with a large wing area, the Sopwith Scout, as it was officially known, could "almost land on a tennis court". It enjoyed brief superiority but was soon overtaken by new designs; 1,770 were built.

Reconnaissance and Fighter Aircraft (cont.)

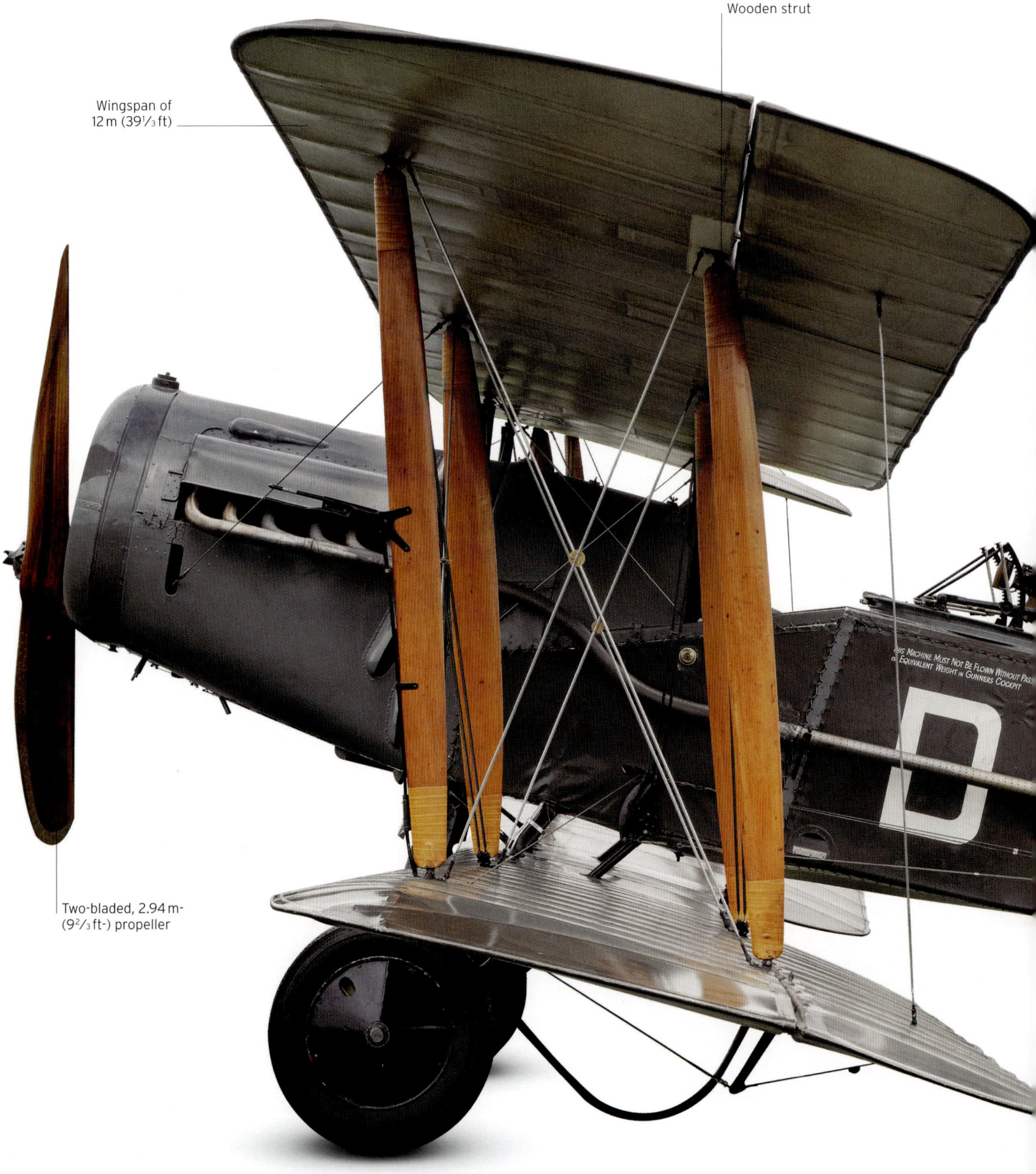

◁ **Anatra Anasal DS**

Date 1916	**Origin** Russia
Engine 150 hp Salmson 9U water-cooled 9-cylinder radial	
Top speed 144 km/h (90 mph)	

Manufactured in Odessa with a French Salmson engine built under licence, the Anasal was used mostly for reconnaissance by Ukraine, Russia, Austro-Hungary (later Austria and Hungary), and Czechoslovakia.

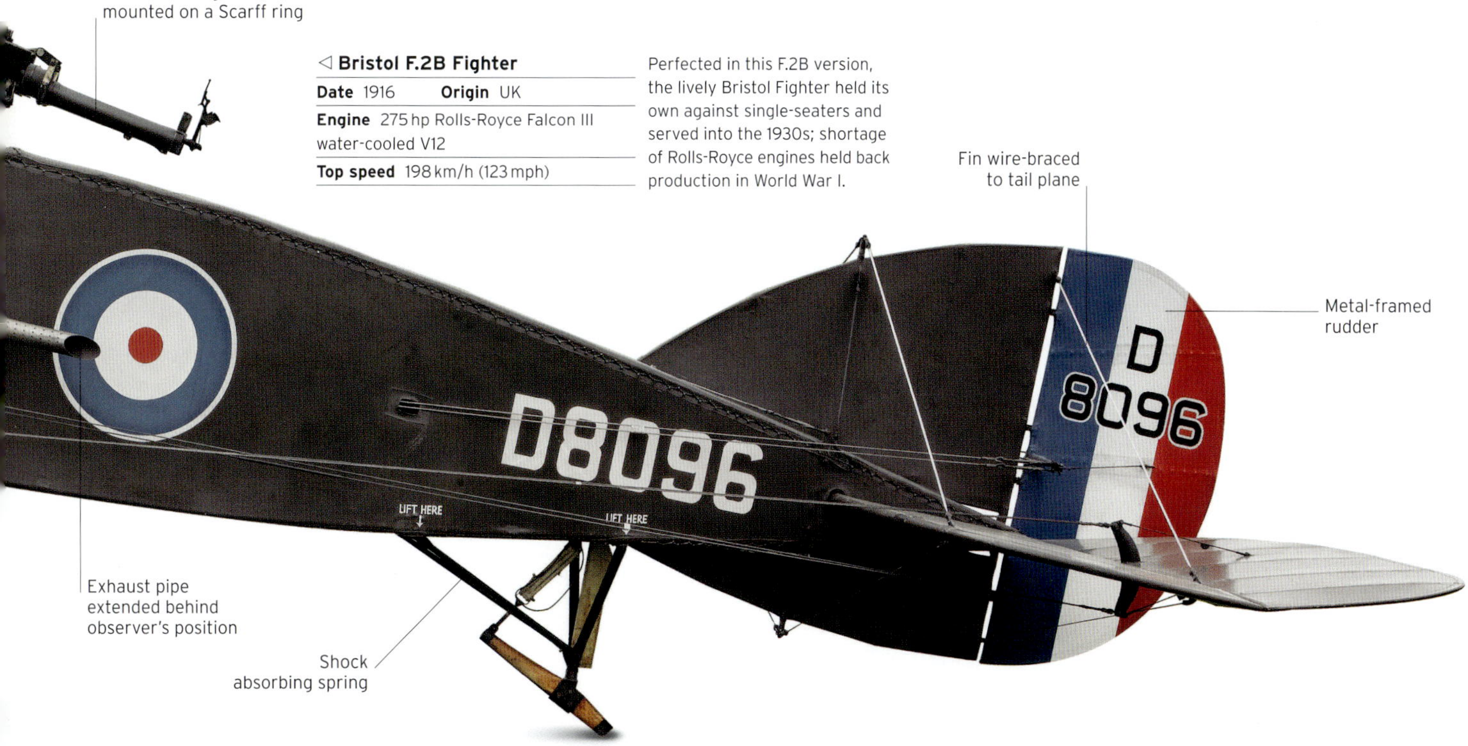

◁ **Bristol F.2B Fighter**

Date 1916	**Origin** UK
Engine 275 hp Rolls-Royce Falcon III water-cooled V12	
Top speed 198 km/h (123 mph)	

Perfected in this F.2B version, the lively Bristol Fighter held its own against single-seaters and served into the 1930s; shortage of Rolls-Royce engines held back production in World War I.

Reconnaissance and Fighter Aircraft (cont.)

▷ **Avro 504k**

Date 1917 **Origin** UK

Engine 110 hp Le Rhône 9Ja single-bank 9-cylinder rotary

Top speed 145 km/h (90 mph)

Early versions of the Avro 504 served as reconnaissance and combat aircraft, but the two-seater 504K came into its own as a trainer. Over 10,000 were built over a period of almost 20 years.

▷ **LVG C.VI**

Date 1917 **Origin** Germany

Engine 200 hp Benz Bz.IV water-cooled 6-cylinder in-line

Top speed 166 km/h (103 mph)

Designed by Willy Sabersky-Müssigbrodt, the C.VI had a semi-monocoque wooden fuselage. Chiefly used for reconnaissance, it continued in service as late as 1940 in Lithuania.

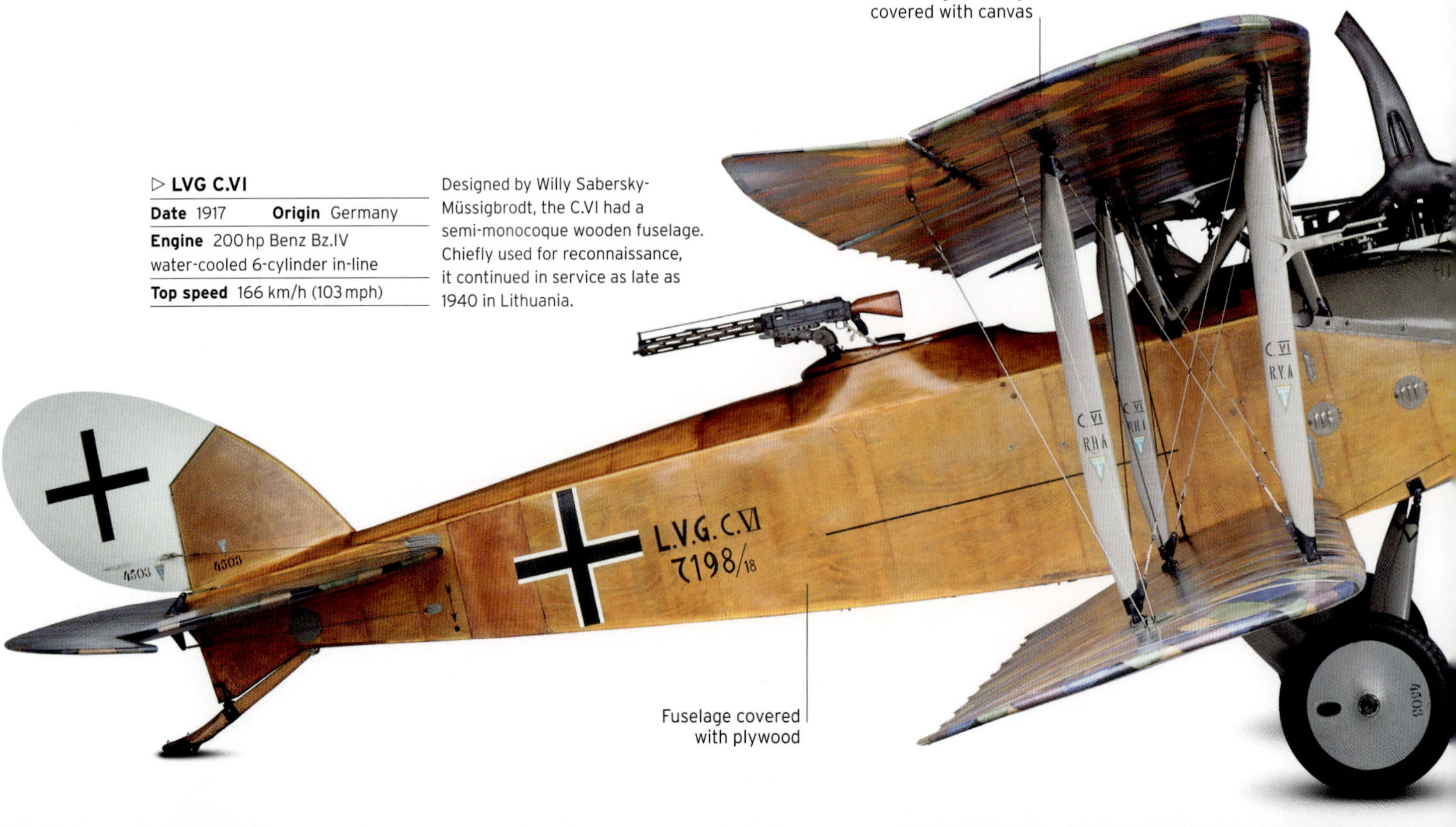

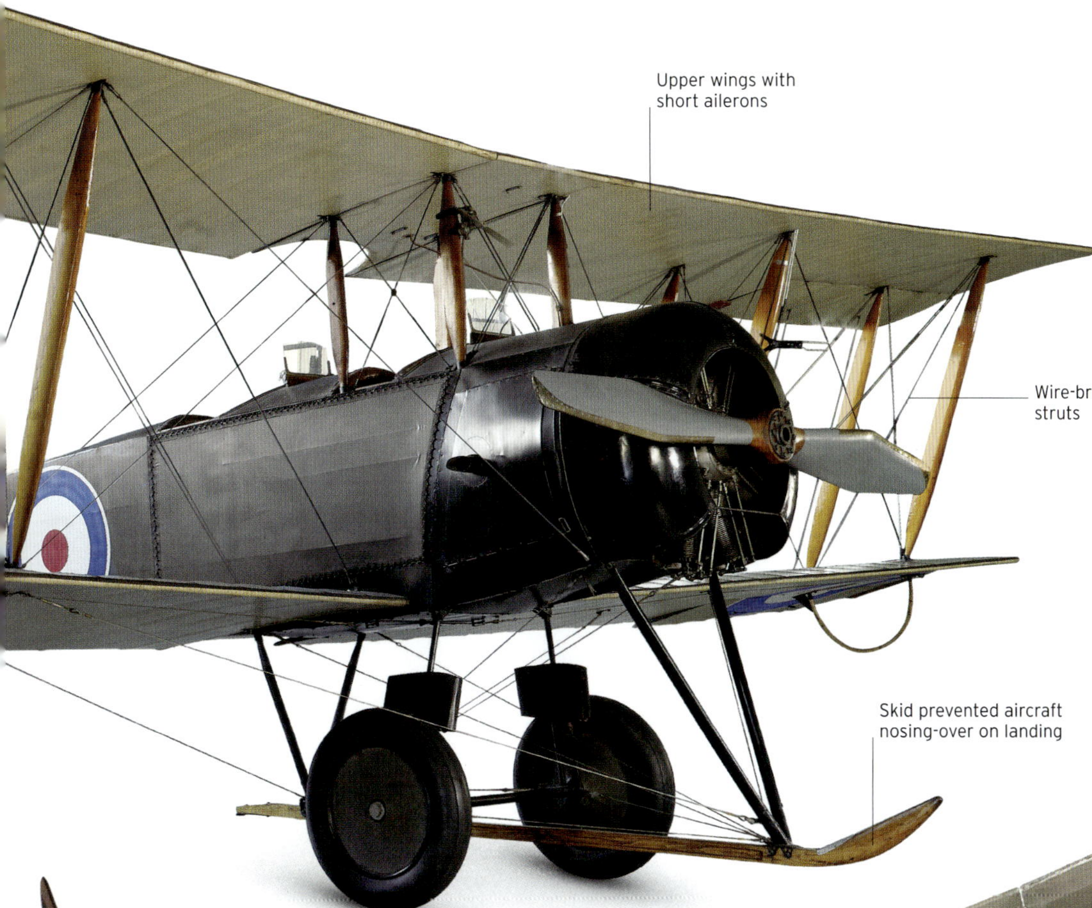

▷ **Sopwith F.1 Camel**

Date 1917 **Origin** UK

Engine 130 hp Clerget 9B/ 150 hp Bentley BR1 air-cooled 9-cylinder rotary

Top speed 185 km/h (115 mph)

Although difficult to fly, the highly manoeuvrable Camel, armed with twin machine-guns, shot down more enemy aircraft than any other in World War I. Some 5,490 were built, giving Allied forces air superiority.

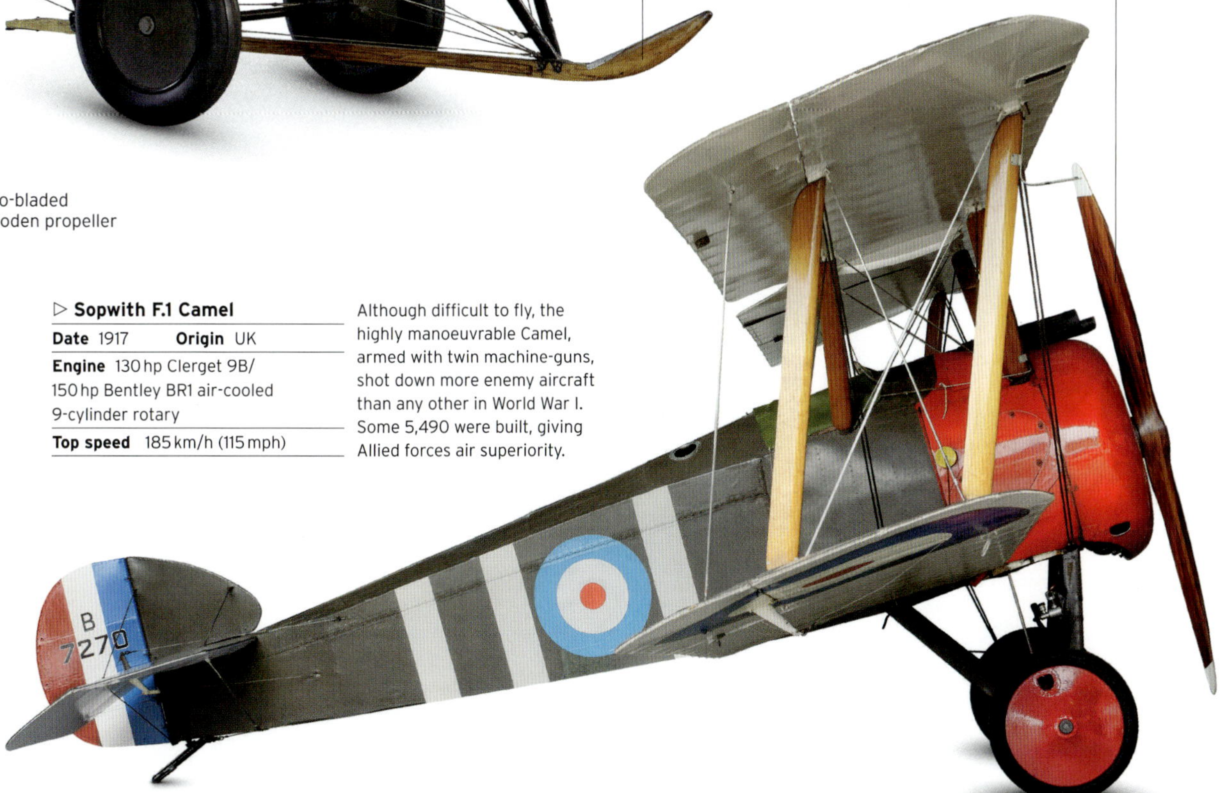

RAF S.E.5a

An especially robust single-seat fighter, the Royal Aircraft Factory (RAF) S.E.5a was also an exceptionally stable gun platform. As such, it is often seen as the World War I equivalent of the later Battle of Britain's Hawker Hurricane, while the lighter and more manoeuvrable Sopwith Camel is equated with the Supermarine Spitfire. Between them the S.E.5a and Camel reestablished Allied air superiority over the Western Front from mid-1917 until the end of the war.

SPECIFICATIONS	
Model	Royal Aircraft Factory S.E.5a
Date	1916
Origin	UK
Production	5,205 (including the S.E.5)
Construction	Wooden frames, fabric covering
Maximum weight	898 kg (1,980 lb)
Engines	1200 hp Hispano-Suiza/Wolseley Viper water-cooled V8
Wingspan	8.1 m (26 ft 7 in)
Length	6.38 m (20 ft 11 in)
Range	483 km (300 miles)
Top speed	222 km/h (138 mph)

DEVELOPED FROM the S.E.5 ("SE" stood for "Scout Experimental"), which had first flown in November 1916, the S.E.5a had a more powerful 200 hp engine in place of the earlier aircraft's 150 hp unit.

Designed under Henry P. Folland at the Royal Aircraft Factory in Farnborough, the S.E.5a was dramatically better than earlier Royal Flying Corps fighters, such as the DH2 and FE8 "pushers" (biplanes with their engines and propellers mounted behind the pilot). Its "tractor" configuration, with the propeller in the front, allowed for a clean, relatively streamlined, fast design. Its blunt, square nose lent it an air of pugnacity.

In the hands of World War I Victoria Cross-holding aces, such as Albert Ball, Billy Bishop, "Mick" Mannock, and James McCudden, the S.E.5 and S.E.5a proved formidable weapons, valued for their strength and steadiness, good all-round field of vision from the cockpit, superior speed, and good performance even at high altitude.

Fin is wire-braced to tailplane

Pilot's headrest is streamlined for speed

Rear decking made of fabric over wooden stringers

Tail is wood/steel-tube frame, fabric-covered

Side panel of fabric fuselage openable for maintenance and inspection

Roundel with blue outer and red inner circle denotes British or Empire aircraft

FRONT VIEW

REAR VIEW

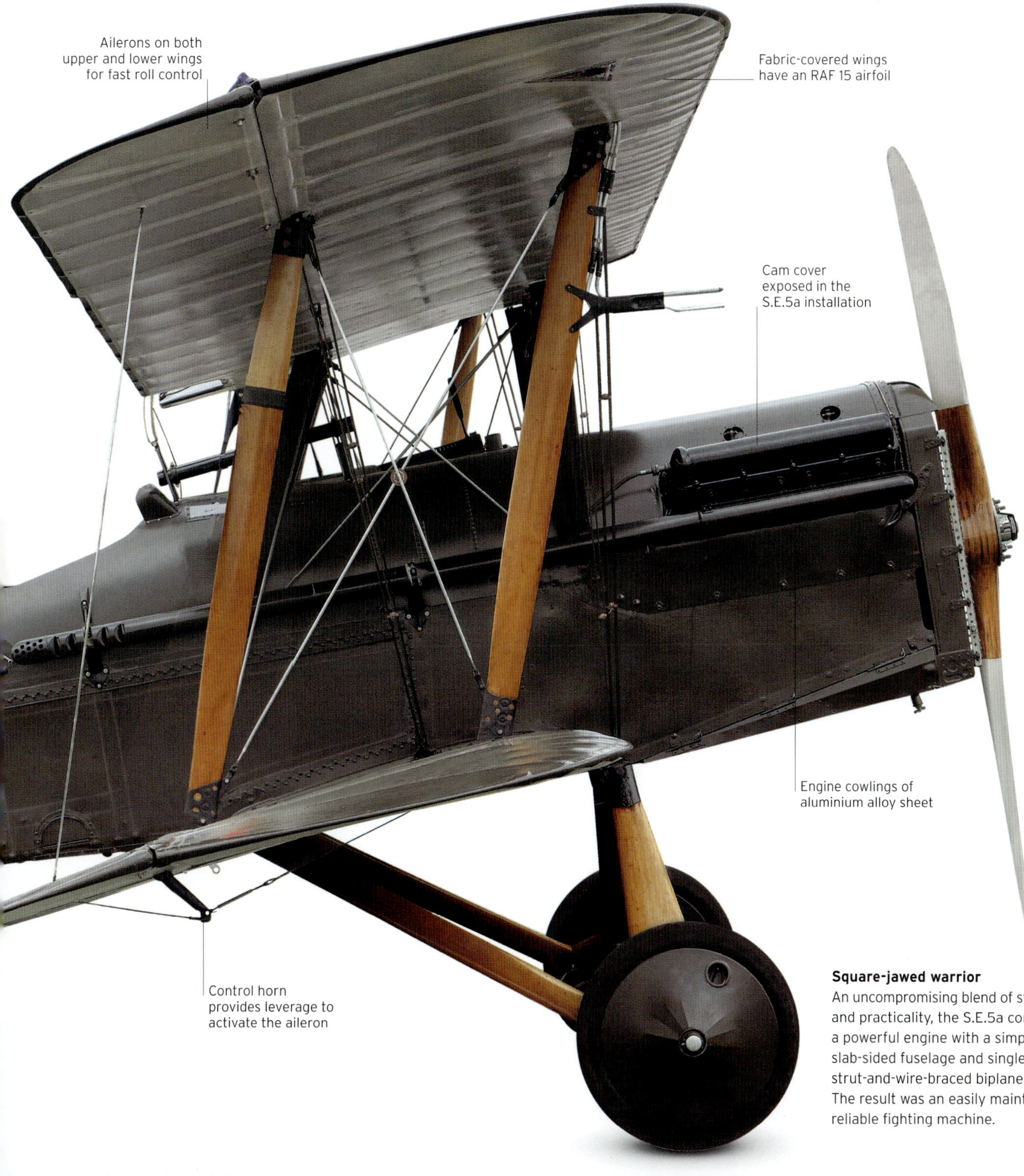

Square-jawed warrior
An uncompromising blend of strength and practicality, the S.E.5a combined a powerful engine with a simple slab-sided fuselage and single-bay, strut-and-wire-braced biplane wings. The result was an easily maintained, reliable fighting machine.

THE EXTERIOR

Careful, efficient detail design is evident everywhere on the S.E.5a, with the emphasis on simplicity, durability, ease of manufacture, and practical serviceability – all vital in getting the aircraft urgently to the front line and keeping it combat-ready. Early problems with the thin structures of the wing and tail on the S.E.5 were soon ironed out, as was a weakness in the steel-tube undercarriage struts. They were replaced with wooden struts, which were more resilient.

1. Bullet spacer on bracing wires **2.** Leather "boots" on bracing-wire ends **3.** Perforated exhaust **4.** Wing strut end **5.** Gun sight **6.** Lewis machine-gun **7.** Cockpit general view **8.** Compass **9.** Airspeed indicator

1

2

3

4

5

6

7

8

9

THE COCKPIT

Spartan by today's standards, all varnished wood and copper tubes and brass fittings, and with instruments and items of equipment seemingly positioned wherever they would fit, the S.E.5a's "office" was typical of the period in its functional approach, with little concession to pilot comfort or ease of use. Both of the aircraft's two machine-guns – the fixed internal Vickers and the movable overwing-rail-mounted Lewis – could be accessed by the pilot in flight to clear jams and, in the case of the Lewis, change the drum-shaped ammunition magazine.

Fields of munitions
The need for munitions to keep the guns firing on the Western Front was keenly felt by both sides in World War I. In Britain, women took the place of absent men in the munitions factories. Here, men and women are working together among the shells in the National Fillings Factory at Chilwell, in Nottingham.

SPECIFICATIONS	
Class	*New York*-class battleship
Commissioned	1914
Origin	US
Displacement	27,000 tons
Length	175 m (574 ft) overall
Beam	29.02 m (95 ft)
Engines	2 x vertical triple-expansion steam engines; 2 x screws
Top speed	21 knots
Range	13,075 km (7,060 nautical miles)
Complement	1,042 officers and men
Armament	10 x 14 in guns; 21 x 5 in guns; 4 x 3-pounder 47 mm; 2 x 1-pounder 37 mm; 4 x 21 in torpedo tubes
Armour	254-305 mm (10-12 in) amidships; 152 mm (6 in) aft; 229 mm (9 in) lower belt

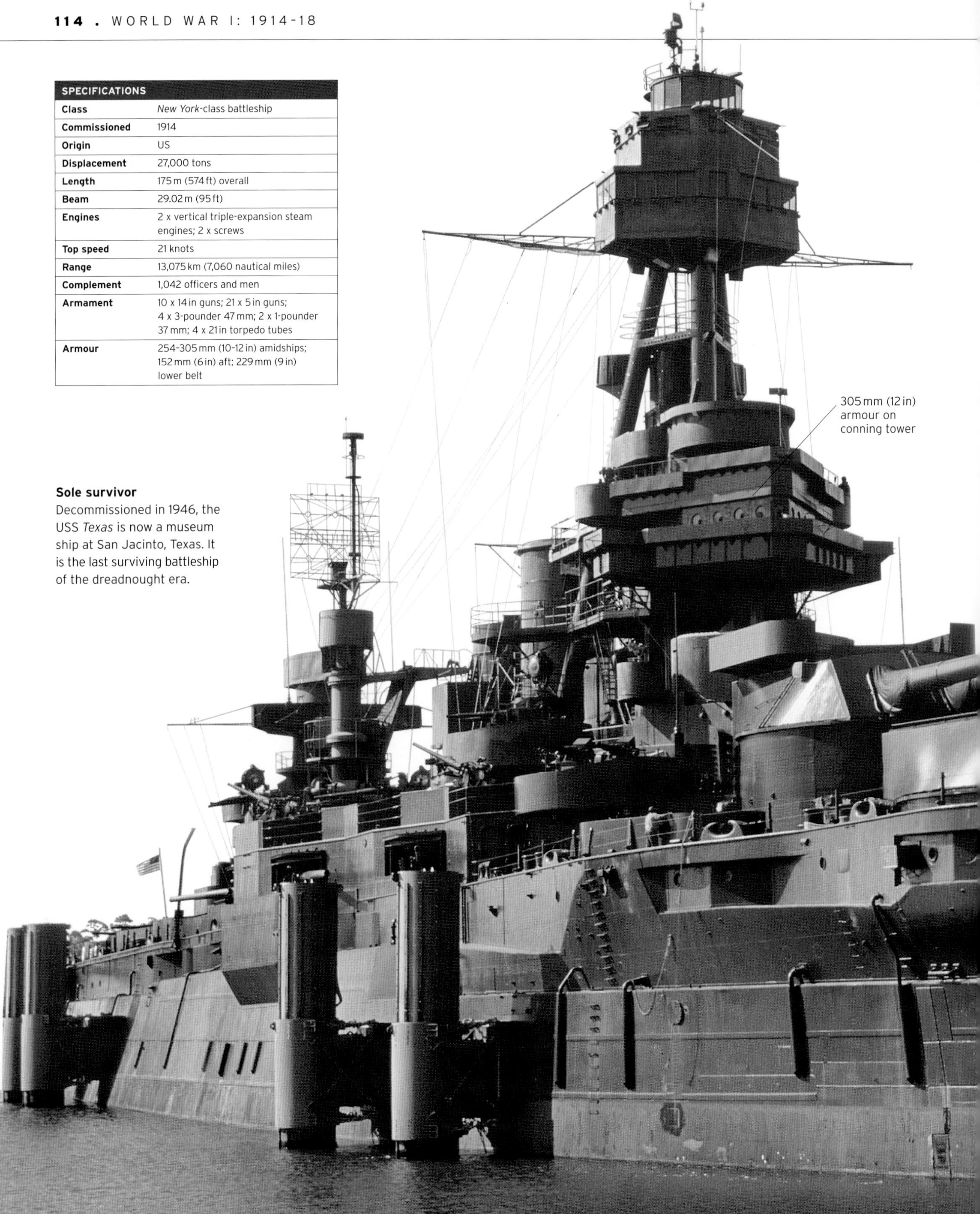

Sole survivor
Decommissioned in 1946, the USS *Texas* is now a museum ship at San Jacinto, Texas. It is the last surviving battleship of the dreadnought era.

USS Texas

The *Texas* was the product of the naval arms race that preceded World War I. A "super-dreadnought", it earned five battlestars during a long service career that spanned more than 30 years.

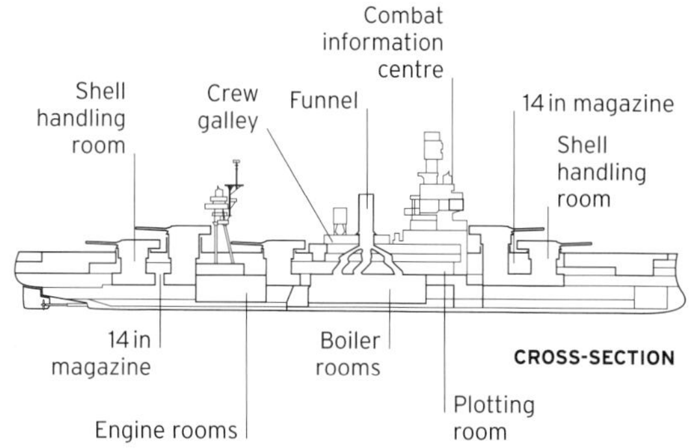

CROSS-SECTION

WITH A MAIN armament of ten 14in guns, the *Texas* entered service in 1914 as the world's most powerful warship. In some respects it was behind the times, especially in using coal-fired reciprocating engines rather than oil-fired steam turbines. An extensive modernization in 1927 installed oil-fired boilers, improved the ship's armour, and upgraded its fire-control systems. Later changes included the addition of many antiaircraft guns and fire-control and air-defence radars.

By World War II, the *Texas* was too slow to keep up with more modern capital ships in combat, but its guns still packed a powerful punch. The *Texas* escorted convoys in the Atlantic before the US entered the war. Later, the ship was prominent in a shore bombardment role, providing fire support for landings in North Africa, Normandy, Iwo Jima, and Okinawa. The *Texas* suffered only one combat fatality, when its conning tower was hit by a shell from a German shore battery in 1944.

1

2

3

4

5

6

THE INNOVATIVE SHIP

USS *Texas* achieved a number of firsts: it was the first US battleship to mount antiaircraft guns and to control gunfire with directors and range-keepers (forerunners of today's computers); it was the first US battleship to launch an aircraft, from a platform on Turret 2; and it was the first US naval vessel to host a permanently assigned contingent of marines. But despite these innovations, the ship soon showed its age and much of its equipment became obsolete.

1. Forward gun turrets **2.** Antiaircraft guns **3.** 20 mm cannon **4.** Battery control **5.** Bofors 40 mm gun **6.** Rear view of foremast **7.** Pilothouse **8.** Emergency steering position **9.** Oil-fired boiler **10.** 14 in shell hoist

7

8

10

9

BELOW DECKS

Home to a complement of about 1,800 men and officers by 1945, the *Texas* was like a small town, with a post office, a dentist, and a barber shop – but no liquor store, because alcohol consumption was banned on all US Navy ships. There were few frills on board: most men ate where they slept, and toilet and bathing facilities were quite primitive. It was, however, a well-organized world in which each man knew his place, and in which basic needs of health and nutrition were properly addressed.

4

BETWEEN THE WARS 1918–39

The lessons learned from World War I led to many developments in the interwar years. Aircraft became stronger and faster, as it was realized that planes would be vital in future conflicts. Medium and heavy tanks were developed to take on enemy armour and fortifications, and armoured cars became increasingly popular. Most rifles had stood up well to World War I, while new pistols improved on their predecessors and submachine-guns were introduced for personal protection.

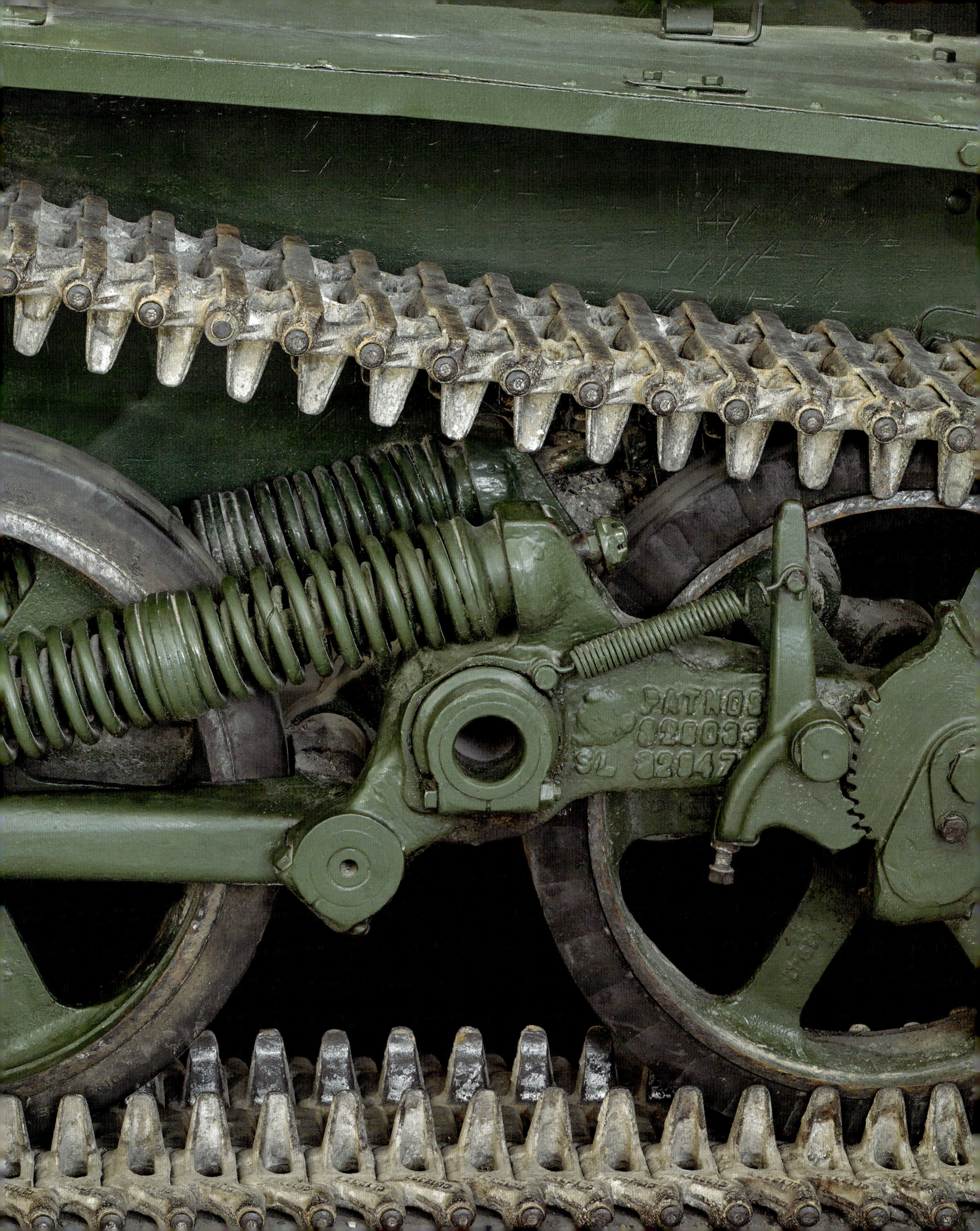

Self-loading Rifles

World War I had severely tested military rifles in service throughout the world. Most had stood up to combat conditions well, and when World War II loomed, most rifles still had the bolt-action mechanism recognizable from 50 years before. While the barrels of many rifles had been reduced in length to make them lighter and easier to handle, this had little adverse effect on their firing accuracy over fighting distances.

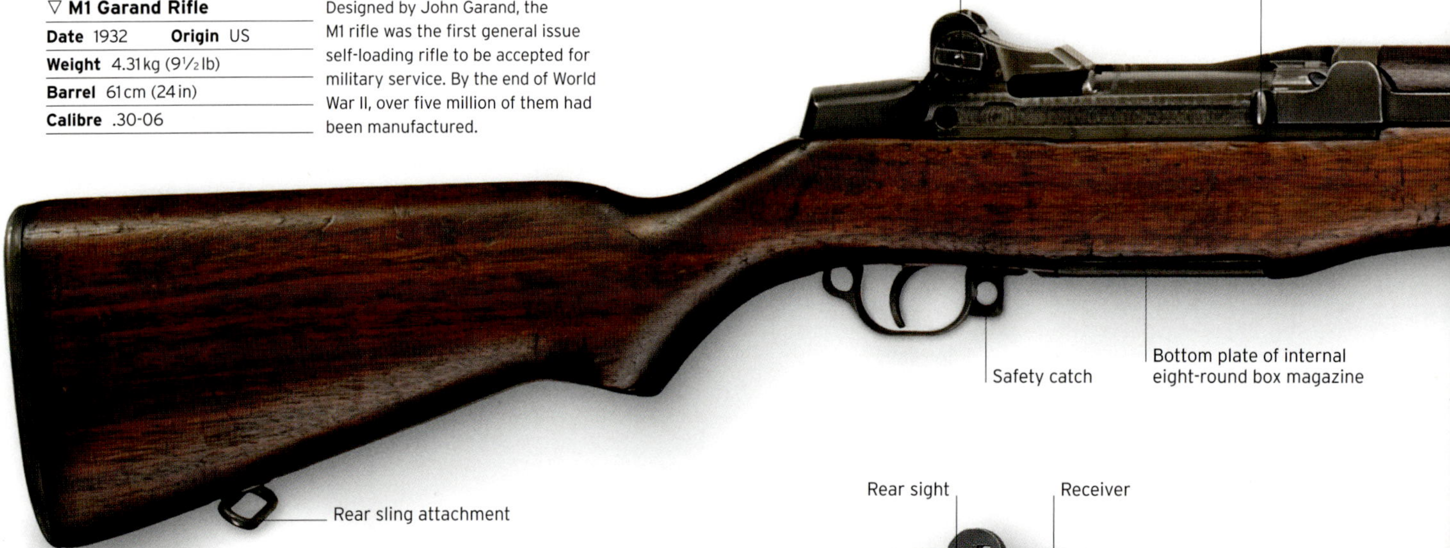

▽ **M1 Garand Rifle**

Date 1932	**Origin** US
Weight 4.31 kg (9½ lb)	
Barrel 61 cm (24 in)	
Calibre .30-06	

Designed by John Garand, the M1 rifle was the first general issue self-loading rifle to be accepted for military service. By the end of World War II, over five million of them had been manufactured.

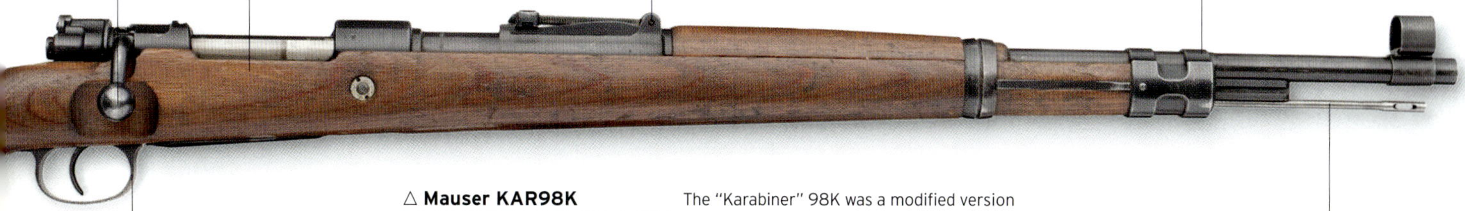

△ Mauser KAR98K

Date 1935	**Origin** Germany
Weight 3.9 kg (8½ lb)	
Barrel 60 cm (23½ in)	
Calibre 7.92 mm x 57	

The "Karabiner" 98K was a modified version of the Gewehr 98, and became the standard German rifle of World War II. More than 14 million were manufactured between 1935 and 1945. During that time, the design was further simplified to speed up production.

△ Lee-Enfield Rifle No. 4

Date 1939	**Origin** UK
Weight 4.1 kg (9 lb)	
Barrel 64 cm (25 in)	
Calibre .303 in	

The new Lee-Enfield, which appeared late in 1939, differed very little from the model it replaced - the SMLE Mark III. The bolt and receiver (the central body of the firearm containing the operating parts) were modified; the rear sight was a new design and was placed on the receiver, and the forestock was shortened, exposing the muzzle. The Number 4 remained in service until 1954.

Self-loading Pistols

If there were any lingering doubts as to the reliability of the self-loading pistol, they were largely dispelled during World War I, when officers of four of the major participating armies (Austria–Hungary, Germany, Turkey, and the US) all carried them. Poorly designed models were still being produced, but few of these found their way into military service (the Japanese Type 94 being an exception). The new types generally proved to be worthy successors to masterpieces like the Luger and the Colt M1911.

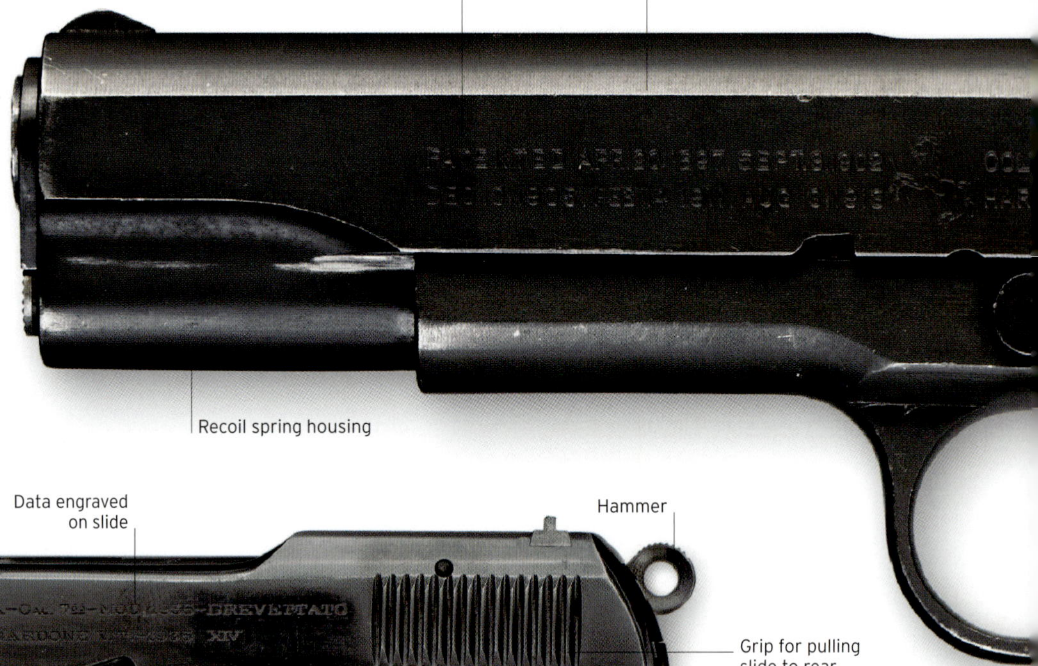

▷ **Colt M1911A1**

Date 1924	**Origin** US
Weight 1.1 kg (2½ lb)	
Barrel 12.7 cm (5 in)	
Calibre .45 in ACP	

Adopted in response to demands for a handgun with guaranteed stopping power, the Browning-designed M1911A1 replaced the M1911 of World War I. It was used by the US armed forces during World War II and after.

▷ **Beretta Model 1934**

Date 1934	**Origin** Italy
Weight 0.65 kg (1½ lb)	
Barrel 15.2 cm (6 in)	
Calibre 9 mm short	

Pietro Beretta SpA is the world's longest established gunmaker. Its M1934 became the official Italian officer's side-arm during World War II. The design evolved from one executed two decades earlier. This recoil-operated weapon was restricted to firing a reduced-power round, originally in 7.65 mm calibre.

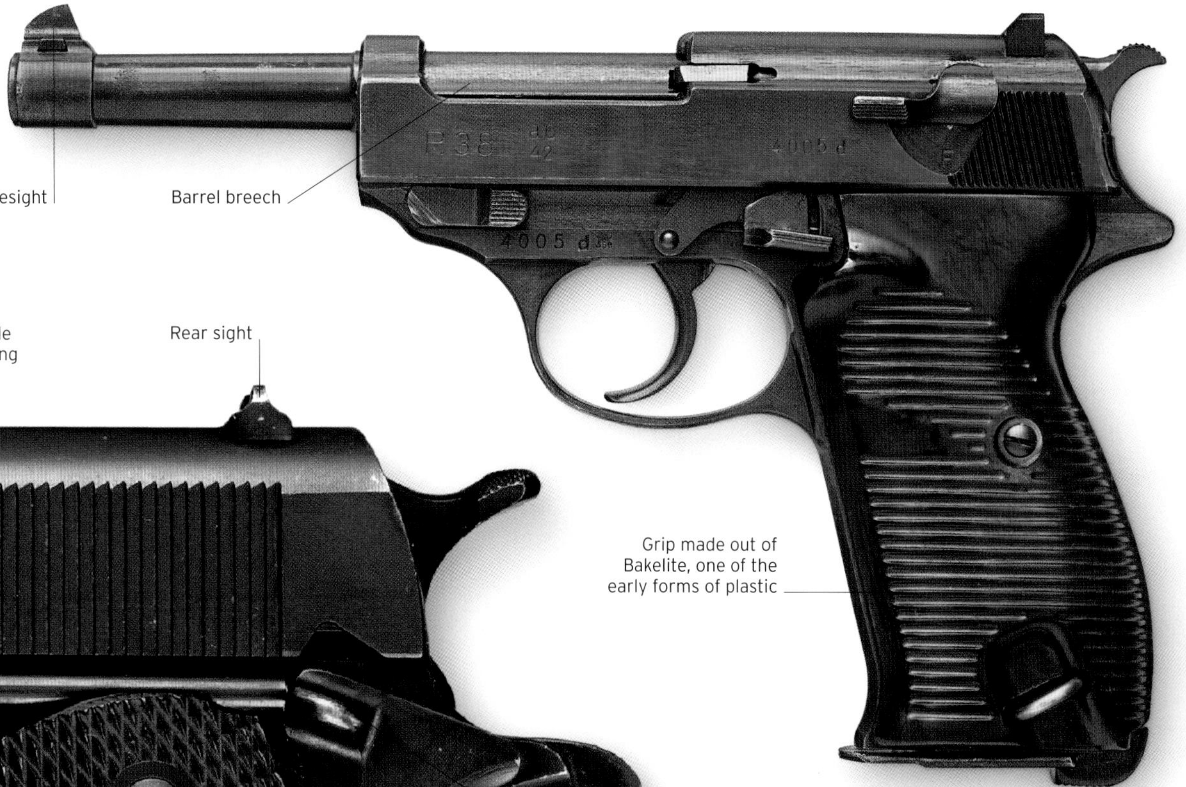

△ Walther P38

Date 1938	**Origin** Germany
Weight 0.8 kg (1¾ lb)	
Barrel 12.4 cm (4¾ in)	
Calibre 9 mm Parabellum	

Developed by the Walther company just prior to World War II, the P38 has come to be recognized as one of the finest semi-automatic pistols ever designed. Simple in construction and ruggedly built, it proved to be reliable under all circumstances.

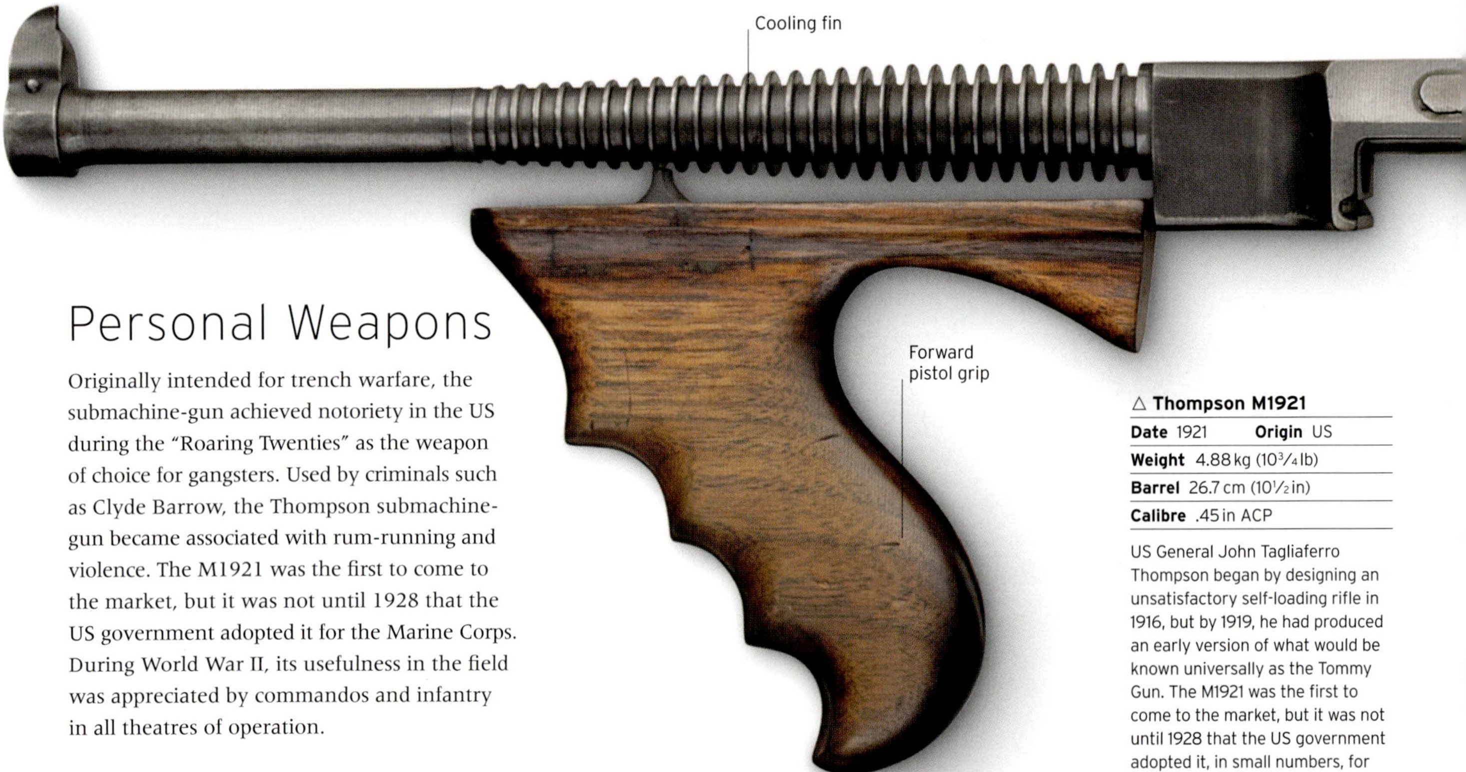

Personal Weapons

Originally intended for trench warfare, the submachine-gun achieved notoriety in the US during the "Roaring Twenties" as the weapon of choice for gangsters. Used by criminals such as Clyde Barrow, the Thompson submachine-gun became associated with rum-running and violence. The M1921 was the first to come to the market, but it was not until 1928 that the US government adopted it for the Marine Corps. During World War II, its usefulness in the field was appreciated by commandos and infantry in all theatres of operation.

△ Thompson M1921

Date 1921	**Origin** US
Weight 4.88 kg (10¾ lb)	
Barrel 26.7 cm (10½ in)	
Calibre .45 in ACP	

US General John Tagliaferro Thompson began by designing an unsatisfactory self-loading rifle in 1916, but by 1919, he had produced an early version of what would be known universally as the Tommy Gun. The M1921 was the first to come to the market, but it was not until 1928 that the US government adopted it, in small numbers, for the Marine Corps.

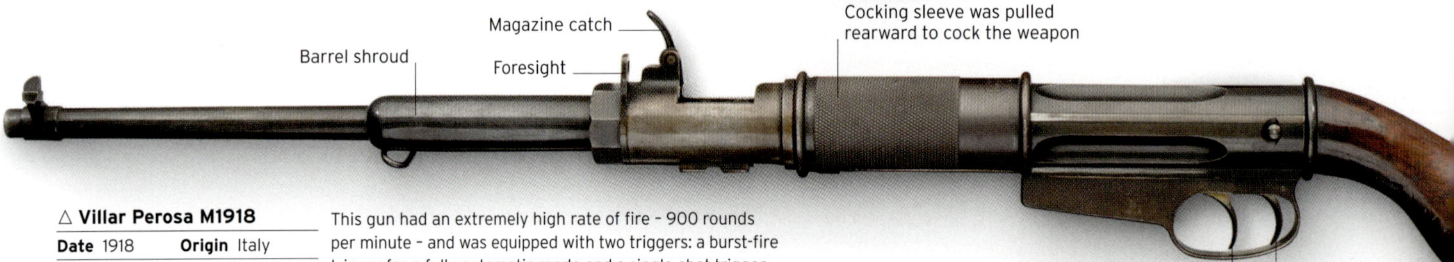

△ Villar Perosa M1918

Date 1918	**Origin** Italy
Weight 3.06 kg (6 lb)	
Barrel 28 cm (11 in)	
Calibre 9 mm Glisenti	

This gun had an extremely high rate of fire - 900 rounds per minute - and was equipped with two triggers: a burst-fire trigger for a fully automatic mode and a single-shot trigger for a semi-automatic mode. This model is a variant of the M1915 Villar Perosa, the first ever submachine-gun (SMG), which was issued to Italian troops in 1915.

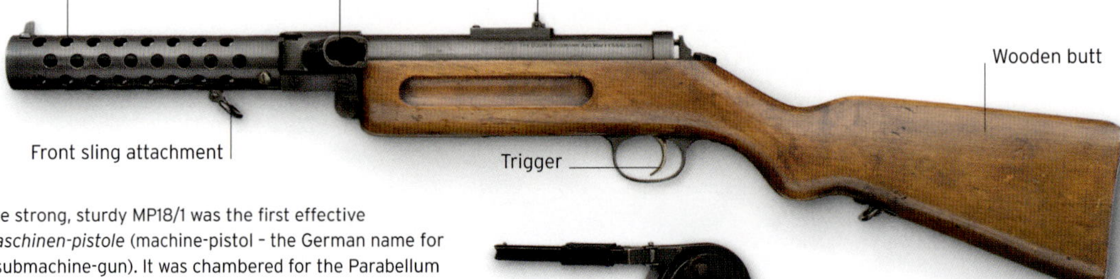

▷ Bergmann MP18/1

Date 1918	**Origin** Germany
Weight 4.2 kg (9¼ lb)	
Barrel 19.6 cm (7¾ in)	
Calibre 9 mm Parabellum	

The strong, sturdy MP18/1 was the first effective *maschinen-pistole* (machine-pistol - the German name for a submachine-gun). It was chambered for the Parabellum round Luger had developed for the P08 pistol, although that resulted in feed problems until a simpler box magazine was designed. Shown to the right is the original drum magazine.

THOMPSON 50-ROUND DRUM MAGAZINE

Naval defence
In the late 1930s, American Forces erected coastal defence batteries in Panama, to protect the strategic Panama Canal, such as this one overlooking the Gulf of Panama on the Pacific coast. This battery was equipped with a 14-in cannon.

NO

Machine-guns

From the 1920s onwards, light machine-guns were redesigned with a view to reducing the size of their crews. While earlier LMGs, such as the Maxim 08/15, required a crew of four, newer LMGs such as the Bren could be operated by a one- or two-man crew. This reduction in crew size was made possible by changing the ammunition feed system from belts, which needed an additional user for ensuring proper loading, to box magazines, which could be loaded and changed exclusively by the main user.

▽ **Browning M1919**	
Date	1919
Origin	US
Weight	14.06 kg (31 lb)
Barrel	61 cm (24 in)
Calibre	.3 in

The M1919 was an air-cooled version of the earlier M1917, and it proved to be a first-rate medium machine-gun, supporting US infantrymen throughout World War II, and remaining in use until the 1960s. It had a firing rate of 400–600 rounds per minute.

FULL VIEW

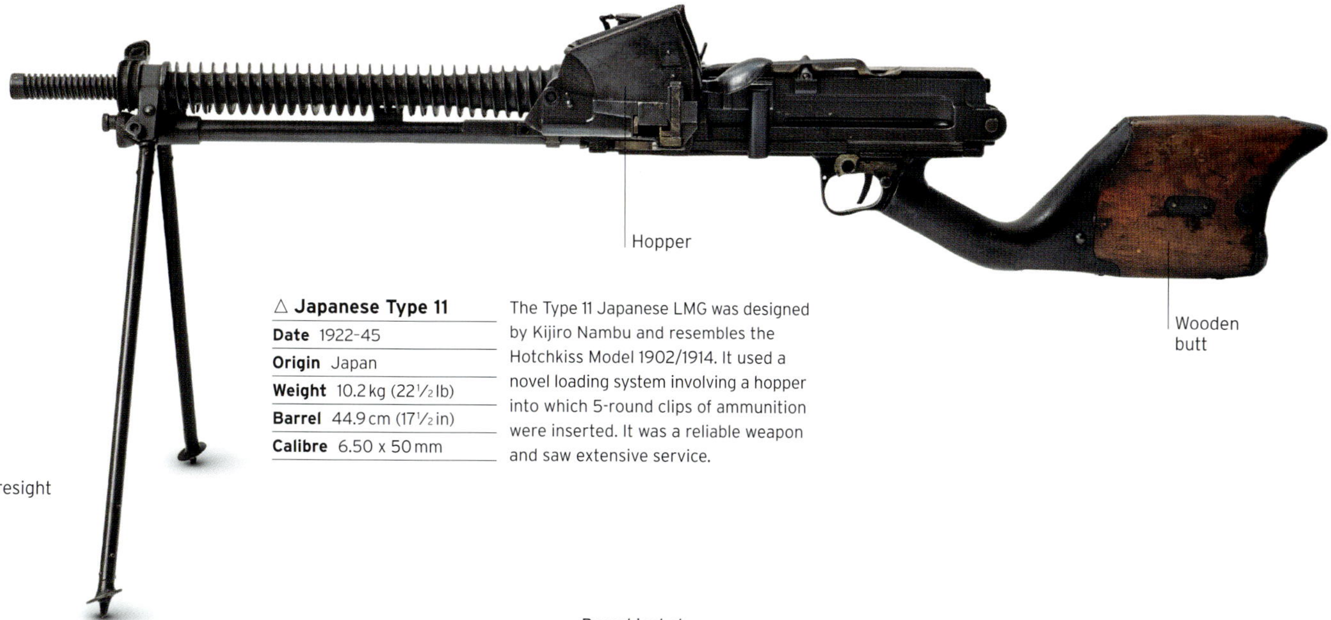

△ Japanese Type 11

Date	1922–45
Origin	Japan
Weight	10.2 kg (22½ lb)
Barrel	44.9 cm (17½ in)
Calibre	6.50 x 50 mm

The Type 11 Japanese LMG was designed by Kijiro Nambu and resembles the Hotchkiss Model 1902/1914. It used a novel loading system involving a hopper into which 5-round clips of ammunition were inserted. It was a reliable weapon and saw extensive service.

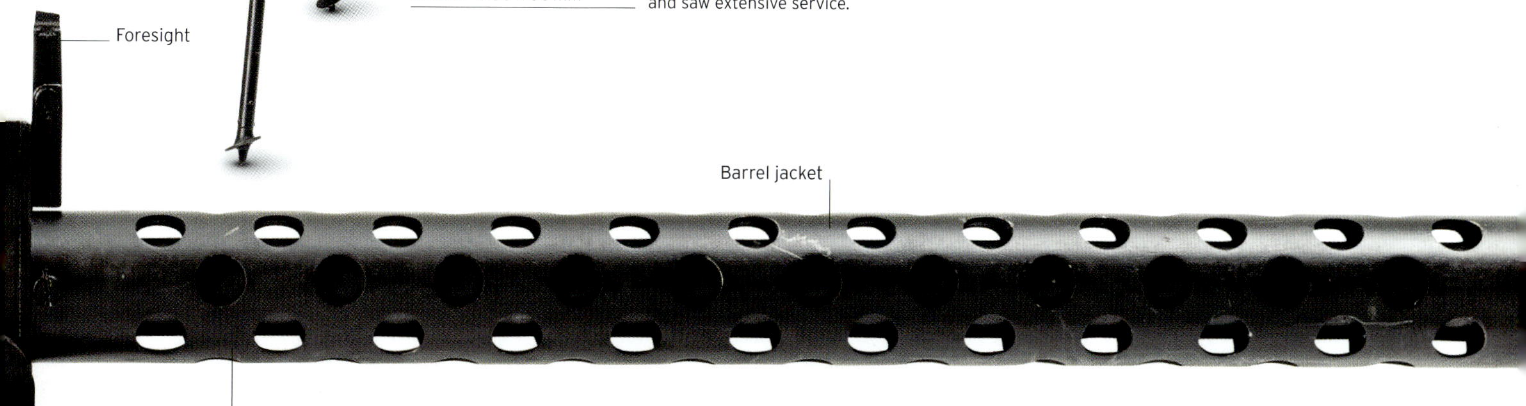

△ Châtellerault Modèle 1924/29

Date	1929
Origin	France
Weight	8.9 kg (19½ lb)
Barrel	50 cm (19¾ in)
Calibre	7.5 x 54 mm

The MLE 1924 was designed as a light machine-gun replacement for the terrible Chauchat MLE 1915 from World War I, but was let down by poor ammunition. The cartridge was redesigned, along with parts of the gun, to produce the MLE 1924/29, which served through World War II and into the 1950s. The gun was unusual in having a dual-trigger arrangement – the forward trigger was for single-shot firing and the rear-set trigger for continuous fire.

Machine-guns (cont.)

▷ Breda Modello 37

Date 1937	**Origin** Italy
Weight 19.4 kg (43 lb)	
Barrel 127 cm (50 in)	
Calibre 8 x 59 mm	

Adopted by the Italian Army in 1937, the Breda was a gas-operated machine-gun fed by 20-round ammunition strips, and later belts. Its primary disadvantage was that the cartridges had to be lubricated with oil prior to firing. Stoppages caused by dust or dirt were therefore a problem. Its low cyclic rate (450 rounds per minute), however, was an advantage for accurate support fire.

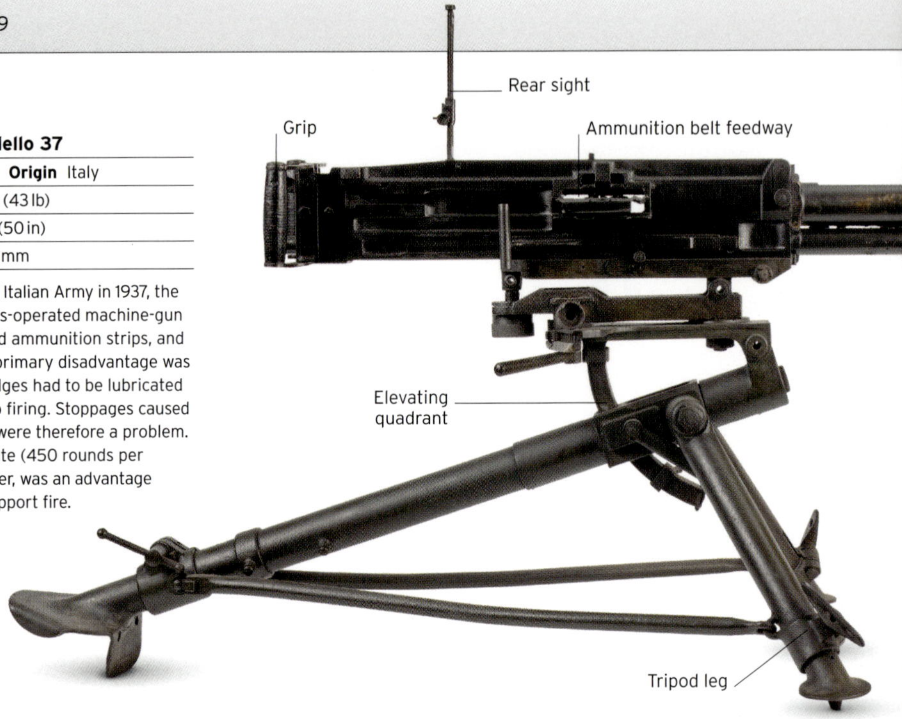

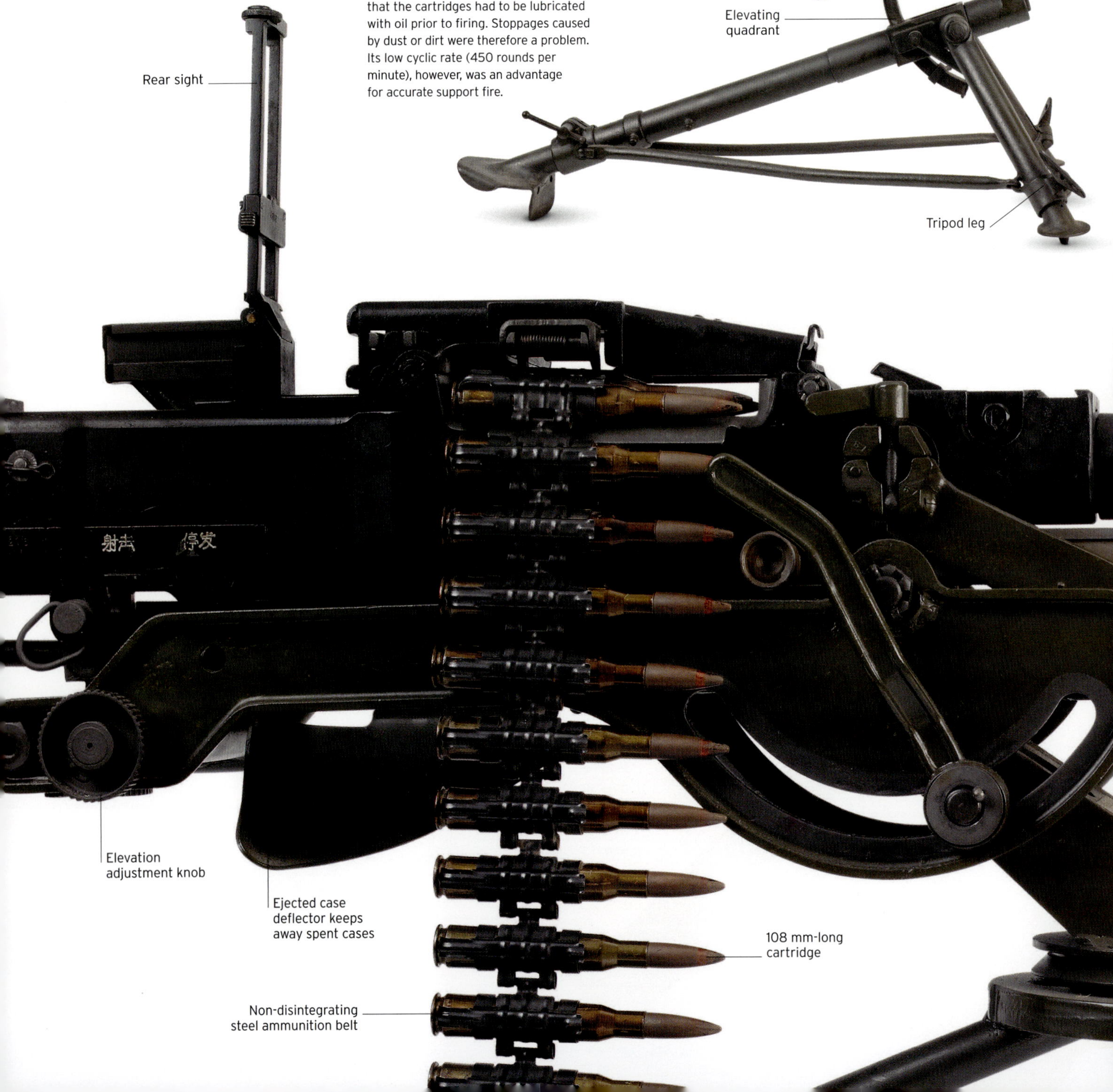

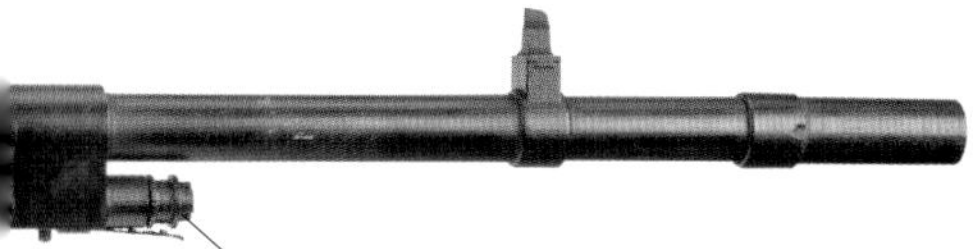

△ Bren Gun

Date 1938 **Origin** UK
Weight 10.15 kg (22¼ lb)
Barrel 63.5 cm (25 in)
Calibre .303 in

Originally developed in Brno, Czechoslovakia, and modified at Enfield in London (hence its name), the dependable Bren was the British Army's light machine-gun during World War II, and remained in service until the 1980s.

△ Degtyarev DShK1938

Date 1938 **Origin** Soviet Union
Weight 33.3 kg (73½ lb)
Barrel 1 m (3½ ft)
Calibre 12.7 x 108 mm

Employed as the Red Army's heavy machine-gun, the gas-operated DShK1938 resembled the .50 in Browning M2. It enjoyed similar longevity – some units are still in service. It fired 600 rounds per minute.

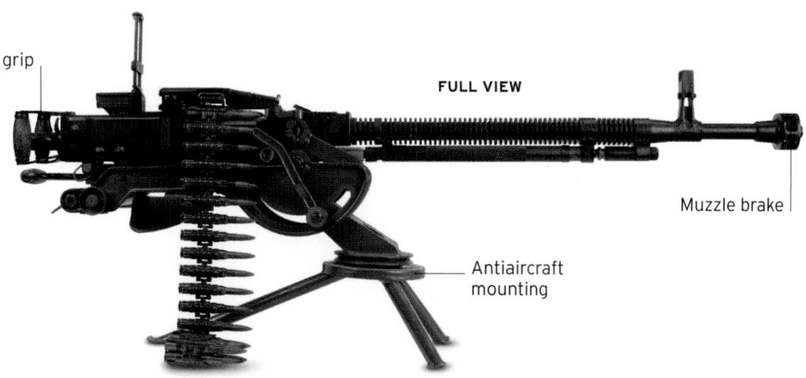

Armoured Cars

Early tanks were unreliable: their tracks were prone to breaking on rough ground or when handled poorly, and they wore out relatively quickly. Wheeled vehicles, on the other hand, were quieter, much more durable, often able to carry similar firepower and armour protection, and were usually faster, except over the roughest terrain. These qualities made armoured cars ideal patrol vehicles, as the British used them in India. Other countries used them for reconnoitering ahead of their tank forces.

▽ Rolls-Royce Armoured Car

Date 1920 **Origin** UK

Weight 4.3 tonnes (4.8 tons)

Engine Rolls-Royce 6-cylinder gasoline, 80 hp

Main armament .303 Vickers machine-gun

The 1920 Pattern Rolls-Royce was very similar to the Royal Navy's 1914 Pattern. It was used by the British Army and Royal Air Force around the world, including in Ireland, Iraq, Shanghai, and Egypt. Some upgraded 1920 and 1924 Pattern vehicles were used in the North African Desert Campaign in 1940 and 1941.

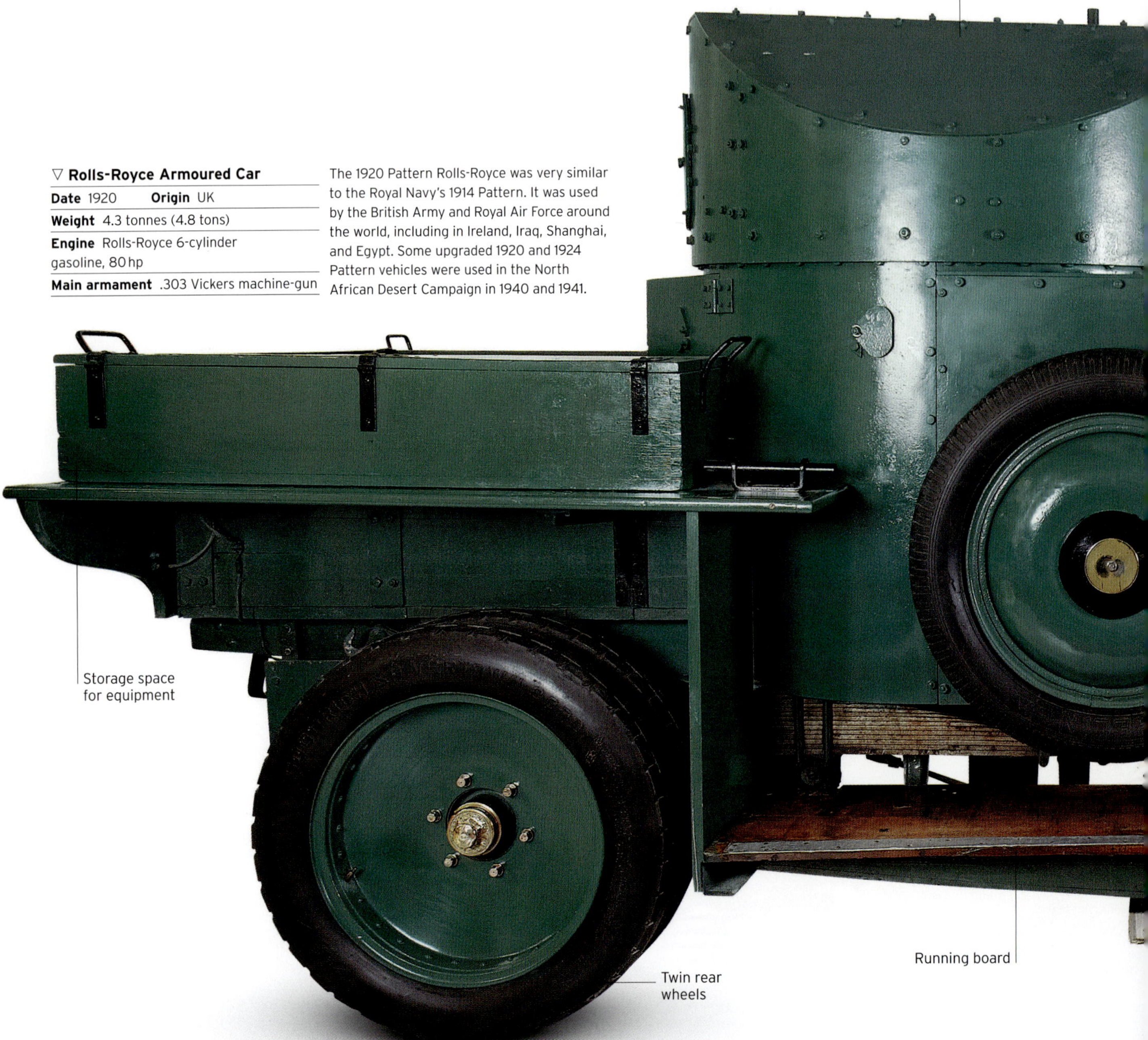

▷ **Crossley-Chevrolet Armored Car**

Date 1939 **Origin** UK

Weight 5.1 tonnes (5.6 tons)

Engine Chevrolet 6-cylinder gasoline, 78 hp

Main armament 2 x Vickers .303 machine-guns

The British Army in India made heavy use of armoured cars, especially on the North West Frontier Province bordering Afghanistan. They were built to "Indian Pattern", including a dome-shaped turret with cupola and an asbestos lining to control the temperature. By 1939, the cars had worn out, and their bodies were attached to new Chevrolet chassis.

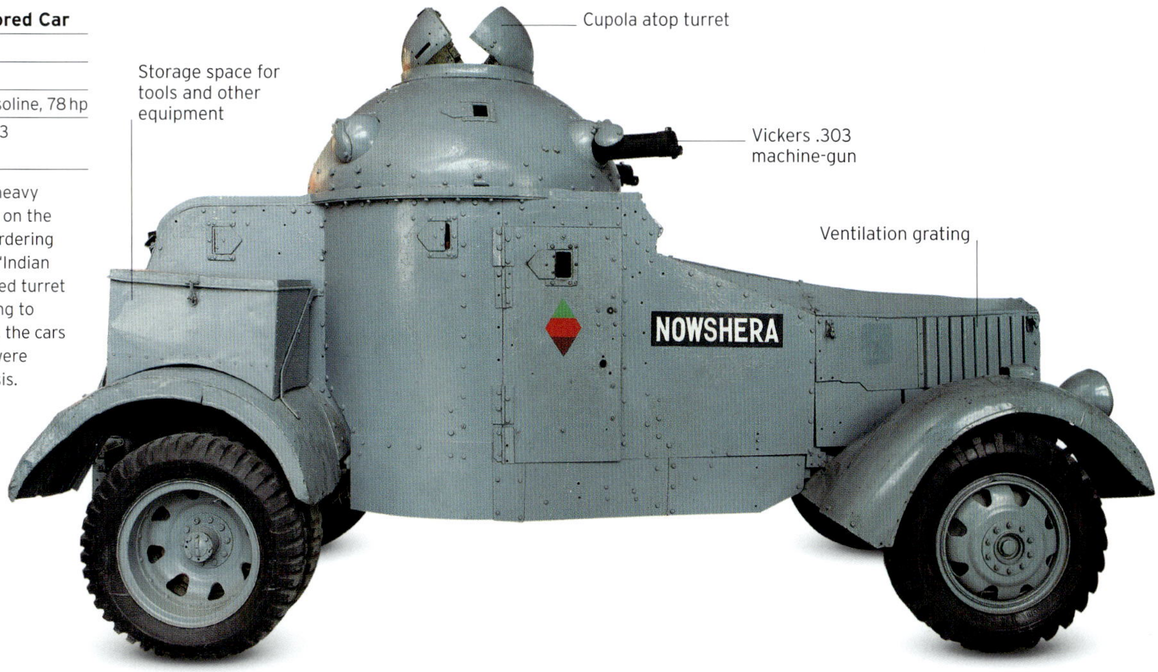

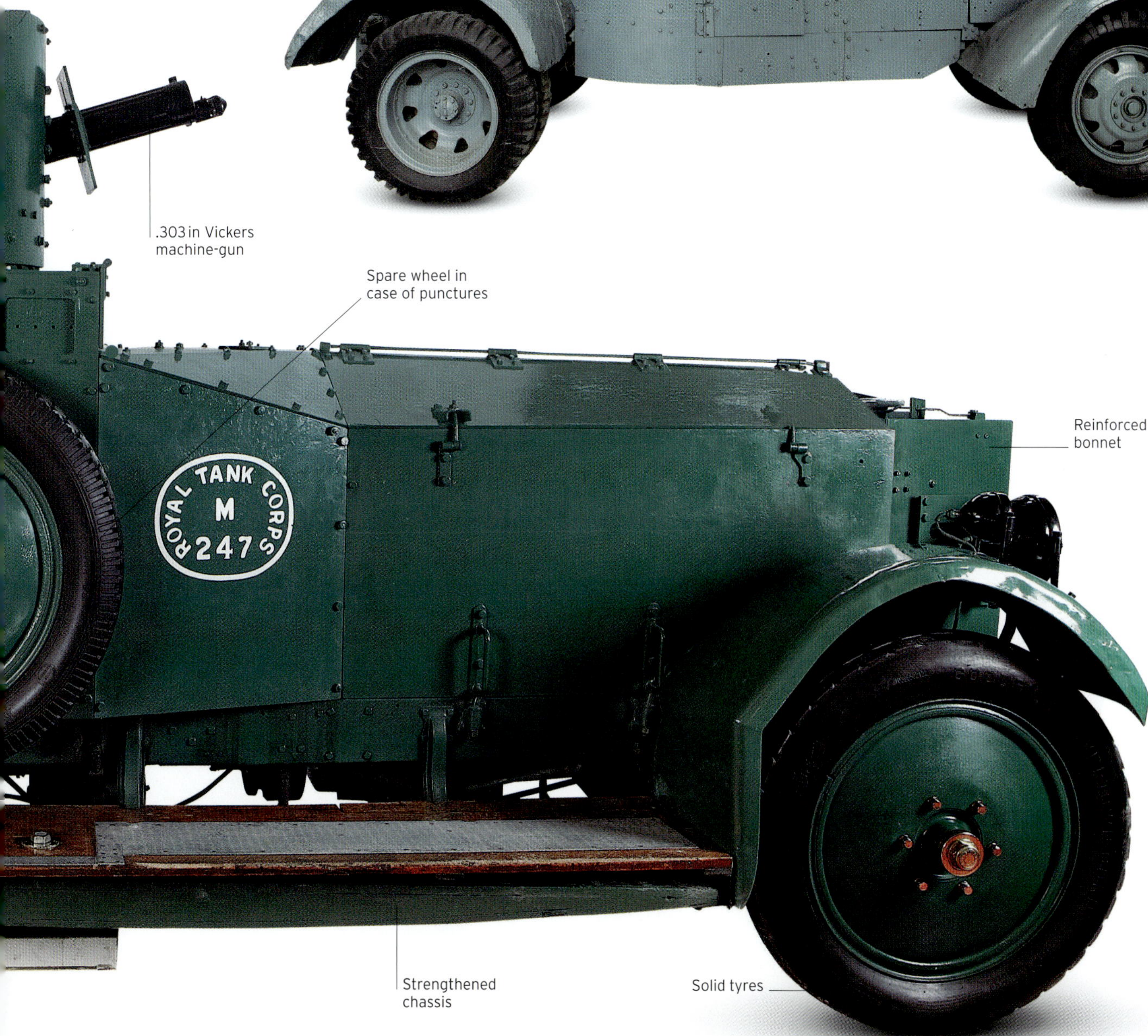

Interwar Tanks

In the interwar period, medium and heavy tanks were intended to take on enemy armour and fortifications, creating the breakthrough for faster vehicles to exploit. In general, armour protection and firepower were therefore emphasized over mobility. As military budgets became increasingly stretched in the 1930s, tankettes proved to be a relatively cheap way to put a lot of armoured firepower onto the battlefield. They were generally used for infantry support and as such became increasingly popular. Light tanks, on the other hand, were larger and better protected, their role to take advantage of breakthroughs made by heavier tanks.

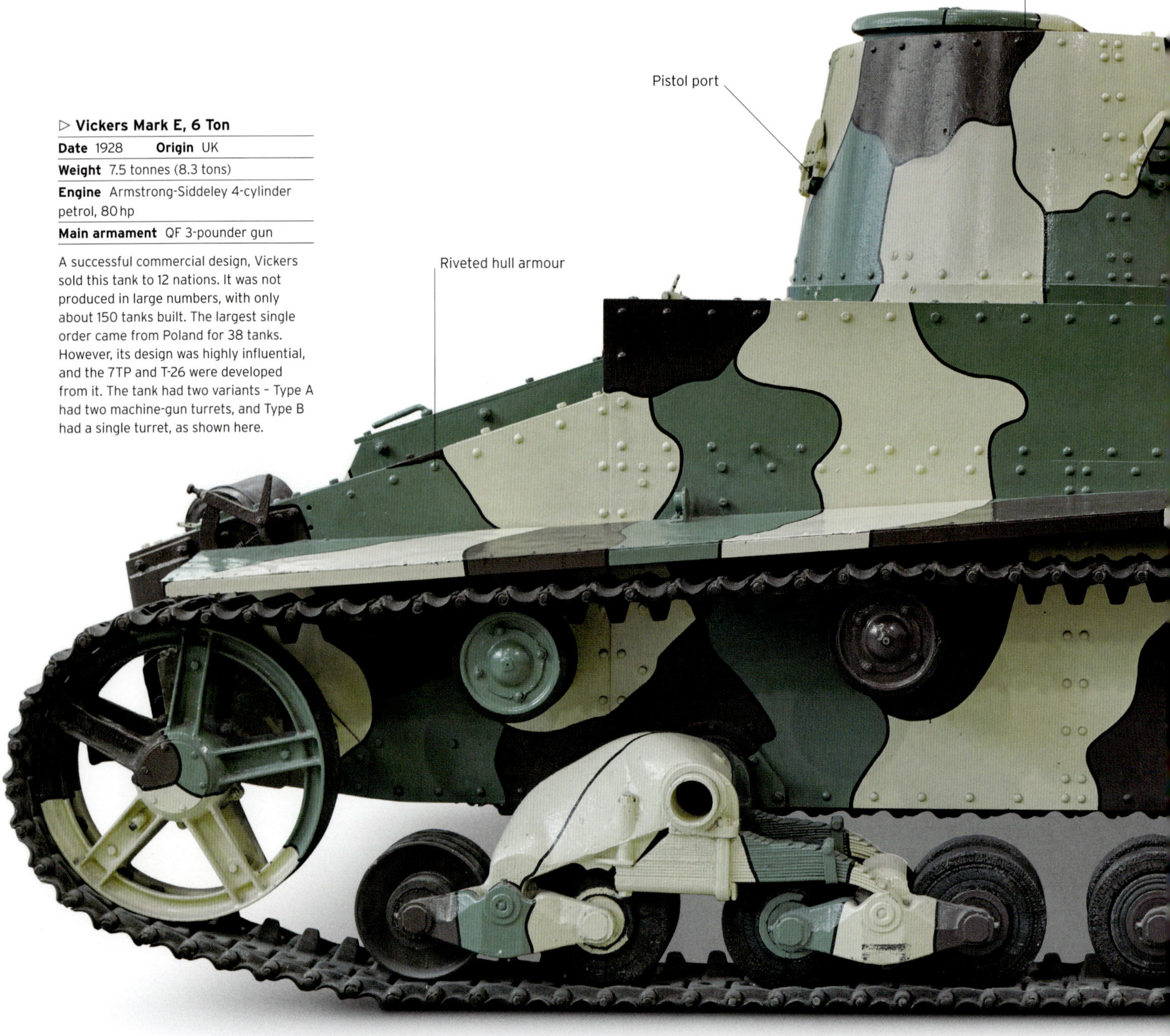

▷ **Vickers Mark E, 6 Ton**

Date 1928 **Origin** UK

Weight 7.5 tonnes (8.3 tons)

Engine Armstrong-Siddeley 4-cylinder petrol, 80 hp

Main armament QF 3-pounder gun

A successful commercial design, Vickers sold this tank to 12 nations. It was not produced in large numbers, with only about 150 tanks built. The largest single order came from Poland for 38 tanks. However, its design was highly influential, and the 7TP and T-26 were developed from it. The tank had two variants - Type A had two machine-gun turrets, and Type B had a single turret, as shown here.

△ **Carden-Loyd Carrier Mark VI**

Date 1928	**Origin** UK
Weight 1.5 tonnes (1.7 tons)	
Engine Ford Model T petrol, 22.5 hp	
Main armament .303 Vickers machine-gun	

The Carden-Loyd Company built a series of one- and two-man tankettes during the mid 1920s. The Mark VI was the most successful (450 were built by 1935) and it was the last before the company was bought by Vickers. The design was sold around the world, where it influenced the development of many vehicles.

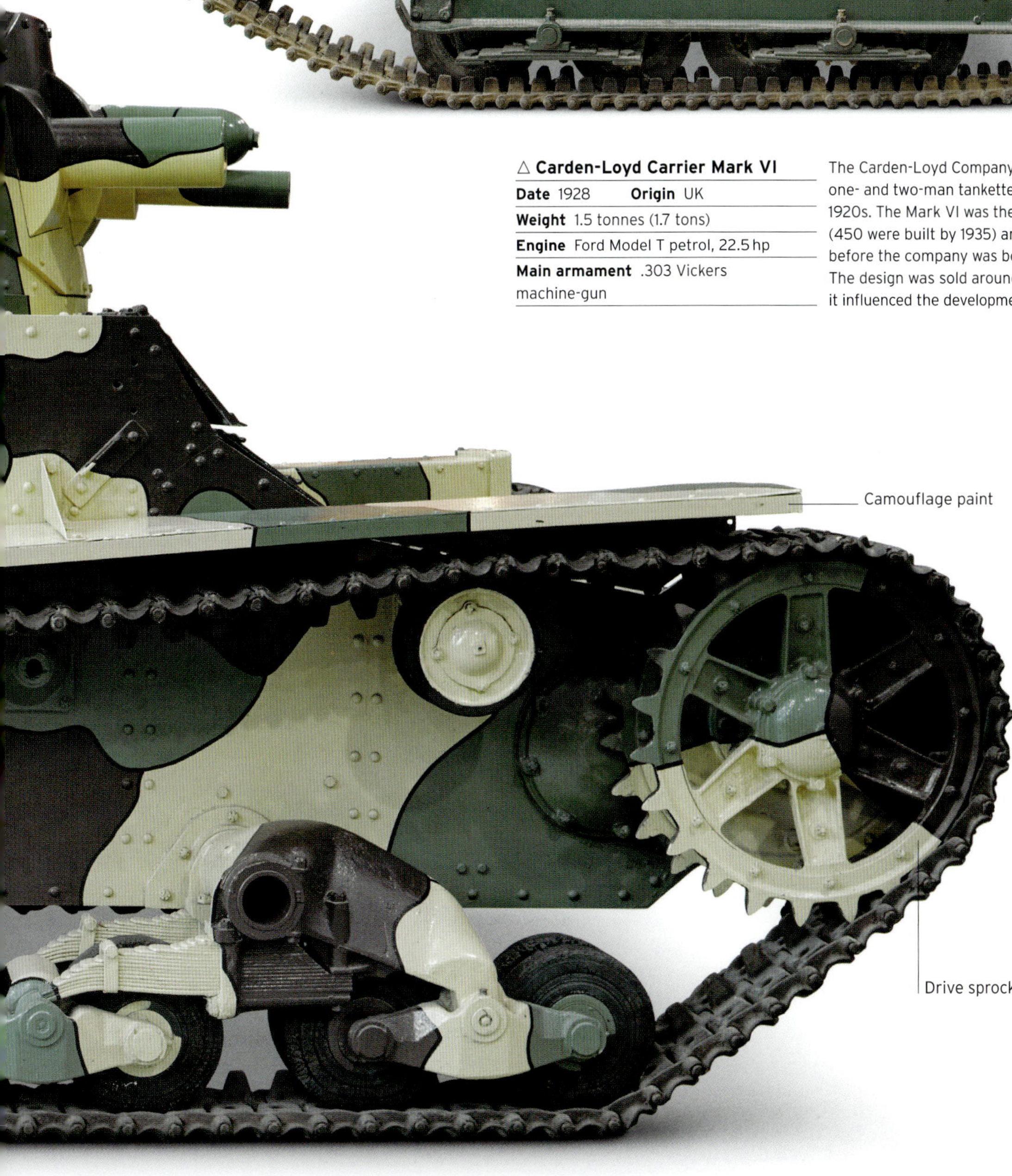

Interwar Tanks (cont.)

▷ **Char B1 bis**

Date 1936 **Origin** France

Weight 31.5 tonnes (34.7 tons)

Engine Renault V12 petrol, 307 hp

Main armament 1 x 75 mm ABS 1929 SA 35 L/17.1 howitzer, 1 x 47 mm SA 35 gun

The most powerful French tank in 1940, the B1 bis was armed with a 75 mm infantry support gun in the hull and a 47 mm antitank gun in the usual one-man turret. It was very heavily armoured, but suffered from slow speed and limited range. This was a result of being in development since the 1920s; by the time it was ready, it had already been overtaken by other models.

▽ **A9 Cruiser**

Date 1937 **Origin** UK

Weight 12.2 tonnes (13.4 tons)

Engine AEC Type 179 petrol, 150 hp

Main armament QF 2-pounder gun

The A9 was the first cruiser tank, a British concept intended for independent operations rather than infantry support. It was therefore fast, but lightly armoured. The A9 had capable suspension and probably the most powerful antitank gun in the world at the time - the 2-pounder.

▽ UE Tankette

Date 1937	**Origin** France
Weight 3.3 tonnes (3.6 tons)	
Engine Renault 4-cylinder petrol, 38 hp	
Main armament None	

Another development of the Carden-Loyd Carrier, the UE was designed as a lightly armoured supply carrier for infantry. It had a stowage container behind the crew that could be tipped automatically, and it could tow a range of gear, such as mortars, antitank guns, and a tracked trailer. Some 5,000 were built, most of which were unarmed.

Vickers Medium Mark II*

Introduced in 1923, the Vickers Medium tank was the first British tank to see service equipped with a sprung suspension and a rotating turret. The design was so successful that the Medium was the main British tank from 1923 to 1935.

SPECIFICATIONS	
Name	Tank, Medium, Mark II*
Date	1923
Origin	UK
Production	100
Engine	Armstrong Siddeley V8 petrol, 90 hp
Weight	11.75 tonnes (13 tons)
Main armament	3-pounder
Secondary armament	3 x Vickers .303 machine-guns
Crew	5
Armour thickness	6.25-8 mm (0.25-0.3 in)

DESIGNED TO FIGHT on the move, the Medium's high speed of 48 km/h (30 mph) came from its air-cooled Armstrong Siddeley engine, which was mounted in the front of the tank. The tank itself had seven variants. The first, the Medium Mark I, had a 3-pounder gun in the turret, a Vickers machine-gun in each side of the hull, and Hotchkiss light machine-guns in the turret. This main gun was adequate against contemporary tanks, but it was useless against field fortifications and antitank guns, so a close support version of the tank was built. The Mark II* dispensed with the Hotchkiss machine-guns and had a coaxial Vickers machine-gun instead. In addition to the gun tanks, command-post and bridge-laying versions were also produced.

Vickers Mediums formed the backbone of the British Army's Experimental Mechanised Force of 1928. This revolutionary combat formation performed manoeuvres on Salisbury Plain that showed the potential of mechanized formations. For this reason, the mechanization of the British Army continued through the 1930s.

FRONT VIEW

Covered sprung suspension

Eminent export

The Vickers Medium was influential not only because it proved the potential of armoured formations, but also because it was widely exported. Fifteen tanks were sold to Russia, and the one sold to Japan led to the country's own Type 89 tank design.

REAR VIEW

EXTERIOR

The Vickers Medium was constructed with riveted armour plate – 6.25 mm (0.25 in) thick on the front, which was protection against bullets but little else. However, the Royal Tank Corps, formed in 1923, became highly skilled at firing the 3-pounder gun on the move, an achievement that enabled them to keep up their mobility and become a harder target for enemy gunners to hit.

1. Engine air intake **2.** Coaxial Vickers machine-gun mount **3.** Hull wall ball-mount Vickers machine-gun **4.** Exhaust **5.** View through rear door **6.** Fighting compartment interior **7.** 3-pounder gun breach **8.** Coaxial Vickers machine-gun **9.** Hull machine-gun position **10.** Vickers .303 machine-gun **11.** Driver's position from above **12.** Driver's controls

1

2

3

4

5

6

7

8

9

10

11

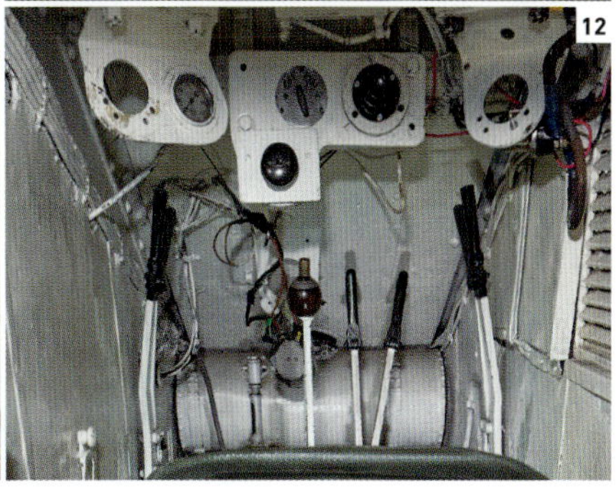

12

INTERIOR

The Medium had a surprisingly roomy interior. Crewed by five men, the driver sat at the front, next to the engine, while the commander and gunner sat in the turret. Two more gunners manned the Vickers .303 machine-guns on each side of the hull.

Training Aircraft

Both the biplane and monoplane training aircraft introduced in the interwar years would for the most part be still serving faithfully more than 50 years later, such was their sturdy design and reliability. Indeed, some are still in active service today rather than retired to leisure use. Most training aircraft had open cockpits and tandem seating, the trainer sitting behind the novice pilot. These aircraft might have been simple, but they taught all the essential skills of pilotage.

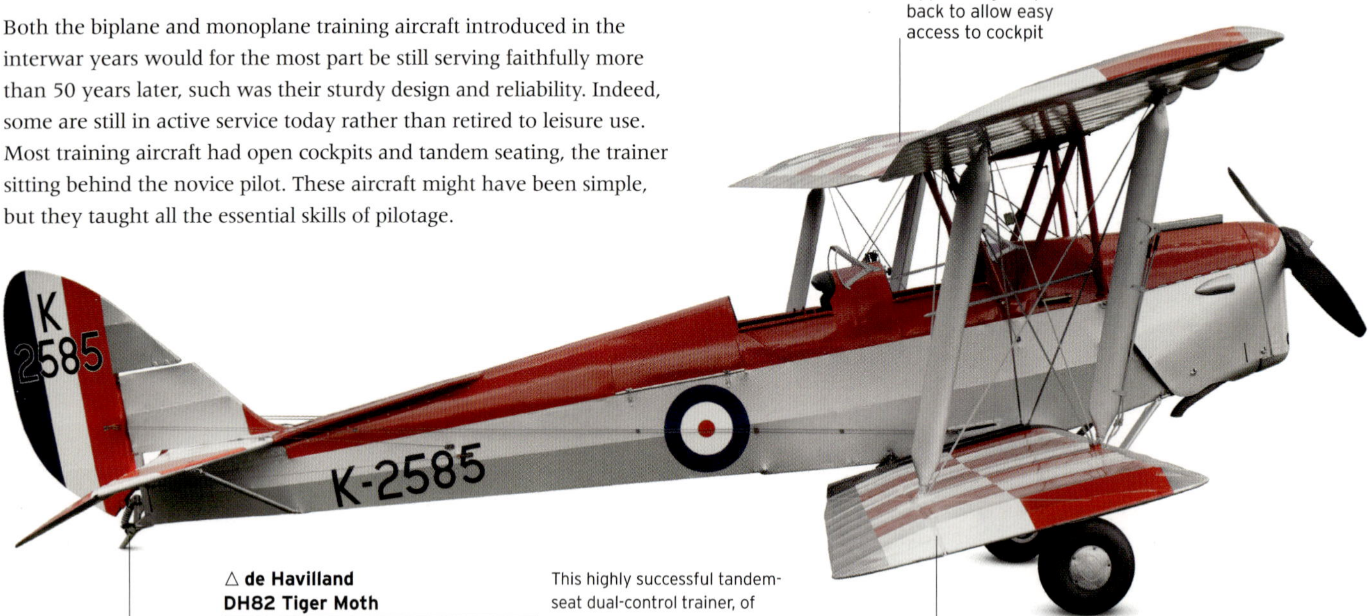

△ **de Havilland DH82 Tiger Moth**

Date 1931 **Origin** UK

Engine 130 hp de Havilland Gipsy Major I air-cooled inverted 4-cylinder in-line

Top speed 175 km/h (109 mph)

This highly successful tandem-seat dual-control trainer, of which 8,868 were built, was used by the RAF and many other air forces. Still sometimes flown for training, it is now principally a leisure aircraft.

▽ **Naval Aircraft Factory N3N-3 Canary**

Date 1935 **Origin** US

Engine 235 hp Wright R-760-2 Whirlwind air-cooled 7-cylinder radial

Top speed 203 km/h (126 mph)

Designed and built (including licence-built engines) by a factory wholly owned by the US government, the yellow Canary was in service with the US Navy as a primary trainer until 1961.

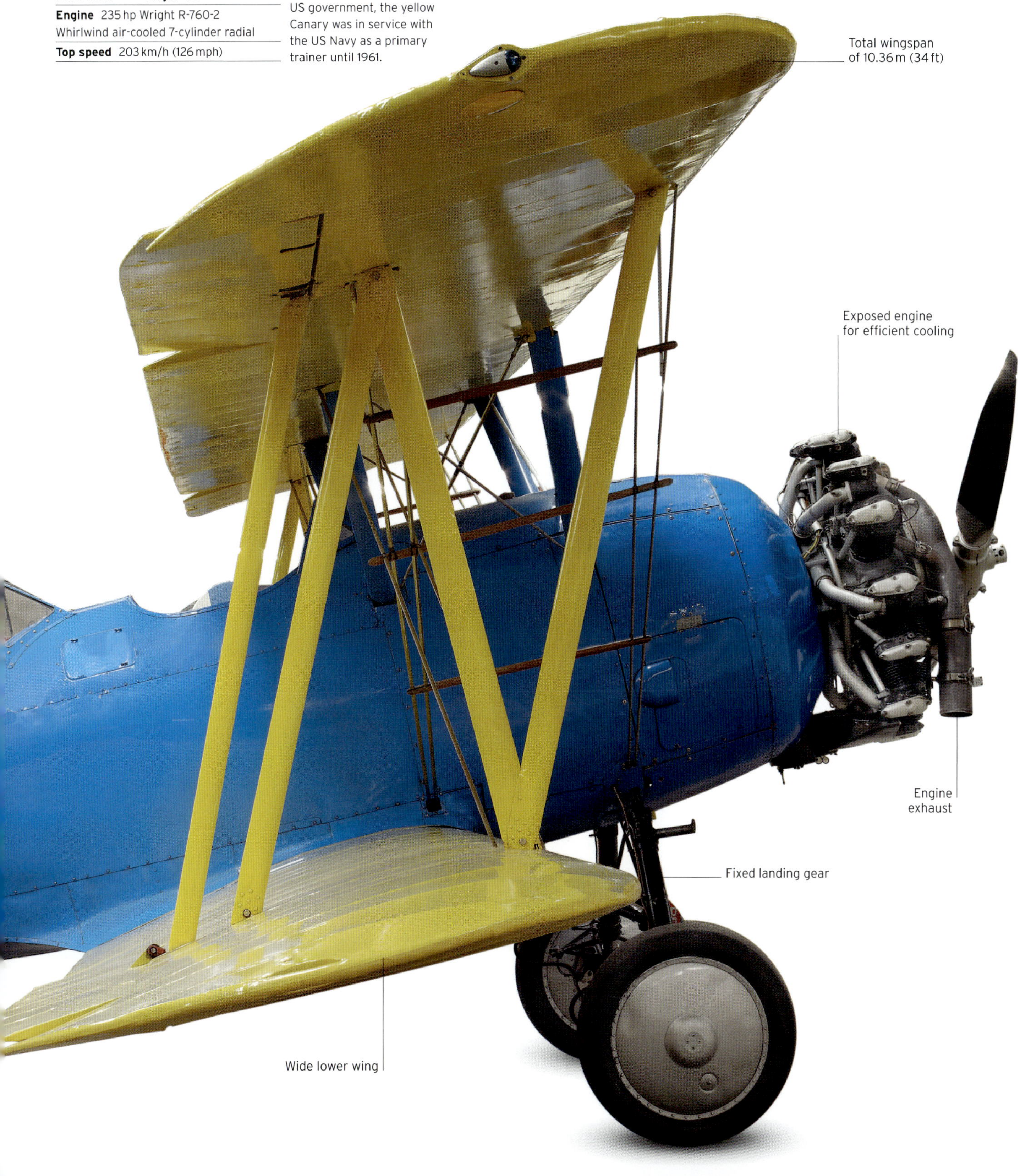

Warplanes

Lessons learned from World War I were consolidated into stronger, faster, and more efficient military aircraft, as it was realised that aircraft would be increasingly important in future conflicts. The 1930s saw rapid development in warplanes, especially from 1935 as the threat of war loomed. The basic bombers and trainers that looked much like late World War I aircraft were replaced with monocoque fuselages, enclosed cockpits, all-metal construction, and advanced monoplane wing designs.

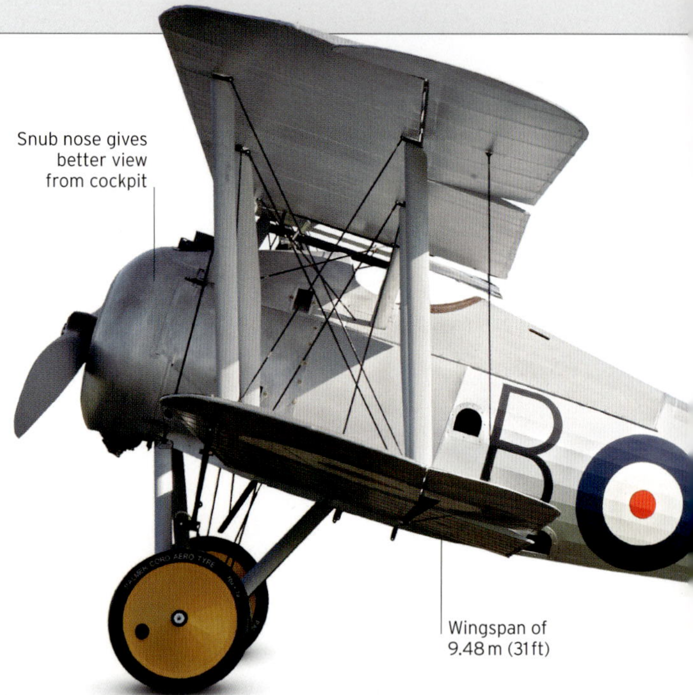

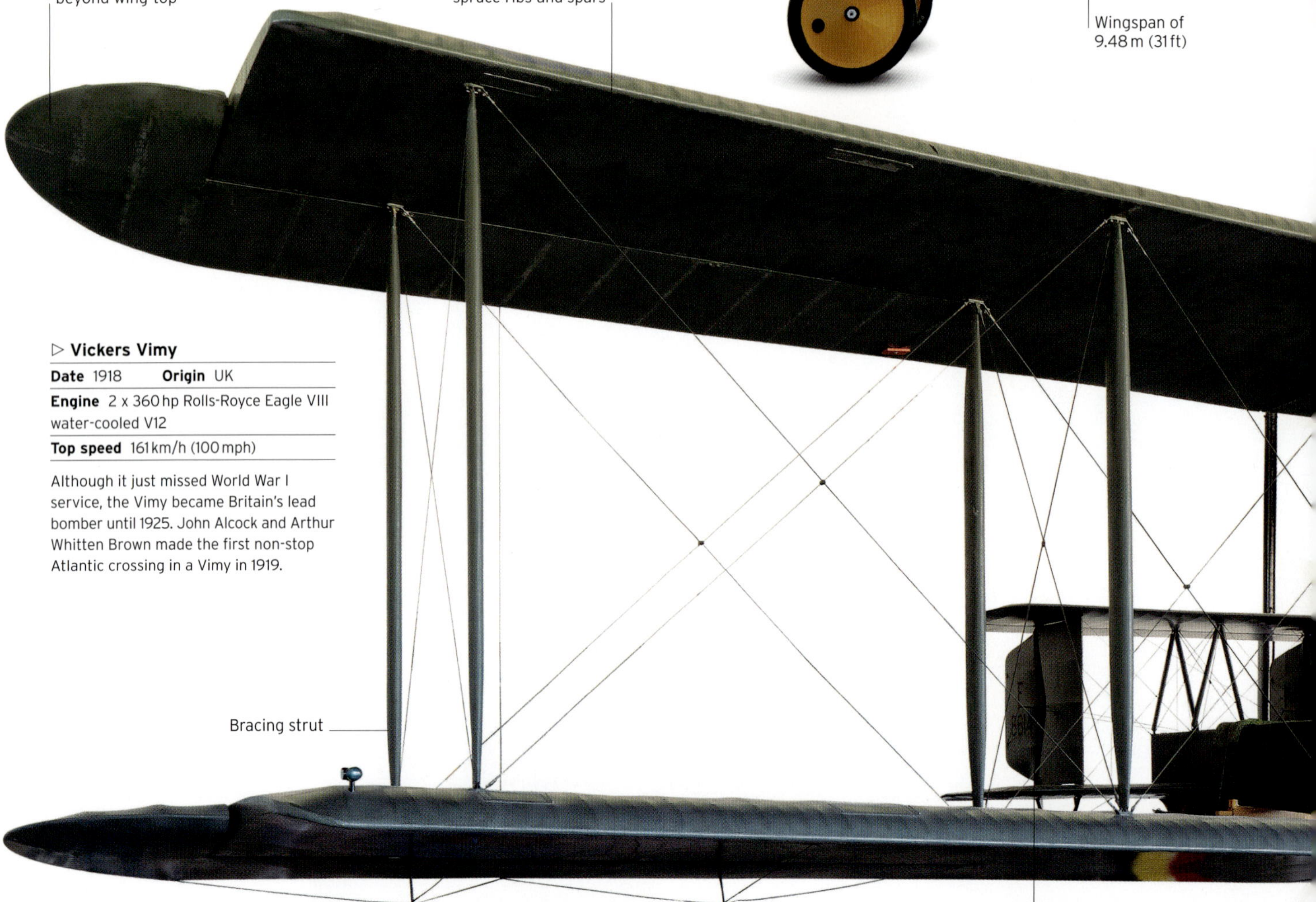

▷ **Vickers Vimy**

Date 1918 **Origin** UK

Engine 2 x 360 hp Rolls-Royce Eagle VIII water-cooled V12

Top speed 161 km/h (100 mph)

Although it just missed World War I service, the Vimy became Britain's lead bomber until 1925. John Alcock and Arthur Whitten Brown made the first non-stop Atlantic crossing in a Vimy in 1919.

▽ Sopwith 7F.1 Snipe

Date 1919	**Origin** UK
Engine 230 hp Bentley BR2 air-cooled 9-cylinder radial	
Top speed 195 km/h (121 mph)	

Introduced a few weeks before the end of World War I, the Snipe became the RAF's main postwar single-seat fighter, finally retired in 1926. Its agility and rate of climb made up for a low top speed.

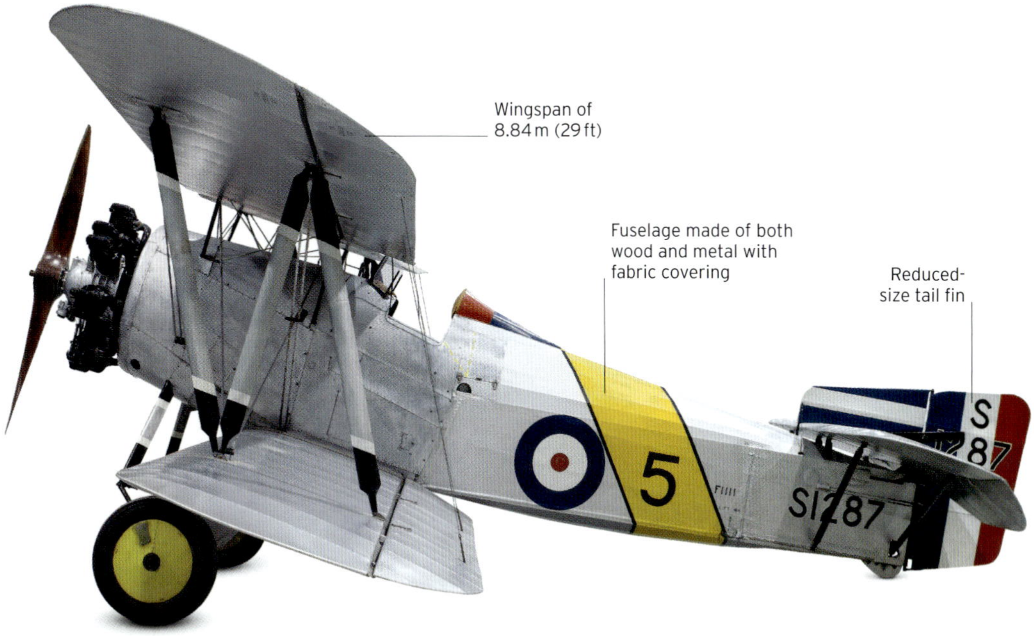

△ Fairey Flycatcher

Date 1923	**Origin** UK
Engine 400 hp Armstrong Siddeley Jaguar IV air-cooled 14-cylinder radial	
Top speed 214 km/h (133 mph)	

Designed for aircraft carrier use with flaps running the full length of both wings and hydraulic wheel brakes, the pioneering Flycatcher could land or take off on just 46 m (151 ft) of deck; 192 were built.

Warplanes (cont.)

Wide upper wing

▽ **Bristol Bulldog**

Date 1929	**Origin** UK
Engine 440-490 hp Bristol Jupiter VII supercharged air-cooled 9-cylinder radial	
Top speed 287 km/h (178 mph)	

Frank Barnwell's design was the RAF's main day/night fighter between the wars. Cheap to maintain, it offered good speed, twin guns, and light bomb capability.

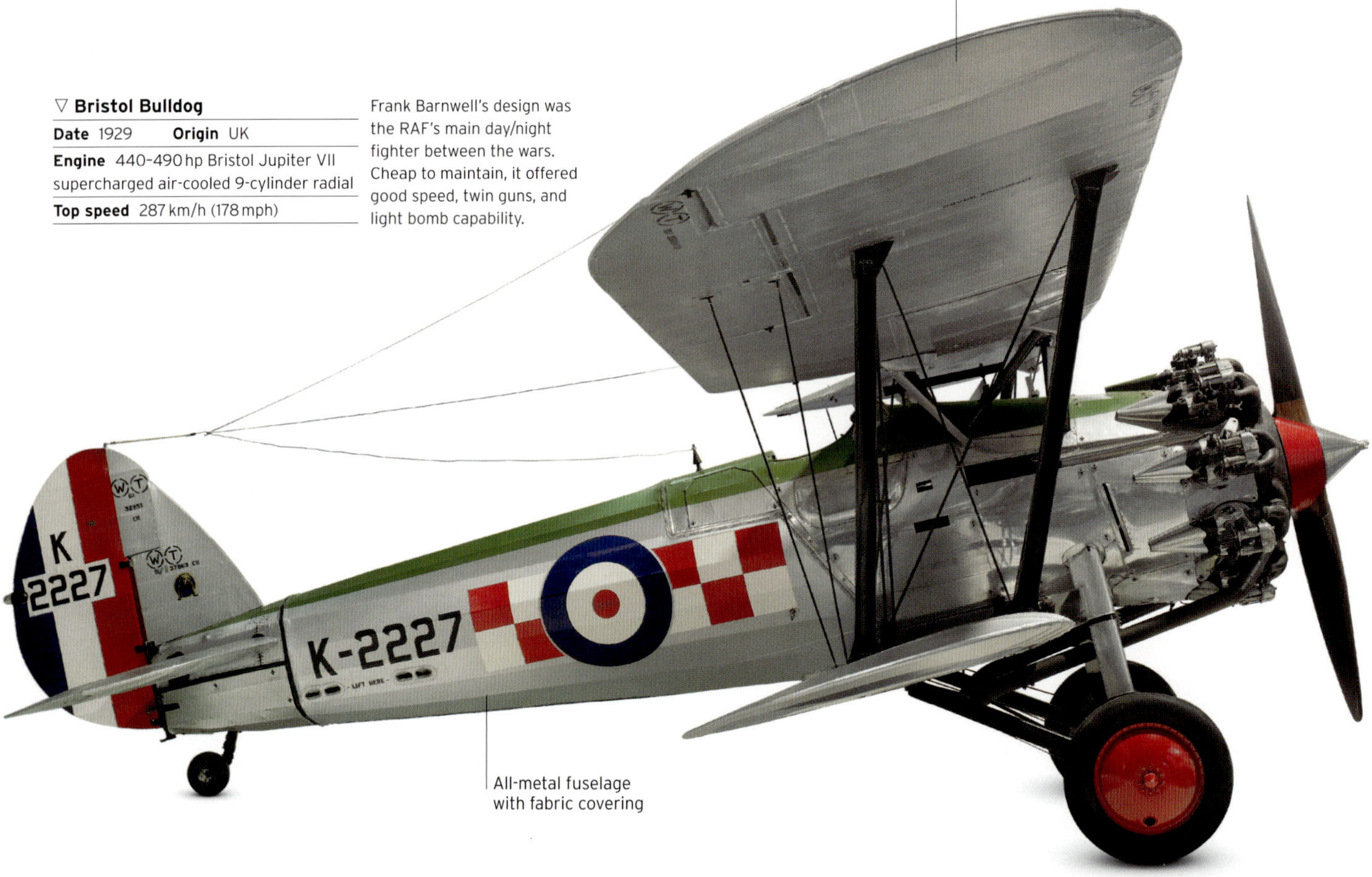

All-metal fuselage with fabric covering

Long, thin fuselage gave aircraft its nickname

Twin tail fin for stability

▽ Hawker Hurricane Mk 1

Date 1936	**Origin** UK
Engine 1,030 hp Rolls-Royce Merlin supercharged liquid-cooled V12	
Top speed 528 km/h (328 mph)	

Sydney Camm's Hurricane was an interceptor, fighter-bomber, night fighter, and ground-attack aircraft. It scored 60 per cent of the victories in World War II's Battle of Britain.

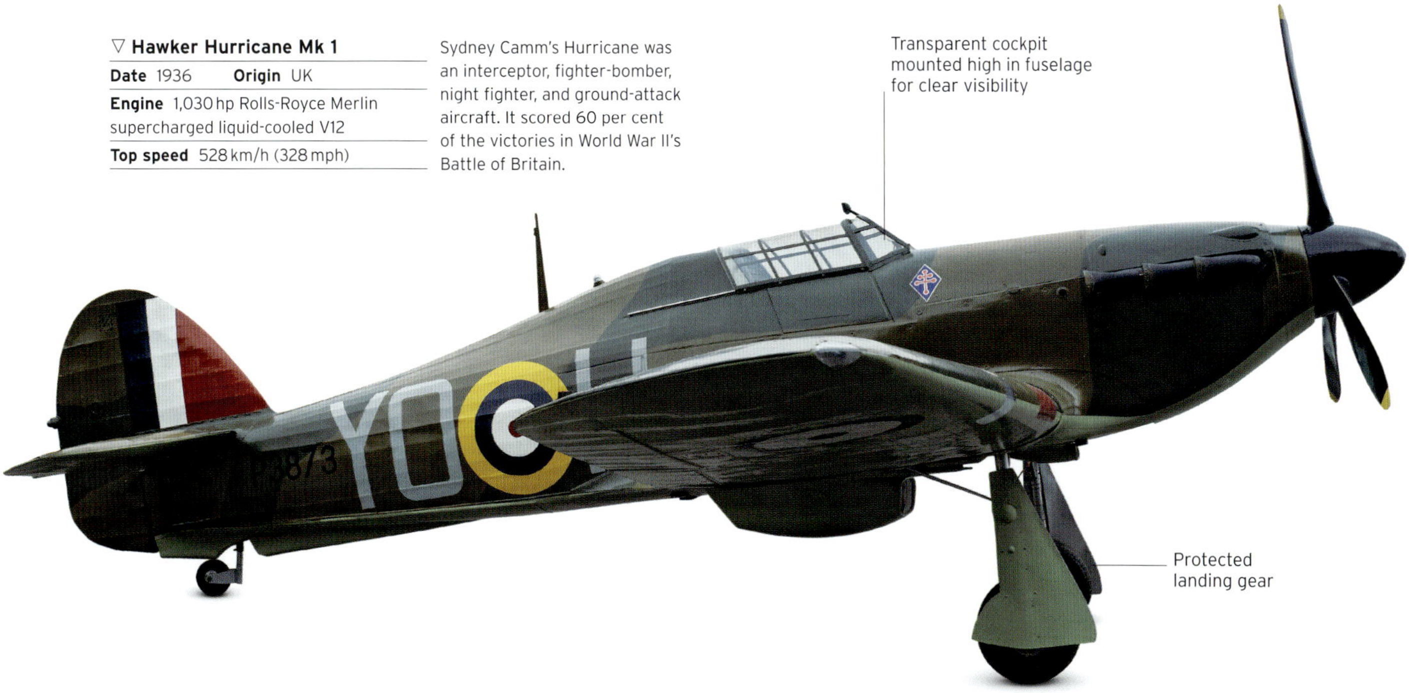

▽ Dornier Do.17

Date 1938	**Origin** Germany
Engine Twin 1,000 hp BMW Bramo 323P "Fafnir" single-bank 9-cylinder radials	
Top speed 410 km/h (255 mph)	

The Do.17 - the "Flying Pencil" - was relatively unimportant when compared to other German bombers of the early war years, especially the He 111. Thanks to its agility, however, it was a favorite with its crew.

Preparing for war
Sailors on board HMS *Repulse* prepare the 15-in guns for firing practice in May 1939, just months before the outbreak of World War II.

Transport, Reconnaissance, and Liaison Aircraft

The first military transport aircraft were commercial aeroplanes, but craft specially designed for military operations soon appeared. Specialist reconnaissance aircraft were developed, too. Some, especially those designed for maritime operations, doubled up in the attack role, while others dispensed with armament completely to fly higher and faster than any interceptor the enemy could send. Light aircraft were also pressed into military service to operate both in and away from the combat zone.

▽ Fieseler Fi.156 Storch

Date 1937 **Origin** Germany

Engine 240 hp Argus As 10 V8

Top speed 175 km/h (110 mph)

The *Storch* (Stork) was designed as an army liaison aircraft. Unusually for a land-based aircraft, it had wings that could be folded back along its fuselage. Its approach speed was so low that in a headwind it appeared to land almost vertically.

Cockpit had space for pilot and observer

Entire aircraft weighed just 1,270 kg (2,800 lb)

▽ Shorts S25 Sunderland

Date 1938 **Origin** UK

Engine 4 x 1,065 hp Bristol Pegasus air-cooled 9-cylinder radial

Top speed 343 km/h (213 mph)

Although loosely based on Shorts's S23 Empire Class flying boat, the Sunderland was significantly different from its civilian ancestor. The aircraft sank many U-boats during World War II.

Underwing racks could accommodate bombs, depth-charges, or torpedoes

Nose turret housed two Browning machine-guns

Four Browning machine-guns in rear turret

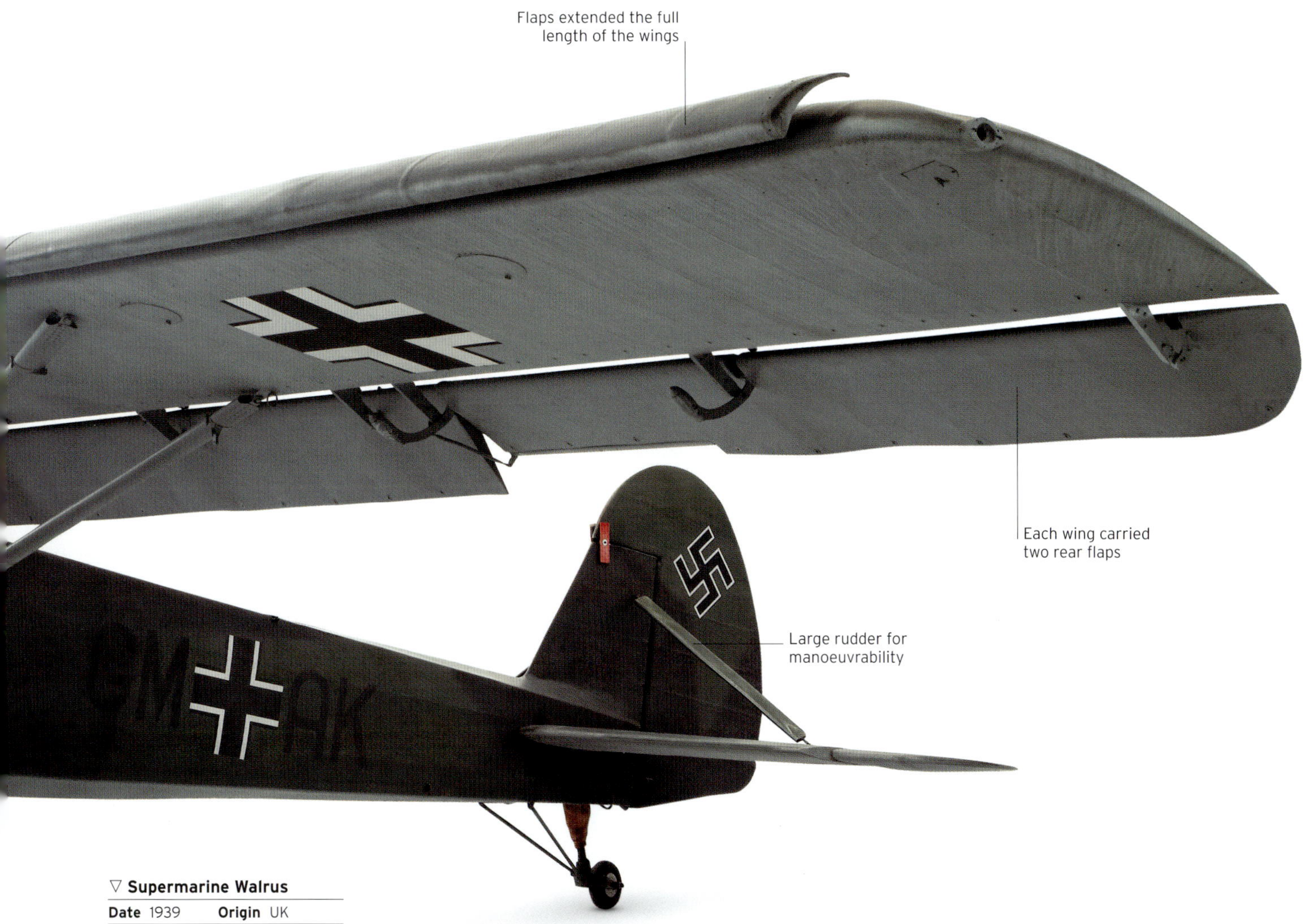

▽ **Supermarine Walrus**

Date 1939 **Origin** UK

Engine 750 hp Bristol Pegasus VI air-cooled 9-cylinder radial

Top speed 215 km/h (135 mph)

The Walrus was designed to be launched by a warship's catapult, and consequently was much stronger than it looked. Rugged and reliable, the Walrus saved countless lives as a search-and-rescue aircraft. Its wings folded for carrier storage.

Military Tractors

Tractor evolution and production started in the US, with the UK close behind. Other European countries, Canada, and Australia followed, with eastern European and South American manufacturers next on the list. Before 1920, the impact of World War I brought large-scale tractor production to the US and sped up the tractor-powered farm mechanization process that eventually replaced both horses and steam.

▽ Holt 75

Date 1918 **Origin** US

Engine Holt 4-cylinder gasoline

Horsepower 75 hp

Transmission 2 forward, 1 reverse

The Holt 75 was the Allies' standard heavy artillery tractor, with 1,651 eventually being delivered from 1915 to November 1918. In the atrocious mud on the Western Front, it was the only tractor capable of hauling the heavy guns into position. As conditions worsened, the 75 was also used to haul supply trains bringing ammunition and other essentials up to the front lines.

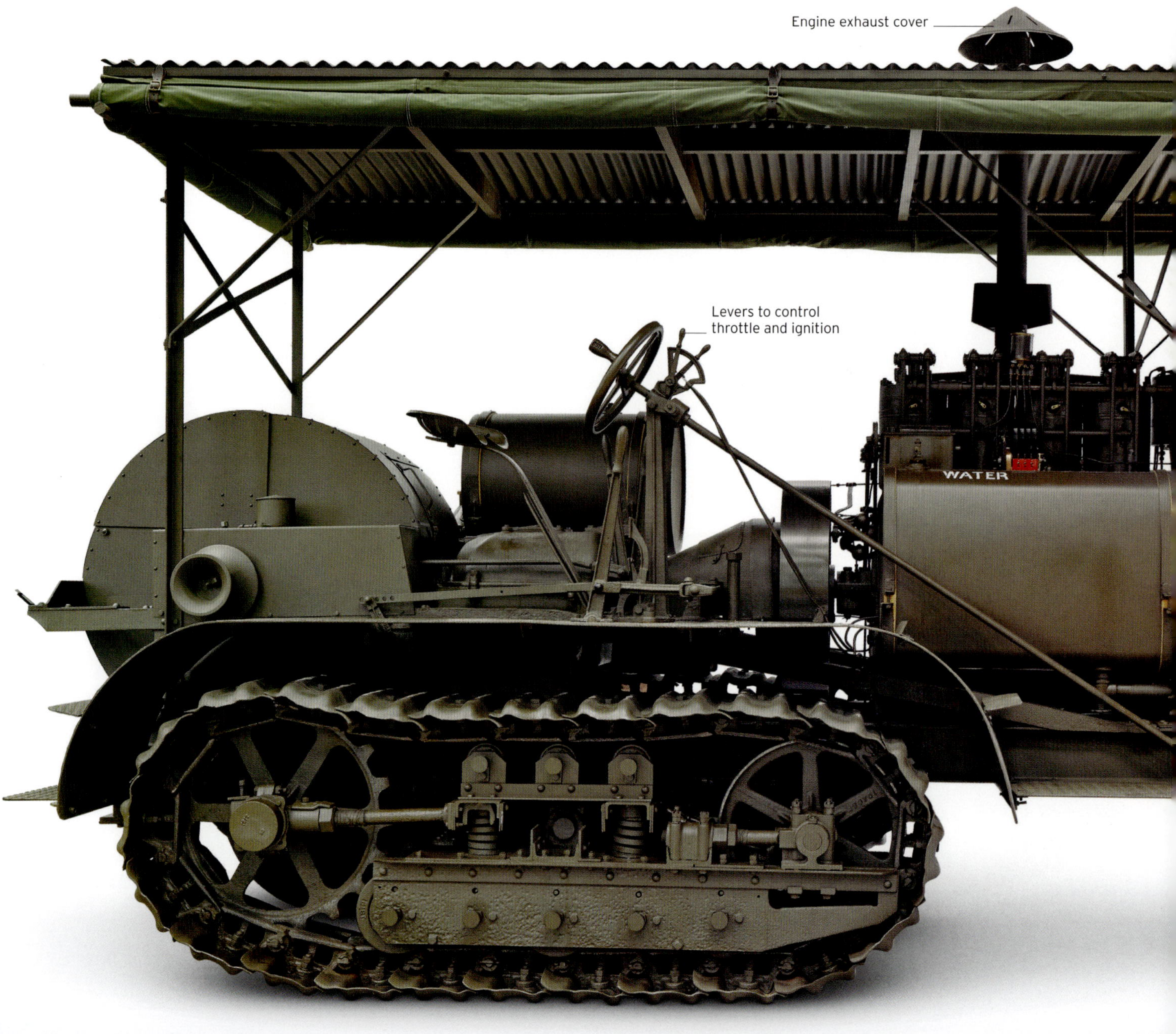

△ Titan 10-20

Date 1919	**Origin** US
Engine International twin-cylinder horizontal petrol/kerosene	
Horsepower 20 hp	
Transmission 2 forward, 1 reverse	

Until the arrival of the Fordson, the 10-20 was the mainstay of the British tractor fleet in World War I, with nearly 4,000 units delivered. It was a simple, reliable, and dependable power unit. More than 78,000 units were produced from 1915 to 1922.

△ International Junior 8-16

Date 1919	**Origin** US
Engine International 4-cylinder petrol/kerosene	
Horsepower 16 hp	
Transmission 3 forward, 1 reverse	

This was a popular tractor on farms in the early 1920s. Featuring a water-washer air cleaner and a mid-mounted radiator, the still chain-driven Junior filled the gap between the "old" type of tractors, the Mogul and Titan, and the gear-drive 15-30 and 10-20 models.

5

1939–45 WORLD WAR II

World War II was the most destructive conflict in human history. It resulted in the spectacular development of aviation and motorized warfare, especially tanks. Submarines established themselves as potentially war-winning commerce raiders. The pressure of war also generated a search for "wonder weapons". The jet aircraft, V-1 flying bomb, and V-2 ballistic missile were all introduced by Germany late in the war. However, the atomic bomb, developed by the US at vast cost, truly heralded a new era.

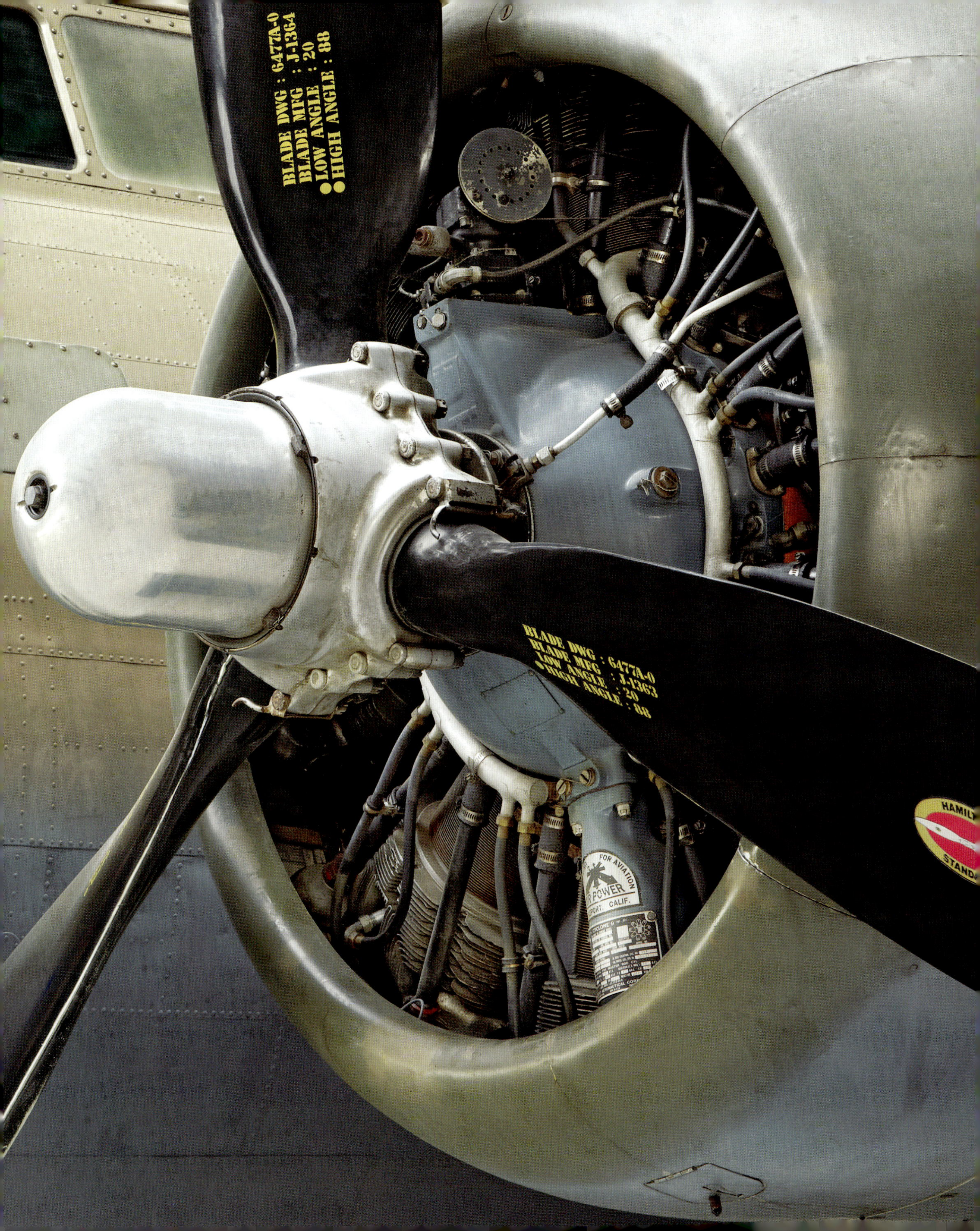
BLADE DWG : 6477A-0
BLADE MFG : J-1364
LOW ANGLE : 20
HIGH ANGLE : 88
BLADE DWG : 6477A-0
BLADE MFG : J-1363
LOW ANGLE : 20
HIGH ANGLE : 88

Self-loading Rifles

The first truly practical self-loading rifle, the M1, was adopted by the US Army in 1936. Further breakthroughs in self-loading rifles came in World War II. The best of these by far was the German Sturmgewehr 44, or StG44, which had fully automatic firing capability and led the way towards today's assault rifles. However it was some time before the intermediate ammunition round, the 44's most important design aspect, achieved universal acceptance.

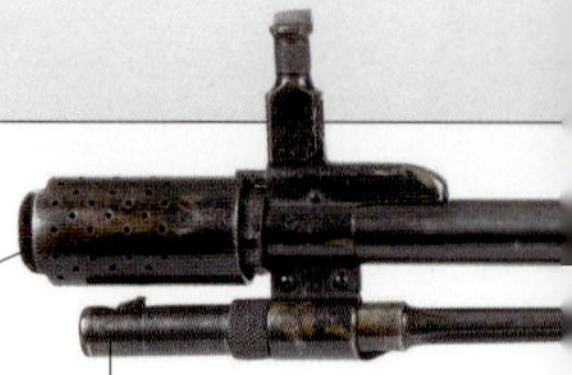

▽ Gewehr 43

Date 1943	**Origin** Germany
Weight 4.35 kg (9½ lb)	
Barrel 56 cm (22 in)	
Calibre 7.92 mm x 57	

The German army's request for a self-loading rifle to increase infantry firepower led to the introduction of the successful Gewehr 43. A number of them were fitted with telescopic sights and used as sniper rifles.

△ **FG42 Automatic Rifle**

Date 1943	**Origin** Germany
Weight 4.53 kg (10 lb)	
Barrel 50.2 cm (19¾ in)	
Calibre 7.9 mm	

The FG42 was a fully automatic weapon designed to provide long-range firepower to paratroopers on the ground. It pioneered a "straight-line" butt-to-muzzle layout and employed a gas-operated firing mechanism.

△ **Sturmgewehr 44 with *Krummlauf* Device**

Date 1944	**Origin** Germany
Weight 4.6 kg (10 lb)	
Barrel 41 cm (16½ in)	
Calibre 7.62 x 33 mm	

The Sturmgewehr 44 was the first true assault rifle, capable of switching between semi-automatic and fully automatic modes. Some examples of this weapon were equipped with curved barrels (the *Krummlauf* device) so that they could be fired indirectly at targets out of the user's direct line of sight by means of a prismatic sight. This device would prove especially useful in house-to-house fighting.

Submachine-guns

The submachine-gun (SMG) was one of World War II's primary offensive weapons. Light in weight, reliable, durable, easy to use, and capable of delivering a massive amount of firepower if needed, the submachine-gun was especially favoured by shock troops and those forces operating in cramped or enclosed surroundings. Soviet forces used the PPSH-41 extensively when attacking, simply because of the volume of fire it could deliver against enemy formations.

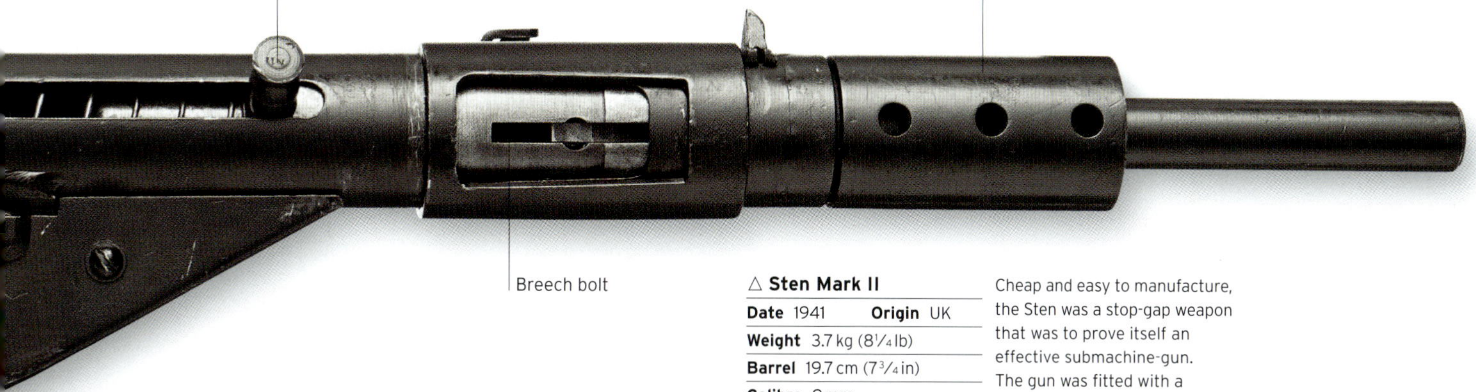

△ Sten Mark II

Date 1941	**Origin** UK
Weight 3.7 kg (8¼ lb)	
Barrel 19.7 cm (7¾ in)	
Calibre 9 mm	

Cheap and easy to manufacture, the Sten was a stop-gap weapon that was to prove itself an effective submachine-gun. The gun was fitted with a 32-round magazine.

△ Beretta Modello 1938/42

Date 1942	**Origin** Italy
Weight 3.27 kg (7¼ lb)	
Barrel 21.3 cm (8½ in)	
Calibre 9 mm	

One of the finest weapons of its type to see service during World War II, the M38/42 was well-made, reliable, and, for a submachine-gun, surprisingly accurate.

Allied Tanks

At the onset of war, the well-developed American automotive industry turned its hand to tank manufacturing. By 1945, it had built more than 60,000 vehicles. Successful design components were kept from model to model to ease production. After massive tank losses in the first few months of the German invasion of the Soviet Union, Soviet tank factories were relocated east beyond the Ural Mountains. Production was standardized as much as possible in order to increase output.

▽ Kliment Voroshilov-1 (KV-1)

Date 1939	**Origin** Soviet Union
Weight 48.3 tonnes (53.2 tons)	
Engine Kharkiv Model V-2K diesel, 500 hp	
Main armament 76.2 mm ZiS-5 L/41.5 gun	

A heavy tank, the KV-1 was virtually immune to the German antitank weapons of 1941. It was one of the few tanks to continue in production after the Soviet factories were relocated. It used the same engine and gun as the T-34, but, being heavier, had poorer mobility. Around 4,700 KV-1s were built before production halted in April 1943.

△ M3 (Grant)

Date 1941 **Origin** US

Weight 27.2 tonnes (30 tons)

Engine Wright Continental R-975 petrol, 340 hp

Main armament 1 x 75 mm M2 L/31 gun, 1 x 37 mm M5 L/56.5 gun

The M3 stemmed from an urgent need to field a 75 mm gun before a suitable turret was ready. The gun was mounted in a sponson on the hull, which limited its field of fire. The M3 kept the successful engine and Vertical Volute Suspension System (VVSS) from the M2 medium. British M3s used a modified turret and named it the Grant. The original version was named the Lee.

◁ T-34

Date 1941 **Origin** Soviet Union

Weight 31.4 tonnes (34.6 tons)

Engine Kharkiv Model V-2-34 diesel, 500 hp

Main armament 76.2 mm F-34 L/41 gun

One of the most important tanks in history, the T-34 began development as early as 1938. Wartime pressures precluded cosmetic considerations, the focus being more on reducing cost and accelerating production.

Allied Tanks (cont.)

▽ M4A1 (Sherman)

Date 1942	**Origin** US
Weight 30.2 tonnes (33.3 tons)	
Engine Wright-Continental R-975 gasoline, 400 hp	
Main armament 75 mm M3 L/40 gun	

The Sherman used the M3 chassis, combined with a turret for the 75 mm gun. There were five main variants of the Sherman, the primary difference being the engine used. The M4A1 had a cast rather than welded hull. Almost 50,000 were built; this tank was the second ever produced and is the oldest survivor.

▷ M5A1 (Stuart)

Date 1942	**Origin** US
Weight 15.3 tonnes (16.9 tons)	
Engine 2 x Cadillac Series 42 gasoline, 148 hp each	
Main armament 37 mm M6 L/56.6 gun	

The M5 was developed from the M3 to free up R-670 engines for aircraft. The hull was also redesigned to improve protection. The new engine arrangement allowed more space inside for the crew and made the tank quieter. Unlike the M3, the M5 was not used by the Soviet Union, but both were used for the same roles in British and American service.

FULL VIEW

▷ Iosif Stalin-3M (IS-3M)

Date 1945 **Origin** Soviet Union

Weight 46.5 tonnes (51.3 tons)

Engine Kharkiv Model V-2IS diesel, 600 hp

Main armament 122 mm D-25T L/45 gun

Limitations in the speed and armour of the IS-2 led to the development of the IS-3, which, although rushed into service, arrived too late for World War II. Initially it developed multiple mechanical problems, but these were resolved in the improved IS-3M model. The IS-3's sloped sides gave better armour protection, and became a feature of postwar Soviet tank designs.

◁ **M14/41**

Date 1940 **Origin** Italy

Weight 14.5 tonnes (16 tons)

Engine SPA 15T M41 diesel, 145 hp

Main armament 47 mm M35 L/32 gun

Italy learned lessons from sending tanks into the Spanish Civil War. New vehicles were designed as a result of that experience, and first saw service in North Africa in 1940. The M14/41 was an upgraded version of the M13/40 that was optimized for desert conditions. It was well armed, but its armour was no match for the Allies' 2-pounder gun.

▽ **Panther**

Date 1943 **Origin** Germany

Weight 46.2 tonnes (51 tons)

Engine Maybach HL230P30 gasoline, 700 hp

Main armament 7.5 cm KwK 42 L/70 gun

Designed in response to the Soviet T-34, the Panther was more heavily armoured and boasted far greater firepower. First used at Kursk in July 1943, it was fast and manoeuvrable, with strong frontal armour and a very accurate and powerful gun. However, like the Tiger, it was often unreliable; engine fires were common.

Armour sloped variably between 25 and 50 degrees

Overlapping steel-rim wheels

Tank supplied with either normal battle tracks (shown here) or narrower transport tracks so it could be transported by train

△ **Tiger II (King Tiger)**

Date 1944 **Origin** Germany

Weight 69.1 tonnes (76.2 tons)

Engine Maybach HL230P30 gasoline, 700 hp

Main armament 8.8 cm KwK 43 L/71

The Tiger II was perhaps the most formidable tank of World War II. Its frontal armour could withstand all Allied antitank weapons, and its 8.8 cm gun was a threat even at long range. Its engine was unreliable, however, and only 489 were built – too few to influence the outcome of the war.

7.5 cm main gun

Bazooka plates

Axis Tanks

The North African Campaign, which began in 1940, was followed, in 1941, by the German invasion of the Soviet Union. As land fighting intensified, tank technology evolved, so much so that by the end of the war, tanks provided the kind of firepower, protection, and reliability that would have been undreamed of in 1939. Although the Germans built ever more formidable vehicles, they were plagued by mechanical failure and problems caused by inexperienced crews.

Tiger I

Of all the tanks of World War II, none has inspired such a fearsome reputation as the Tiger. With its 88 mm gun, thick frontal armour, wide tracks, and sheer size, it was a devastating weapon that struck terror into Allied forces on the battlefield. However, it was dogged by technical difficulties that compromised its tactical effectiveness.

SPECIFICATIONS	
Name	PzKpfw VI Tiger Ausf E
Date	1942
Origin	Germany
Production	1,347
Engine	Maybach HL210P45 V-12 petrol, 650 hp
Weight	57.9 tonnes (63.8 tons)
Main armament	8.8 cm KwK 36
Secondary armament	7.92 mm MG34
Crew	5
Armour thickness	Max 120 mm (4.72 in)

HITLER ORDERED the production of a heavy tank in May 1941, after the failure of German weaponry to penetrate the armour of the Matilda 2 and Char B. The Tiger's boxy shape and layout were similar to earlier German tanks, but on a huge scale – over twice the weight of the Panzer IV. The heavy tank was a stable platform for the accurate 88 mm KwK 36 gun, for which it carried 92 rounds. Its engine was upgraded from 650 hp to 700 hp during production: even so, the engine and transmission struggled to cope with the vehicle's weight, which grew from a planned 50 tonnes (55 tons) to 57.9 tonnes (63.8 tons).

The Tiger was rushed into service and suffered numerous growing pains. It was mainly used defensively, rather than to punch through enemy lines as intended: the cost of production, and a shortage of skilled crews, meant that it failed to have the desired impact on the battlefield. However, it had a huge psychological effect on the enemy, and remains the most mythologized tank of the war.

One of a kind
This tank, Tiger 131, was captured in Tunisia in April 1943. As the first complete Tiger captured, it was taken to Britain for extensive analysis. An early example, it had the original HL210P45 engine rather than the more common HL230P30 700 hp. The tank has been restored to running order.

REAR VIEW

FRONT VIEW

EXTERIOR

To spread out the large weight of the tank, the road wheels are positioned in an interleaved system, copied from earlier German half-track designs. Sixteen torsion bars provide suspension – eight arms on each side, each arm holding three wheels, which meant that to replace just one of the inner wheels, nine had to be removed. The size of the tank led to innovations such as removing outer road wheels and installing thinner transportation tracks for train travel. This tank, Tiger 131, still shows exterior battle damage from the day of its capture.

1. Drive sprocket and interleaved road wheels **2.** Radio operator's machine-gun **3.** Smoke grenade dischargers **4.** Commander's hatch **5.** Turret pistol port **6.** Loader's position and main gun breech **7.** Commander's hatch (open) **8.** Commander's periscope **9.** Binocular gun sight **10.** Driver's controls and vision port **11.** Radio operator's machine-gun (from interior)

1

6

2

3

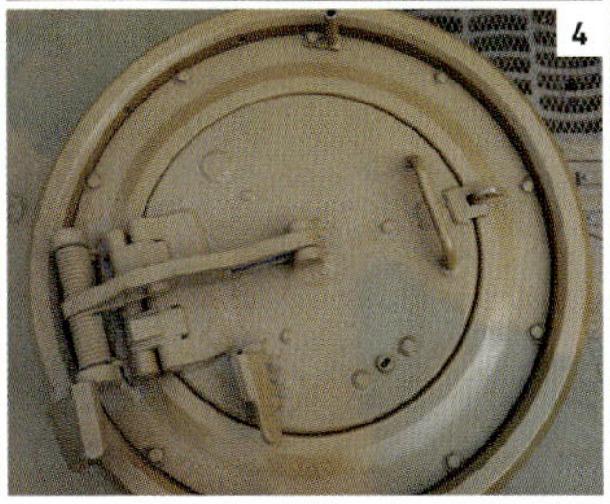
4

5

7

8

9

10

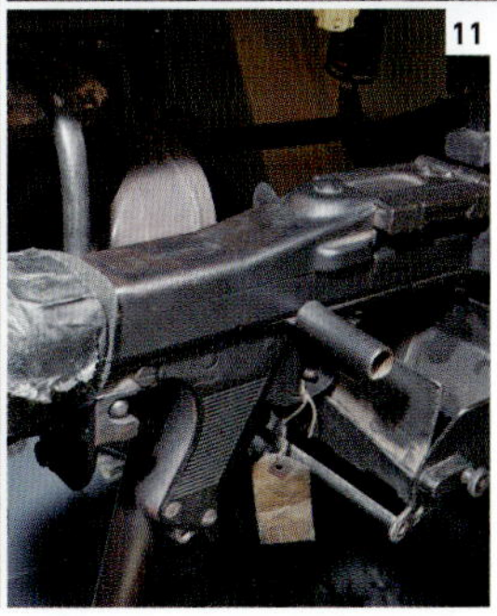
11

INTERIOR

The commander and gunner sat in the left side of the turret, with the commander at the rear, while the loader was positioned in the space to the right. The driver and radio operator were stationed in the front of the main hull, and the latter operated the ball-mounted machine-gun.

Antitank Weapons

Some antitank weapons used a spring-driven firing pin to ignite a propellant charge attached to a self-propelled projectile. Others, such as the Bazooka, released projectiles with solid rocket motors. In both cases, when the projectile met its target, a shaped-charge warhead focused the explosive's energy so that it could penetrate armour effectively. This made launchers lighter to manufacture. As tanks evolved and their armour became thicker, older designs of antitank rifles, such as the PTRD, became obsolete, as they could rarely destroy a tank, even at short range.

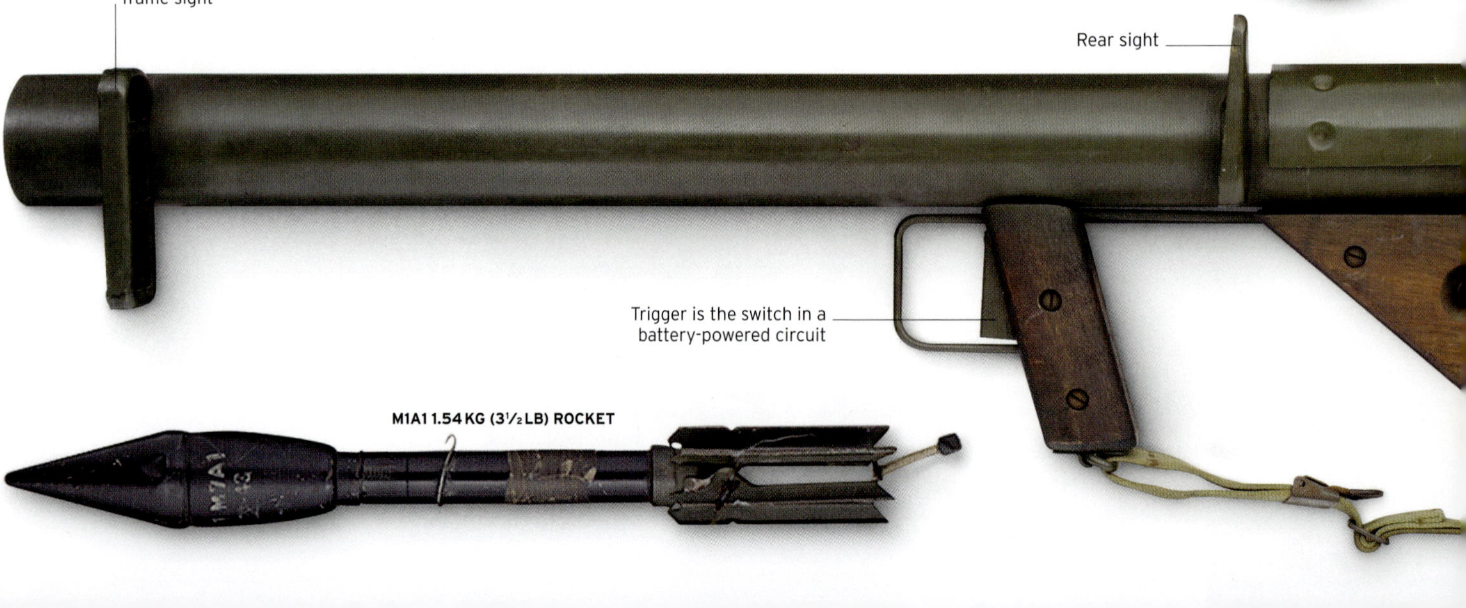

△ Panzerbüchse 39 Antitank Rifle

Date 1940	**Origin** Germany
Weight 12.6 kg ($27\frac{3}{4}$ lb)	
Barrel 1.08 m ($3\frac{1}{2}$ ft)	
Calibre 7.92 x 94 mm	
Armour penetration 25 mm (1 in) at 300 m (328 yards)	

The Panzerbüchse 39 relied on its very high muzzle velocity and tungsten-cored bullet to penetrate enemy armour. It was, however, expensive to manufacture, and was only produced in small numbers. By 1944 it had become inadequate against all but the lightest armoured vehicles.

△ PTRD Antitank Rifle

Date 1941	**Origin** Soviet Union
Weight 17.3 kg ($38\frac{1}{4}$ lb)	
Barrel 1.23 m (4 ft)	
Calibre 14.5 mm	
Armour penetration 35–40 mm (1.3–1.5 in) at 100 m (110 yards)	

The PTRD was a more complicated weapon than it appeared. It had a barrel that recoiled into the receiver and unlocked the bolt in the process. The bolt was held back when the barrel returned to its original position, opening the breech and ejecting the spent round. A fresh round was then introduced by the loader and the bolt closed by hand.

△ M1A1 "Bazooka"

Date 1942	**Origin** US
Weight 6 kg ($13\frac{1}{4}$ lb)	
Length 1.37 m ($4\frac{1}{2}$ ft)	
Calibre 60 mm	
Armour penetration 120 mm ($4\frac{3}{4}$ in) at 138 m (150 yards)	

The Bazooka was the forerunner of the German *Raketenpanzerbüchse* and the Soviet RPG rocket launchers. It was no more than a tube from which a solid fuel rocket, with a shaped-charge warhead, was launched. It was operated by two men: one to fire, the other to load.

32
26
SERVON

Tank warfare
Whereas infantry had previously advanced towards the enemy on foot, World War II saw armoured divisions of tanks drive into battle. These French tanks are advancing in May 1940 to face the German invaders. The resulting battle at Hannut, in central Belgium on 12–13 May, involved about 1,500 armoured vehicles, making it the largest tank battle yet fought.

Tank Destroyers and Assault Guns

There was a clear difference in design between Soviet and US tank destroyers. The Soviets favoured turretless vehicles: they were quicker and cheaper to build and could mount a larger gun and heavier armour than the tank they were based on. In contrast, American tank destroyers were used in outmanoeuvring enemy tanks and emphasized mobility over protection. Both countries employed them as artillery pieces and to support infantry. Early German tank destroyers, meanwhile, used captured or obsolete light-tank hulls, with antitank guns affixed on top.

▽ **StuG III**

Date 1940 **Origin** Germany

Weight 24.3 tonnes (26.8 tons)

Engine Maybach HL120TRM petrol, 300 hp

Main armament 7.5 cm StuK 40 L/48 gun

The first StuGs were armed with the same short-barrelled 7.5 cm L/24 gun as early Panzer IVs. The StuG's low height and armour made it an ideal tank destroyer, and in 1942 the longer-barrelled L/48 gun was attached to optimize it for that role. With over 11,000 built, it was Germany's most-produced armoured vehicle.

◁ **SU-76M**

Date 1943 **Origin** Soviet Union

Weight 10.4 tonnes (11.4 tons)

Engine 2 x GAZ-203 6 cylinder diesel, 85 hp each

Main armament 76.2 mm ZiS-3Sh L/42.6 gun

With over 12,600 built, the SU-76M was the second most-produced Soviet armoured vehicle of the war. Based on a stretched T-70 light tank chassis, it was used as a light assault gun and mobile artillery piece, and had the capability to destroy lighter German tanks. Although reliable and popular with the infantry, due to its light armour and open top its crew did not always feel the same.

Arctic camouflage

▽ **M18 Hellcat**

Date 1943 **Origin** US

Weight 17.8 tonnes (19.6 tons)

Engine Wright Continental R-975 petrol, 400 hp

Main armament 76 mm M1A2 L/52 gun

One of the fastest ever armoured vehicles, the M18 was well suited to US tank destroyer doctrine. However, its speed and mobility – enhanced by very thin armour and torsion bar suspension – proved to be of limited value, and its firepower was inadequate against the heaviest German tanks.

Main gun proved inadequate against strong frontal armour of later German tanks

.50 Browning M2HB machine-gun

Light armour to facilitate increased speed

Tank Destroyers and Assault Guns (cont.)

FULL VIEW

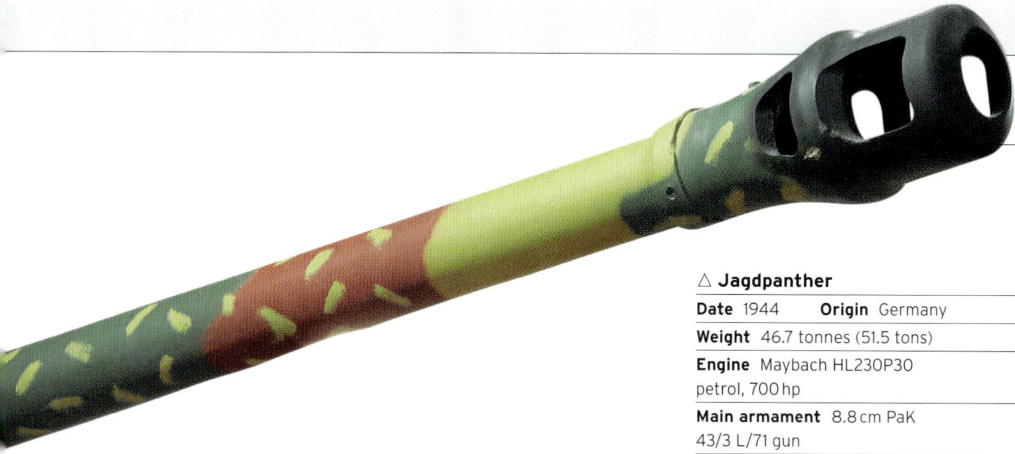

△ Jagdpanther

Date 1944 **Origin** Germany
Weight 46.7 tonnes (51.5 tons)
Engine Maybach HL230P30 petrol, 700 hp
Main armament 8.8 cm PaK 43/3 L/71 gun

The Jagdpanther was based on the Panther chassis, and was well armoured, mobile, and possessed heavy firepower. It was a capable weapon, especially when used in ambush or defensive positions. However, only 392 were built and they were plagued by poor maintenance and crew training. The Jagdpanther was thus too scarce to affect the course of the war.

◁ SU-100

Date 1944 **Origin** Soviet Union
Weight 31.5 tonnes (34.7 tons)
Engine Kharkiv Model V-2-34 diesel, 500 hp
Main armament 100 mm D-10S L/53.5 gun

The design of SU-85 was upgraded to become the SU-100. Both vehicles provided long-range antitank support to formations, and were also held in reserve to defend against the heaviest German tanks. Around 1,200 were built during the war. Production and upgrades continued afterwards, and the vehicle remained in service around the world for decades.

◁ Jagdpanzer IV/70

Date 1944 **Origin** Germany
Weight 24.4 tonnes (26.9 tons)
Engine Maybach HL120TRM petrol, 300 hp
Main armament 7.5 cm PaK 42 L/70 gun

Like the StuG IV, the Jagdpanzer IV was also based on the Panzer IV chassis. A total of 769 of the original vehicle were built. A dedicated tank hunter, it was armed with a PaK 39 L/48 gun. This version was equipped with the longer and more powerful PaK 42 L/70, and replaced the earlier vehicle from 1944. Around 1,200 of these tanks were built.

Artillery of World War II

Artillery evolved between World War I and World War II. Field pieces gradually became more mobile, ranges increased, and radio communications improved tactical flexibility. One new development, however, was the widespread introduction of rocket artillery, such as the German *Nebelwerfer*, which was able to cover large areas with a carpet of high explosive. Artillery continued to play a key role in both attack and defence, which was the reason that the Soviet armed forces described it as the "Red God of War".

▷ 25-pounder Gun-howitzer (Mk II)

Date 1940	**Origin** UK
Weight 1.8 tonnes (2 tons)	
Length 4.6 m (15 ft)	
Calibre 88 mm	
Range 12.25 km (7¾ miles)	

An effective compromise between the gun and the howitzer, the 25-pounder came into its own in the North African Campaign, where it was pressed into service as an ad hoc antitank gun.

▷ 2 cm Flak 38 2 cm Antiaircraft Gun

Date 1943	**Origin** Germany
Weight 420 kg (926 lb)	
Length 4.08 m (13¼ ft)	
Calibre 20 mm	
Range 2.2 km (1½ miles)	

The German term for antiaircraft guns, Flak (*Flugzeugabwehrkanone*), gave its name to the bursting shells of antiaircraft guns in general. The German arms manufacturer Rheinmetall started an adaptation of the naval 2 cm Antiaircraft (AA) gun for army use, producing the Flak 30 and later, the Flak 38.

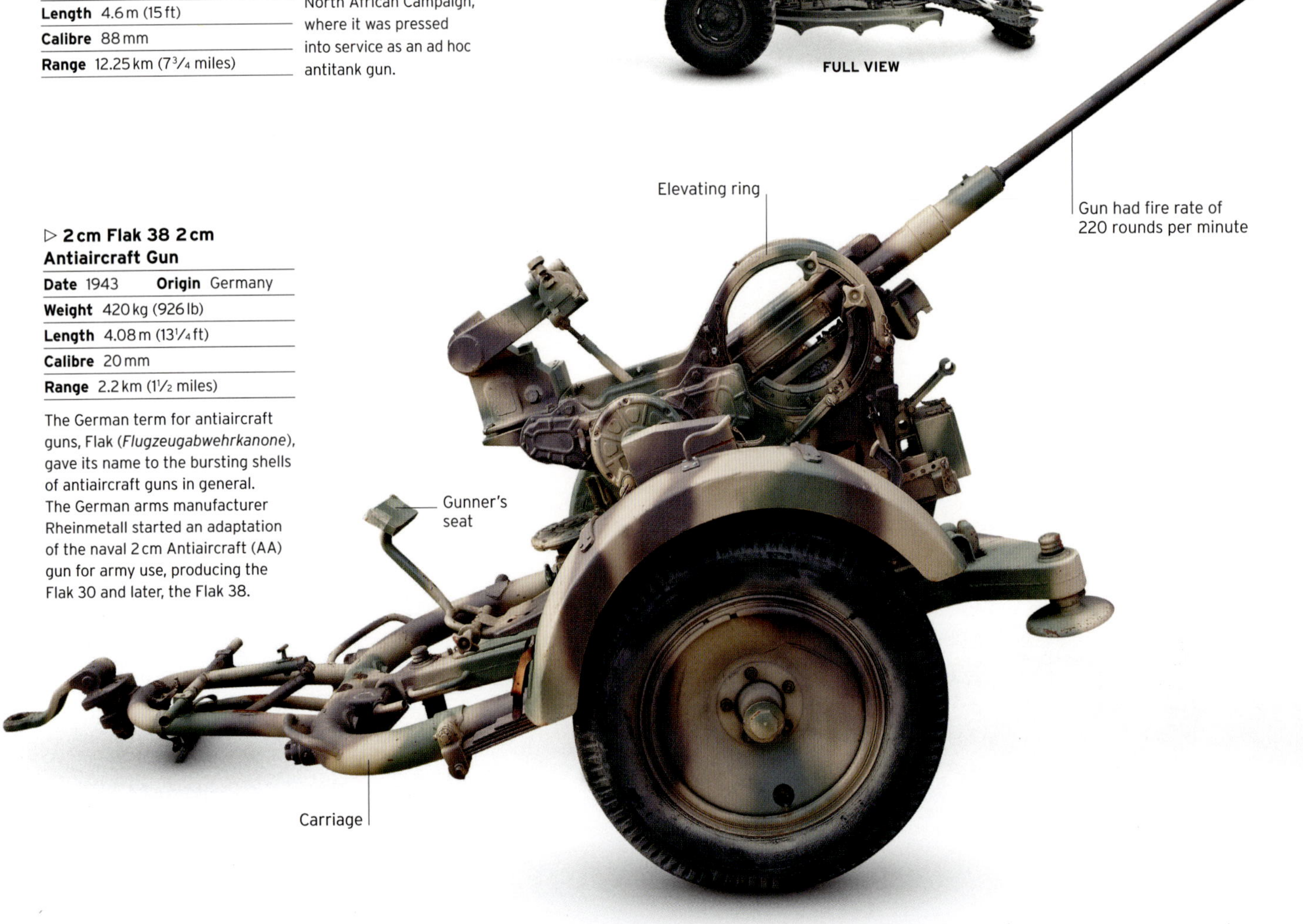

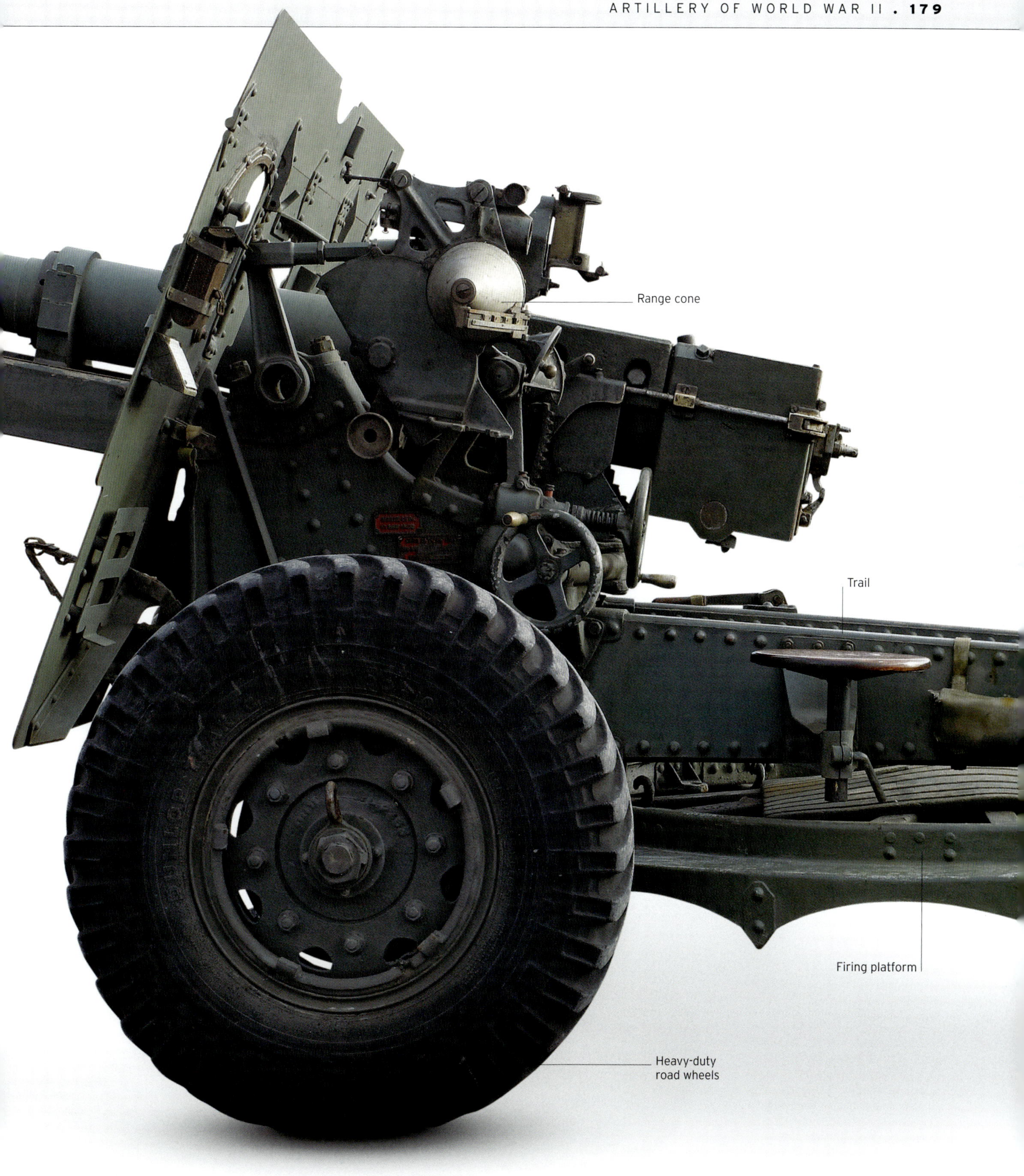
Range cone
Trail
Firing platform
Heavy-duty road wheels

Armoured Vehicles and Troop Carriers

World War II saw the widespread use of armoured vehicles for transport, reconnaissance, and armoured infantry support. Some carried light or no firepower, while others were as well armed as contemporary tanks. Their main role was to find the enemy and survive to report back, so binoculars, a radio, and good tactics were their main weapons. Armoured half-tracks were used by Allied and Axis nations to carry infantry across country and under fire.

▷ Universal Carrier, Mark II

Date 1939 **Origin** UK

Weight 4 tonnes (4.4 tons)

Engine Ford flathead V8 petrol, 85 hp

Main armament .303 Bren machine-gun

One of the most-produced armoured vehicles in history, the Universal Carrier descended from the Carden-Loyd. A number of different carriers were developed and amalgamated into one "universal" design. Highly versatile, it was used to carry machine-guns, mortars, infantrymen, supplies, and artillery observation equipment, among other roles. Carriers were popular with the infantry and in high demand.

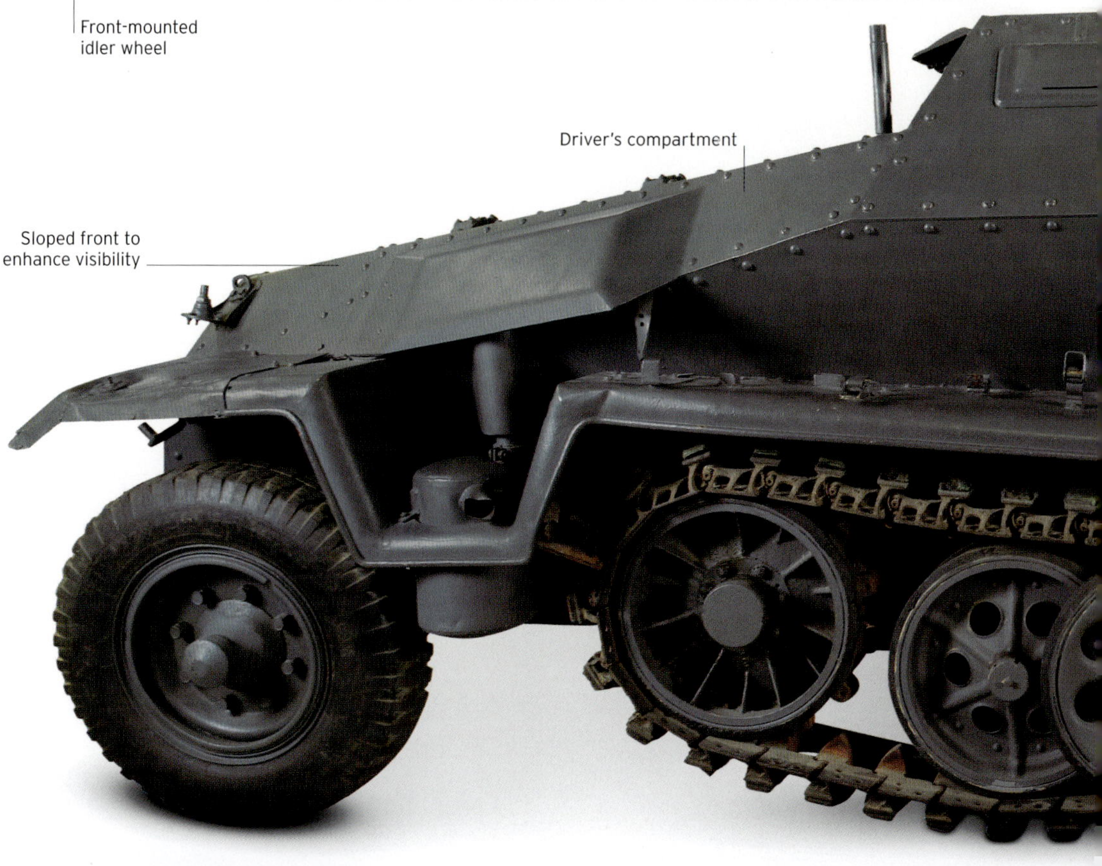

▷ Sd Kfz 251/8 Mittlere Krankenpanzerwagen Ausf C

Date 1939 **Origin** Germany

Weight 7.9 tonnes (8.7 tons)

Engine Maybach HL42 TUKRM petrol, 100 hp

Main armament None

Designed as an armoured personnel carrier for German Panzergrenadiers to accompany the tanks, this vehicle had a capacity to carry 10 infantrymen. It was well armoured, but open-topped, and its half-track design gave it good cross-country mobility. More than 15,000 of these were built, including around 2,500 in postwar Czechoslovakia.

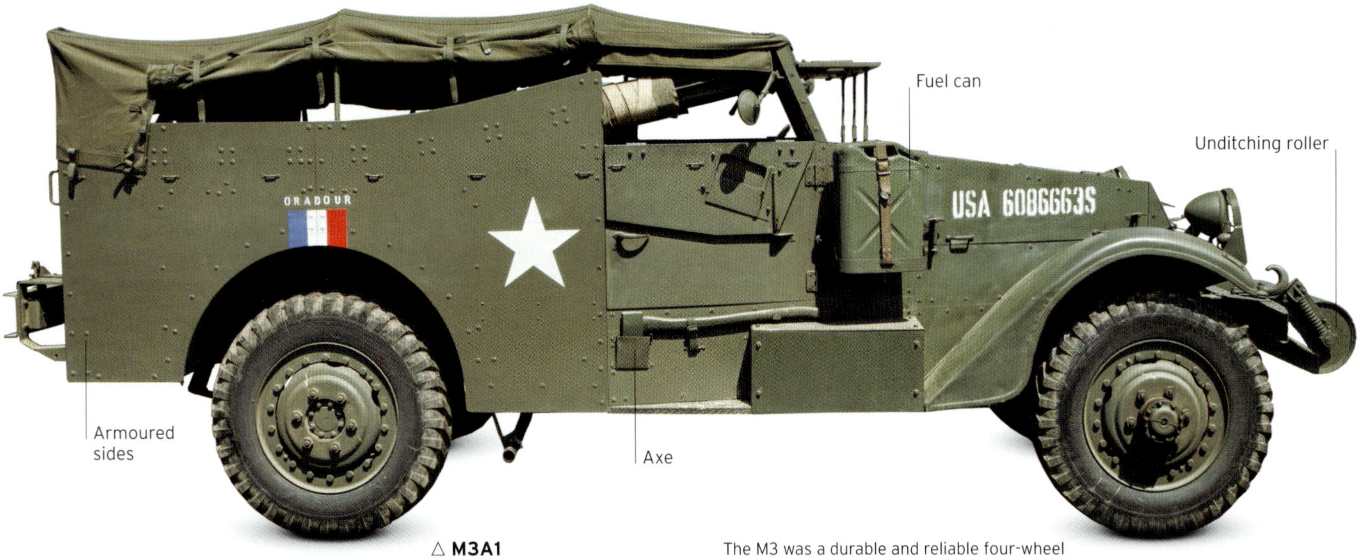

△ **M3A1**

Date 1940 **Origin** US

Weight 4.1 tonnes (4.5 tons)

Engine Hercules JXD gasoline, 87 hp

Main armament None

The M3 was a durable and reliable four-wheel scout car with an open-topped, armoured body. It was widely used by the Americans, British, and Soviets to ferry troops, as well as other roles such as ambulance, command, and forward observation. The roller at the front of the vehicle helped prevent it from ditching.

Armoured Vehicles and Troop Carriers (cont.)

▷ **Willys Jeep**

Date 1941 **Origin** US

Weight 1.04 tonnes (1.14 tons)

Engine Willys 4-cylinder 60 hp petrol engine

Main armament None

Technically known as a truck, but more commonly called a jeep, this iconic World War II vehicle was rugged, reliable, and eminently versatile. It had space for four crew.

▽ **Dodge T214-WC56 Command Reconnaissance Light Truck**

Date 1942 **Origin** US

Weight 2.45 tonnes (2.7 tons)

Engine Dodge T214 6-cylinder 92 hp petrol engine

Main armament None

One of a series of light trucks, the command reconnaissance (WC56) was often used by senior officers. It was fitted with map boards and internal lighting, as well as a canvas top and side-screens.

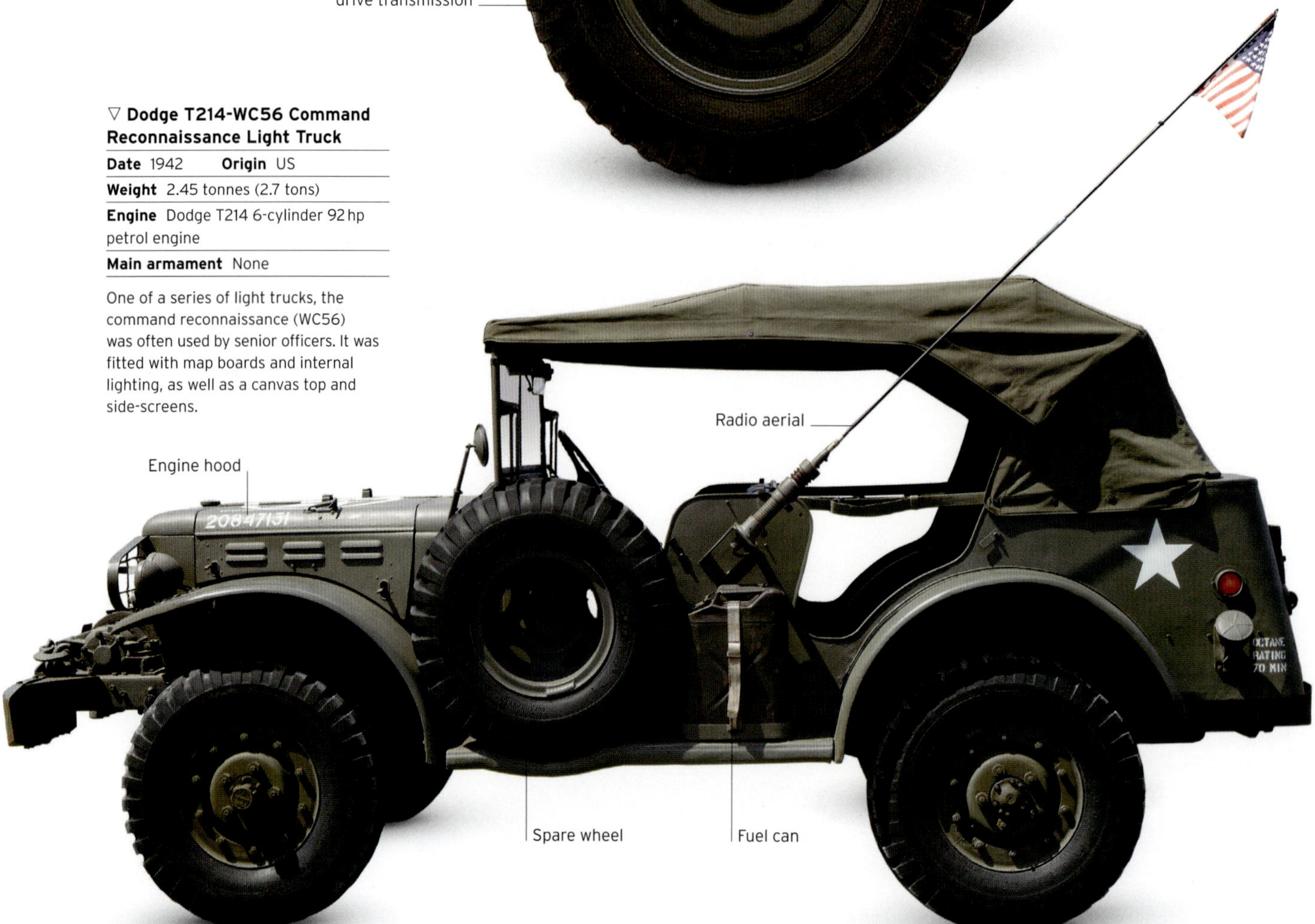

▽ Sd Kfz 234/3 Schwerer Panzerspahwagen, 8-rad

Date 1944	**Origin** Germany
Weight 11.7 tonnes (12.9 tons)	
Engine Tatra 103 diesel, 220 hp	
Main armament 7.5 cm Kwk 51 L/24 gun	

The Sd Kfz 234 replaced the Sd Kfz 231 in 1944. It had more advanced suspension and steering, giving greater mobility, as well as a more powerful engine and thicker armour. There were four variants, with different armament. This version was used against fortifications and area targets to support other variants, which were armed with dedicated antitank guns.

Military Utility Aircraft

While the wartime news was filled with tales of frontline fighters and bombers, a multitude of workhorse aircraft performed equally vital roles, from training pilots to transporting equipment, ground troops, and parachutists. In most cases, these were civilian models from the 1930s, usually strengthened and fitted with more powerful engines to withstand the rigours of military service.

▽ Douglas C-47 Skytrain

Date 1940 **Origin** US

Engine 2 x 1,200 hp Pratt & Whitney R-1830-90C Twin Wasp air-cooled 14-cylinder radial

Top speed 360 km/h (224 mph)

The commercial DC-3 airliner entered military service as the much-loved C-47 Skytrain, or Dakota. More than 10,000 were built, with a cargo door and strengthened floor to carry troops and equipment.

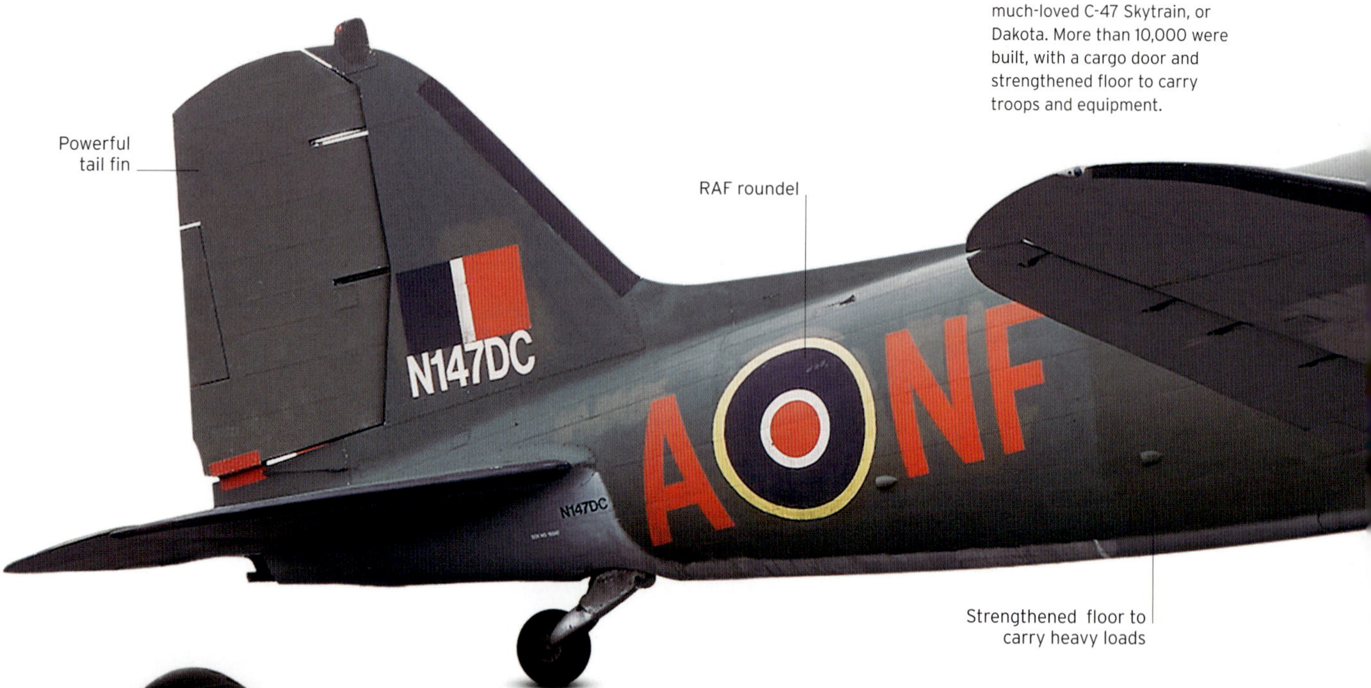

▽ Airspeed Horsa Glider

Date 1941 **Origin** UK

Engine None

Top speed 160 km/h (100 mph)

The *Luftwaffe* used gliders during the invasion of Belgium and France in 1940, and the British soon followed. The Horsa was larger than the German DFS 30, and could carry 25 troops. Some 4,000 were built, over 1,200 of which were expended in Operation Market Garden.

Crew of two
Cabin could accommodate 32 paratroopers
Three-bladed propeller driven by radial engine

Glider pilots were also combat soldiers
Wings and fuselage of fabric-on-wood construction
Fuselage could accommodate equipment, such as bicycles, as well as troops

Military Utility Aircraft (cont.)

△ Douglas C-54 Skymaster

Date 1942 **Origin** US

Engine 4 x 1,450 hp Pratt & Whitney R-2000-9 Twin Wasp air-cooled 14-cylinder radial

Top speed 442 km/h (275 mph)

The Skymaster was the first aircraft type to carry the US President. It was a civilian DC-4 in military guise, used for many roles from transport and research to missile tracking and recovery. The C-54 was in service until 1975.

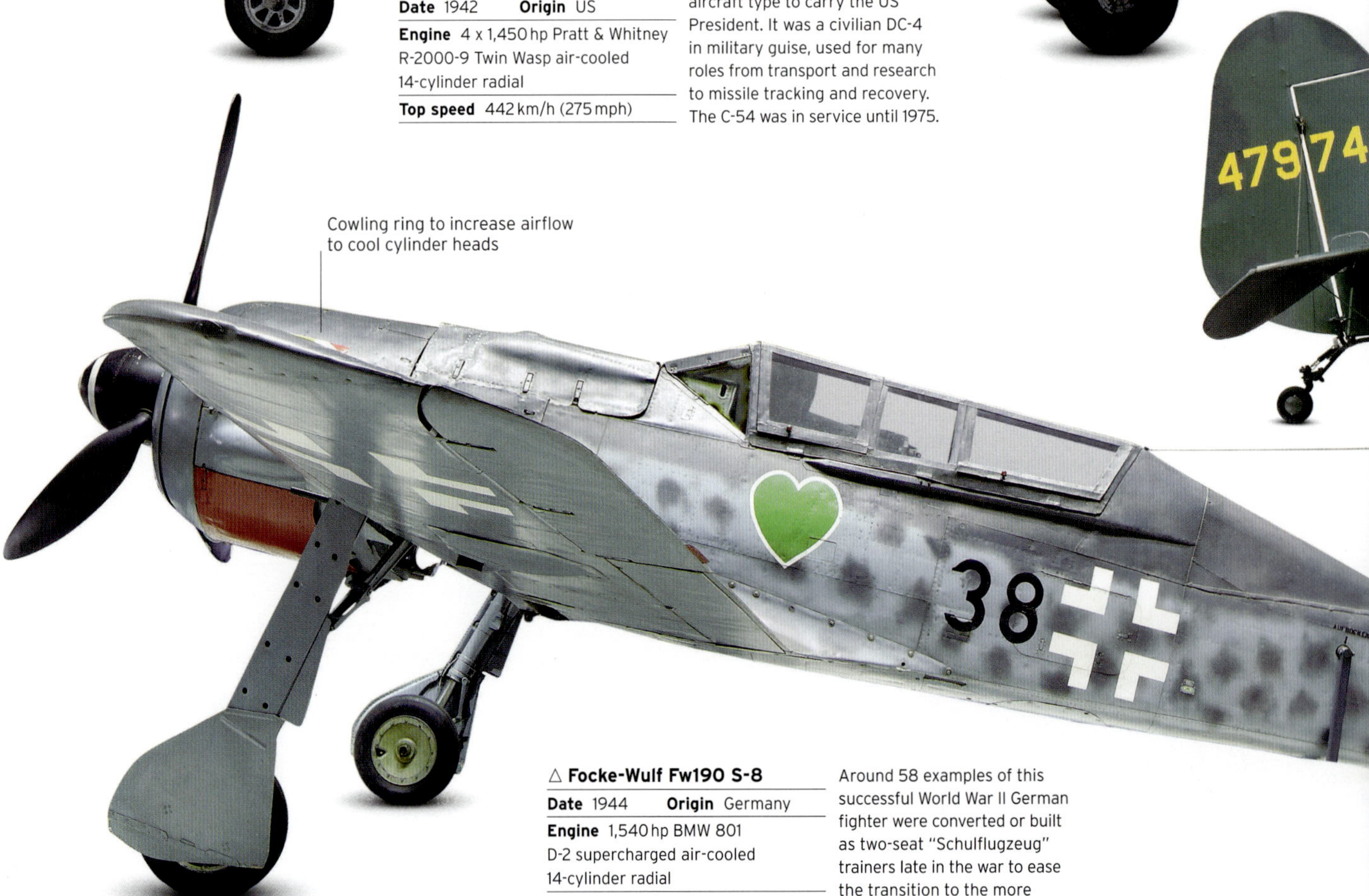

△ Focke-Wulf Fw190 S-8

Date 1944 **Origin** Germany

Engine 1,540 hp BMW 801 D-2 supercharged air-cooled 14-cylinder radial

Top speed 657 km/h (408 mph)

Around 58 examples of this successful World War II German fighter were converted or built as two-seat "Schulflugzeug" trainers late in the war to ease the transition to the more powerful fighter aircraft.

Carried up to 26 troops, later increased to 50

Entry door near rear of fuselage

Plexiglass greenhouse skylight and rear windows for improved visibility

Welded steel-framed fuselage covered in fabric

△ Piper L-4H Grasshopper

Date 1944	**Origin** US
Engine 65 hp Continental A-65	
Top speed 137 km/h (85 mph)	

US forces used this military liaison aircraft based on the Piper Cub for artillery spotting, short-range reconnaissance, and transport during World War II, alongside types from other light plane manufacturers. It proved to be a rugged workhorse.

Triangular hinged panel to allow access to tailwheel retraction mechanics

Supermarine Spitfire

Arguably the most famous aircraft of all time, the iconic Spitfire was instrumental – along with the Hawker Hurricane – in defending Britain during the Battle of Britain in 1940. More prominent than the Hurricane because of its instantly recognizable, curvaceous lines, the Spitfire was a wartime propagandist's dream. Its basic design lent itself to continuous development and it remained in production from the beginning to the end of World War II.

SPECIFICATIONS	
Name	Supermarine Spitfire Mk II
Date	1940
Origin	UK
Production	20,351
Construction	Aluminium alloy stressed-skin
Maximum weight	2,799 kg (6,172 lb)
Engine	1,440–1,585 hp Rolls-Royce Merlin 45 supercharged liquid-cooled V12
Wingspan	11.23 m (36 ft 10 in)
Length	9.12 m (29 ft 11 in)
Range	651 km (405 miles)
Top speed	575 km/h (357 mph)

DESIGNED BY R. J. MITCHELL, creator of Supermarine's Schneider Trophy-winning racing floatplanes of the 1920s and early 1930s, the Spitfire fighter epitomized elegant stressed-skin construction. In contrast to a fabric covering over wood or metal frames, an eggshell-thin, aluminium-alloy outer surface carried much of the load imposed on the aircraft.

The beautiful elliptical wing shape was chosen not for its looks but because it offered low drag while still allowing room for the retracted undercarriage and eight 0.303-in Browning machine-guns (later a combination of guns and 20-mm cannon).

The type's potential for development meant that by the time Mitchell's successor Joseph Smith had produced the final variant in 1946 – the Mk24 – it had more than twice the horsepower of the prototype, and its maximum weight had increased by the equivalent of 30 passengers.

Every inch a thoroughbred
With its compound curves, the Spitfire was difficult and costly to make, but its pilots, such as Douglas Bader, Bob Stanford-Tuck, "Sailor" Malan, and "Johnnie" Johnson, loved it.

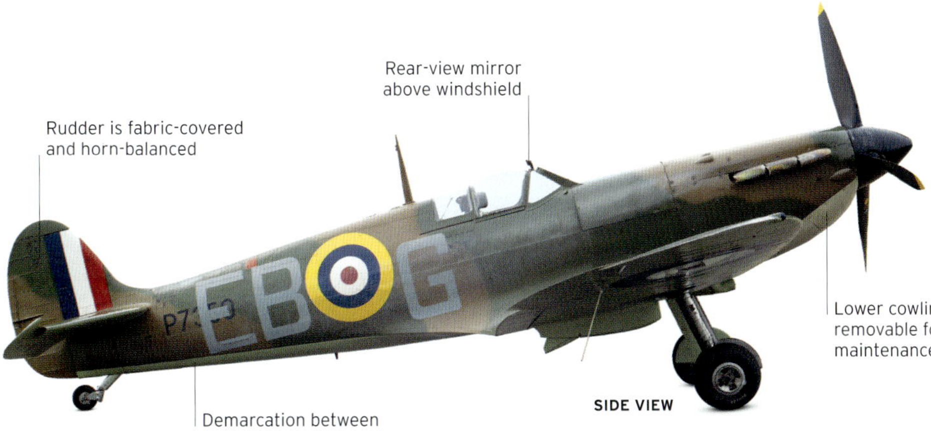

SIDE VIEW

REAR VIEW

FRONT VIEW

THE EXTERIOR

Speed means the difference between life and death for a fighter pilot, so attention was paid to squeezing an extra few miles per hour from the aircraft. Streamlining reduced drag, so flush-rivets were used on the wings, and then on later versions on the fuselage, to make the skin smoother. Other ways of increasing speed included adding ejector exhausts and a "Meredith Duct" around the radiator, which added to the main thrust provided by the propeller.

1. Ejector engine exhausts **2.** Fabric patch over machine-gun port to reduce drag (rounds break fabric when gun fires) **3.** IFF (Identification friend or foe) aerial grommet **4.** Cockpit door with escape crowbar **5.** Instrument panel (with modern avionics in place of gun sight) **6.** Instrument panel (left) **7.** Instrument panel (right) **8.** Undercarriage selector **9.** Rudder pedal **10.** Gun-camera indicator **11.** Pilot's bucket-seat with height adjustment lever **12.** Headrest and armour

1

2

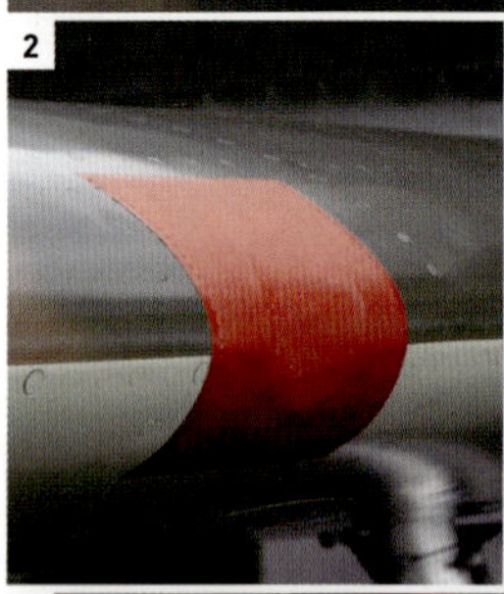

3

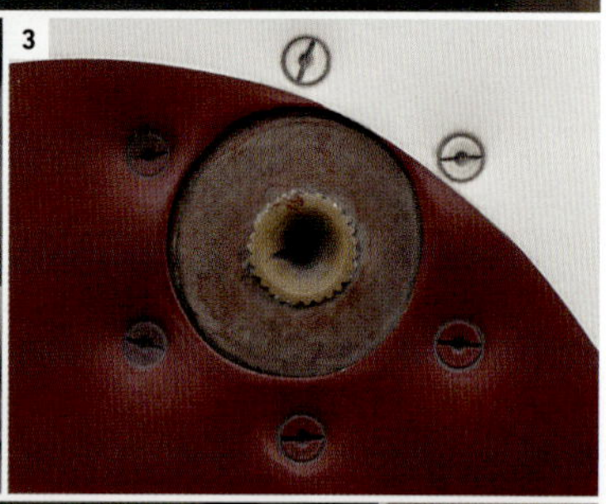

4

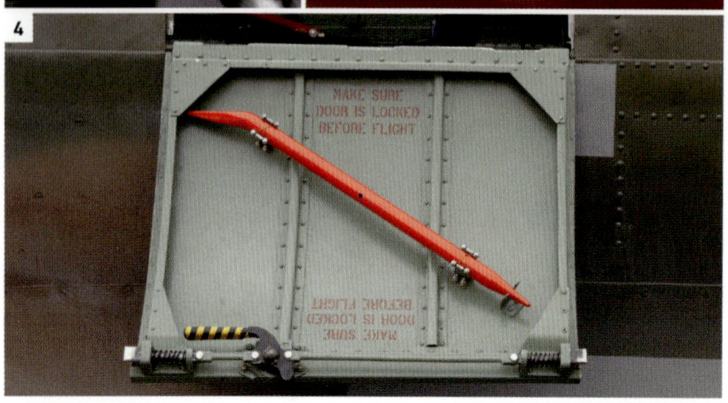

THE COCKPIT

Following typical RAF practice for the time, the Spitfire's cockpit featured a central, "Basic Six" group instrument panel comprising airspeed indicator, artificial horizon, vertical speed indicator, altimeter, heading indicator, and turn-and-slip indicator. Engine instruments were to the right, and oxygen/undercarriage/flaps and other instruments to the left. The cockpit had no floor – just rudder pedals on which to rest the feet, with structure and systems beneath.

5

6

7

8
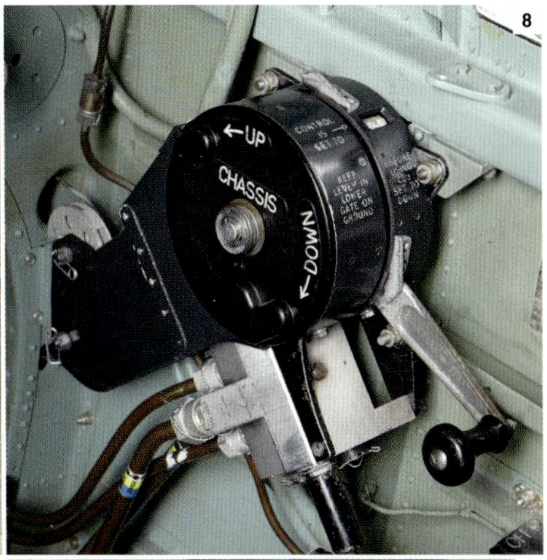

9

10

11

12

Fighter and Fighter-bomber Aircraft

Some combatant nations – notably Japan – initially favoured lightweight, lightly armoured fighter aircraft, on the grounds that manoeuvrability was all-important; others preferred better protection and more powerful weaponry. It was the latter that were to prove more effective. Such fighter aircraft were also more easily adapted to ground attack, and this became increasingly important on both European fronts and in the Pacific theatre. After the brief appearance of rocket-powered aircraft, jet propulsion technology took its first faltering steps towards the war's end.

△ Messerschmitt Me262 Schwalbe

Date 1942	**Origin** Germany
Engine 2 x 898 kg (1,980 lb) thrust Junkers Jumo 004 B-1 turbojets	
Top speed 900 km/h (559 mph)	

This very advanced aircraft was the world's first operational jet fighter. Although much faster than any piston machine, it was hampered by the lack of dive brakes, and also the short life and inherent unreliability of its Jumo turbojets.

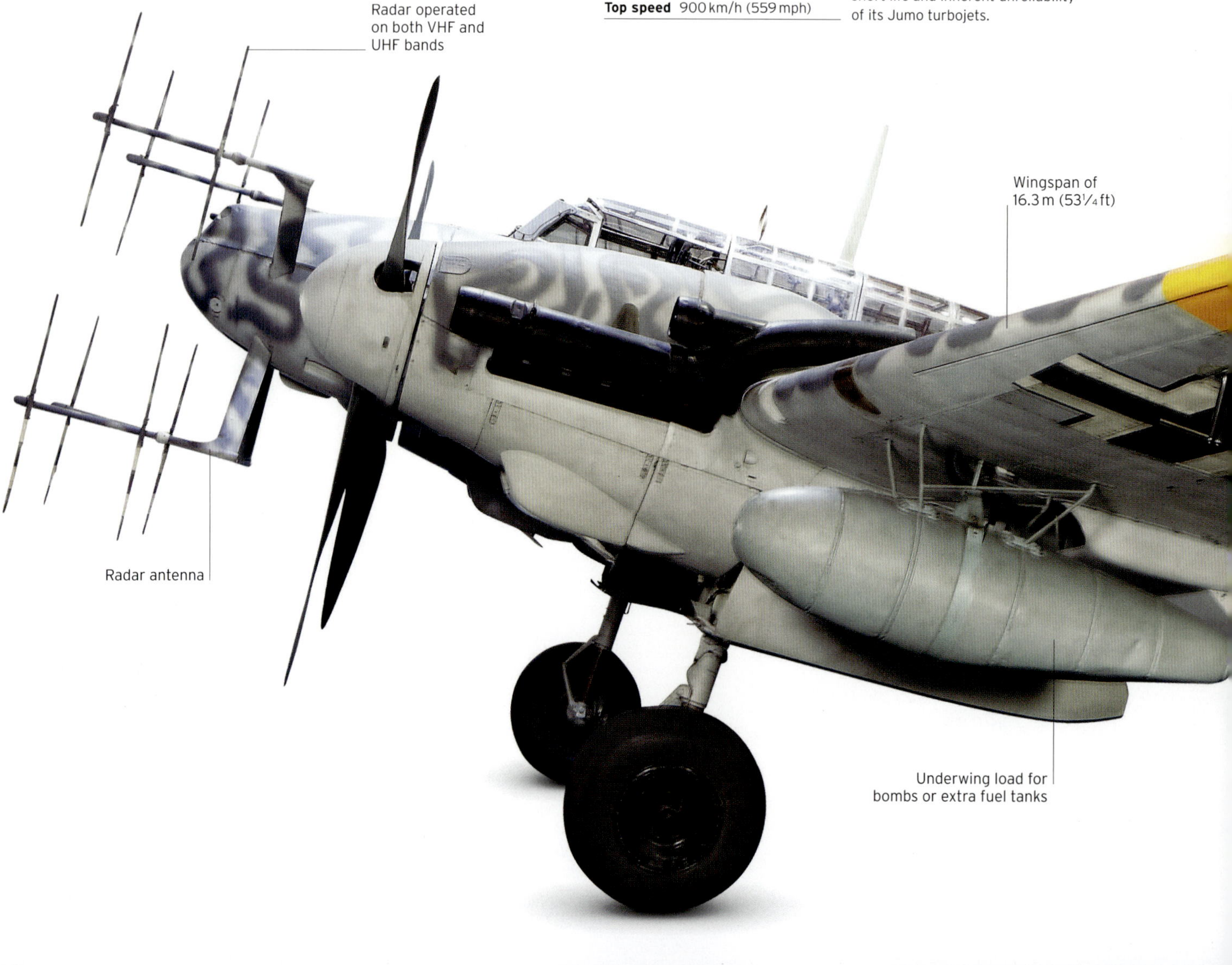

Tailplane mounted high, out of jet exhaust

▽ de Havilland Mosquito B.16

Date 1942 **Origin** UK

Engine Two 1,710 hp Rolls-Royce Merlin 76 V-12s

Top speed 670 km/h (415 mph)

The Mosquito was an anomaly: a modern aircraft built largely from wood. Its first flight was in November 1940. It was to become one of the most successful aircraft the British RAF operated during World War II, serving in bomber, day- and night-fighter, and reconnaissance roles.

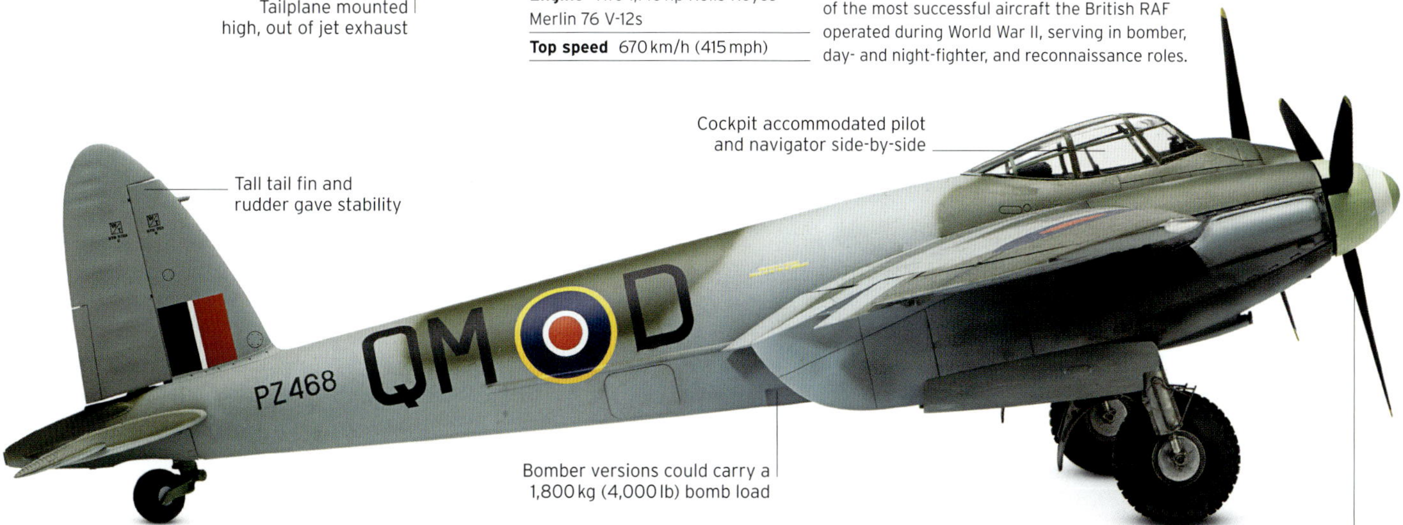

Cockpit accommodated pilot and navigator side-by-side

Tall tail fin and rudder gave stability

Bomber versions could carry a 1,800 kg (4,000 lb) bomb load

Three-bladed variable-pitch propeller

◁ Messerschmitt Bf 110G

Date 1943 **Origin** Germany

Engine 2 x 1,085/1,455 hp Daimler-Benz DB 601/605 liquid-cooled inverted V12

Top speed 560 km/h (348 mph)

In production ahead of World War II, this twin-engined fighter-bomber was effective in early engagements but lacked agility, changing to ground support and night-fighting with radar, at which it excelled.

Tailplane had twin fins and rudders

Fighter and Fighter-bomber Aircraft (cont.)

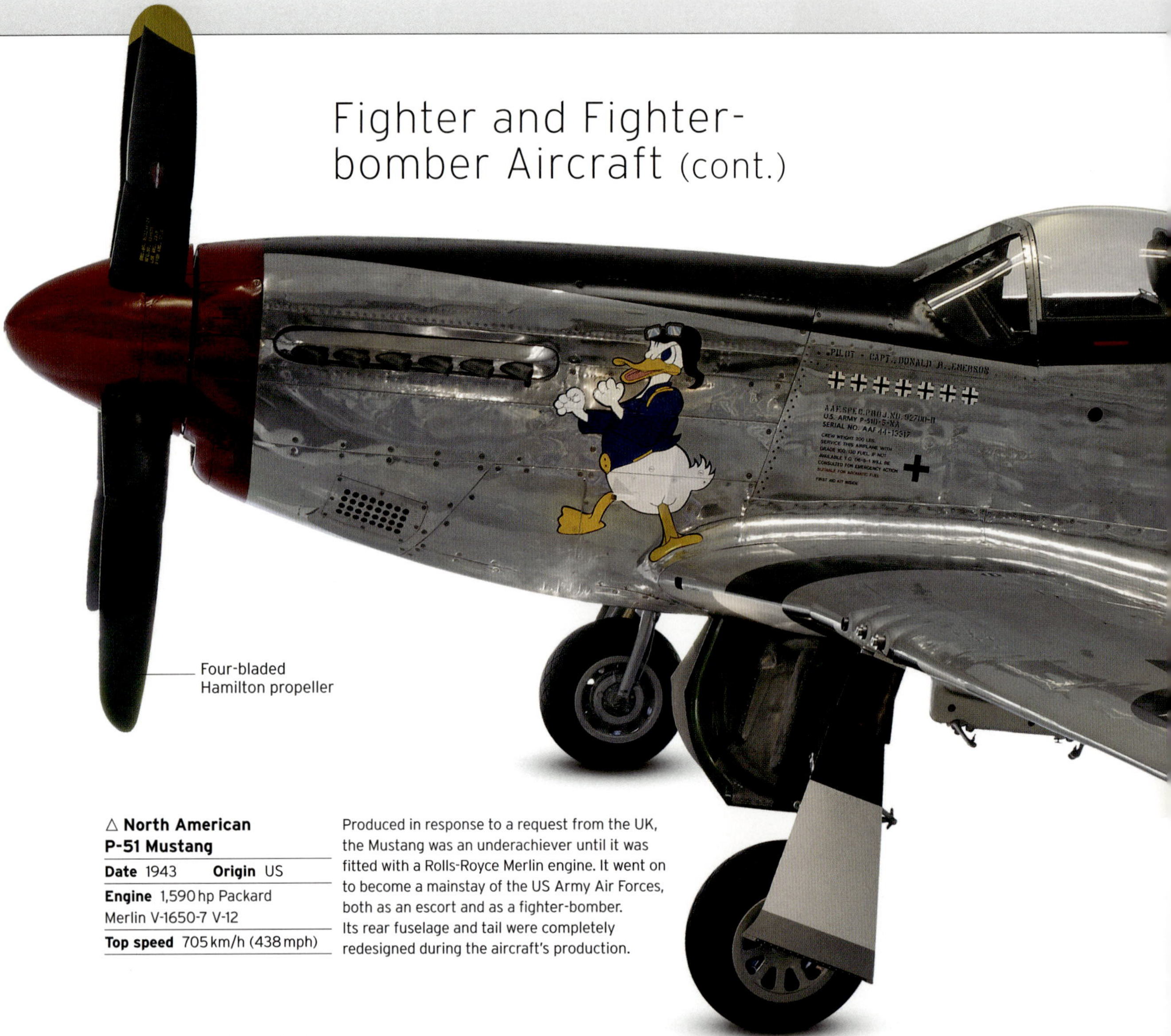

△ North American P-51 Mustang

Date 1943 **Origin** US

Engine 1,590 hp Packard Merlin V-1650-7 V-12

Top speed 705 km/h (438 mph)

Produced in response to a request from the UK, the Mustang was an underachiever until it was fitted with a Rolls-Royce Merlin engine. It went on to become a mainstay of the US Army Air Forces, both as an escort and as a fighter-bomber. Its rear fuselage and tail were completely redesigned during the aircraft's production.

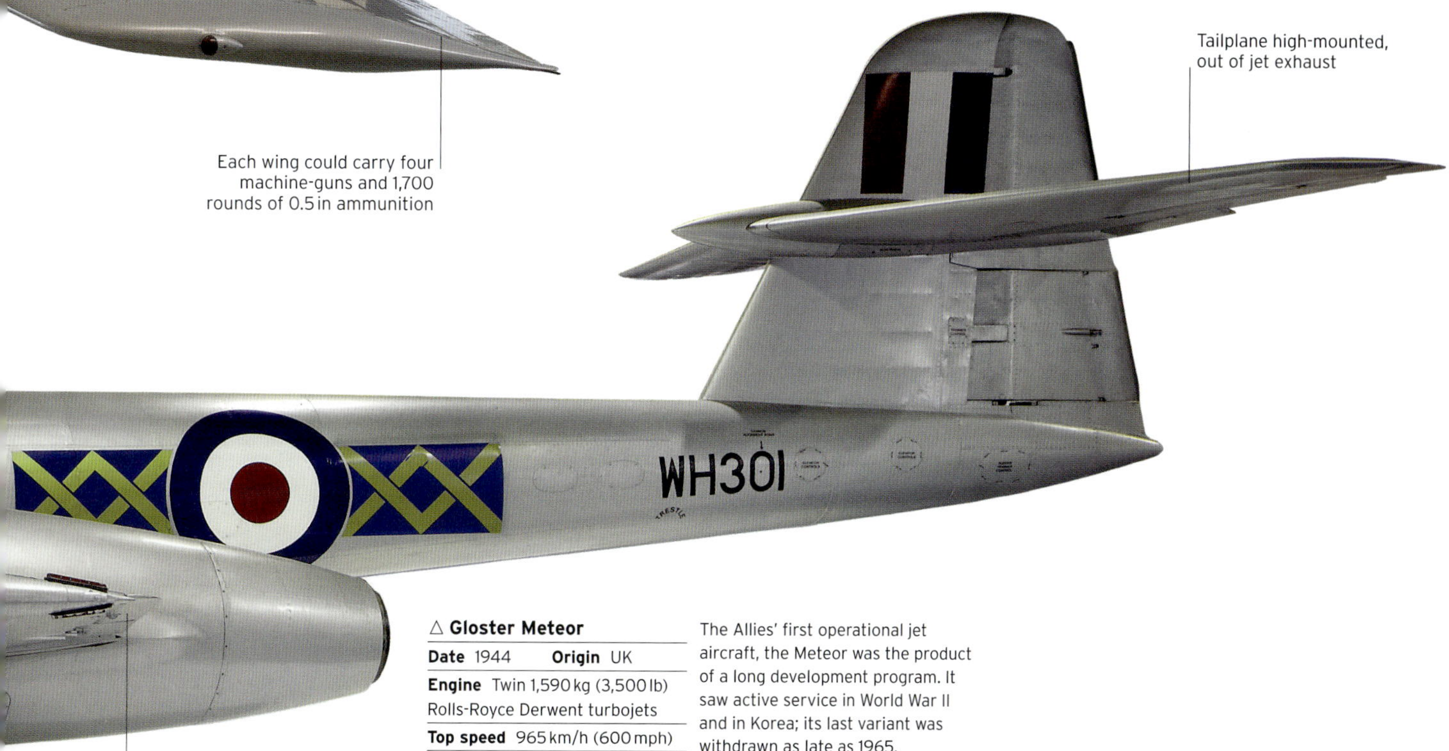

△ Gloster Meteor

Date 1944	**Origin** UK
Engine Twin 1,590 kg (3,500 lb) Rolls-Royce Derwent turbojets	
Top speed 965 km/h (600 mph)	

The Allies' first operational jet aircraft, the Meteor was the product of a long development program. It saw active service in World War II and in Korea; its last variant was withdrawn as late as 1965.

Bomber Aircraft

During World War II, two different types of bomber aircraft emerged: those designed to fly long-range "strategic" missions against infrastructure targets and industrial cities; and "tactical" bombers employed around the battlefield. Both had vital roles to play, but it was the "heavies" which came to define the type. Strategic bombers evolved during the war, their capacities enhanced by the development of more powerful engines, and their capabilities improved by the introduction of radar-based guidance systems and effective predictive bombsights.

△ **Heinkel He 111**

Date 1941 **Origin** Germany

Engine Two 1,300 hp Junkers Jumo 211F-1 in-line V-12s (inverted)

Top speed 440 km/h (275 mph)

The most numerous of the medium bombers with which the *Luftwaffe* entered the war, the He 111 was built in a bewildering array of variants, the most outlandish of which was the twin-fuselage, five-engined He 111Z.

△ **Consolidated B-24 Liberator**

Date 1941 **Origin** US

Engine 4 x 1,200 hp Pratt & Whitney R-1830-65 Twin Wasp turbosupercharged air-cooled 14-cylinder radial

Top speed 467 km/h (290 mph)

The B-24 Liberator was lighter, faster, with a greater range and bomb load than the B-17. However, it was also harder to fly and more liable to catch fire or crash if hit. More than 18,400 of this most prolific World War II Allied bomber were built.

△ Junkers Ju 87D Stuka

Date 1941	**Origin** Germany
Engine 1,400 hp Junkers Jumo 211J V-12	
Top speed 390 km/h (240 mph)	

Perhaps the most recognizable of all German aircraft of the period, the Ju 87 *Sturzkampfflugzeug* first saw combat in Spain, in 1937. It was still operational – armed with twin 3.7 cm cannon – in the last days of World War II, by which time around 6,500 had been built in six main variants.

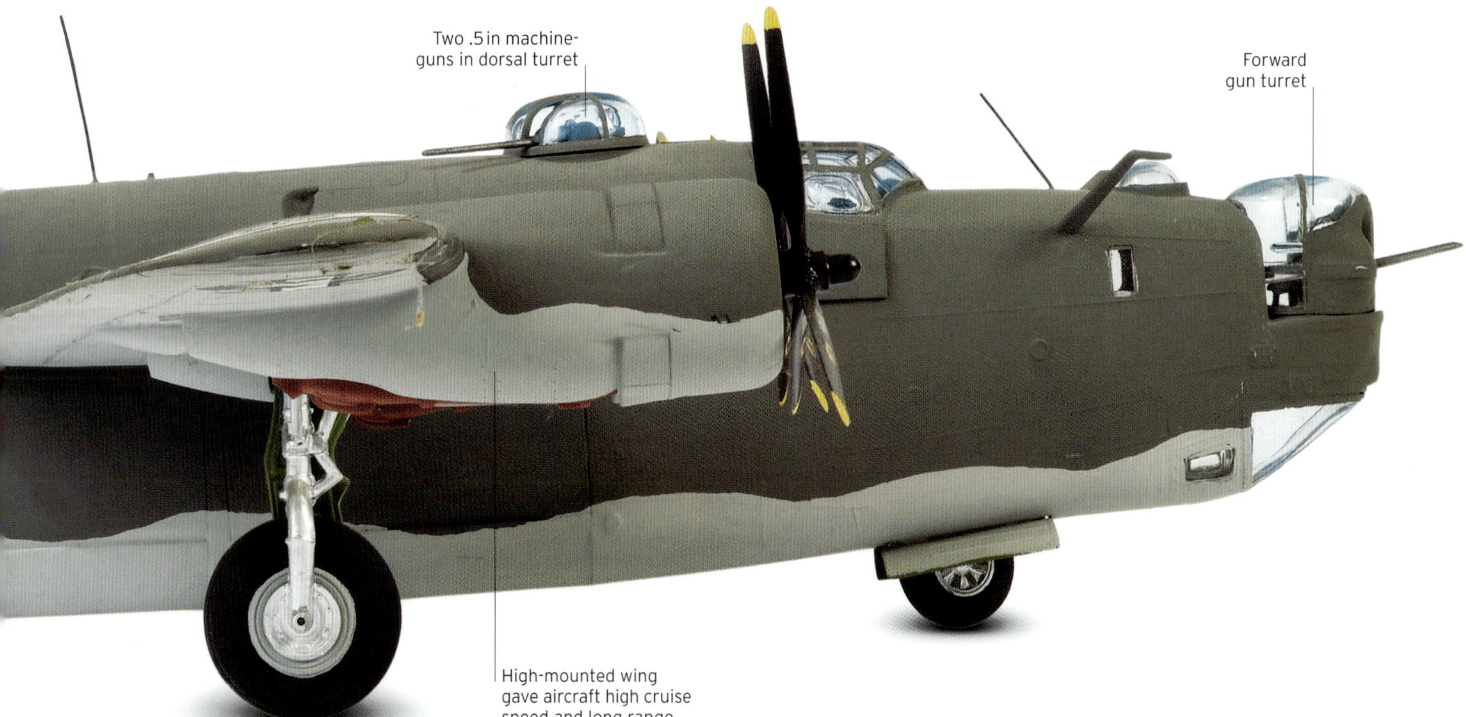

Bomber Aircraft (cont.)

△ **Heinkel He 177 *Greif***

Date 1942 **Origin** Germany

Engine Two 2,600 hp Daimler-Benz DB 610 W-24s

Top speed 565 km/h (350 mph)

The *Greif* (Griffin) was the only specially built long-range heavy bomber operated by the *Luftwaffe* during World War II. An inspired design that was flawed in execution, many of its shortcomings could be traced to its overcomplicated engine and to the requirement that it function as a precision dive bomber.

▽ Avro Lancaster

Date 1942 **Origin** UK

Engine Four 1,280 hp Rolls-Royce Merlin XX in-line V-12s

Top speed 460 km/h (285 mph)

Perhaps the best bomber aircraft of World War II, the Lancaster carried a 6,350 kg (14,000 lb) bomb load to targets in Germany and beyond from British Royal Air Force Bomber Command's bases in the east of England.

△ Boeing B-17G Flying Fortress

Date 1945 **Origin** US

Engine 4 x 1,200 hp Wright R-1820-97 Cyclone turbocharged air-cooled 9-cylinder radial

Top speed 462 km/h (287 mph)

First flown in 1935, the B-17 was the USAAF's main precision daytime bomber in World War II. It was well defended and able to survive much damage, but it had only half the bomb capacity of an Avro Lancaster.

Boeing B-17

Known as the "Flying Fortress," the Boeing B-17 was an extraordinary fighting machine. It bristled with machine-guns and could fly at an altitude of more than 9,000 m (30,000 ft). When in mass formation, it was capable of delivering a staggering tonnage of explosives. Since the B-17 was employed in large fleets, mass production was essential, and, for every B-17 shot down, American factories produced more than two.

SPECIFICATIONS	
Model	Boeing B-17G Flying Fortress
Date	1945
Origin	US
Production	12,731
Construction	Aluminium and steel
Maximum weight	24,948 kg (55,000 lb) loaded
Engines	4 x 1,200 hp Wright R-1820-97 Cyclone turbocharged air-cooled 9-cylinder radial
Wingspan	31.6 m (103 ft 9 in)
Length	22.7 m (4 ft 4 in)
Range	2,950 km (1,850 miles)
Top speed	462 km/h (287 mph)

FOR THE B-17'S CREW of 10, conditions were cramped and uncomfortable. The Flying Fortress was not pressurized and the effects of altitude sickness were highly unpleasant. The USAAF crews had to endure hours in freezing temperatures but always be alert and ready to battle the *Luftwaffe*'s fighter force once over enemy territory. Nevertheless, the B-17 gained the abiding affection of those who flew in it, and the dependable Fortress became a symbol of America's ability to take the war to Germany. Indeed, the B-17 was to take on the lion's share of the day bombing campaign.

Although built in fewer numbers than its contemporary, Consolidated's B-24 Liberator, and despite its bomb load often being little more than that carried by the much smaller and faster de Havilland Mosquito, the B-17 was immensely strong and had a reputation for being able to take a great deal of punishment and still get its crew home.

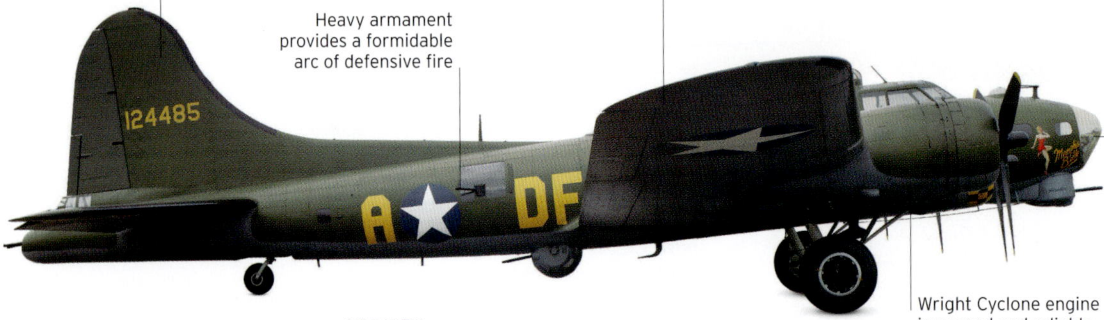

SIDE VIEW

FRONT VIEW

REAR VIEW

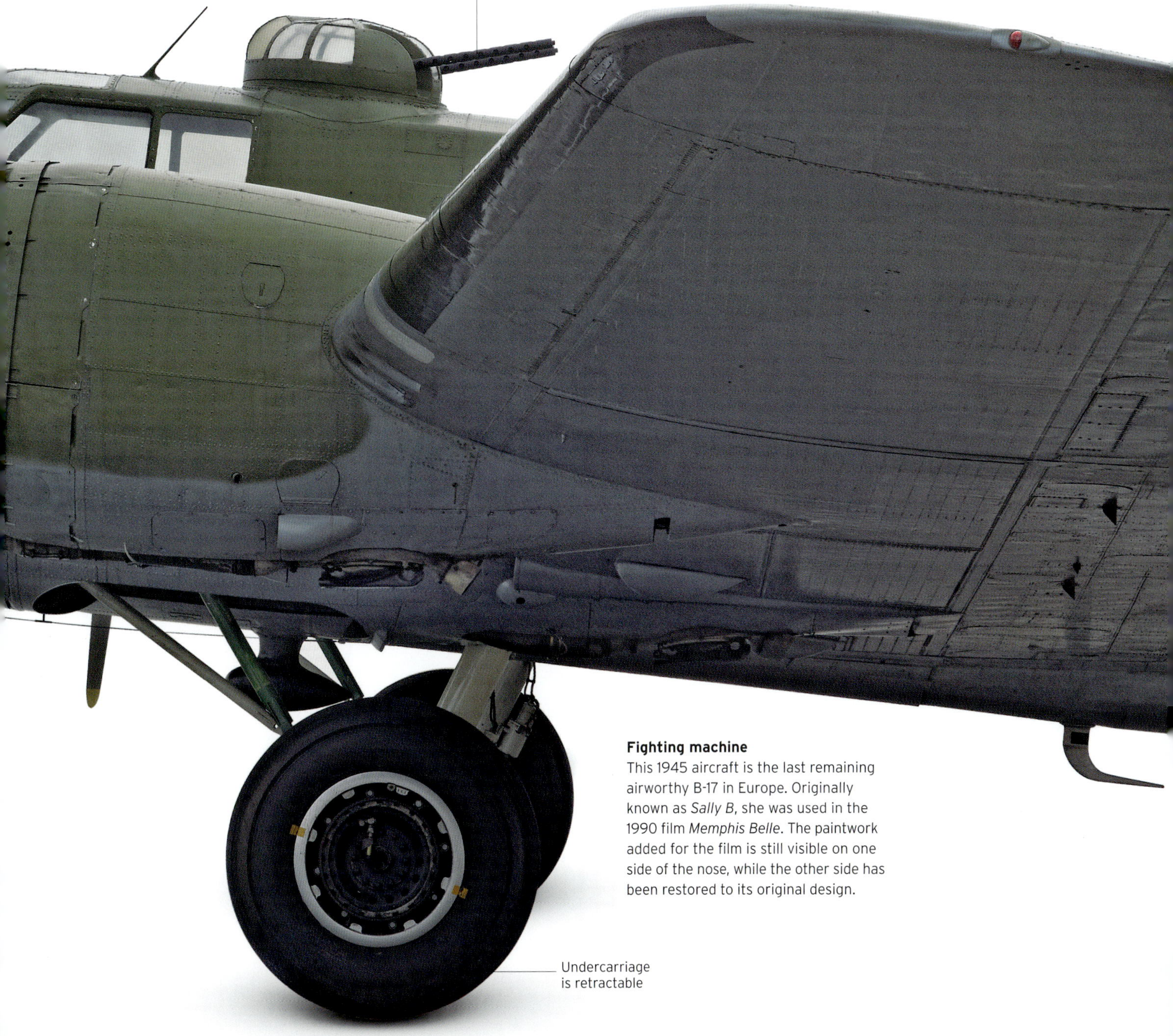

Fighting machine
This 1945 aircraft is the last remaining airworthy B-17 in Europe. Originally known as *Sally B*, she was used in the 1990 film *Memphis Belle*. The paintwork added for the film is still visible on one side of the nose, while the other side has been restored to its original design.

THE EXTERIOR

The B-17 belonged to a new generation of all-metal monoplane aircraft with enclosed cockpits, and was built to be tough. From the outset, Boeing had envisioned the new bomber as an aerial battleship. When a journalist reported that the prototype looked like a "flying fortress," Boeing saw the value in the name and trademarked it.

1. Chin guns remotely controlled by bombardier **2.** Waist machine-gun position **3.** Wright Cyclone radial engine with Hamilton Standard hydromatic propeller **4.** Sperry swivelling ball turret **5.** Bombardier's seat and Norden bombsight in nose compartment **6.** Sophisticated waist-gun sight **7.** Rear gunner's station in the tail **8.** Bomb bay – typically carried 2,722 kg (6,000 lb) of bombs **9.** The "office" – the B-17 flight deck

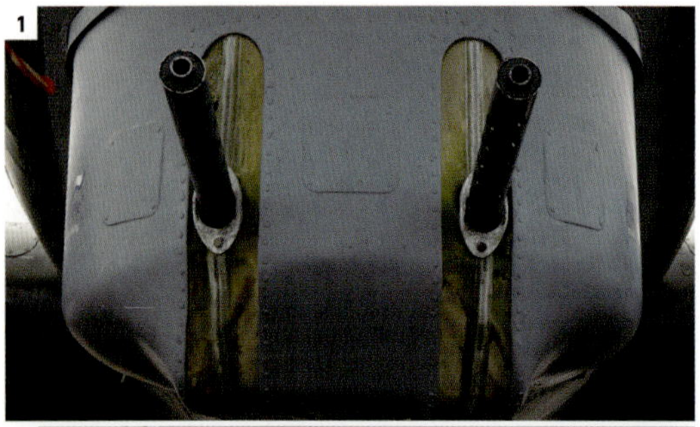

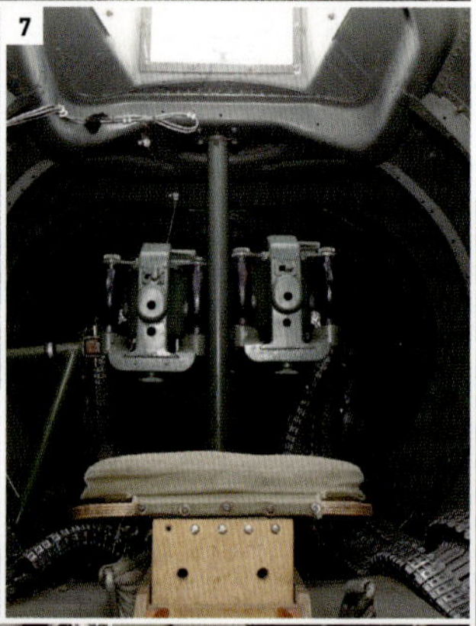

THE INTERIOR

Packed with bombs and fuel, the B-17 offered the crew limited space. The bombardier and navigator had to crouch to reach their seats in the bomber's nose. The ball-turret gunner had to be small to fit into his cramped station beneath the fuselage while the tail gunner had to crawl through the rear of the fuselage to reach his remote position. The pilot and copilot sat on the flight deck – the only area designed to be spacious – with the flight engineer above and behind them. The pilot operated from the left seat with the basic flight instruments, such as altimeter, airspeed indicator, and turn-and-bank indicator located in the central panel.

9
HYDRAULIC PRESSURE WARNING
FEATHERING MOTOR NOT FUSED. IF NO FEATHERING WITHIN 90 SECONDS OPEN THIS SWITCH BY PULLING
PROP FEATHER ENG 1. ENG 2.
PUSH
PROP FEATHER ENG 3. ENG 4.
VCMA 110
VLOF 115
V2 120
COMM
121.400
NOT TO BE FLOWN ABOVE 10000 FT
PRESS TO TEST LIGHTS
UNDERCARRIAGE DOWN
TAILWHEEL LOCK
UP
FLAP POSITION
DOWN
T 1
T-2
OPEN
POWER SETTINGS
CLOSED
THROTTLE
CLOSED
LOCK
LOCKED LOW PITCH
HIGH R.P.M.
PROP. PITCH
LOCKED
LOCK
BOEING

Bombs and Missiles

Initially, aerial bombs were simple iron cylinders filled with explosives and fused to detonate on impact. Some had rudimentary fins, but they were still only suitable for hitting areas rather than specific targets. As soon as appropriate technologies became available, bombs were fitted with guidance systems, some of them built-in, others requiring a controlling hand in the launch aircraft. By 1944, following much experimentation with rocketry, the first generation of surface-to-surface missiles appeared that promised to change the nature of the war in the air.

▷ **Ruhrstahl/Kramer X-1 "Fritz X"**

Date 1943

Origin Germany

Charge 320 kg (705 lb)

Length 3.3 m (11 ft)

The most successful guided bomb of the war, the "Fritz X" was steered to its target by an operator aboard the launching aircraft. It was a marked success, with the *Luftwaffe*'s specialist unit, *Kampfgeschwader* 100, sinking the British ship HMS *Warspite* at Salerno.

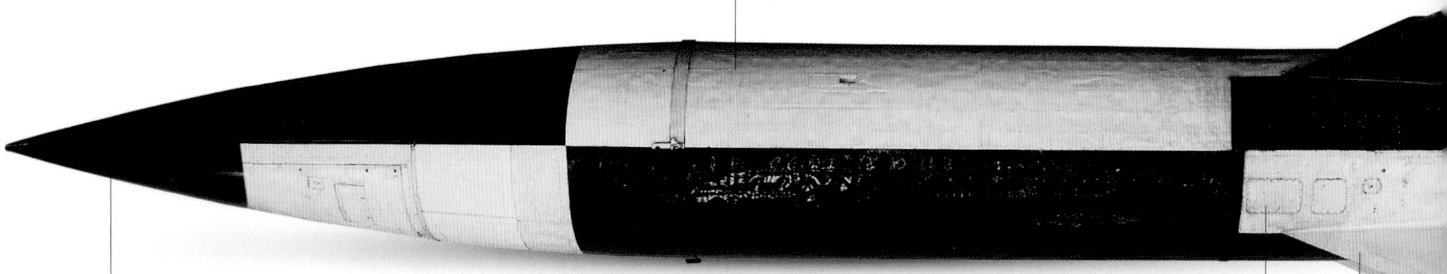

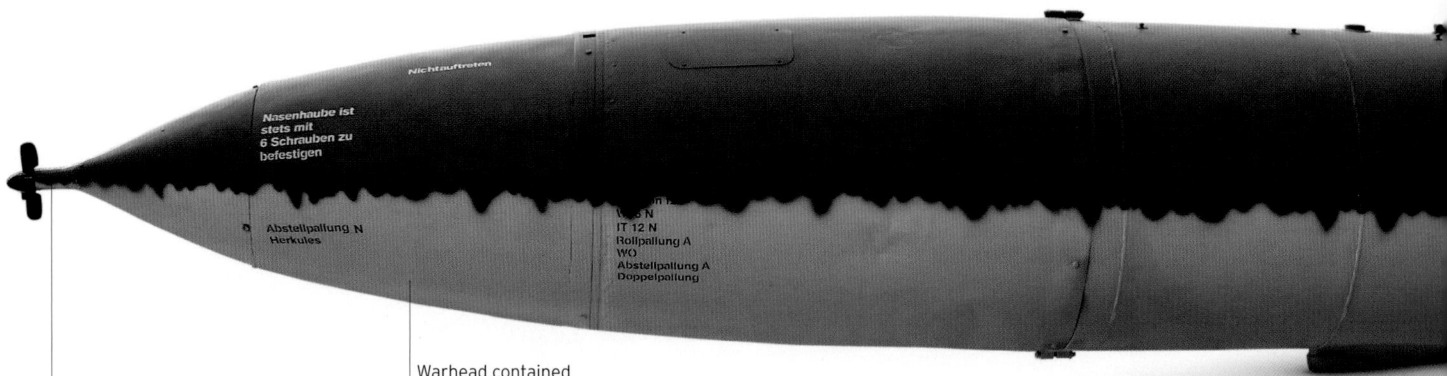

◁ **A4 (V2)**

Date 1944
Origin Germany
Charge 1,000 kg (2,205 lb)
Length 14.05 m (46 ft)

The A4 was the world's first ballistic missile, with a maximum range of 330 km (205 miles), which allowed it to hit London from launch sites in the Netherlands. Horizontal and vertical gyroscopes guided the rocket.

△ **Fieseler Fl103 (V1)**

Date 1944
Origin Germany
Charge 850 kg (1,874 lb)
Length 8.32 m ($27\frac{1}{3}$ ft)

The first long-range surface-to-surface missile, the Fl103 was launched from a ramp by a steam catapult and was powered by a simple pulse-jet motor. It was deployed from June 13, 1944 against targets in the UK and later against Antwerp.

Pearl Harbor
The Japanese attack on the US naval base at Pearl Harbor, in Hawaii, on the morning of 7 December 1941 took the US by surprise, forcing them to enter World War II. A total of 2,403 military personnel and 69 civilians were killed. Eight battleships were damaged and four sunk, including the USS *Arizona*, shown here.

Destroyers and Escorts

By 1939, destroyers displaced 1,000 tons or more. They were built for speed – well over 30 knots was normal – and had 4 in or larger guns, as well as torpedoes mounted on their decks. Their primary function was to defend naval craft against attack from similar ships or torpedo-boats, although they were also used to hunt submarines. They were enlarged still further during the war, up-gunned, and armed with an array of depth-charges. These improved destroyers were mainly employed to guard convoys of merchant ships against attack from submarines and aircraft, along with a new generation of smaller escorts.

▷ **HMS *Acanthus***

Commissioned	1940
Origin	UK
Displacement	1,245 tons
Length	62.5 m (205 ft)
Top speed	16.5 knots

Corvettes such as HMS *Acanthus* were the smallest specially built warships used for convoy escort duties during World War II. Their design was based on that of commercial whale-catchers, and they were powered by piston engines, rather than turbines.

▽ **HMS *Avon Vale***

Commissioned	1941
Origin	UK
Displacement	1,625 tons
Length	85.3 m (280 ft)
Top speed	27 knots

Avon Vale was the first of the second group of *Hunt*-class destroyer-escorts built in the early years of World War II. This multirole ship was designed to protect merchant convoys from attack from both submarines and aircraft.

Mast in traditional
position behind bridge
4 in gun
Open foredeck
K01

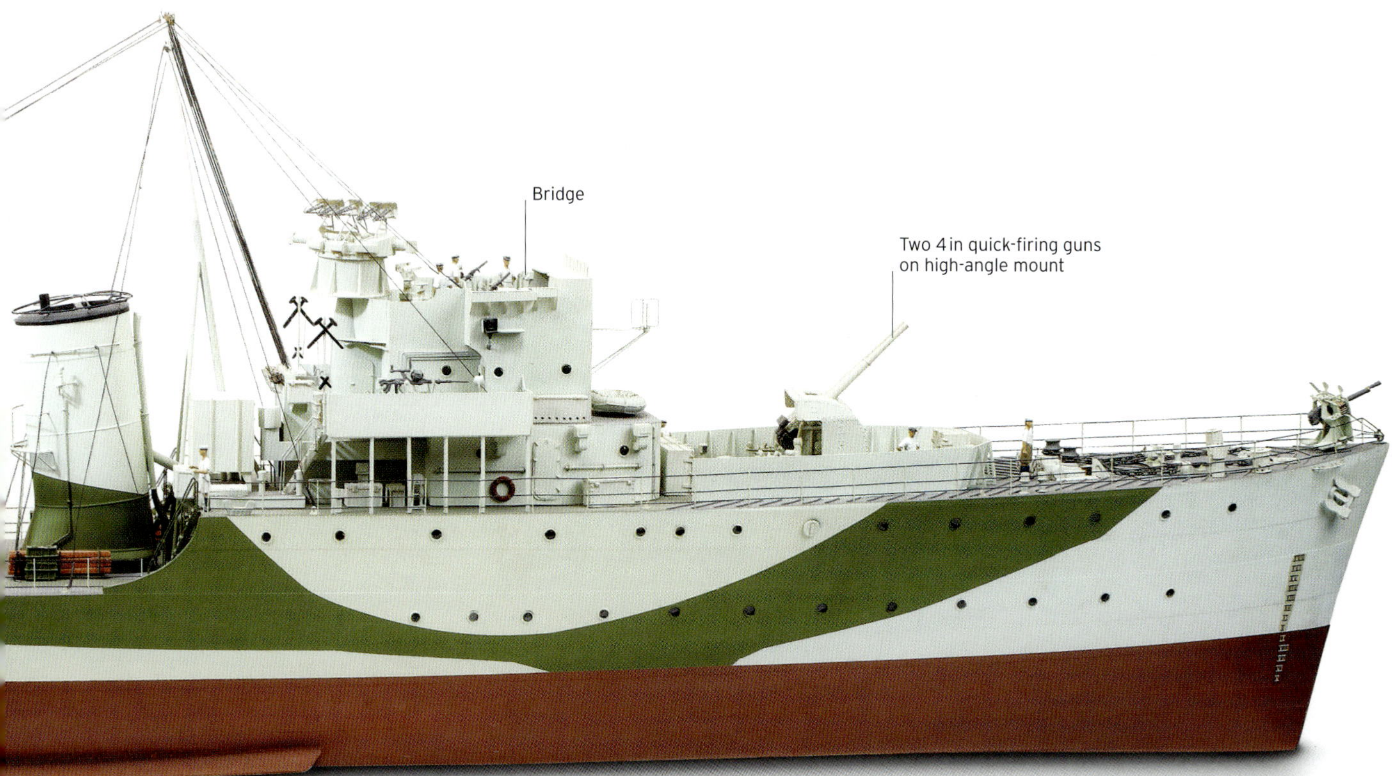
Bridge
Two 4 in quick-firing guns
on high-angle mount

Capital Ships and Cruisers

The term "capital ship" was defined in the 1920s and was applied to the most powerful craft in the fleet: battleships and battlecruisers. In the early stages of World War II, such ships proved themselves worryingly vulnerable to air attack, and the pride-of-place they once enjoyed passed to the aircraft carrier. Traditionally, cruisers were warships big enough to be able to undertake protracted voyages and operate for long periods. They were described as "light" if armed with 6 in guns and "heavy" if they mounted anything larger.

△ *Bismarck*

Commissioned	1940
Origin	Germany
Displacement	50,900 tons
Length	248 m (814 ft)
Top speed	29 knots

The pride of the *Kriegsmarine*, *Bismarck* and its sister-ship *Tirpitz* achieved iconic status. Both ships acted as a deterrent that drained British naval resources, although *Bismarck*'s effective action was limited to the destruction of HMS *Hood*. It was sunk in 1941 after being holed by British torpedo bombers.

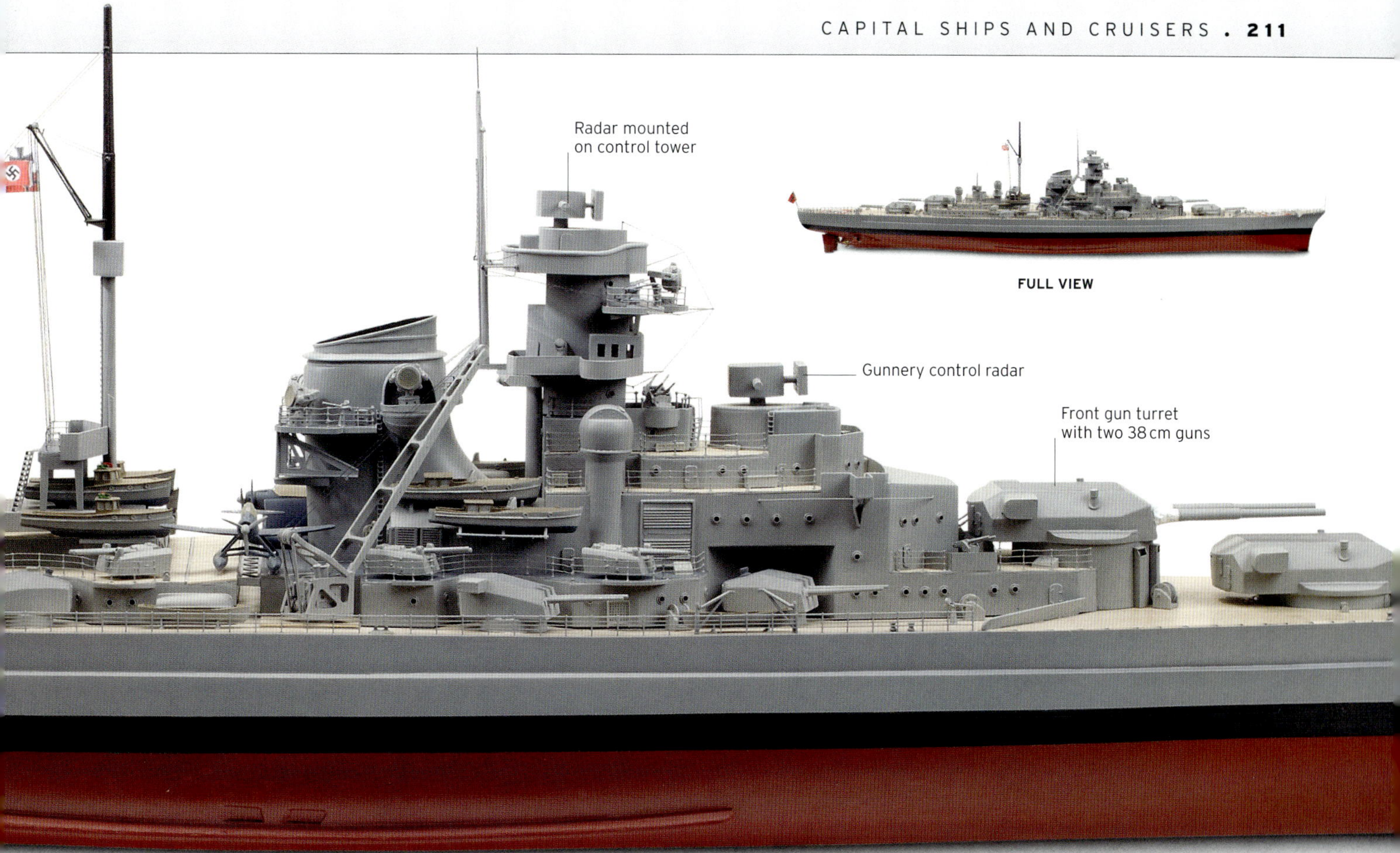

▽ ***Yahagi***	
Commissioned 1943	
Origin Japan	
Displacement 8,535 tons	
Length 174.1 m (571¼ ft)	
Top speed 35 knots	

Yahagi was one of four light cruisers of the *Agano* class that were built as fast destroyer squadron leaders, all but one of which were war losses. Mountings for two aircraft were added during construction in place of one of the ship's twin 6 in gun turrets.

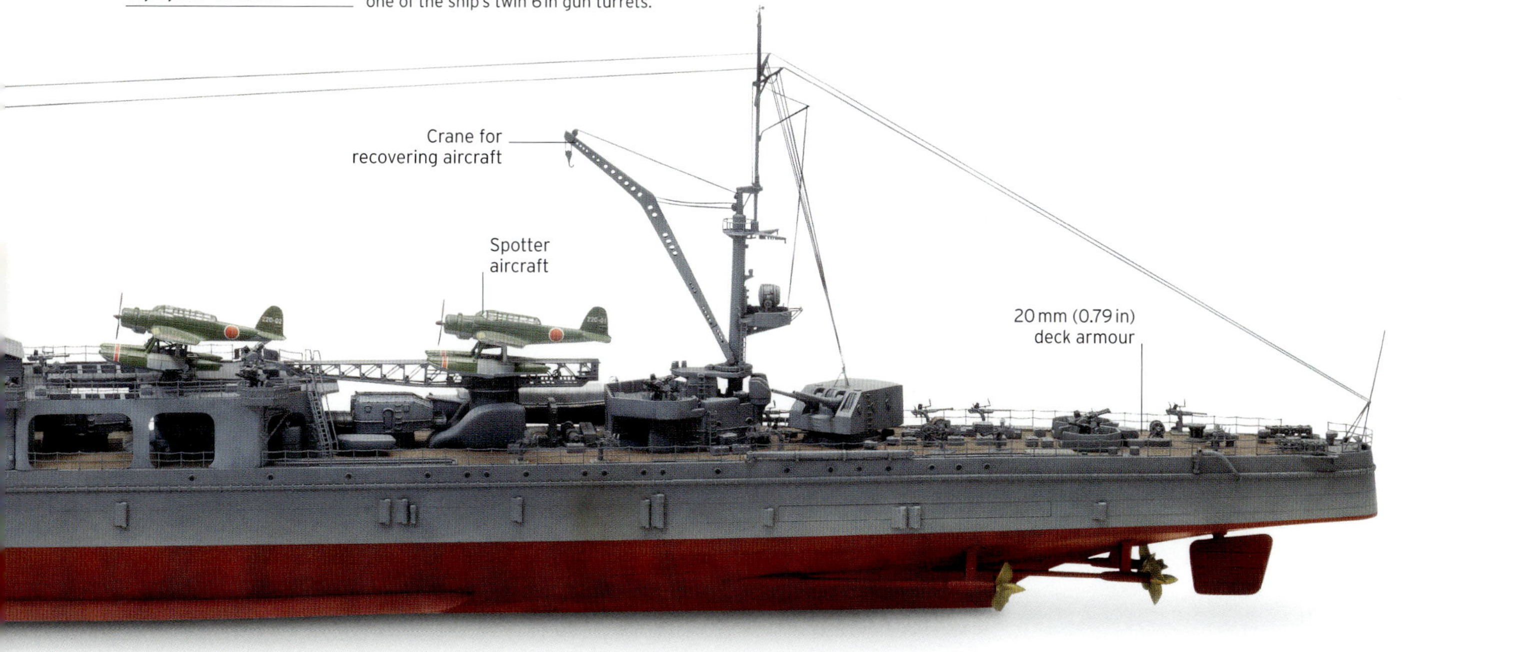

Submarines of World War II

During World War II, when Germany's surface fleet was severely limited by Hitler's prejudice against it, the U-boats provided the *Kriegsmarine* (navy of Nazi Germany) with its victories. It is a widely held view that they came close to bringing Britain to its knees. As a consequence, both Britain's Royal Navy and the US Navy were forced to invest in measures to combat this "submarine menace", which took some time to take effect. The Battle of the Atlantic could be fully declared won only after these measures had yielded results.

▽ German Type VIIC

Commissioned 1940–44

Origin Germany

Displacement 749 tons (851 tons submerged)

Length 67.1 m (220 ft)

Top speed 17 knots (7.6 knots submerged)

The Type VII boats were built in very large numbers from 1936 to 1943. The VIICs predominated, and no less than 663 were completed. They were the workhorses of the German submarine service. Operating chiefly in the Atlantic from ports in western France, they came close to cutting the vital supply chain from North America on which Britain depended.

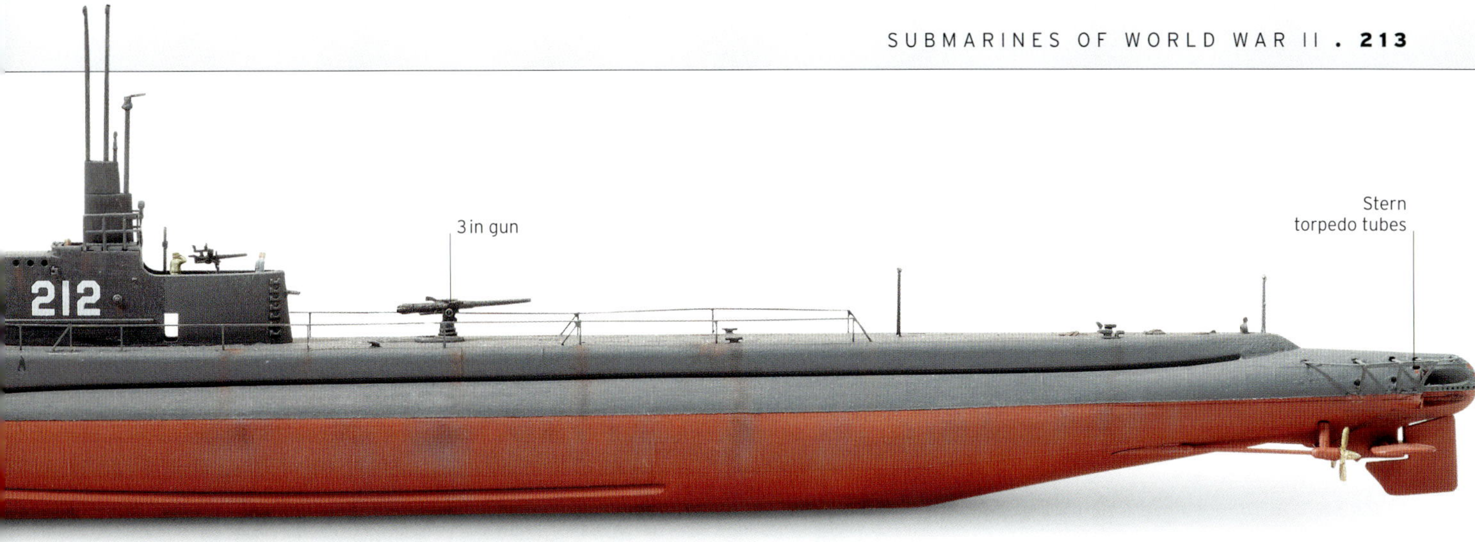

△ USS *Gato*

Commissioned 1941

Origin US

Displacement 1,810 tons (2,410 tons submerged)

Length 95 m (311½ ft)

Top speed 20 knots (8.75 knots submerged)

USS *Gato* was the leader of one of three near-identical classes of "fleet boats" that equipped the US Navy during World War II. Each class was modified extensively during and after the war. *Gato* itself survived as a training boat until the 1960s, but some in the class were transferred to other navies in the 1970s and remained in service until the 1990s.

▽ I-400

Commissioned 1944

Origin Japan

Displacement 5,225 tons (6,560 tons submerged)

Length 122 m (410¼ ft)

Top speed 18.7 knots (6.5 knots submerged)

The *Sen Toku* class consisted of submarine aircraft carriers built to launch airstrikes on the locks in the Panama Canal linking the Atlantic and the Pacific oceans. Eighteen were ordered, but just three were completed, one of which was converted into a tanker during construction. They were the largest submarines constructed until the US Navy's nuclear-powered *George Washington* class appeared in the 1960s.

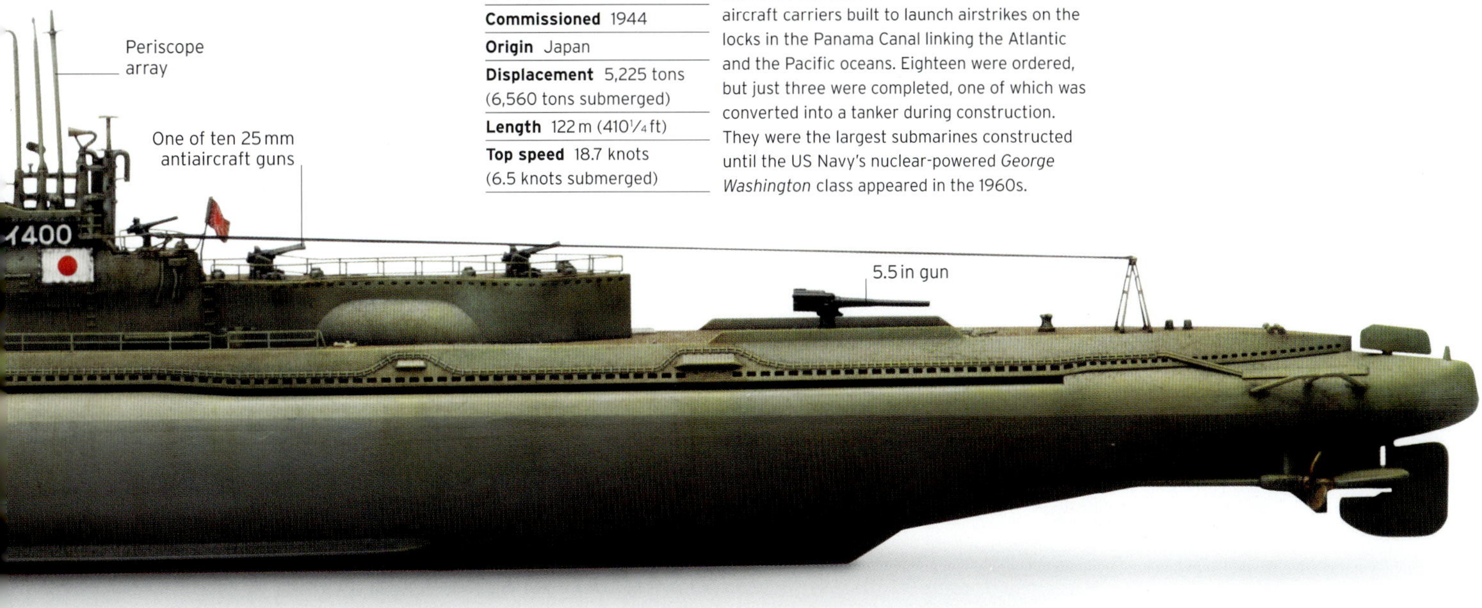

Bicycles at War

During World War II, bicycle use in Europe was limited mainly to messenger duties and air-drop operations. This involved paratroopers jumping out of planes with specially-designed folded bicycles that they could quickly unfold in order to pedal quickly to comrades behind enemy lines. Bicycles continued to be used widely by the military after the war, especially in Asia. The last dedicated bicycle infantry unit, belonging to the Swiss army, was only disbanded in 2003.

BSA MK2 PARA BIKE FOLDED FOR TRANSPORTATION

▽ Royal Enfield Rifle Bike

Date c.1940	**Origin** UK
Frame Steel	
Gears Single speed	
Wheels 70 cm (28 in)	

This special military model was basically a standard roadster bicycle with a rear carrier, rifle clips, and heavy-duty tires. It had a sprung saddle, stove-enamelled paintwork, and rubber pedal grips. Gearing was limited to a single-speed freewheel.

◁ **BSA MK2 Para Bike**

Date 1943	**Origin** UK
Frame Steel	
Gears Single speed	
Wheels 65 cm (26 in)	

This model was specially developed for and used in all major airborne landings during World War II including D-Day and Arnhem. Paratroopers could fold the bicycle in half and carry it with them as they jumped from aircraft. Once on the ground, they could easily unfold the bike for use.

▽ **Schwinn Military Touring WWII**

Date 1940s	**Origin** US
Frame Steel	
Gears Single speed	
Wheels 65 cm (26 in)	

Founded in 1895, the Schwinn Co. was noted for its high standards of bicycle construction. Its Military Touring model featured an all-welded frame, chainguard, and kickstand. Braking was provided by a rear coaster hub brake. Schwinn produced 10,000 of these bicycles per year during World War II.

Military Bikes

Most military motorcycles were used for communication. The machines needed to be tough, reliable, and capable of crossing rough terrain, and, because they were entrusted to inexperienced riders, simple to ride. Manufacturers produced no-frills machines, usually based on existing models, and equipped them with accessories deemed necessary for military use. Some sidecar outfits were developed to carry heavy guns, and they were sometimes equipped with a driven sidecar wheel to allow them to be used in battlefield terrain.

Integral sidecar unit to carry two soldiers

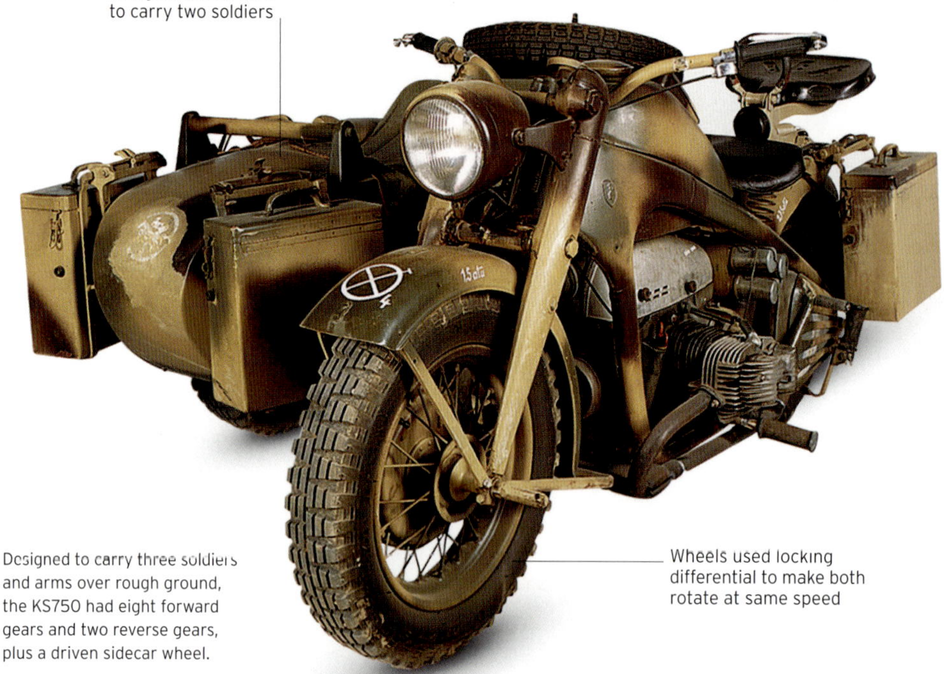

Wheels used locking differential to make both rotate at same speed

▷ **Zündapp KS750**

Date 1940	**Origin** Germany
Engine 751cc, ohv flat-twin	
Top speed 97km/h (60mph)	

Designed to carry three soldiers and arms over rough ground, the KS750 had eight forward gears and two reverse gears, plus a driven sidecar wheel.

Heavy-duty luggage rack for radio

◁ **Harley-Davidson WLA**

Date 1942 **Origin** US

Engine 738 cc, side-valve V-twin

Top speed 105 km/h (65 mph)

To convert the civilian WL model to military specification, Harley added a bash plate under the engine, modified the mudguards, and added a gun holster.

Leather holster for submachine-gun

Front light for use in blackout

Harley-Davidson WLC

Harley-Davidson's military WL motorcycles were some of the finest workhorses of World War II. Although most were used by US Forces in WLA form, a large number of these 45-cubic-inch V-twins were issued to the Canadian military and, like this model, were designated WLCs. Rugged, practical, and utterly dependable, the WLC was a fine example of how the simplicity of Harley's side-valve power plant made it perfectly suited to the rigours of warfare.

SPECIFICATIONS	
Model	Harley-Davidson WLC
Date	1942
Assembly	Milwaukee, WI
Production	More than 80,000
Construction	Tubular cradle frame
Engines	45 cu in (739 cc) side-valve V-twin
Power output	23 hp
Transmission	Three-speed
Suspension	Leading-link front forks, rigid rear
Brakes	Drums, front and rear
Maximum speed	105 km/h (65 mph)

THREE YEARS after Harley-Davidson unveiled its W-series 750 cc twins in 1937, the Milwaukee-based marque was forced to turn its attention to manufacturing motorcycles for the war effort. The straightforward nature of the side-valve engines at the heart of the W-series made them an obvious choice for military use, and by the end of the conflict more than 80,000 had been deployed by the Allies. The WLC model was produced for the Canadian forces between 1941 and 1944, Harley-Davidson stepping up to the mark when British manufacturers Norton and BSA were struggling to meet the huge demand for wartime machines from Britain and Canada. Among the bike's military specifications were olive-drab paint for camouflage, blackout lighting, and extended forks for greater ground clearance over rough terrain, while some examples also sported a rifle holster on the front forks.

The Canadian variant differed in several respects, including an alternative throttle-lever position, an auxiliary clutch hand lever, and wheels that were interchangeable. By 1945, the WLA and WLC Harley bikes had been recognized as extremely successful combat motorcycles, and in the postwar era many continued to be used by civilians.

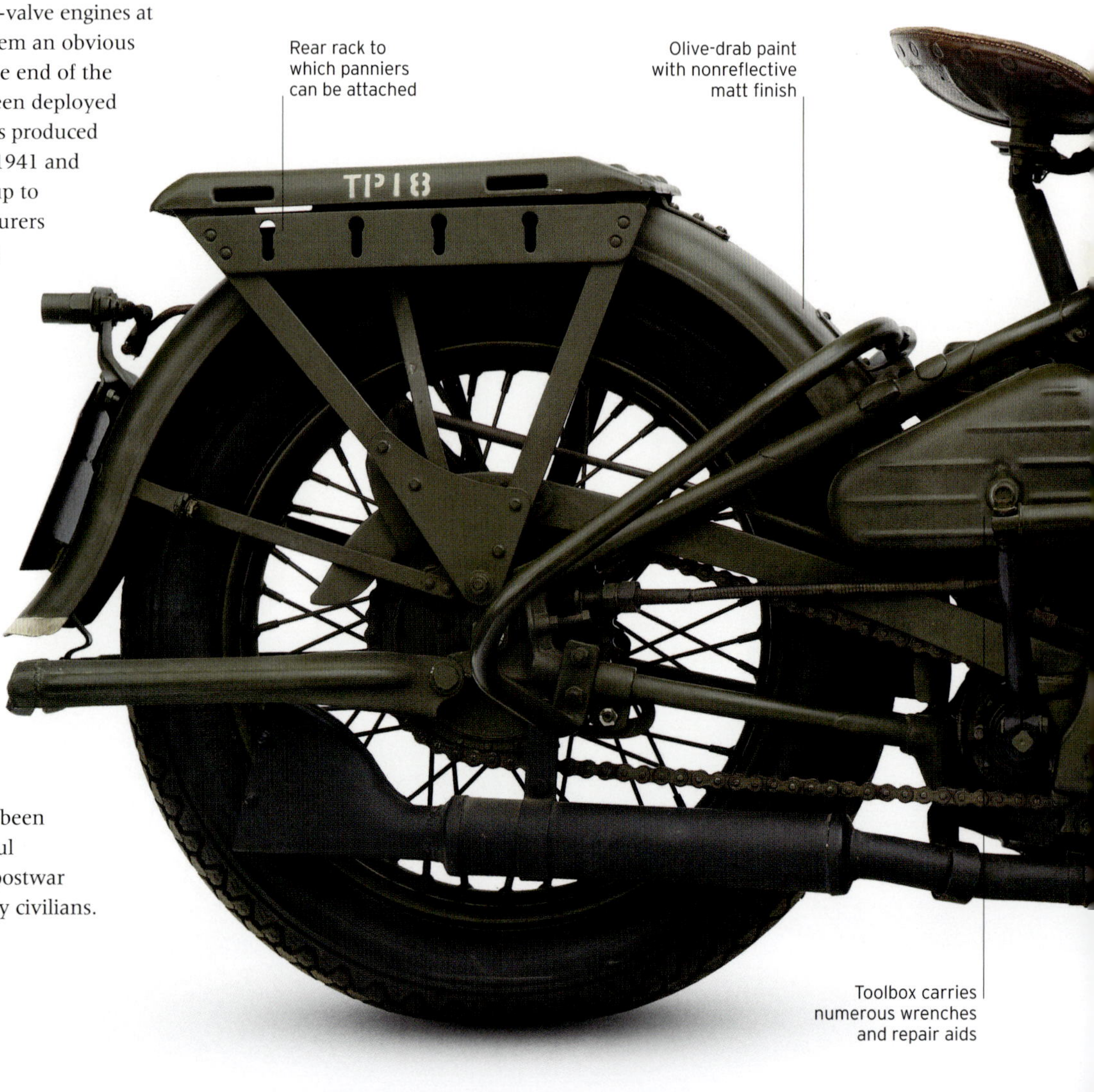

Rear rack to which panniers can be attached

Olive-drab paint with nonreflective matt finish

Toolbox carries numerous wrenches and repair aids

Light approach
Canadian Army WLC riders were equipped with a "blackout kit" that contained shrouds for the front and rear lights that directed light downward during blackout conditions. To compensate for this, small marker lights were positioned on the front and rear mudguards.

FRONT VIEW

REAR VIEW

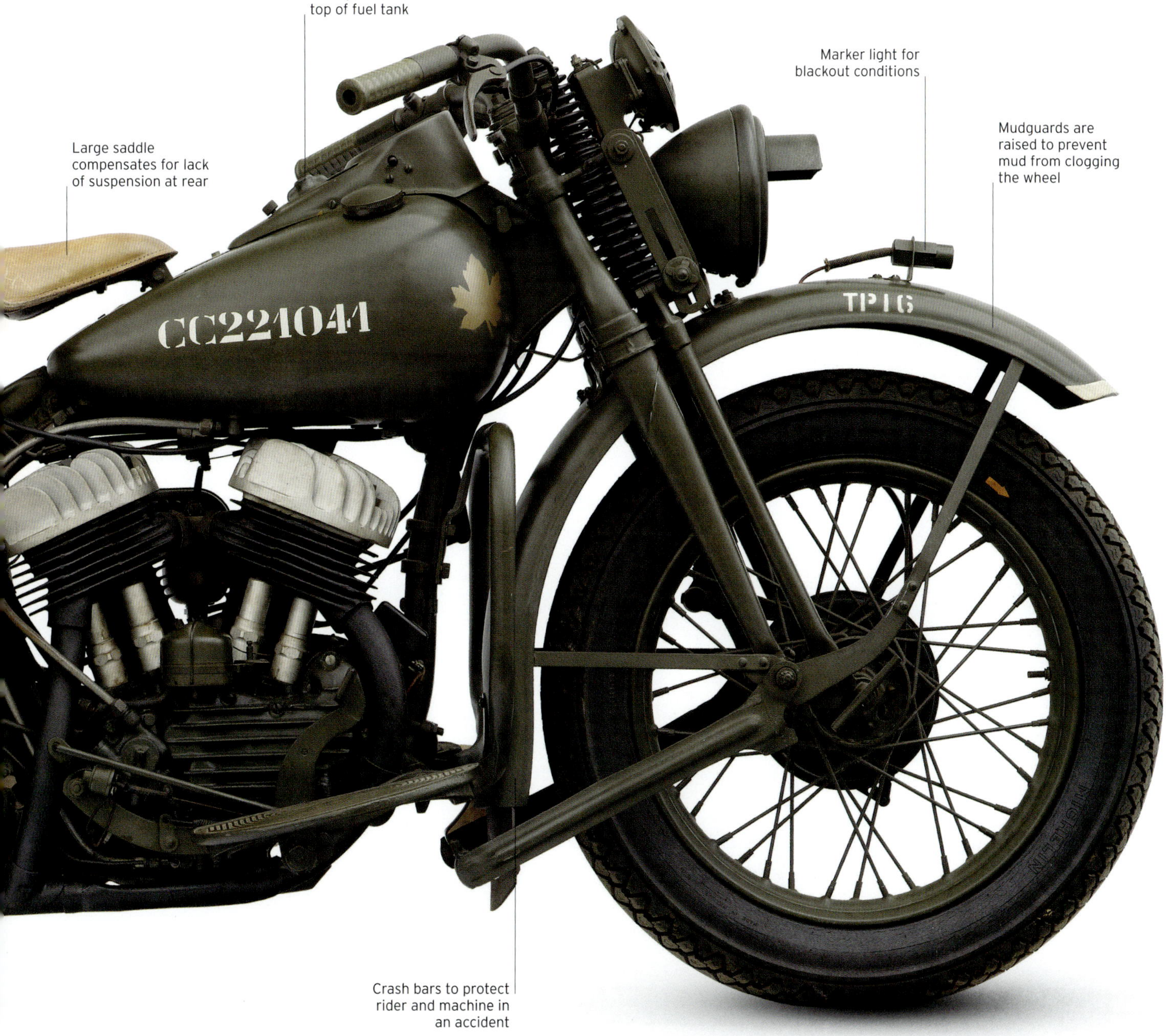

THE BIKE

The military WLs were based on the W Series "Baby Flathead" twins already in production. Special equipment included a revision to Harley-Davidson's traditional leading-link forks to allow increased ground clearance, as well as footboards and protective crash bars. The WLC saw action in several theatres of war from 1941 to 1945, including the Normandy landings and many other major conflict zones across Europe.

1. Speedometer **2.** Gear change **3.** Rear sprocket **4.** Clutch control **5.** Canadian emblem displayed on either side of tank **6.** Kick-starter **7.** Rear lights **8.** Air intake hose **9.** Ignition timing unit **10.** Carburettor floatbowl **11.** Inlet manifold **12.** Rugged side-valve engine

3

5

1

4

6

2

7

8

9

THE ENGINE

Key to the success of Harley's side-valve (or "Flathead") V-twin was the absence of any moving parts in its cylinder head, which simplified maintenance in battlefield conditions. The bike's reliability was further enhanced by an upgraded lubrication system and an oil-bath air filter to keep out dust, grit, and sand.

10

11

12

Military Tractors

The tractors supplied to the military during World War II fell into two categories: they were either built to standard civilian specifications or adapted for specific tasks. For example, tractors used to tow aircraft required different transmissions and extra weight to cope with heavy starting loads, and tracked machines were favoured for towing. The ability to start instantly was important, so many ran on pure petrol. Civilian models that were normally fuelled by kerosene after warm-up had modified manifolds for continuous petrol running.

△ **Ford 9N Moto-Tug B-NO-25**

Date 1941 **Origin** US

Engine Ford 4-cylinder petrol

Horsepower 23 hp

Transmission 3 forward, 1 reverse

The Moto-Tug was a light machine with a pull of about 1,100 kg (2,500 lb). As such, it could handle only light loads such as fighter planes and their ammunition supply carts on the airfield and concrete hangar standings. The Moto-Tug saw extensive service on US aircraft carriers and at overseas civilian airports.

▷ Allis-Chalmers Model M

Date 1942 **Origin** US

Engine Allis-Chalmers UM 4-cylinder petrol/kerosene

Horsepower 35 hp

Transmission 4 forward, 1 reverse

The Model M was robust, simple, and reliable, and was popular with farmers on both sides of the Atlantic. Produced in both 101 cm (40 in) and 121 cm (50 in) gauges, it was extensively used by the US military between 1941 and 1945. Production ceased in 1942 to free factory capacity for war work.

Caterpillar tracks for muddy ground

Powerful back wheels to gain traction on the ground

▷ Fordson Model N

Date 1944 **Origin** UK

Engine Fordson 4-cylinder petrol/kerosene

Horsepower 25 hp

Transmission 3 forward, 1 reverse

Known as the "Standard" Fordson, this tractor was the backbone of the British agricultural tractor fleet during World War II. Production peaked at 2,500 a month in 1943. The model N was available with the low-ratio "Red Spot" and the higher-ratio "Green Spot" gearbox options. Almost all of the wartime production was delivered on steel wheels.

High exhaust pipe

High rear mudguard

High ground clearance for engine

Specialized Vehicles

After the failed Dieppe Raid of 1942 exposed the difficulty of landing vehicles during an amphibious invasion, Allied commanders knew that getting tanks across the beaches of France would be a challenge. The job of developing suitable vehicles was given to Percy Hobart, the commander of the British 79th Armoured Division. Known as "Hobart's Funnies", these vehicles were based on tank hulls, which gave them similar mobility and protection, and made logistics easier. They were used in northwest Europe, Italy, and the Far East.

▽ Matilda CDL

Date 1940	**Origin** UK
Weight 26.9 tonnes (29.7 tons)	
Engine 2 x AEC 6 cylinder diesel, 95 hp each	
Main armament None	

The Canal Defence Light (CDL) was an attempt to dazzle the enemy during night fighting. The turret of the Matilda contained a 13-million candle power searchlight that flickered at a frequency that increased the blinding effect.

◁ **Valentine Bridgelayer**

Date 1943 **Origin** UK

Weight 19.9 tonnes (20 tons)

Engine AEC A189 gasoline, 135 hp

Main armament None

The first bridgelaying tanks were developed at the end of World War I, but it was not until World War II that they were used. The Scissors Bridge shown here could span a 9.2 m (30 ft) gap and support 30 tonne (33 ton) vehicles.

▽ **Sherman V Crab**

Date 1943 **Origin** US

Weight 32.2 tonnes (35.5 tons)

Engine Chrysler A57 Multibank gasoline, 425 hp

Main armament 75 mm M3 L/40 gun

Clearing minefields was a dangerous job, both because of the mines and because they were usually protected by enemy fire. Flail tanks, such as this Sherman V Crab, had to move in a straight line at less than 3.2 km/h (2 mph), while the rotating chains beat the ground with enough force to set off any mines.

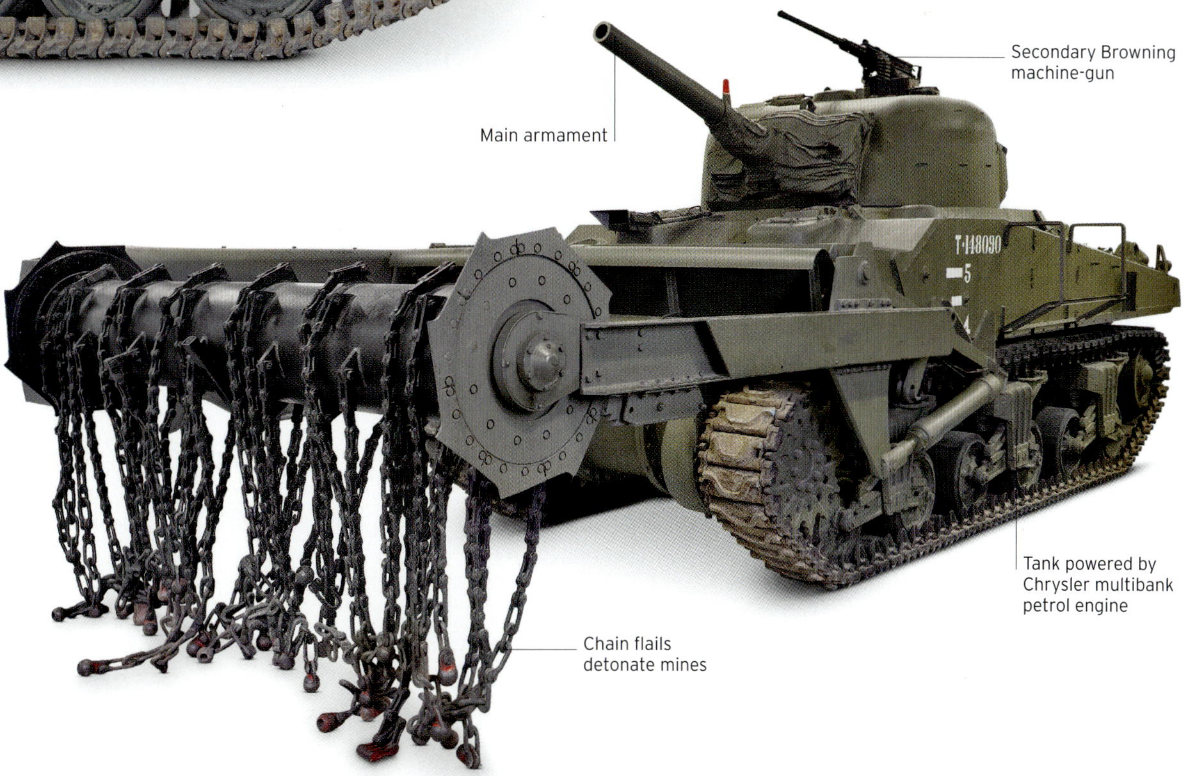

1945–91 THE COLD WAR

After World War II, developments in military technology were driven by the Cold War confrontation between the US and the Soviet Union. A nuclear arms race created weaponry of awesome destructive power, with peace maintained by the certainty of unbearable losses in the event of a nuclear war. At the same time, each side sought to surpass the other in every area of conventional military technology, from the performance of aircraft and submarines to the latest tanks and firearms.

EXHAUST
CLEAR
STEP

△ **AK47 Type 56S**

Date 1957	**Origin** China
Weight 5.13 kg (11¼ lb)	
Barrel 41.4 cm (16¼ in)	
Calibre 7.62 x 39 mm	

The most famous assault rifle in the world, the AK47 has undergone a number of changes over the years and has been widely copied. This Type 56S civilian variant was made in China.

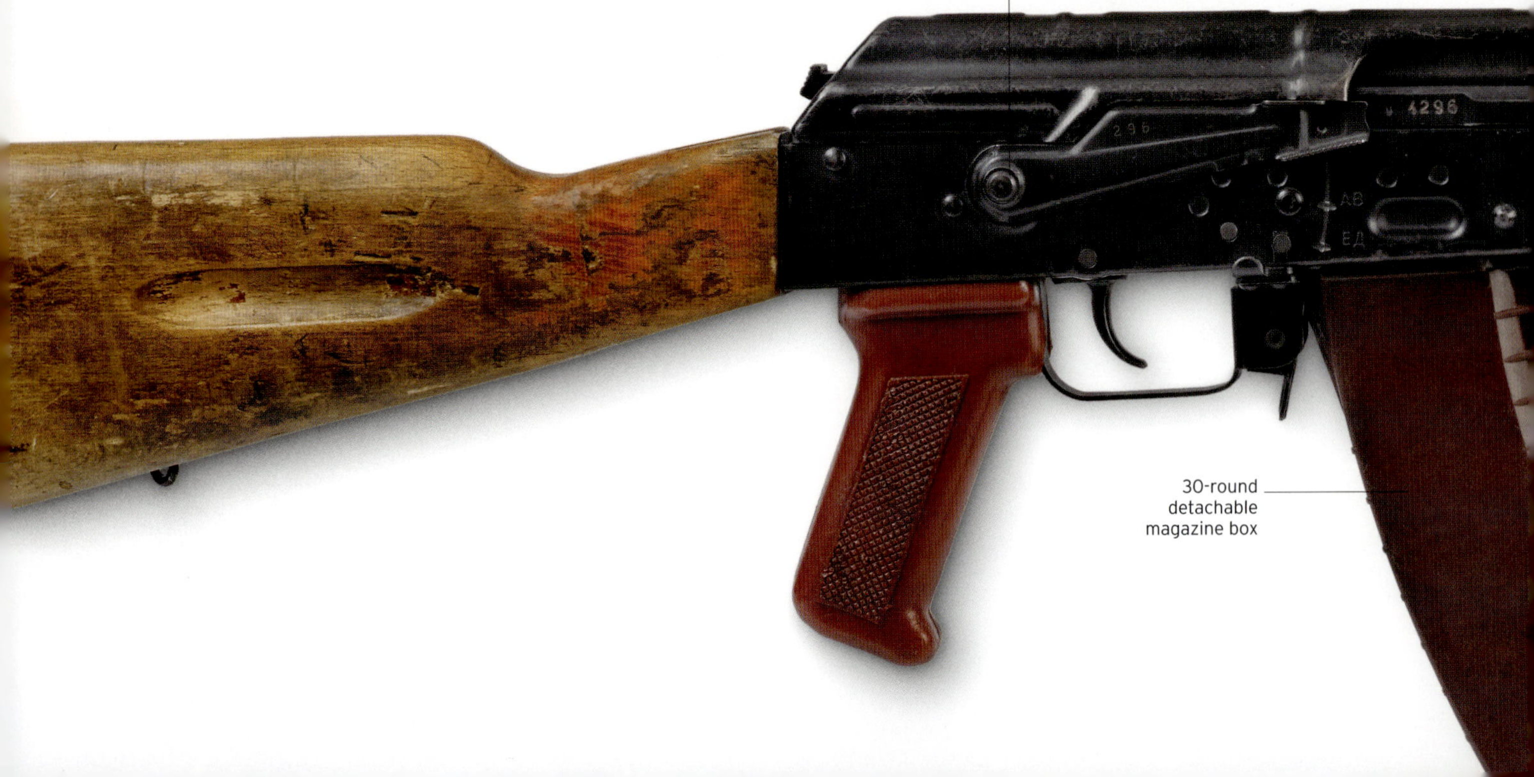

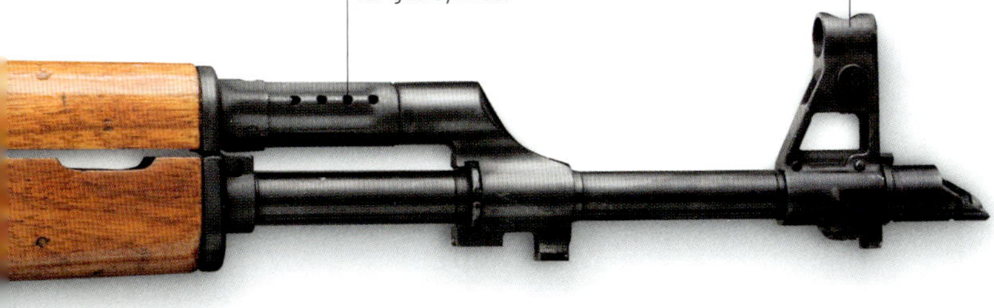

Assault Rifles

If there is a quintessential firearm of the Cold War period, it is the assault rifle, distinguished by its high-capacity magazine and ability to function in semi- or fully-automatic modes. Though the idea was first developed at the end of World War I, the assault rifle was technically born in 1949 when the AK47, designed by Soviet arms engineer Mikhail Kalashnikov, entered service. Now the weapon of choice on five continents, the assault rifle has become so well known that even its silhouette is immediately recognized by most people.

△ Stoner 63

Date 1963	**Origin** US
Weight 3.52 kg (7¾ lb)	
Barrel 50.8 cm (20 in)	
Calibre 5.56 x 45 mm	

Designed as a modular firearm, the Stoner 63 can be assembled to produce different variants that include a carbine, assault rifle (shown here), and several machine-gun configurations.

△ AK74

Date 1974	**Origin** Soviet Union
Weight 3.07 kg (6¾ lb)	
Barrel 41.5 cm (16¼ in)	
Calibre 5.45 x 39 mm	

In 1974, the design of the Kalashnikov (AK47) was modified to improve its performance. The calibre was reduced to 5.45 mm, stamped components replaced those that had been previously machined from solid steel, and a plastic magazine was substituted for the earlier metal version. This resulted in a much lighter rifle that still had the reliability of its predecessor.

FULL VIEW

Assault Rifles (cont.)

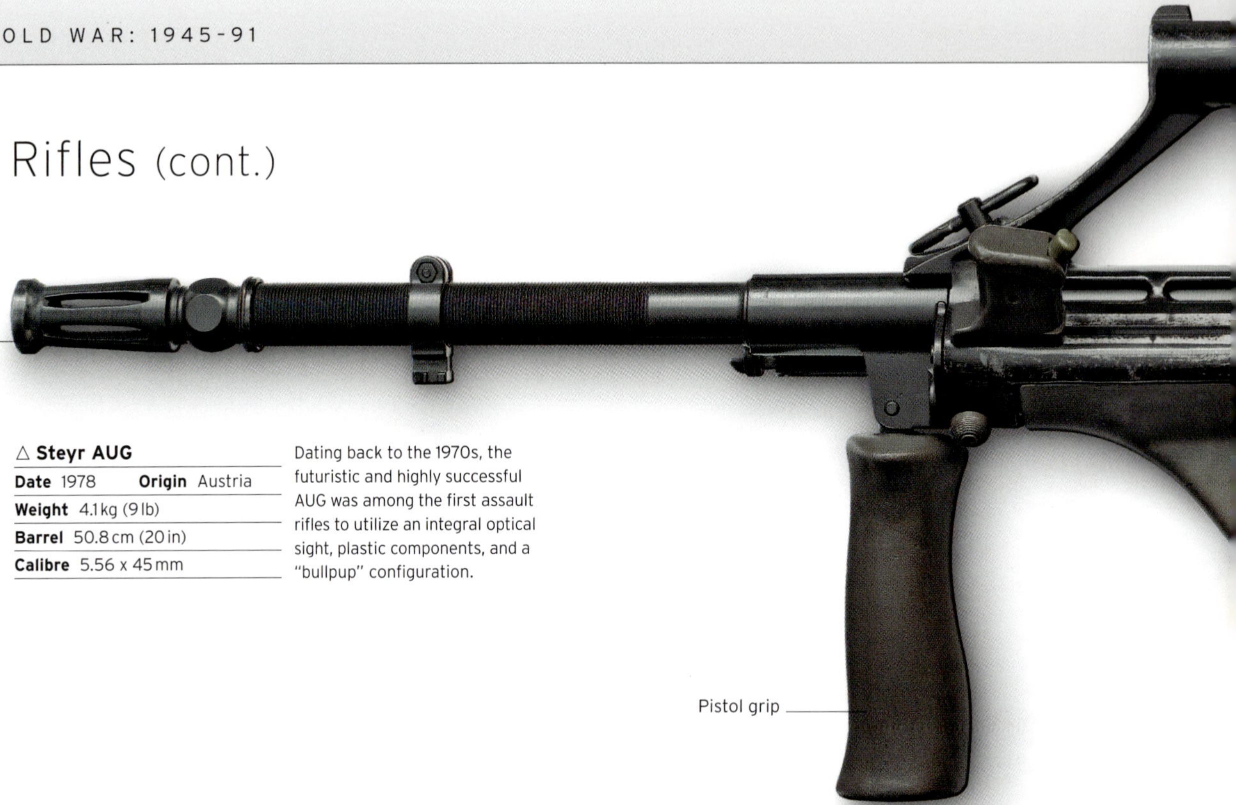

△ Steyr AUG

Date 1978	**Origin** Austria
Weight 4.1 kg (9 lb)	
Barrel 50.8 cm (20 in)	
Calibre 5.56 x 45 mm	

Dating back to the 1970s, the futuristic and highly successful AUG was among the first assault rifles to utilize an integral optical sight, plastic components, and a "bullpup" configuration.

▽ FAMAS F1

Date 1978	**Origin** France
Weight 3.61 kg (8 lb)	
Barrel 48.8 cm (19¼ in)	
Calibre 5.56 x 45 mm	

A "bullpup" design, the FAMAS F1 is a very compact weapon, and has been used by the French armed forces since the late 1970s. Like many assault rifles, it makes full use of plastics and metal stampings.

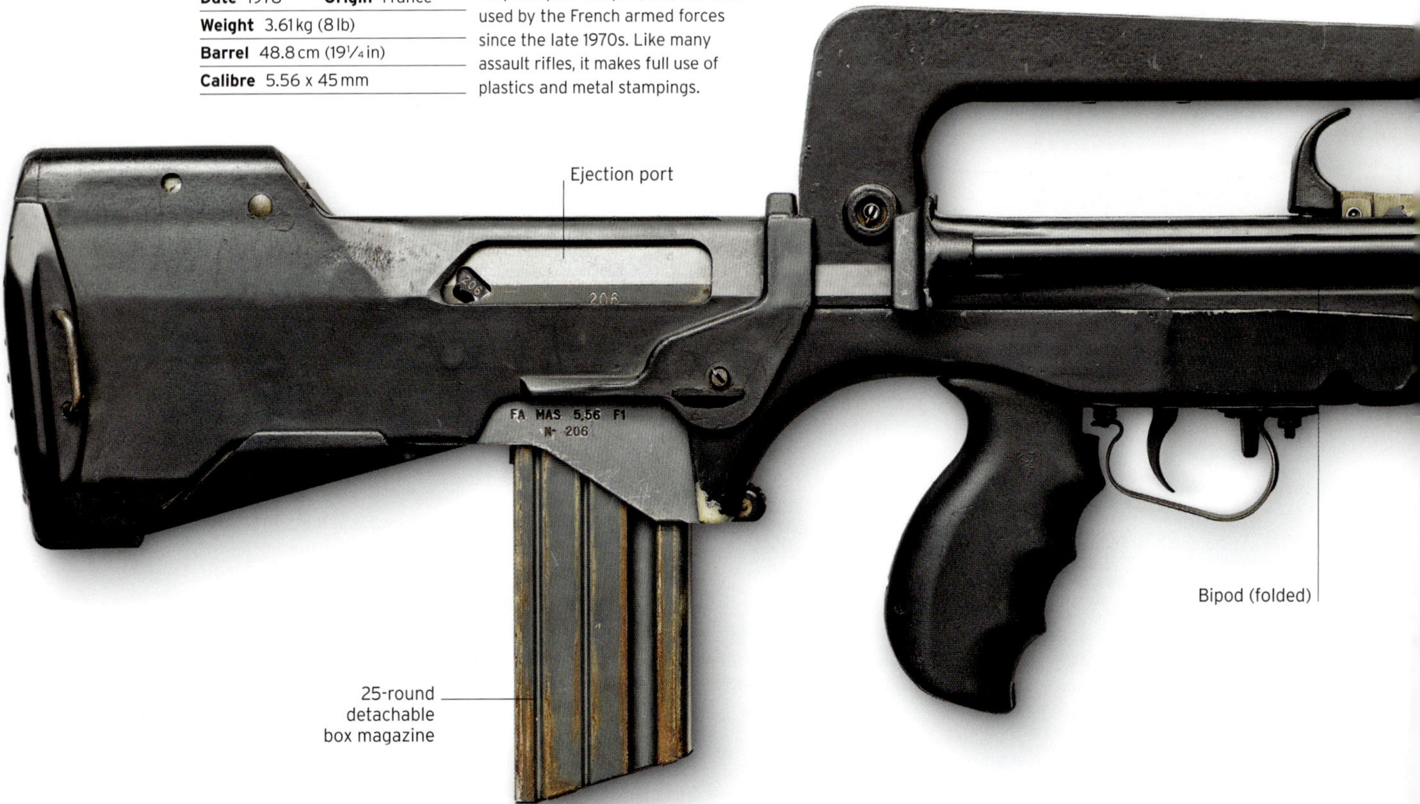

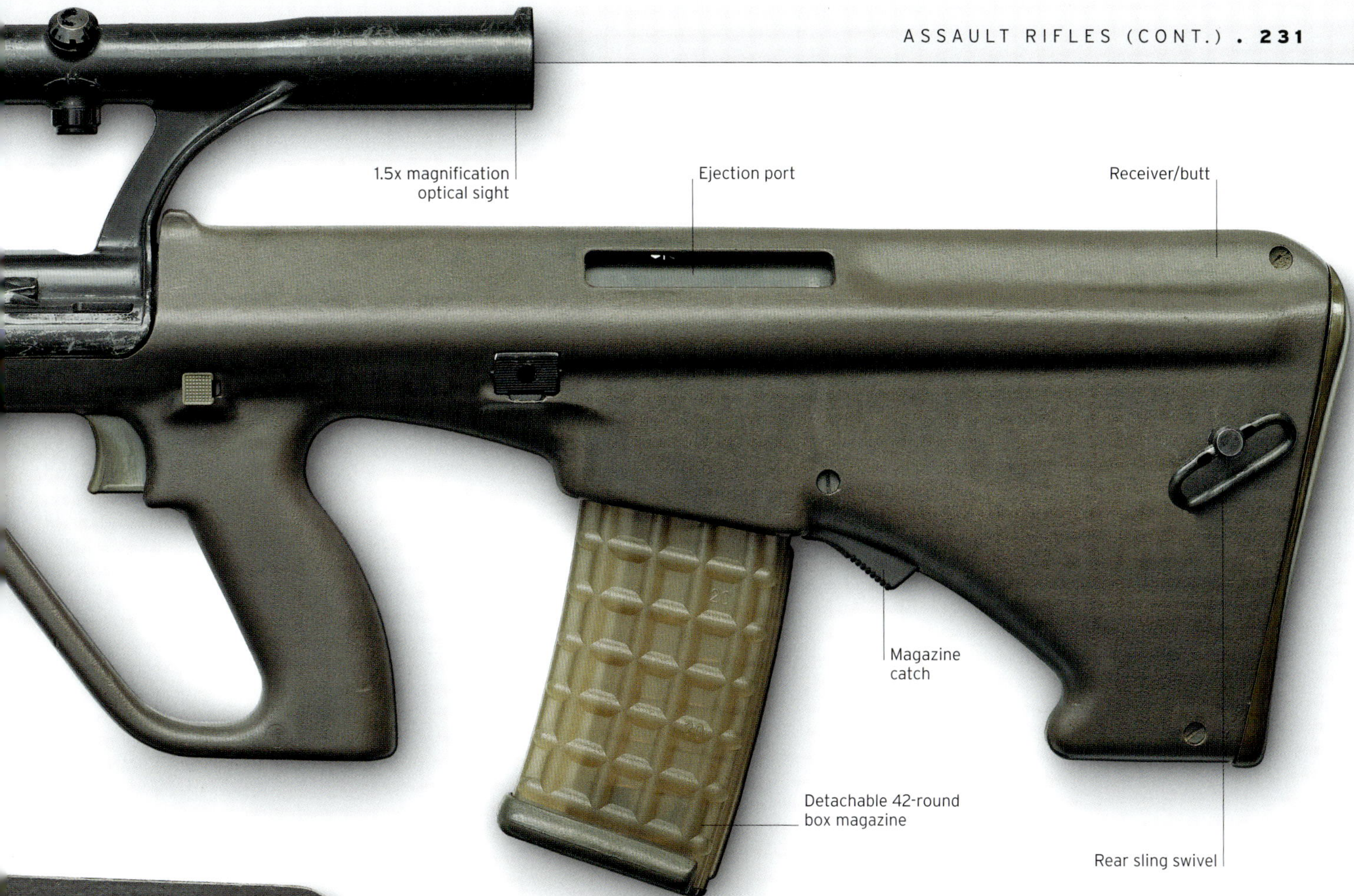

△ Heckler & Koch G41

Date 1981	**Origin** Germany
Weight 4.1kg (9lb)	
Barrel 45cm (18in)	
Calibre 5.56 x 45mm	

A progression from H&K's 7.62mm G3 rifle, the G41 was rechambered to take the 5.56 x 45mm NATO round, and could be fitted with other NATO standard features including a universal sight mount and magazine. It had limited military use.

△ **Degtyarev RP46**

Date 1946

Origin Soviet Union

Barrel 60.5 cm (23¾ in)

Calibre 7.62 x 54 mm

The Red Army adopted the Degtyarev DP in 1928. It was modified in 1945, and the following year it received a heavier barrel and was adapted to take belts as well as drum magazines, evolving into the RP46. It was still not entirely satisfactory, however, and was soon replaced by the RPD.

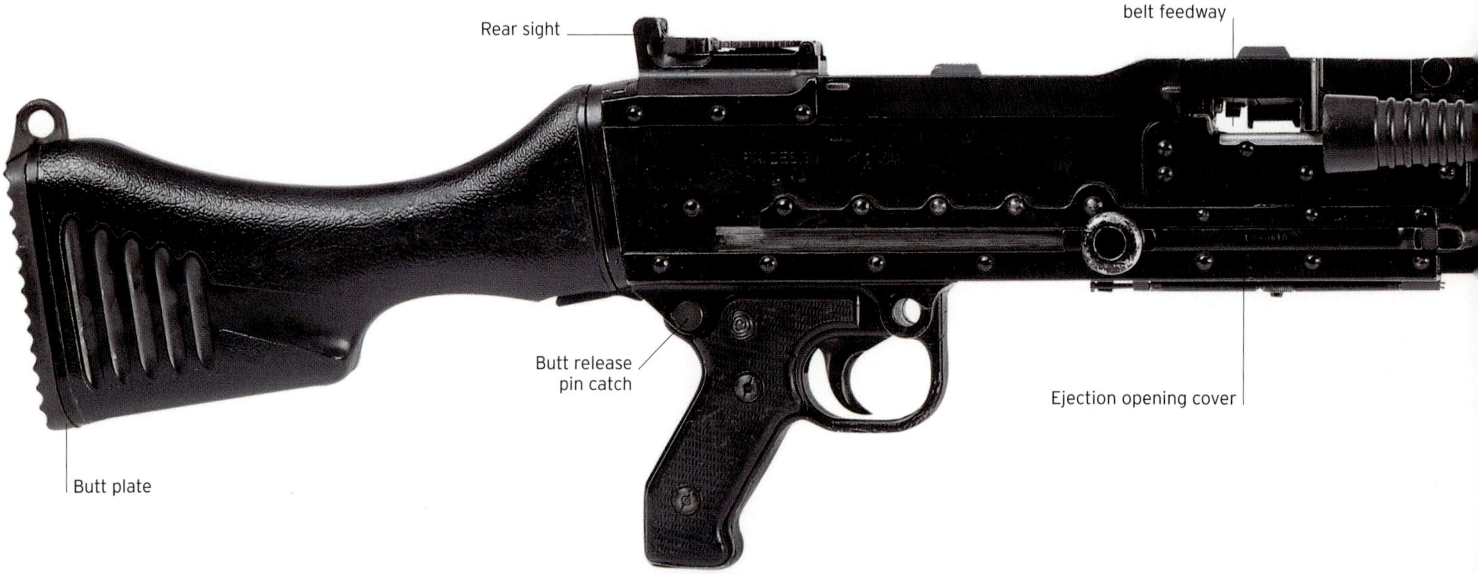

Machine-guns

During World War II, engagements took place at shorter ranges than before. This had two consequences after the war: the barrels of rifles and light machine-guns became shorter, and the rounds they fired became lower-powered and lighter. For the individual soldier, this meant a welcome reduction in the load he had to carry. More recently, weapons became lighter still when plastic replaced wood and bullpup configurations were introduced.

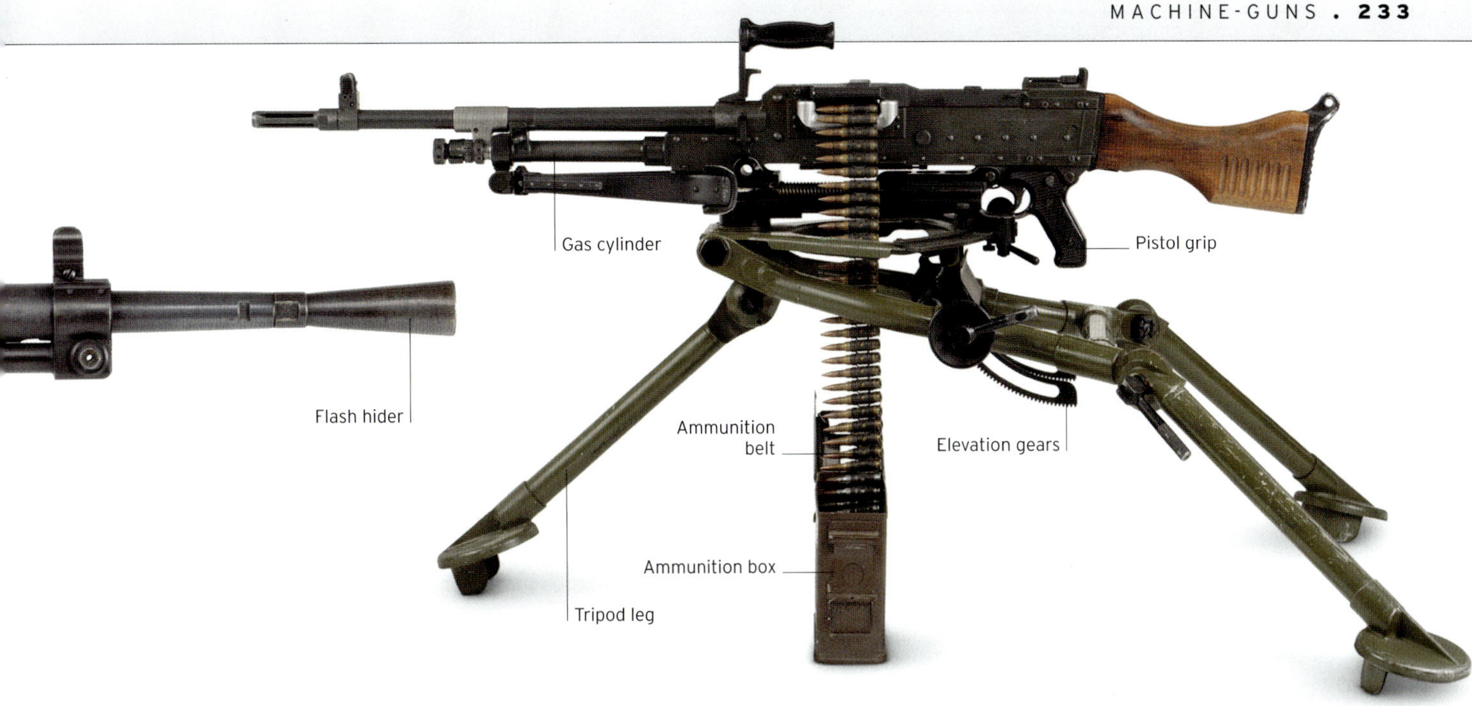

△ **FN MAG**

Date	1958
Origin	Belgium
Barrel	55 cm (21½ in)
Calibre	7.62 x 51 mm NATO

The MAG (*Mitrailleuse à Gaz*, meaning gas-operated machine-gun), produced by FN, used a modified form of the locking system developed by John Browning for his Automatic Rifle; this was married to the feed mechanism of the MG42.

△ **L7A2 Light Machine-gun**

Date	1960
Origin	UK
Barrel	70 cm (27½ in)
Calibre	7.62 x 51 mm NATO

The British L7A2 light machine-gun is essentially a copy of the Belgian FN MAG made under licence in Britain. It is a platoon support weapon of considerable versatility since it can also be used with fixed mounts on vehicles.

▷ **Uzi**	
Date	1950s
Origin	Israel
Barrel	26 cm (10¼ in)
Calibre	9 mm Parabellum

The secret of the Uzi's legendary stability lies in its bolt being wrapped around its barrel; this brings the centre of gravity forward and helps to cure the tendency for the barrel to rise during automatic fire. Heavy moving parts keep its rate of fire to a manageable 600 rounds per minute.

△ **Uzi 9 mm Steel Stock**	
Date	1950
Origin	Israel
Barrel	26 cm (10¼ in)
Calibre	9 mm Parabellum

While the original version of the Uzi was fitted with a conventional wooden butt, this proved unwieldy in confined quarters, such as aircraft or armoured vehicles. Consequently, a modified model was designed with a collapsible metal butt that greatly reduced the firearm's overall length when folded.

Submachine-guns

The second generation of submachine-guns, introduced during and just after World War II, were unsophisticated weapons, designed for mass-production rather than military efficiency. They produced devastating short-range firepower and a great deal of noise, but were notoriously inaccurate and difficult to control and, as a result, were of limited military value. More recently, developments have concentrated on applications for security forces and police.

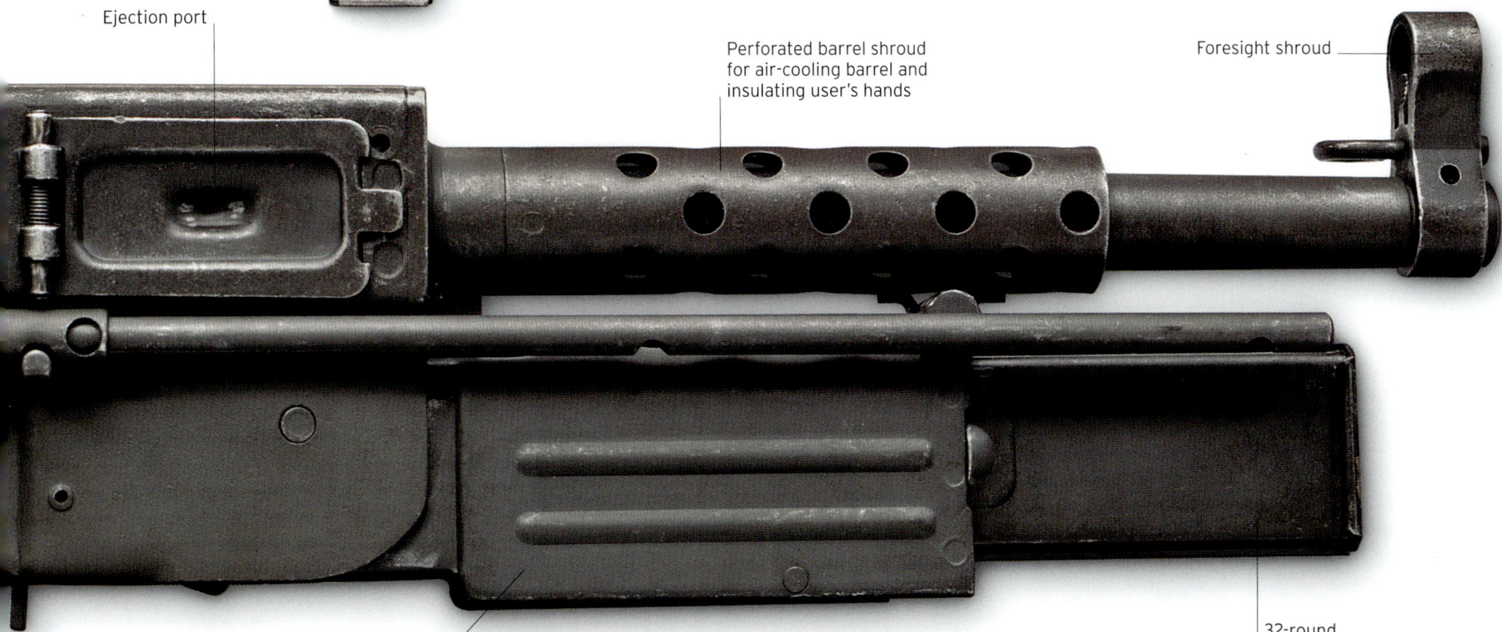

△ Manufacture Nationale d'Armes de Tulle (MAT) 49

Date 1950s

Origin France

Barrel 23 cm (9 in)

Calibre 9 mm Parabellum

The MAT 49's distinctive feature is its pivoting magazine housing; in addition to making the weapon easier to conceal, it's a very positive safety device because it takes the magazine out of the firing position. The gun saw widespread combat use during the First Indochina War (1946–54) and the Algerian War (1954–62), as well as in the 1956 Suez Crisis.

Optical sight
Safety catch and selective fire level
Magazine release catch
Composite shoulder stock
45-round box magazine

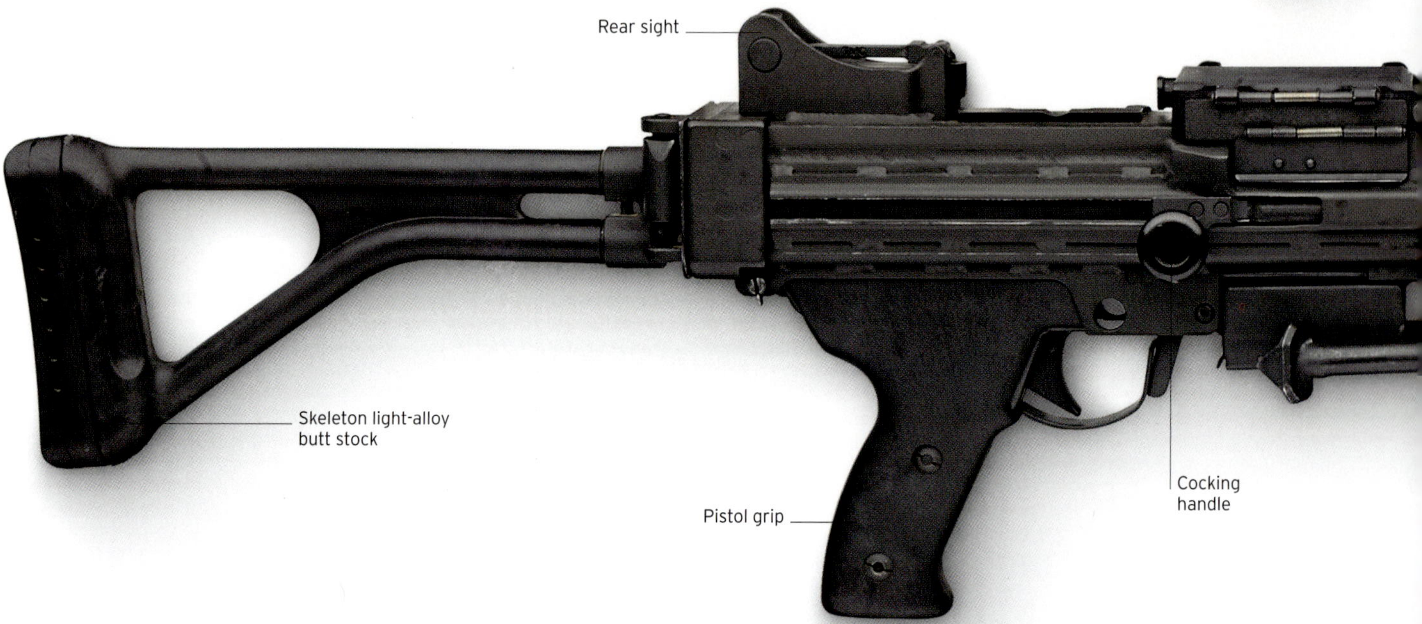
Rear sight
Skeleton light-alloy butt stock
Pistol grip
Cocking handle

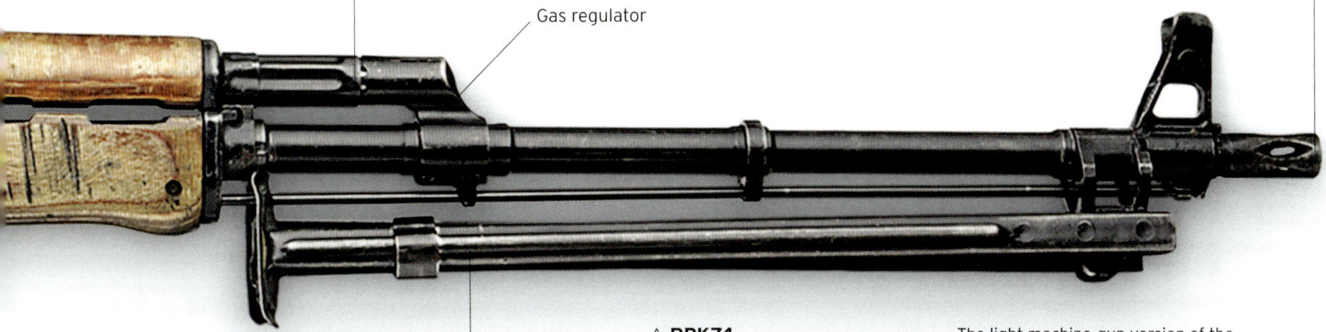

△ **RPK74**

Date 1974	**Origin** Soviet Union
Weight 4.7 kg (10¼ lb)	
Barrel 59 cm (23¼ in)	
Calibre 5.45 x 39 mm	

The light machine-gun version of the infantryman's AK74 assault rifle, this weapon features a heavier barrel, which is chrome-lined like the band of the AK74. It also has a modified receiver, a bipod, and an extended magazine. It fires up to 650 rounds per minute.

▽ **Negev**

Date 1988	**Origin** Israel
Weight 7.2 kg (15¾ lb)	
Barrel 46 cm (18 in)	
Calibre 5.56 mm	

Israel Military Industries' Negev is one of a breed of lightweight automatic weapons that has blurred the distinction between LMG and GPMG. Chambered for the SS109 NATO bullet in 5.56 mm calibre, it can deliver automatic fire at 700 or 900 rounds per minute (rpm).

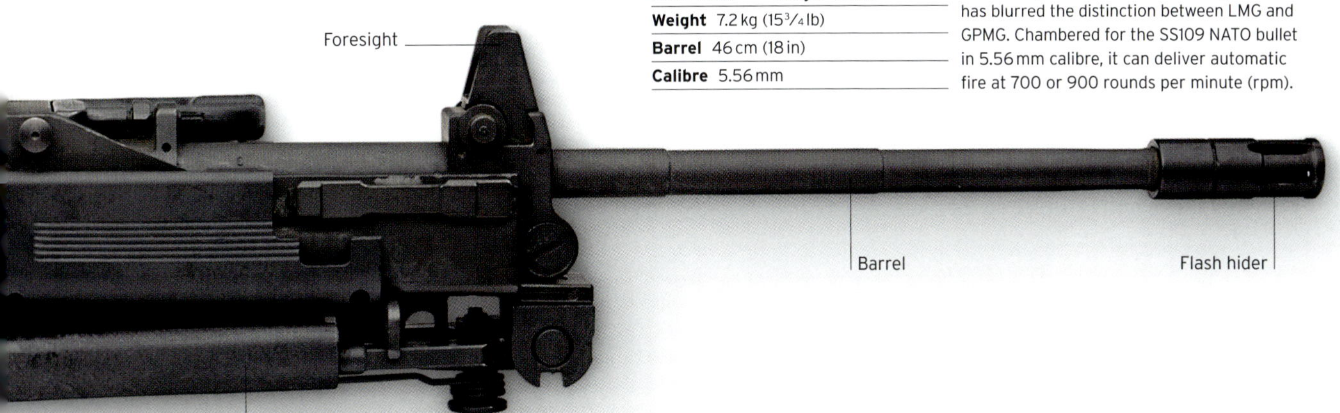

Infantry Firepower

Although the modern assault rifle is a highly capable weapon, it lacks sufficient firepower to support infantry fighting on its own. For this reason, portable weapons with greater firepower were developed. The light machine-gun (LMG) is one of the oldest support weapons capable of providing sustained automatic fire. At the next level is the grenade launcher that is more powerful, followed by the mortar, which provides infantry with miniaturized artillery.

Self-loading Pistols

Modern self-loading pistols differ little from their predecessors visually. However, their construction now involves an increased use of carbon composites, plastics, and lightweight metal alloys. Another key development is that their grips are designed to allow the use of high-capacity magazines capable of holding up to 20 rounds. The profile of the forward trigger guard bow has also become more vertical and grooved, a configuration that allows shooters to hold a pistol securely with both hands.

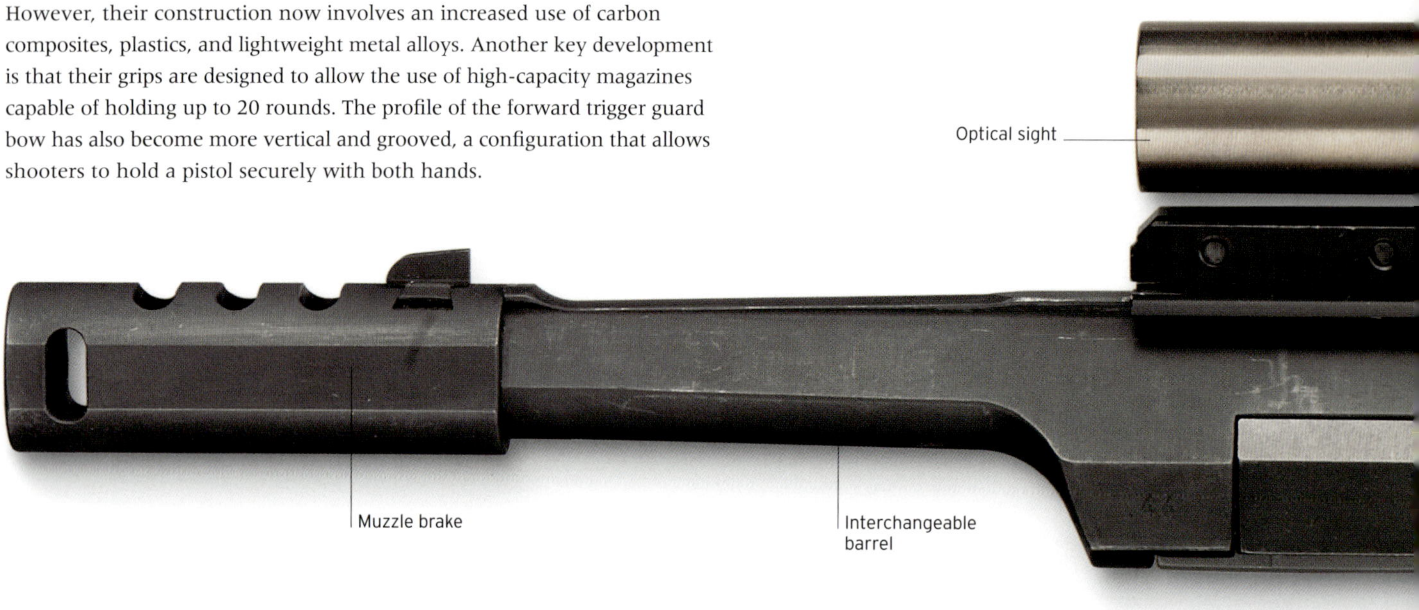

▽ Heckler & Koch VP70M

Date 1970s	**Origin** Germany
Weight 1.55 kg (3 lb) including stock	
Barrel 11.6 cm (4½ in)	
Calibre 9 mm Parabellum	

The VP70M, the first pistol to make extensive use of plastic, was an attempt to produce a fully automatic handgun, although limited to firing three-round bursts. The mechanism that controlled this was housed in the detachable butt; when it was removed, the pistol reverted to normal semi-automatic operation.

△ **IMI Desert Eagle**

Date 1983	**Origin** Israel
Weight 2.66 kg (5 lb)	
Barrel 25.4 cm (10 in)	
Calibre .44 in Magnum	

Unlike almost all other self-loading pistols, the Desert Eagle, made by Israel Military Industries (IMI), was gas-operated, and of modular design. Its standard frame was able to accept sets of components for different ammunition, from .357 in Magnum to .5 in Action Express (AE), and barrels of different lengths.

US Marines Weapons

One of the four armed service branches of the US Department of Defense, the United States Marine Corps was founded in 1775 during the Revolutionary War and has been in active service since 1798. The Marines are part of the US Department of the Navy and work closely with naval forces for the purposes of training, transport, and logistics. Working on land and sea, they are one of the main exponents of amphibious warfare.

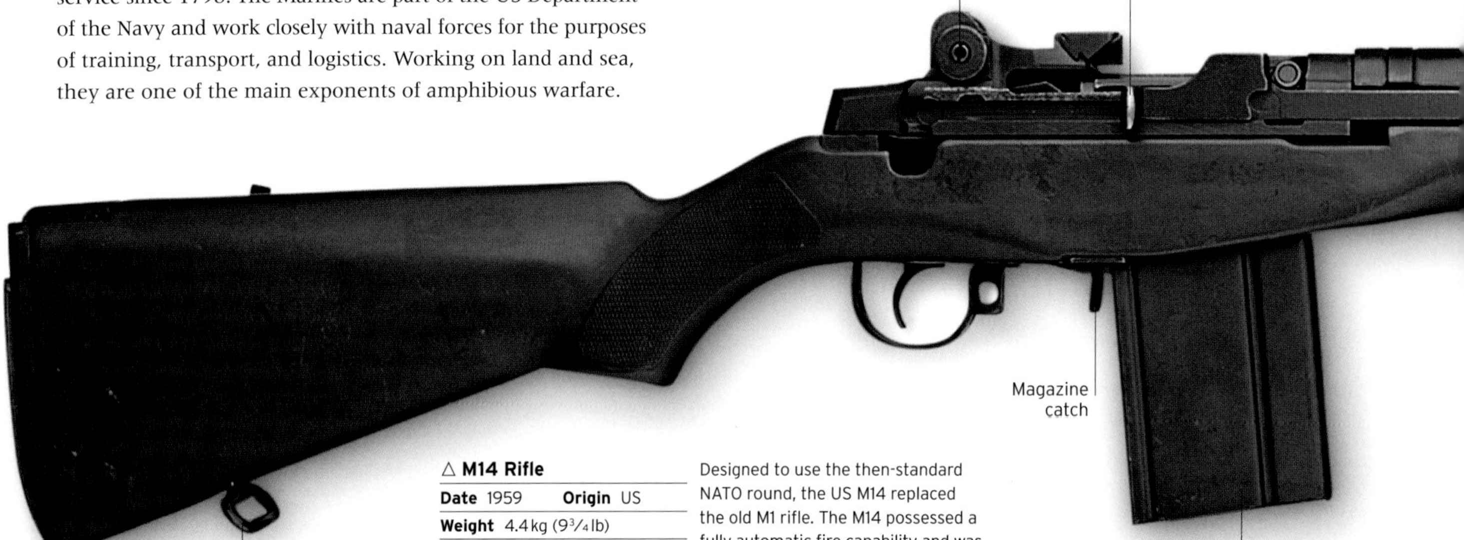

△ **M14 Rifle**

Date 1959	**Origin** US
Weight 4.4 kg (9¾ lb)	
Barrel 55.8 cm (22 in)	
Calibre 7.62 mm	

Designed to use the then-standard NATO round, the US M14 replaced the old M1 rifle. The M14 possessed a fully automatic fire capability and was equipped with a larger magazine. By the late 1960s, it was replaced by the M16.

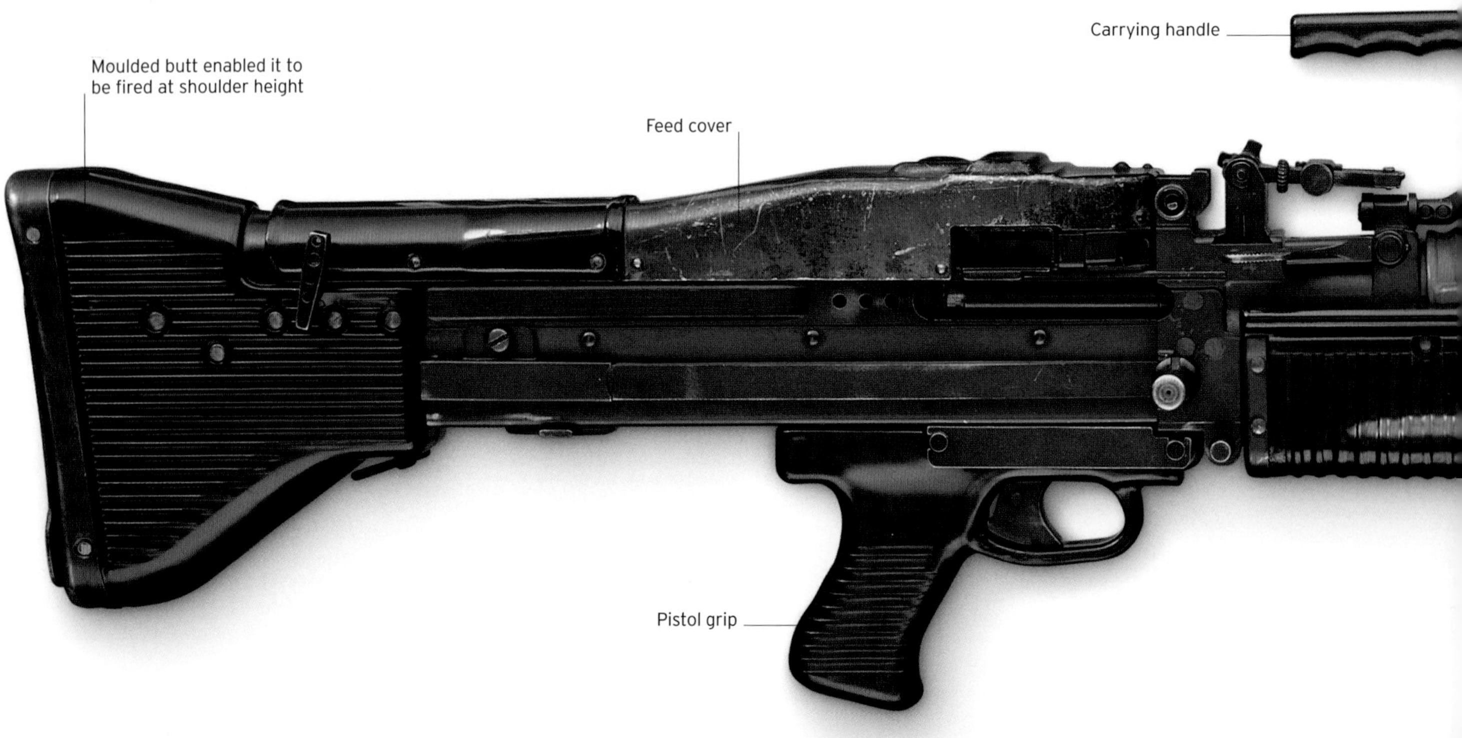

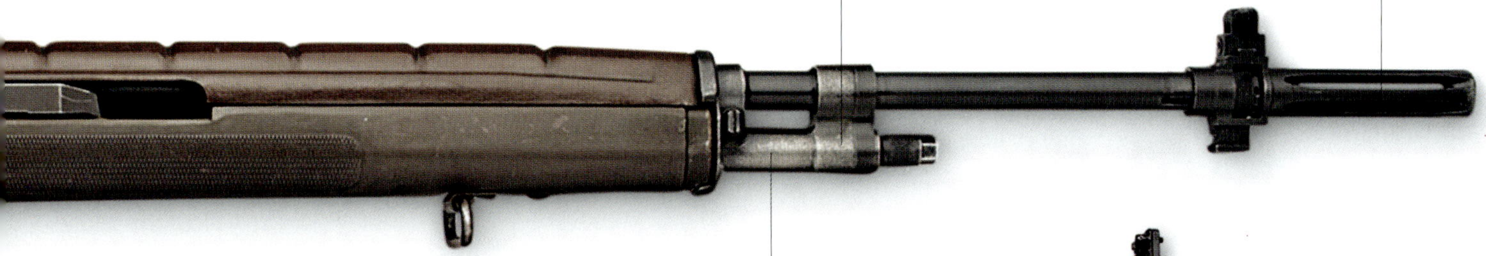

△ M79 Grenade Launcher

Date 1961	**Origin** US
Weight 2.75 kg (6 lb)	
Barrel 30.5 cm (12 in)	
Calibre 40 mm	

With a maximum range of 300 m (985 ft), the M79 grenade launcher bridged the gap between the hand grenade and the mortar. As well as firing high explosive, the M79 could fire antipersonnel, smoke, and illuminating rounds. Two were issued to each rifle squad.

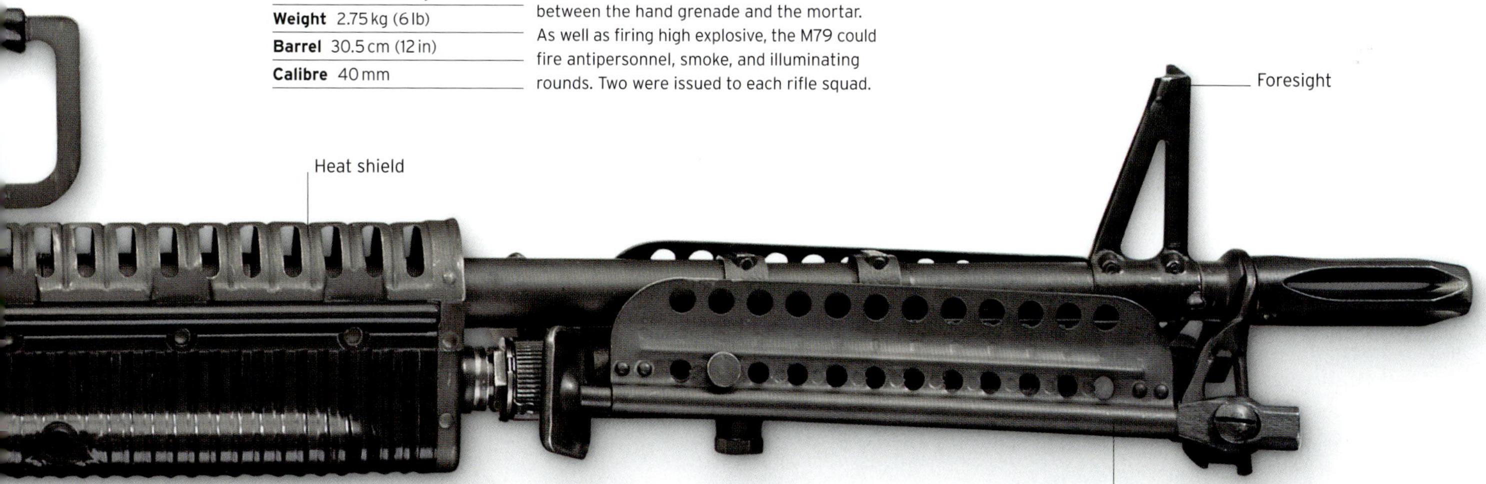

△ M60 Machine-gun

Date 1963	**Origin** US
Weight 10.51 kg (23 lb)	
Barrel 59.9 cm (23½ in)	
Calibre 7.62 mm	

The M60 was the US example of the general-purpose machine-gun – inheriting some design features from the German MG42. It was widely used by the US Marine Corps in Vietnam and is still in service today.

Helicopter power
Helicopters proved useful to the US Forces fighting in Vietnam after 1965. They were used to carry in troops and supplies, and to airlift out casualties. Here, a Chinook lowers supplies to the US Marine Corps in the Khe Sanh Combat Base, in South Vietnam, as the GIs try to avoid the airstream created by the rotor blades.

△ Franchi SPAS 12

Date 1978 **Origin** Italy

Weight 4.4 kg ($9\frac{3}{4}$ lb)

Barrel 54.5 cm ($21\frac{1}{2}$ in)

Calibre 12-bore

Developed as a close-combat weapon for both police and military, the Special Purpose Automatic Shotgun (SPAS) is gas-operated (with an optional pump mode) and holds eight rounds in an under-barrel tubular magazine.

▽ Heckler & Koch MP5A5

Date 1966 **Origin** Germany

Weight 2.82 kg ($6\frac{1}{4}$ lb)

Barrel 22.5 cm ($8\frac{3}{4}$ in)

Calibre 9 mm Parabellum

The MP5A5 is a plastic-stock version of the MP5. Here the multi-purpose arm is featured in combination with a mounted grenade launcher built by the British company ISTEC.

Special Forces Weapons

Special Forces units are sometimes required to deploy specialized weapons. Rock-solid reliability is a precondition for any such selection; a high level of firepower makes small arms such as the Franchi shotgun and the Glock pistol popular choices. At other times, stealth weapons are needed. The most interesting recent development has been the Personal Defense Weapon (PDW), an example of which is the FN P90. This dispenses with the old Parabellum submachine-gun cartridge in favour of a smaller but more powerful round that can penetrate body armour.

▷ FN P90

Date	1990	**Origin**	Belgium
Weight	2.68 kg (6 lb)		
Barrel	26.3 cm (10¼ in)		
Calibre	5.7 x 28 mm		

A ground-breaking PDW, the FN P90's nonmechanical body components are all moulded from plastic, and its unique horizontal ammunition feed allows the magazine to be incorporated within the receiver.

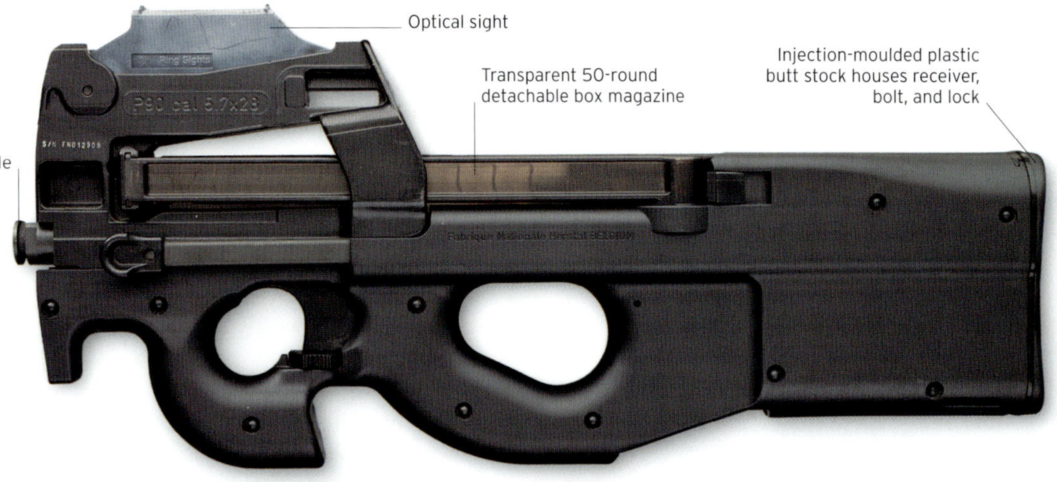

Disguised Firearms

Since the 16th century, attempts have been made to disguise firearms as other objects. Although early ignition systems prevented any degree of effective disguise, the introduction of the self-contained metallic cartridge made it possible. As a result, from the mid-19th century onwards, firearms have been made in the form of canes, umbrellas, pens, and more. These arms are effective only at close range, and civilian use of them is frowned upon because the weapons could be utilized for nefarious purposes, such as assassinations.

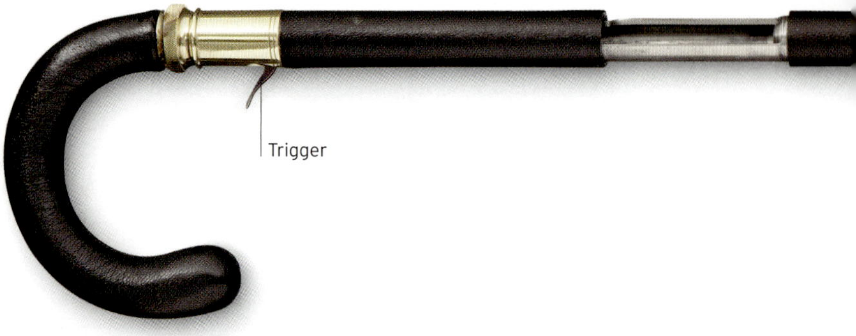

▽ **Cigarette Lighter Pistol**	
Date	1970s
Origin	Not known
Barrel	4 cm (1½ in)
Calibre	.22 in

What appears to be a cigarette lighter actually contains a single-shot pistol. The trigger is of a clasp type and runs up the side of the "gun" body. It is not known which country produced this firearm, but it was made in the 1970s.

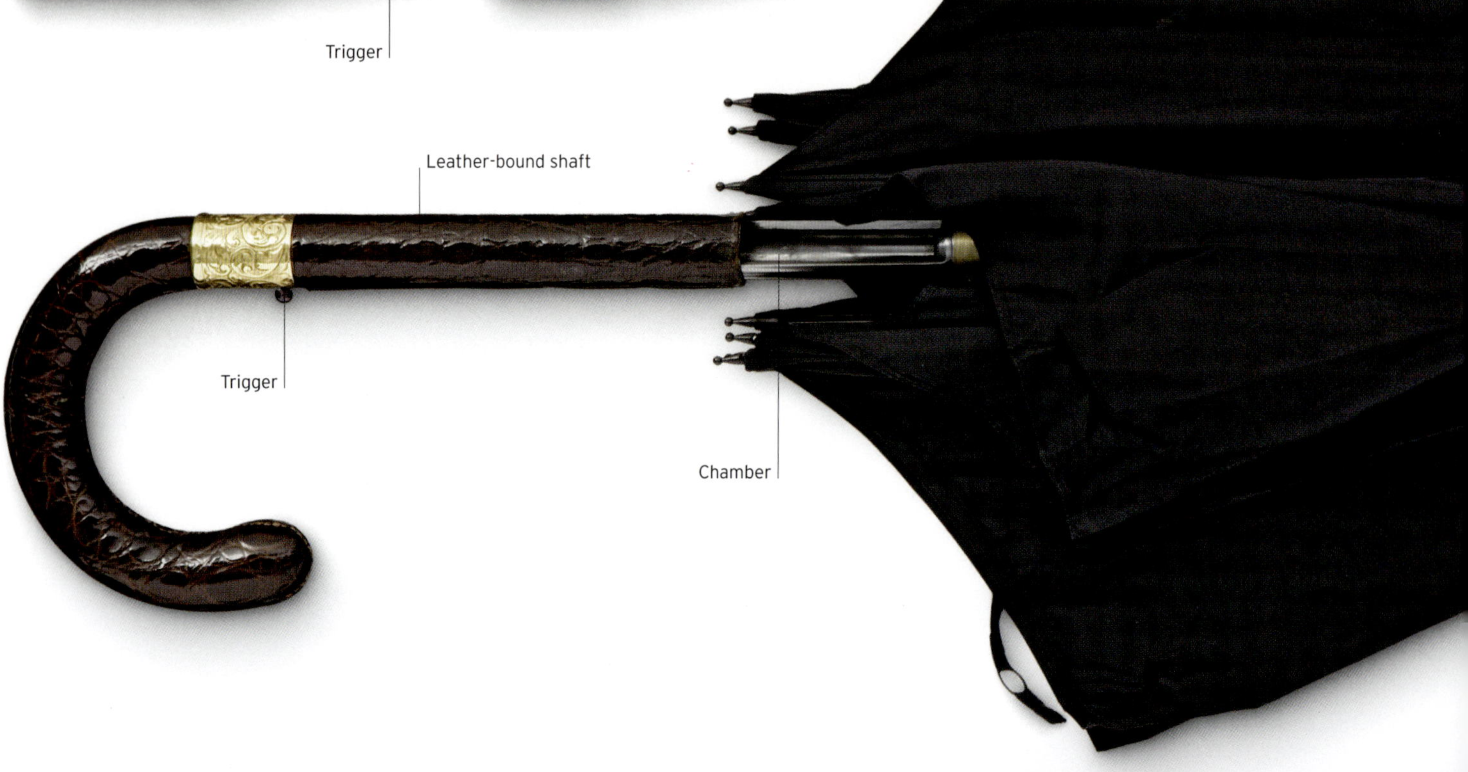

△ Wilson Cane Gun

Date 1984

Origin UK

Barrel Not known

Calibre .410 in

This cane gun is a "gentry gun" produced by the same gunmaker who made the Wilson umbrella gun (below). With a calibre of .410 in and a range of up to 23 m (25 yards), it would have been suitable for poaching.

△ Flashlight Stinger

Date 1980s

Origin US

Barrel 5 cm (2 in)

Calibre .22 in

This covert weapon is disguised as a flashlight and actually contains a .22in single-shot firearm. The bullet is loaded behind the flashlight's bulb section and is fired by depressing the light switch.

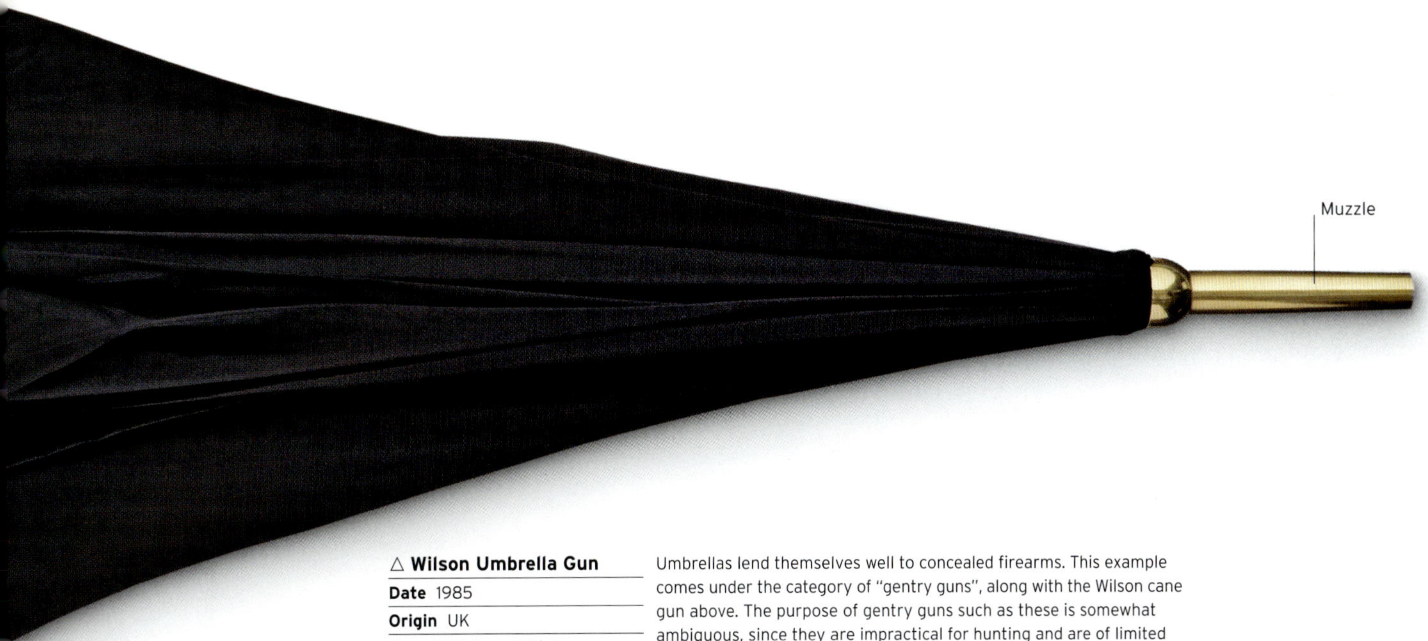

△ Wilson Umbrella Gun

Date 1985

Origin UK

Barrel 76.2 cm (30 in)

Calibre .410 in

Umbrellas lend themselves well to concealed firearms. This example comes under the category of "gentry guns", along with the Wilson cane gun above. The purpose of gentry guns such as these is somewhat ambiguous, since they are impractical for hunting and are of limited power for self-defence. This umbrella gun has a centre-fire mechanism around its barrel. However, it is not licensed for sporting use in the US.

Cold War Sniper Rifles

Whether used by military forces or the police, bolt-action sniper rifles, such as the L96A1, represent the epitome of accuracy. Though some are quite plain and closely resemble sporting arms, others are equipped with stocks that can be adjusted to the user's personal preferences and bipods to provide steady support. In common with their single-shot counterparts, self-loading sniper rifles are capable of firing multiple rounds in quick succession and are designed to provide accurate fire at long distances.

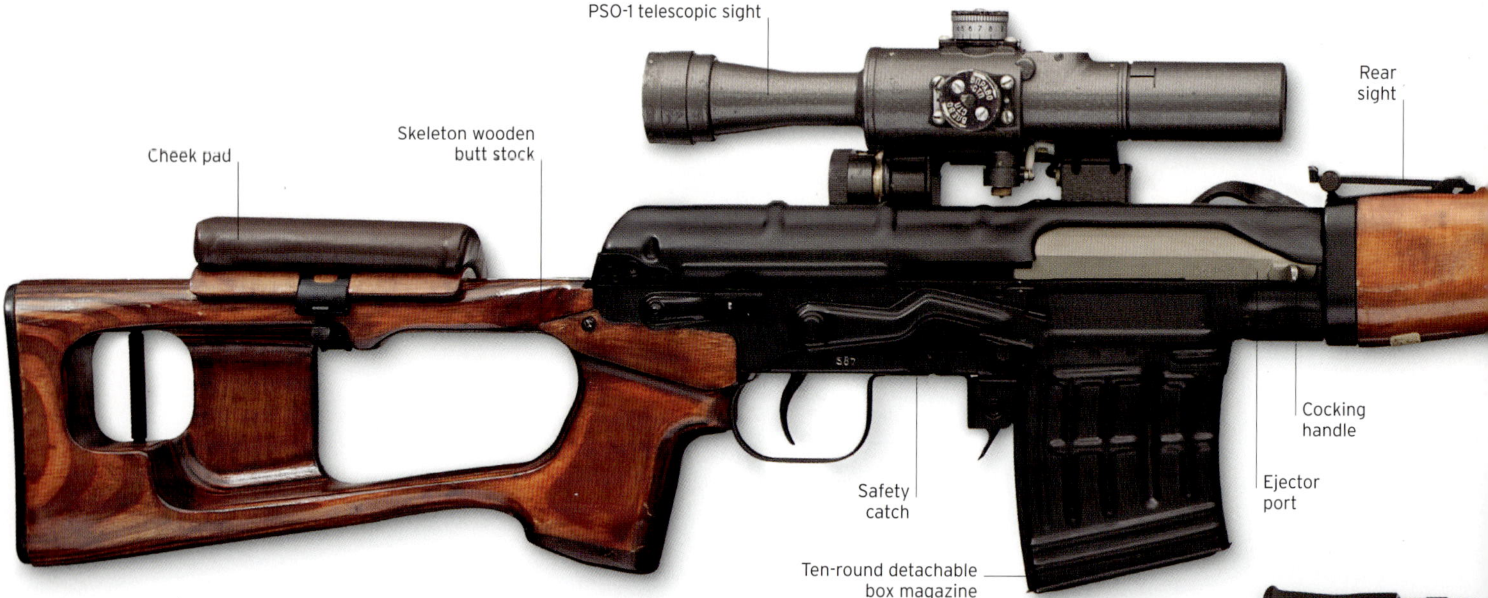

△ Dragunov SVD

Date	1963	**Origin**	Soviet Union
Weight	4.3 kg (9½ lb)		
Barrel	61 cm (24 in)		
Calibre	7.62 x 54R		

The Snaiperskaya Vintovka Dragunova (chambered for the rimmed 7.62 mm round developed for the "3-line" Mosin-Nagant rifle in 1891) was adopted by the Soviet bloc armies in 1963. Its PSO-1 telescopic sight has a limited infrared capability.

▷ Walther WA2000

Date	1978	**Origin**	Germany
Weight	6.95 kg (15¼ lb)		
Barrel	65 cm (25½ in)		
Calibre	.300 Win Mag/7.62 mm		

Developed primarily for police use, the WA2000 employed a "bullpup" configuration and a semi-automatic action fed by a six-round magazine. High manufacturing costs ended its production in 1988.

△ **L96A1**

Date 1984	**Origin** UK
Weight 6.5 kg (14¼ lb)	
Barrel 65.5 cm (25¾ in)	
Calibre 7.62 x 51 mm	

The British Army's L96A1 sniper rifle was the first to be developed specifically for sniping, and it became the forerunner of a whole series of sniper rifles produced in a variety of calibres.

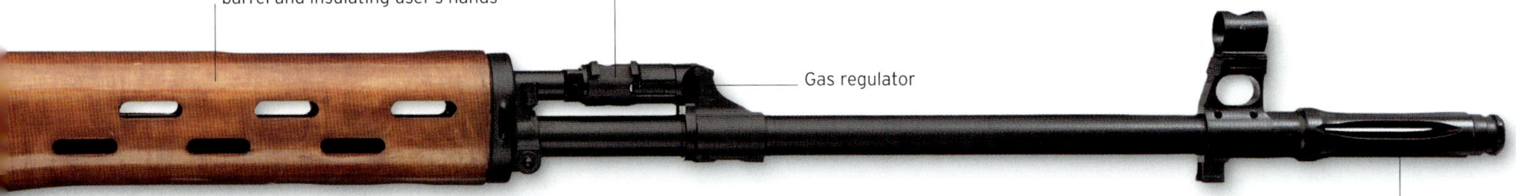

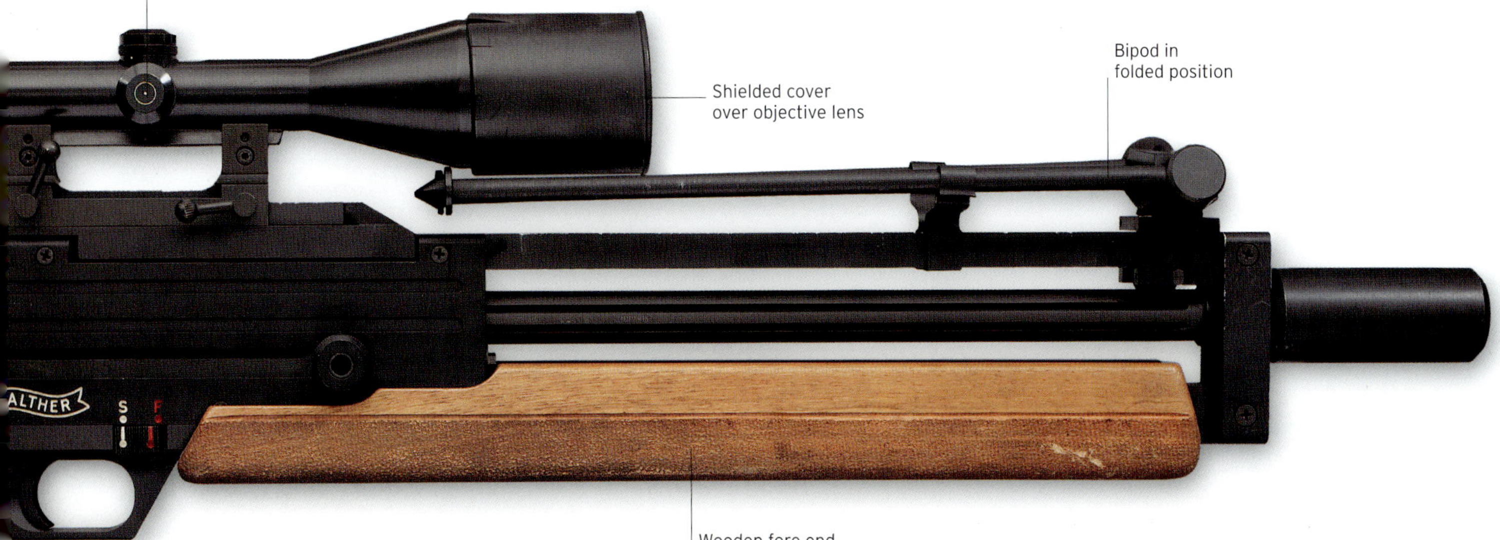

Improvised Firearms

When ammunition is at hand, there is a temptation to fashion a weapon capable of firing it. In its crudest form, this need be no more than a piece of tubing of roughly the right diameter, a nail to act as a striker, and a means of propelling it with enough force to detonate the primer in the cartridge. Discharging such a device is likely to be at least as dangerous to the person holding the weapon as to the intended victim.

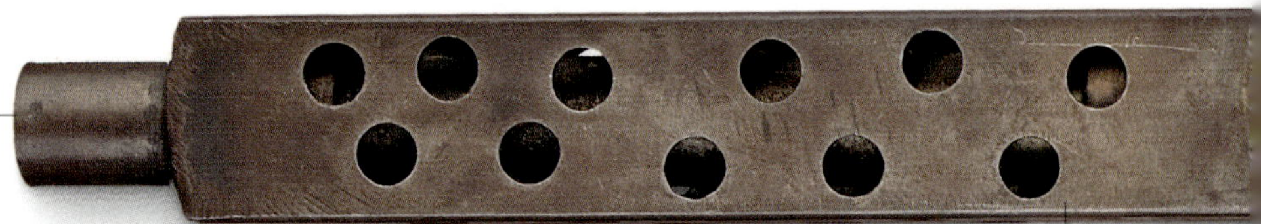

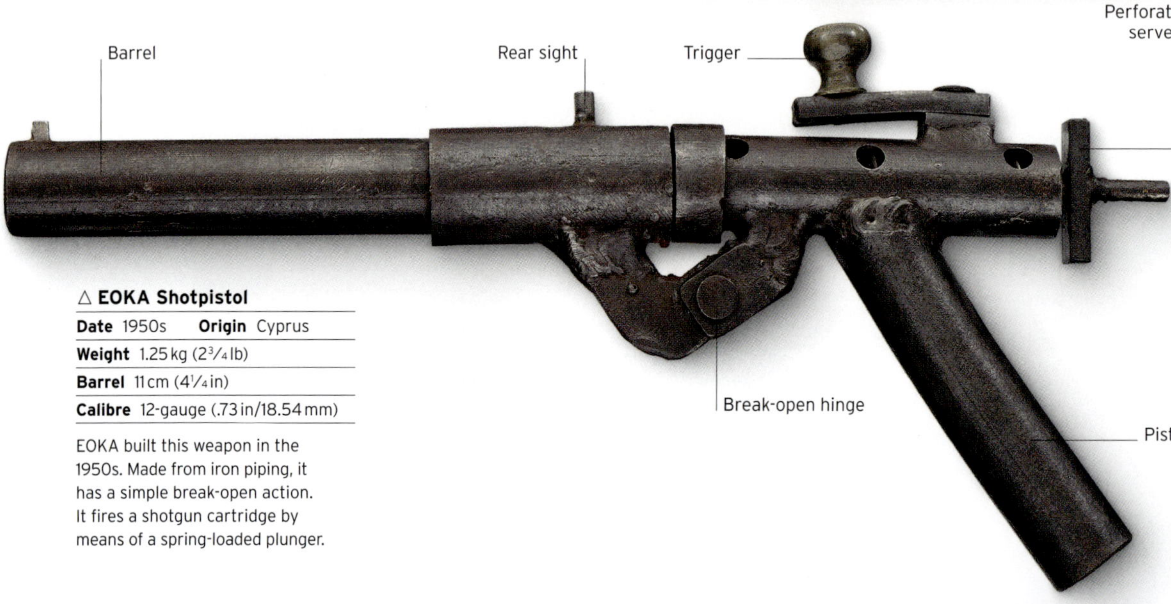

△ EOKA Shotpistol

Date 1950s	**Origin** Cyprus
Weight 1.25 kg (2³⁄₄ lb)	
Barrel 11 cm (4¹⁄₄ in)	
Calibre 12-gauge (.73 in/18.54 mm)	

EOKA built this weapon in the 1950s. Made from iron piping, it has a simple break-open action. It fires a shotgun cartridge by means of a spring-loaded plunger.

△ Mau-Mau Carbine

Date 1950s	**Origin** Kenya
Weight 1.6 kg (3½ lb)	
Barrel 51.2 cm (20¼ in)	
Calibre .303 in	

Somewhat more sophisticated than many of its type, this short-barrelled, bolt-action, single-shot carbine was made in Kenya during the time of the Mau-Mau insurrection against British rule in the 1950s. Most of the improvised weapons made by the rebels, the majority of whom were from the Kikuyu people, exploded when they were fired.

△ Loyalist Submachine-gun

Date 1970s	**Origin** UK
Weight 2.6 kg (5¾ lb)	
Barrel 20 cm (7¾ in)	
Calibre 9 mm Parabellum	

Modelled on the vintage Sten gun from World War II, this homemade machine-pistol was produced by a loyalist paramilitary group in Northern Ireland. The barrel shroud and receiver have been fashioned from square-framed tubing. This gun uses a magazine from an L2 Stirling submachine-gun.

Grenade Launchers

Although rifle-mounted grenade launchers remain widely used, there are times when they are not suitable: for example, when non-lethal 40 mm grenades are used for riot-control purposes. On the battlefield, rapid-fire launchers have come to supersede light mortars, since not only can they be used in the direct- and indirect-fire role (against visible and invisible targets, the latter on a compass bearing) but they can also put down a greater weight of bombs.

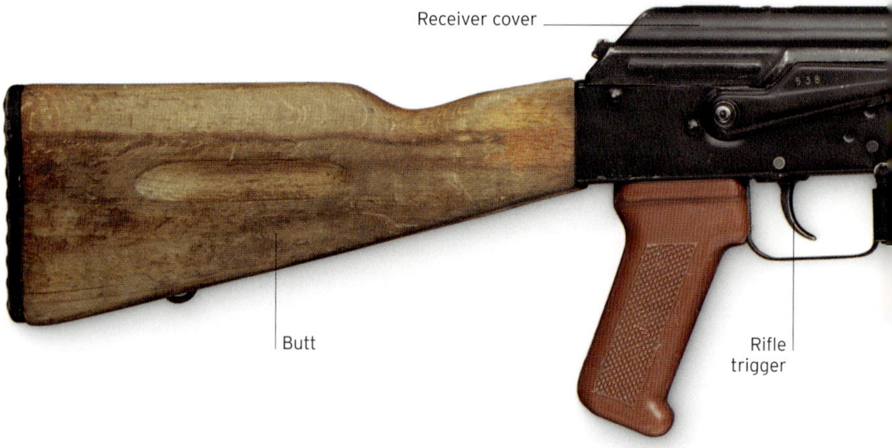

▷ **AGS-17 "PLAMYA"**

Date	1975
Origin	Soviet Union
Barrel	30 cm (11¾ in)
Calibre	30 mm
Grenade range	1.7 km (1 mile)

This recoil-operated gun is the Soviet equivalent of the American 40 mm M19 that was first used in the Vietnam War. Like the M19, the AGS-17 is a belt-fed, air-cooled launcher. Such weapons are commonly mounted in ground vehicles, boats, and hovercraft, and aboard helicopters and fixed-wing aircraft.

FULL VIEW

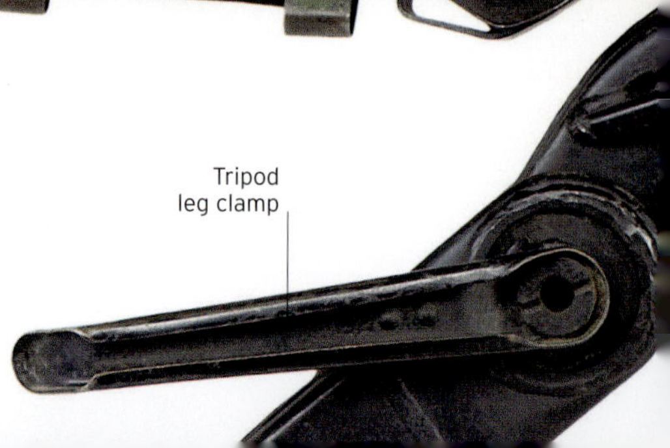

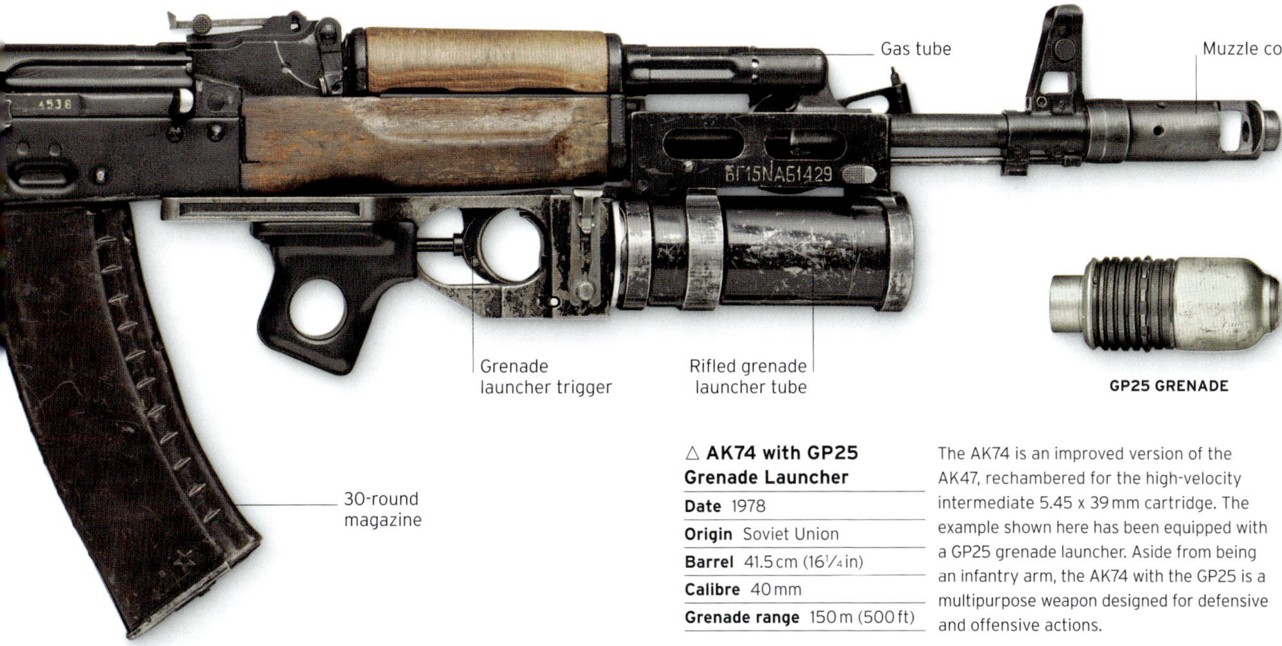

GP25 GRENADE

△ AK74 with GP25 Grenade Launcher

Date	1978
Origin	Soviet Union
Barrel	41.5 cm (16¼ in)
Calibre	40 mm
Grenade range	150 m (500 ft)

The AK74 is an improved version of the AK47, rechambered for the high-velocity intermediate 5.45 x 39 mm cartridge. The example shown here has been equipped with a GP25 grenade launcher. Aside from being an infantry arm, the AK74 with the GP25 is a multipurpose weapon designed for defensive and offensive actions.

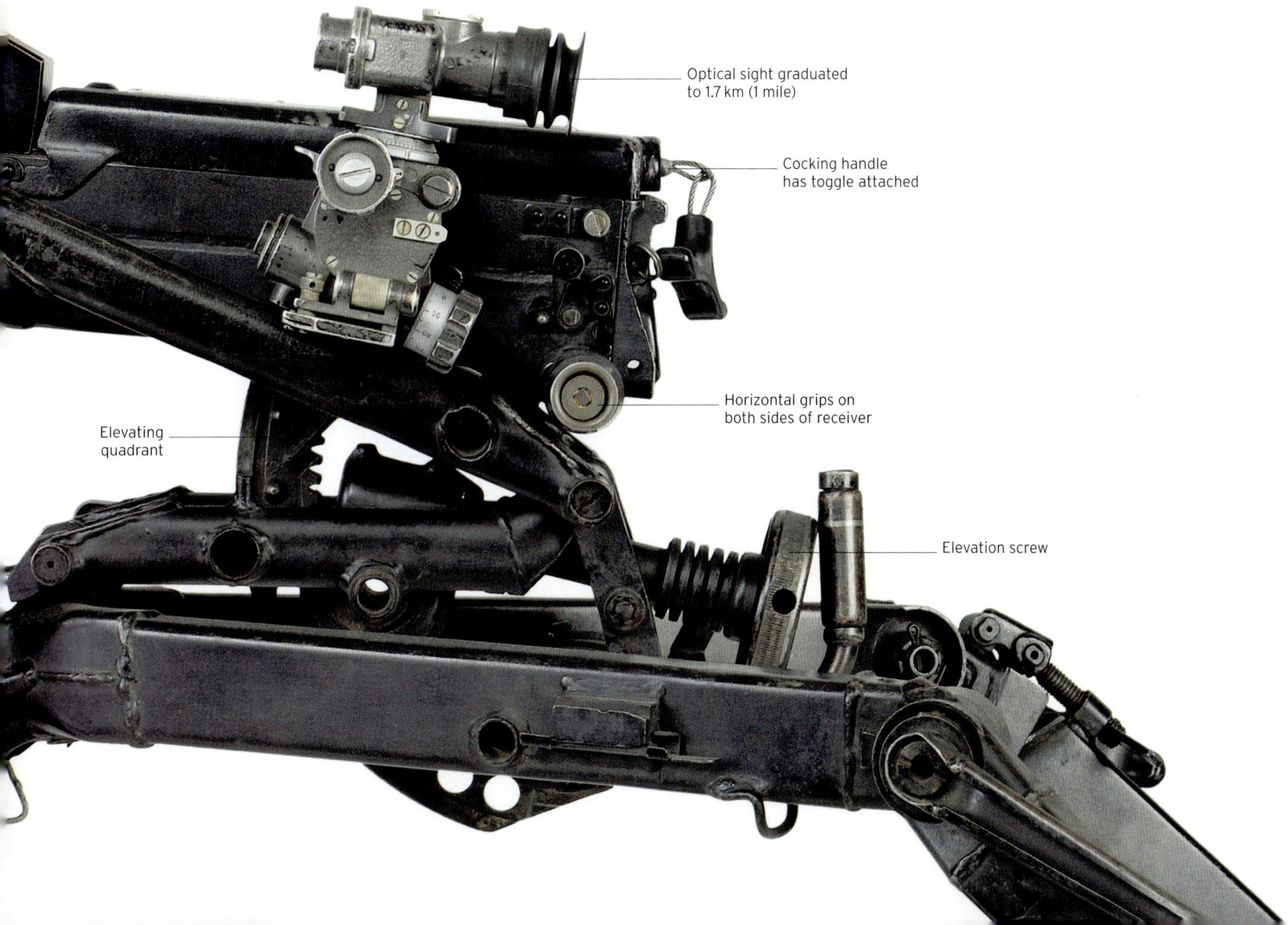

Tanks of the NATO Alliance

NATO nations produced a wide range of tanks, all of which were intended to defend Western Europe against a Soviet threat. Differing national doctrines led to a variety of different designs. The German Leopards, for example, emphasized mobility and had very light armour, whereas the British Chieftain was far more heavily armoured and much less mobile. Many of these tanks were exported to other NATO members and Western allies across the world.

▷ M48 Patton

Date 1952 **Origin** US

Weight 44.7 tonnes (49.3 tons)

Engine Continental AV-1790-5B petrol, 810 hp

Main armament 90 mm M41 L/50 rifled gun

The M48 was being developed even before M47 production began. It had an improved hull design and suspension. Almost 12,000 tanks were built and used by 26 nations, seeing service in several wars. An AVDS-1790 diesel engine and 105 mm gun were added to later versions.

△ Leopard 1

Date 1965 **Origin** West Germany

Weight 42.4 tonnes (46.7 tons)

Engine MTU MB838 multifuel, 830 hp

Main armament 105 mm L7A3 L/52 gun

Unlike Germany's wartime tanks, the Leopard was fast with thin armour. Around 5,000 of these were produced and they served over a dozen nations. In more than 30 years of service, it received upgrades in armour protection, sights, and fire control system. Two turret variants were produced – this one was cast, the other, with an angular shape, was welded.

▽ Centurion Mark 13

Date 1966	**Origin** UK
Weight 52.6 tonnes (58 tons)	
Engine Rolls-Royce Meteor Mark IVB petrol, 650 hp	
Main armament 105 mm L7 L/52 rifled gun	

The 105 mm L7 gun was developed after the British analysed the Soviet T-54 tank. It was attached to the Centurion in 1959. Subsequent Centurions were equipped with ranging machine-guns for accurate gunnery, an infrared searchlight for night fighting, and thicker armour. Upgraded Israeli versions of the Centurion saw heavy combat and earned a stellar reputation.

Leopard 1

The German Leopard, in all its many forms, is undoubtedly one of the most successful postwar tank designs. When the West German Army was re-formed in 1955, it was initially equipped with American tanks, but two years later a Franco-German tank development programme began. However, this partnership ended in 1962, and France went its own way to build the rival AMX-30 design.

SPECIFICATIONS	
Name	Leopard 1A1A2
Date	1965
Origin	West Germany
Production	6,486
Engine	MTU MB838 10-cylinder multifuel, 830 hp
Weight	42.4 tonnes (46.7 tons)
Main armament	105 mm L7A3
Secondary armament	2 x 7.62 mm MG3
Crew	4
Armour thickness	10-70 mm (0.39-2.76 in)

GERMANY CONTINUED the wartime practice of ordering prototypes from different companies (or, in this case, groups of companies) and then selecting the best model. In 1963, Krauss-Maffei of Munich was awarded the contract for the new Standard Panzer, the tank that became known as Leopard 1. In contrast to late-World War II German tank design, the Leopard emphasized mobility over protection. However, in terms of firepower, the Germans selected the best weapon available at that time – the British 105 mm L7 gun, as used in the Centurion.

Although it began life as a relatively simple tank, new technologies, increased armour protection, and individual countries' requirements led to the Leopard developing many subvariants. This version is the Leopard 1A1A2, which has a gun stabilization system, additional layers of armour around the turret, and improved gun sights and observation equipment.

REAR VIEW

FRONT VIEW

Enduring appeal
The Leopard was a great export success, with variants being operated by 15 countries. Many were then taken out of service, refurbished, and sold in modified forms, including engineer-vehicle and recovery models.

EXTERIOR

With its emphasis on lightness and mobility, the Leopard 1 had minimal armour protection. To compensate for this, the front-most part of the tank, known as the glacis plate, is sloped at 60 degrees to the vertical. This helps deflect enemy projectiles, and effectively thickens the hull by forcing projectiles to take a diagonal route through its surface.

1. Driver's periscopes **2.** Commander's TRP 2A panoramic sight-head **3.** Commander's cupola (closed) **4.** Range-finder aperture **5.** Smoke launchers **6.** Rear stowage box **7.** Gunner's position **8.** Looking down into commander's cupola **9.** Commander's TRP 2A panoramic sight eyepiece **10.** Driver's position **11.** 105 mm gun breech **12.** Driver's controls

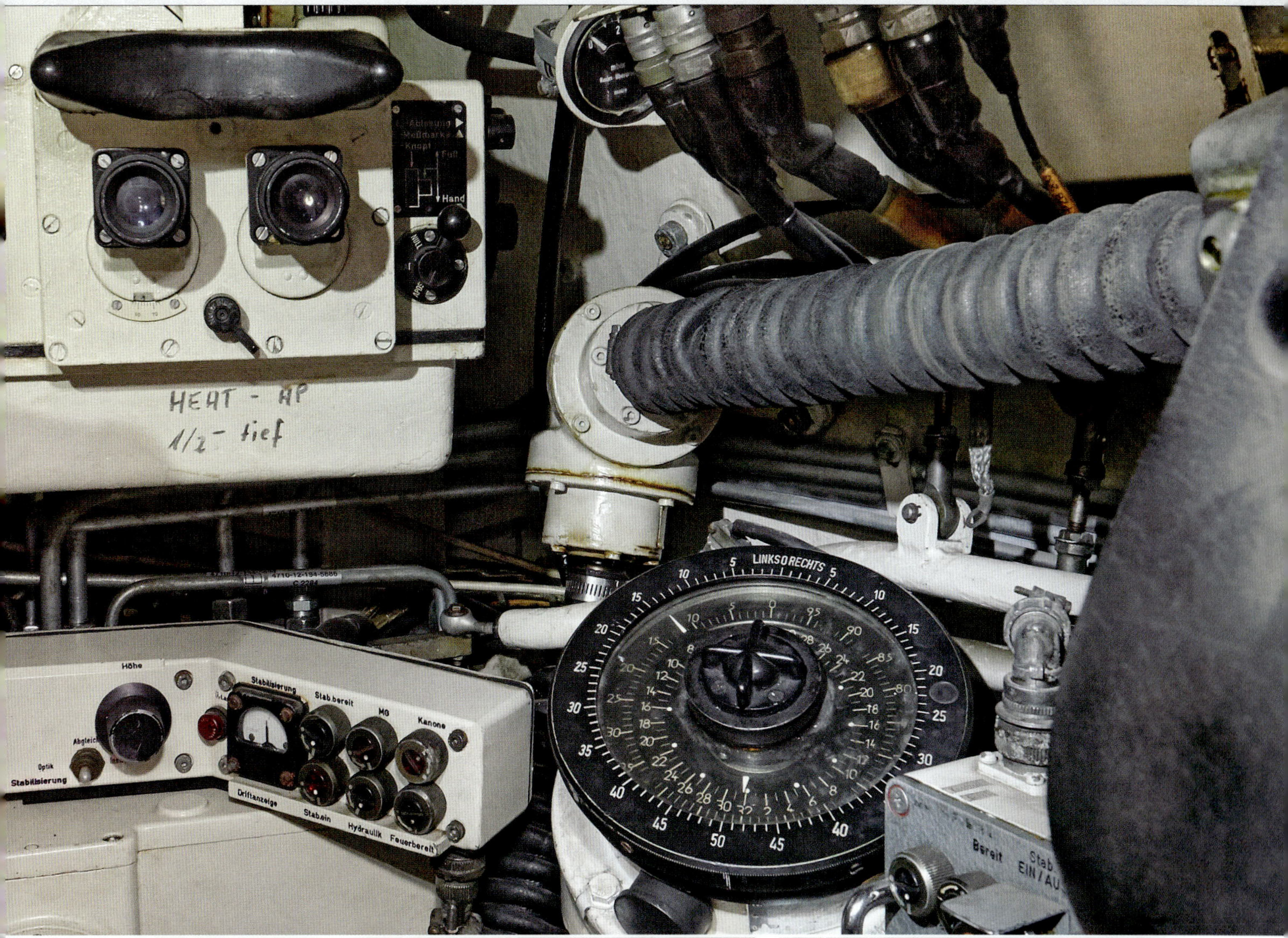

9

10

11

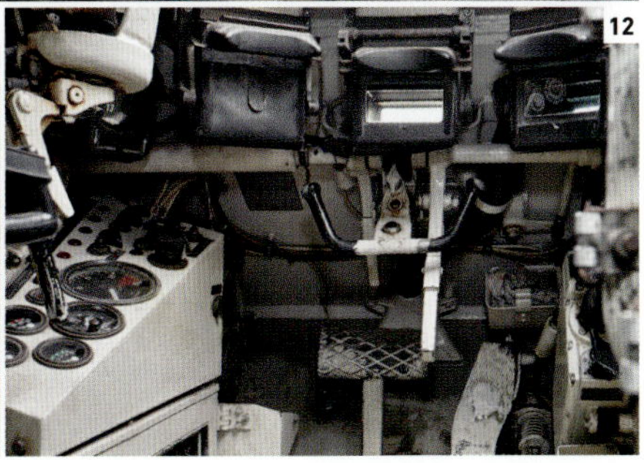
12

INTERIOR

The interior is divided into two compartments, with a fire wall in between. The engine is situated in the rear compartment, while the crew are in the front: the commander in the turret, with the gunner in front of him and loader to his left, and the driver positioned forward and to the right.

Tanks of the Warsaw Pact

After World War II, the Soviet Union introduced the T-54. This was the first of a series of tanks that were mass-produced and exported to the Warsaw Pact. Soviet doctrine envisaged using tanks, supported by artillery and infantry, to break through frontline defences and to make long advances into the enemy's rear positions. This influenced their design, which emphasized mobility and low height so that the tanks would be harder to hit. As a result, their crews usually found them cramped and uncomfortable.

▽ PT-76

Date 1951 **Origin** Soviet Union

Weight 14.6 tonnes (16.1 tons)

Engine Model V-6 diesel, 240 hp

Main armament 76.2 mm 2A16 L/42 rifled gun

A light tank, the PT-76 was able to swim with the help of two water jets. This made it highly mobile and versatile, but its buoyancy requirements resulted in a large hull and thin armour that could barely protect the tank against heavy machine-guns.

△ T72

Date 1971	**Origin** Soviet Union
Weight 41.5 tonnes (45.7 tons)	
Engine 12-cylinder 780 hp diesel engine	
Main armament 125 mm smoothbore gun	

The three-man T72 was an effective, if not particularly advanced, tank that dispensed with the usual fourth crew member in favour of an automatic loader. It was widely exported to countries around the world.

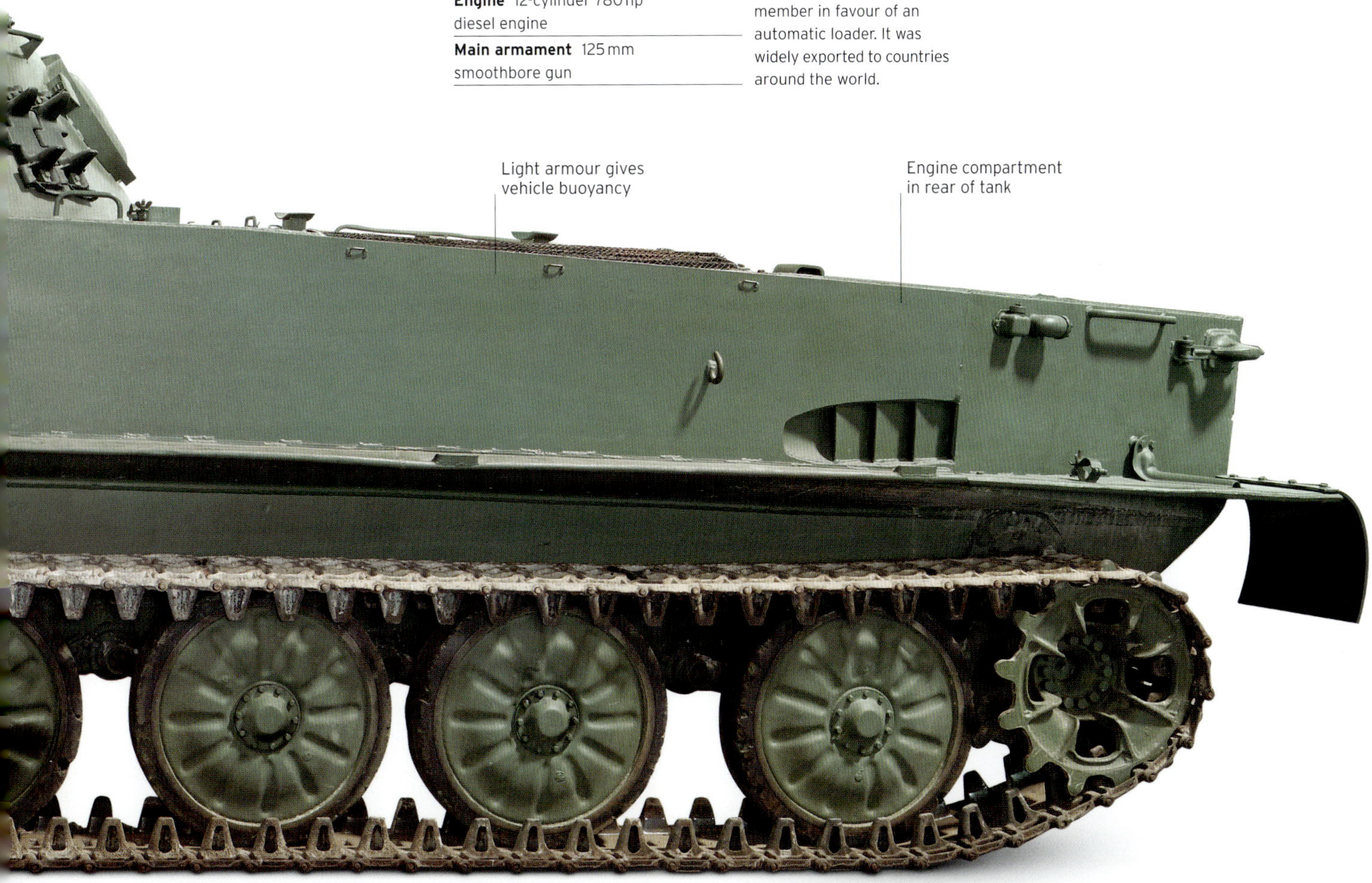

T-72

The T-72 was a Soviet tank designed for use if the Cold War had escalated into open conflict. Simple to manufacture and maintain, it followed the T-64, a more expensive and complex tank. The T-72 entered service with the Red Army in the 1970s and is still used by over 40 countries. Versions of the T-72, often with lower standards of protection, were built in the Soviet Union for exportation, while Poland and Czechoslovakia also manufactured T-72s.

SPECIFICATIONS	
Name	T-72M1
Date	1973
Origin	Soviet Union
Production	Over 25,000
Engine	V46.6 V-12 diesel, 780 hp
Weight	41.5 tonnes (45.7 tons)
Main armament	125 mm 2A46M smoothbore
Secondary armament	12.7 mm NSVT machine-gun
Crew	3
Armour thickness	Max 280 mm (11 in)

THE T-72 INCLUDED FEATURES from earlier Soviet tank designs – a low profile, a frying pan-shaped turret, and a reliable diesel engine. At just over 41 tonnes (45 tons), it was relatively light compared to contemporary Western tanks. It was also considered less effective than its Western rivals in one-on-one encounters, as with many Soviet tanks of the Cold War. However, it was fit for purpose: Soviet commanders intended to use it in huge massed attacks to swamp Western defences.

The T-72 was equipped with an autoloader system for the main gun, with 22 rounds housed in a circular, horizontal carousel; 17 extra rounds were stored in the hull. This allowed a maximum rate of fire of up to three shots in 13 seconds. It also meant that a three-man crew could be used (commander, gunner, and driver), reducing the need for crew space and enabling a smaller, lighter design. This was so effective that official guidelines specified a maximum height of 175 cm (5 ft 9 in) for crewmen, to ensure they could fit into the T-72's cramped interior.

THREE-QUARTER VIEW

Stealth and mobility
The front view of the T-72 reveals one of its major tactical assets – its low profile. At just over 2 m (6 ft) in height, it presents a difficult target for an enemy. The autoloader allows a reduction in height since there is no need for a standing crew member in the turret.

REAR VIEW

EXTERIOR

Tanks often feature improvements and additions, and this T-72 from Polish service shows added "gill" armour along the sides. These rubber squares can be angled forward to detonate or disrupt hollow charge rounds before they meet the main body of the tank. The external machine-gun bracket was originally mounted with an antiaircraft 12.7 mm NSVT, and the turret also housed a 7.62 mm PKT coaxial machine-gun.

1. Commander's hatch (closed) **2.** Machine-gun bracket **3.** Deep wading snorkel (stowed) **4.** Gunner's hatch (closed) **5.** Looking down into commander's position **6.** Looking down into gunner's position **7.** Looking down into driver's position **8.** Gearshift **9.** Driver's instrument panel **10.** Commander's sight

1

2

3

4

5

6
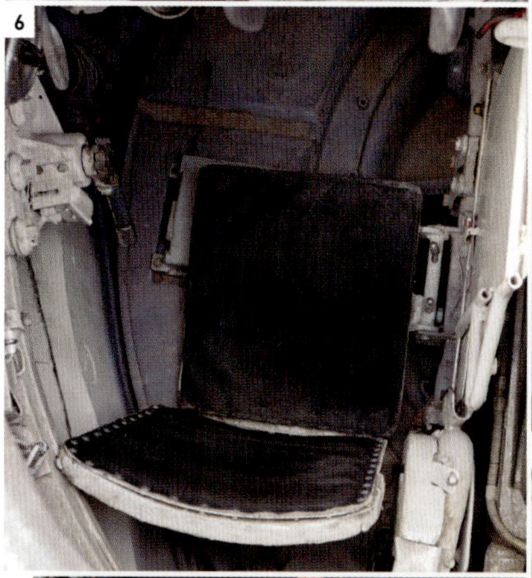

7
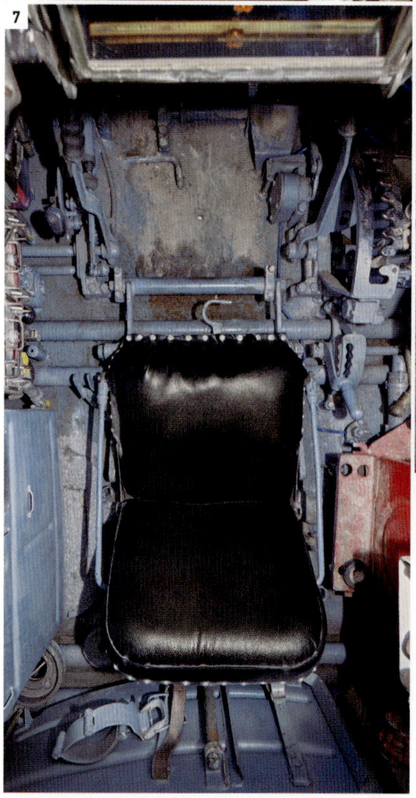

8

9

INTERIOR

Housing just three crew, the interior of the T-72 was cramped and made few concessions to human comfort. Its crew compartment offered nuclear, biological, and chemical (NBC) protection, and the gunner had access to gun sights and a laser range finder for use in the day, as well as infrared sights for use at night.

10

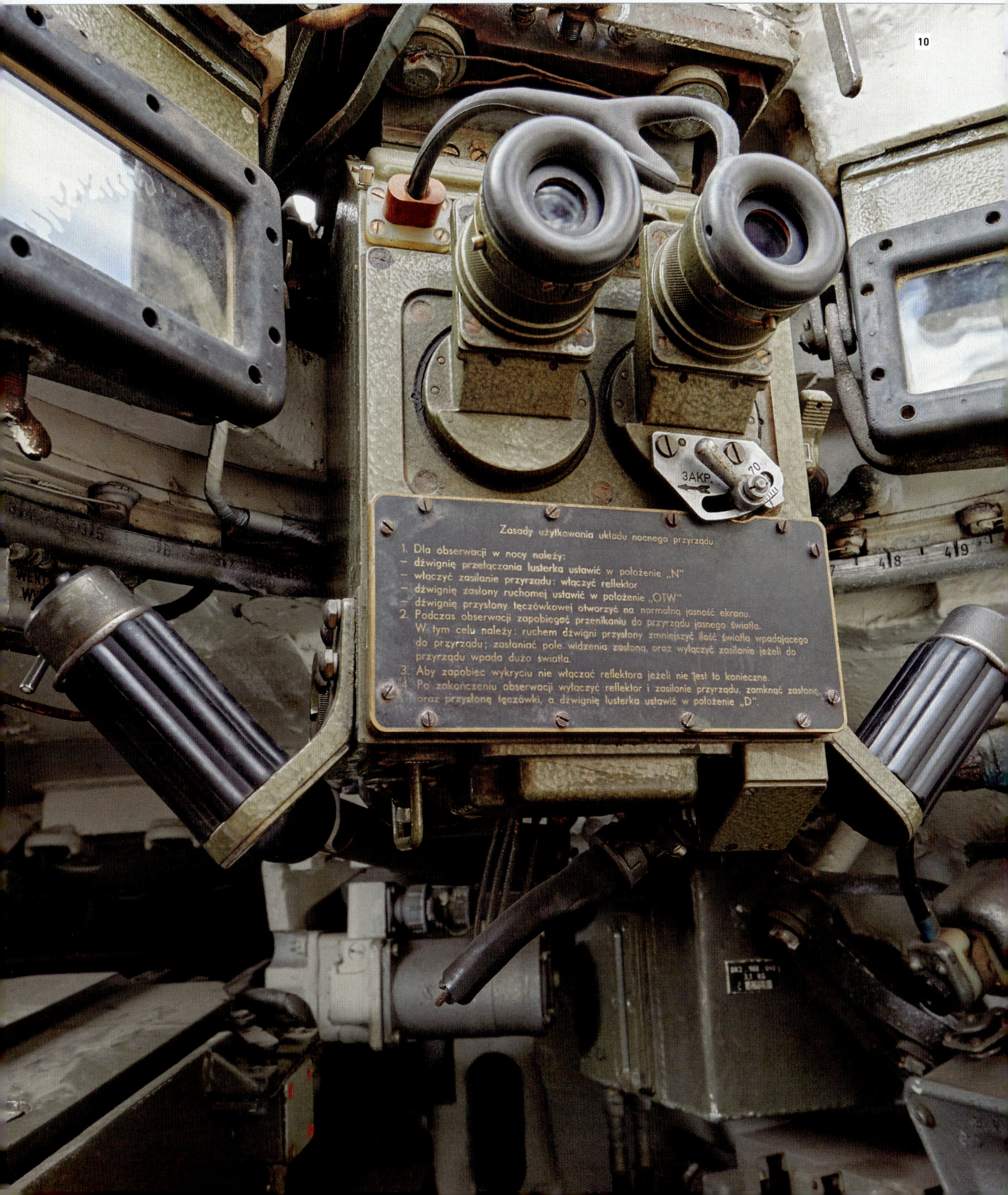
ЗАКР.
70
Zasady użytkowania układu nocnego przyrządu
1. Dla obserwacji w nocy należy:
– dźwignię przełączania lusterka ustawić w położenie „N"
– włączyć zasilanie przyrządu: włączyć reflektor
– dźwignię zasłony ruchomej ustawić w położenie „OTW"
– dźwignię przysłony tęczówkowej otworzyć na normalną jasność ekranu.
2. Podczas obserwacji zapobiegać przenikaniu do przyrządu jasnego światła.
W tym celu należy: ruchem dźwigni przysłony zmniejszyć ilość światła wpadającego
do przyrządu; zasłaniać pole widzenia zasłoną, oraz wyłączyć zasilanie jeżeli do
przyrządu wpada dużo światła.
3. Aby zapobiec wykryciu nie włączać reflektora jeżeli nie jest to konieczne.
4. Po zakończeniu obserwacji wyłączyć reflektor i zasilanie przyrządu, zamknąć zasłonę,
oraz przysłonę tęczówki, a dźwignię lusterka ustawić w położenie „D".

▷ **Panzer 61**

Date 1961 **Origin** Switzerland

Weight 38.6 tonnes (42.6 tons)

Engine MTU MB837 Ba-500 diesel, 630 hp

Main armament 105 mm L7 L/52 rifled gun

The Panzer 61 was developed for Swiss terrain – steep mountains and narrow train tunnels. It replaced the Centurion, with 150 built. The original coaxial 20 mm cannon was later replaced with a more conventional 7.5 mm machine-gun. It served until the 1990s.

▷ **Strv 103C (S-Tank)**

Date 1967 **Origin** Sweden

Weight 39.6 tonnes (43.7 tons)

Engine Rolls-Royce K60 multifuel, 240 hp, and Caterpillar 553 gas turbine, 490 hp

Main armament 105 mm Bofors L/62 rifled gun

The Strv 103 was intended to fight defensively, ambushing the enemy then escaping; its low profile and second, rear-facing driver made it very effective in this role. The autoloading gun was aimed by steering and adjusting the height of the hydropneumatic suspension.

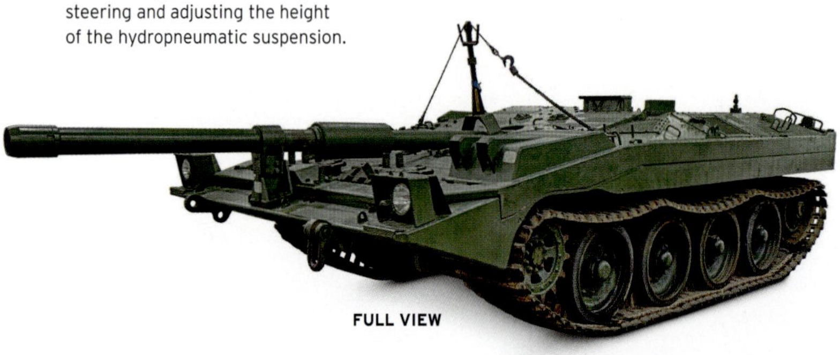

FULL VIEW

Tanks of the Non-aligned World

Many nations attempted to steer between the two Cold War powers. Some, such as Yugoslavia, purchased equipment from both sides, while others, such as Switzerland, continued designing and building their own weapons. Other nations used both domestic and foreign vehicles. As well as being a symbol of industrial and military power, a domestically designed tank could be optimized for the conditions a country expected to face on the battlefield. The unique design of the Swedish Strv 103 illustrates this most clearly.

Combat Vehicle Reconnaissance (Tracked)

Developed during the 1960s for the British Army, the Combat Vehicle Reconnaissance (Tracked) family was a range of lightweight vehicles that were constructed from common components for ease of manufacture. They were lightly armoured and made of aluminium, and so could readily be moved by air. After decades of service with forces around the world, these vehicles were upgraded: the petrol engine was replaced by a more powerful diesel one, while some models were developed with a lengthened chassis to make them longer, bulkier, and heavier.

▽ **FV101 Scorpion**

Date 1972 **Origin** UK

Weight 8.1 tonnes (8.9 tons)

Engine Jaguar J60 No1 Mk100B petrol, 190 hp

Main armament 76 mm L23A1 rifled gun

The world's fastest tank, at 82 km/h (51 mph), the Scorpion was a light reconnaissance vehicle with a three-man crew. It was by far the most widely exported CVR(T) vehicle, sold to around 20 countries. An upgraded variant with a 90 mm gun was later developed.

◁ FV102 Striker

Date 1976 **Origin** UK

Weight 8.3 tonnes (9.2 tons)

Engine Jaguar J60 No1 Mk100B petrol, 190 hp

Main armament Swingfire antitank guided missile launcher

The Striker carried the Swingfire antitank guided missile in a five-round launcher box on the Armoured Personnel Carrier (APC) hull. Swingfire was a wire-guided missile that could turn in flight to hide the launcher's location. It was used in the Persian Gulf in 1991 and 2003.

△ FV105 Sultan

Date 1977 **Origin** UK

Weight 8.6 tonnes (9.5 tons)

Engine Jaguar J60 No1 Mk100B petrol, 190 hp

Main armament 7.62 mm L7 machine-gun

The Sultan is used by commanders at all levels, including in units that are not equipped with other CVR(T) variants. It provides enough room for a map board and desk, space for multiple radios, and has a tent that can be attached to the rear to provide more space for the commanders.

Specialized Vehicles

Hobart's Funnies (tanks developed by the British 79th Armoured Division during World War II) had more than proven their worth, and so, after the war, the idea of building specialized vehicles based on a tank chassis became common. Armoured Personnel Carriers (APCs) often received this treatment, too, with a dizzying array of vehicles developed. These versatile vehicles have been used as mortar carriers, antitank missile launchers, signals vehicles, artillery observation posts, command posts, antiaircraft missile launchers, and in many other roles.

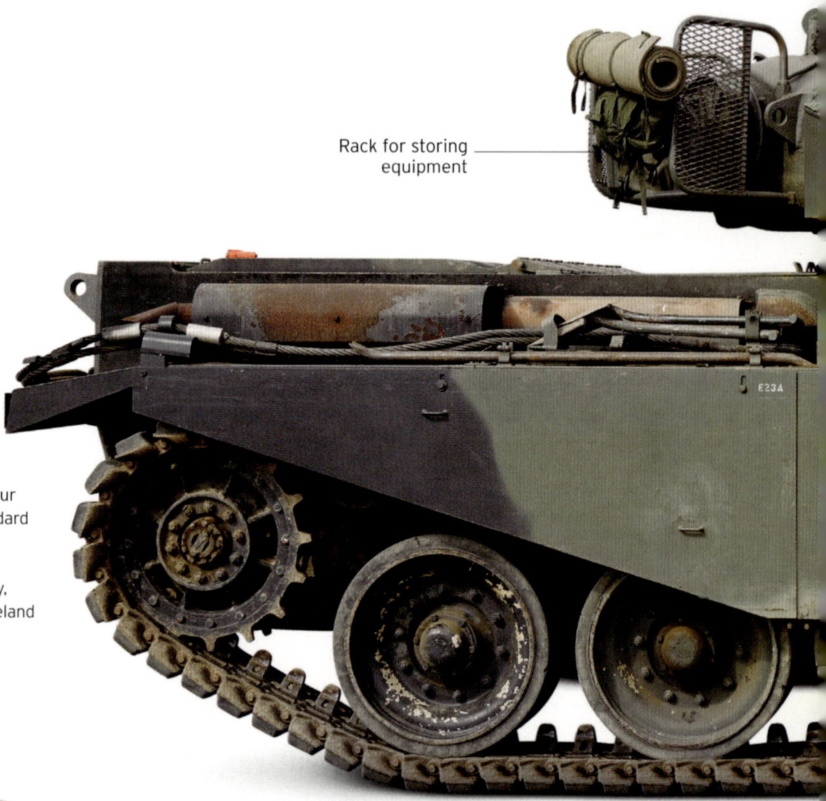

▷ Centurion Armored Vehicle Royal Engineers (AVRE)

Date 1963 **Origin** UK

Weight 50.8 tonnes (56 tons)

Engine Rolls-Royce Meteor Mark IVB petrol, 650 hp

Main armament 165 mm L9 demolition gun

The AVRE carried a wide range of equipment to allow engineers to do their work, with similar armour protection and mobility to the standard tank. It was equipped with a dozer blade or a mine plough, and could carry a fascine or a roll of trackway. The AVRE was used in Northern Ireland in 1972 and the Gulf War in 1991.

△ M548

Date 1965 **Origin** US

Weight 13.4 tonnes (14.8 tons)

Engine General Motors Model 6V-53 diesel, 215 hp

Main armament .50 Browning M2 machine-gun

An unarmoured cargo carrier using the running gear of M113 APC, the M548 was originally intended to carry artillery ammunition and gunners. Its mobility and 5.4-tonne (6-ton) capacity meant it was adapted for a wide range of roles, including launchers for the Chaparral and Rapier surface-to-air missiles. It has seen service in Vietnam, the Yom Kippur War, and the Gulf War.

▽ **MT-LB**

Date 1970	**Origin** Soviet Union
Weight 13.3 tonnes (14.7 tons)	
Engine YaMZ 238 V diesel, 240 hp	
Main armament 7.62 mm PKT machine-gun	

The amphibious MT-LB was developed as an armoured, all-terrain artillery tractor. It was widely used as a command post vehicle, chemical warfare reconnaissance vehicle, electronic warfare vehicle, and missile carrier. It also saw service as an APC, especially in Arctic regions where its low ground pressure gave it better mobility than other vehicles.

△ BTR-152

Date 1950	**Origin** Soviet Union
Weight 10.1 tonnes (11.1 tons)	
Engine ZIS-123 petrol, 110 hp	
Main armament 7.62 mm SGMB machine-gun	

Larger and more mobile than the BTR-40, the BTR-152 could carry 15 infantrymen. Later models had an armoured roof and the first Soviet central tire pressure regulation system. Over 12,500 BTR-152s of all variants were built, and saw decades of service around the world.

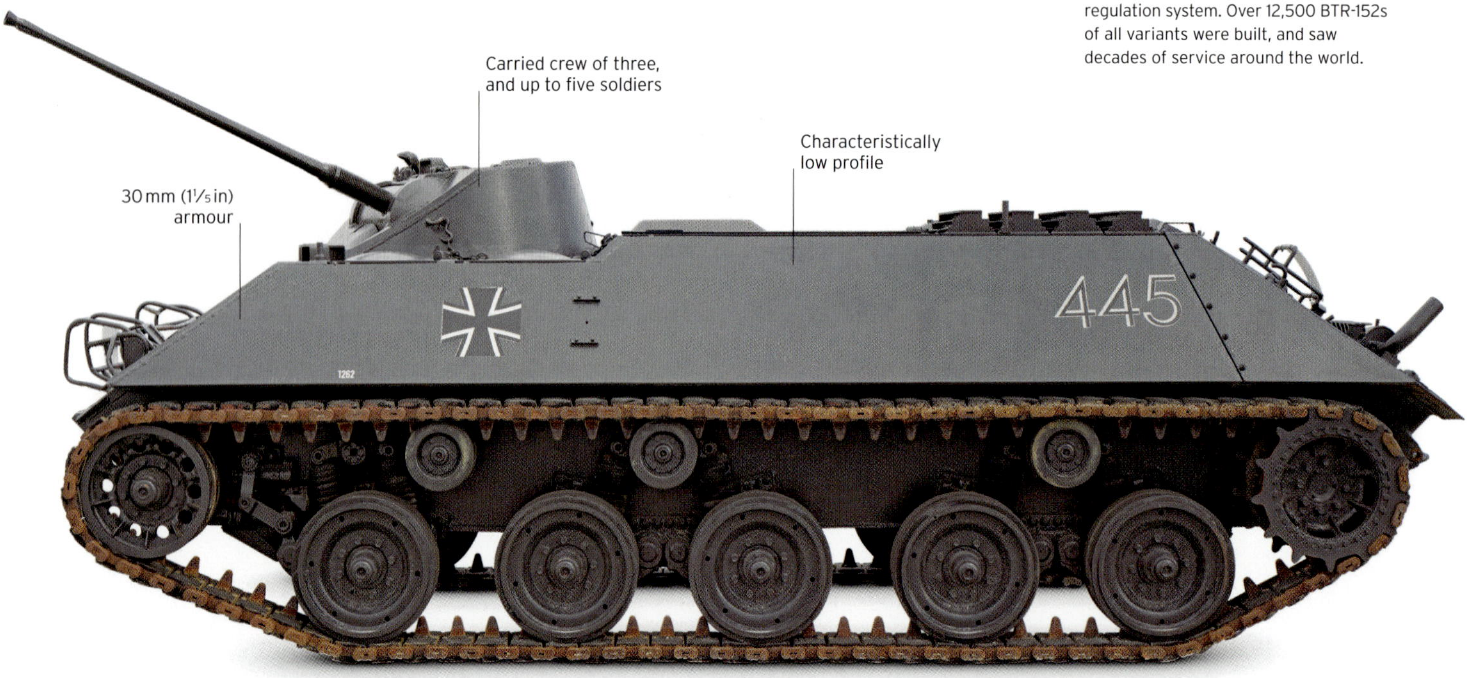

△ Schützenpanzer Lang HS.30

Date 1958	**Origin** West Germany
Weight 14.6 tonnes (16.1 tons)	
Engine Rolls-Royce B81 Mark 80F petrol, 220 hp	
Main armament 20 mm Hispano-Suiza HS.820 cannon	

According to West German military doctrine, tanks, infantry, and infantry carriers were to fight alongside each other. Accordingly, the Schützenpanzer Lang was more heavily armed and armoured than contemporary APCs, and had a lower profile. It had a capacity for five infantry, who entered and left via roof hatches. Unreliable at first, it improved after costly modification.

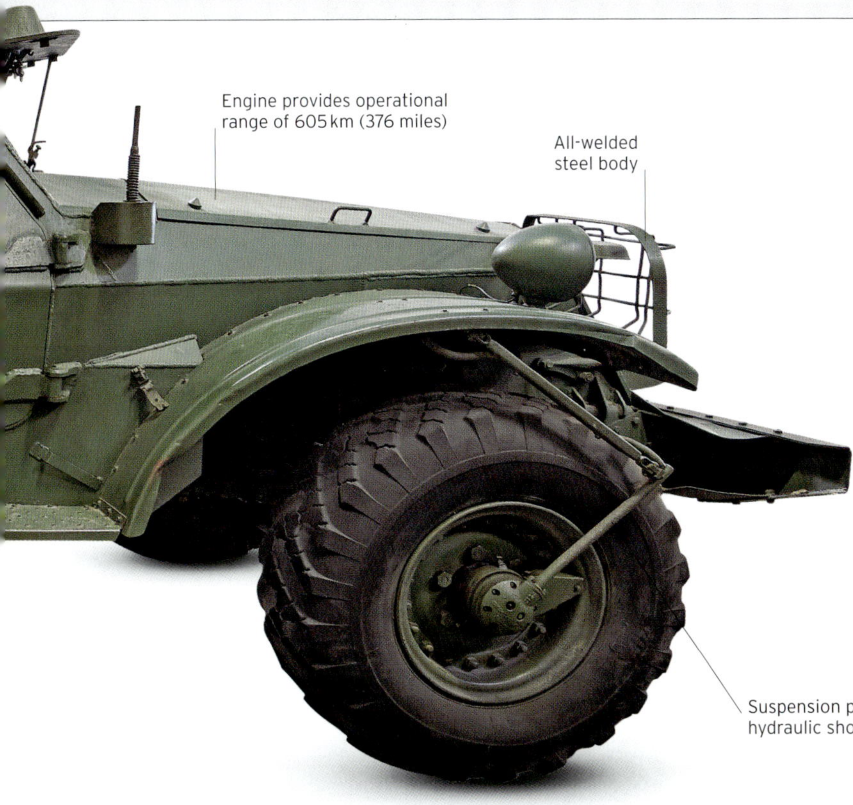

Armoured Personnel Carriers and Infantry Fighting Vehicles

Armoured Personnel Carriers (APCs) allowed infantry to operate alongside tanks, but their thinner armour, lighter firepower, and limited mobility left them vulnerable to attack. To rectify this, designers turned their attention to developing infantry fighting vehicles (IFVs) that could not only fight alongside tanks, but allowed their infantry to engage the enemy without leaving the vehicle. Wheeled personnel carriers remained in widespread use throughout the Cold War. However, few of them had the armour or firepower to operate on the front line.

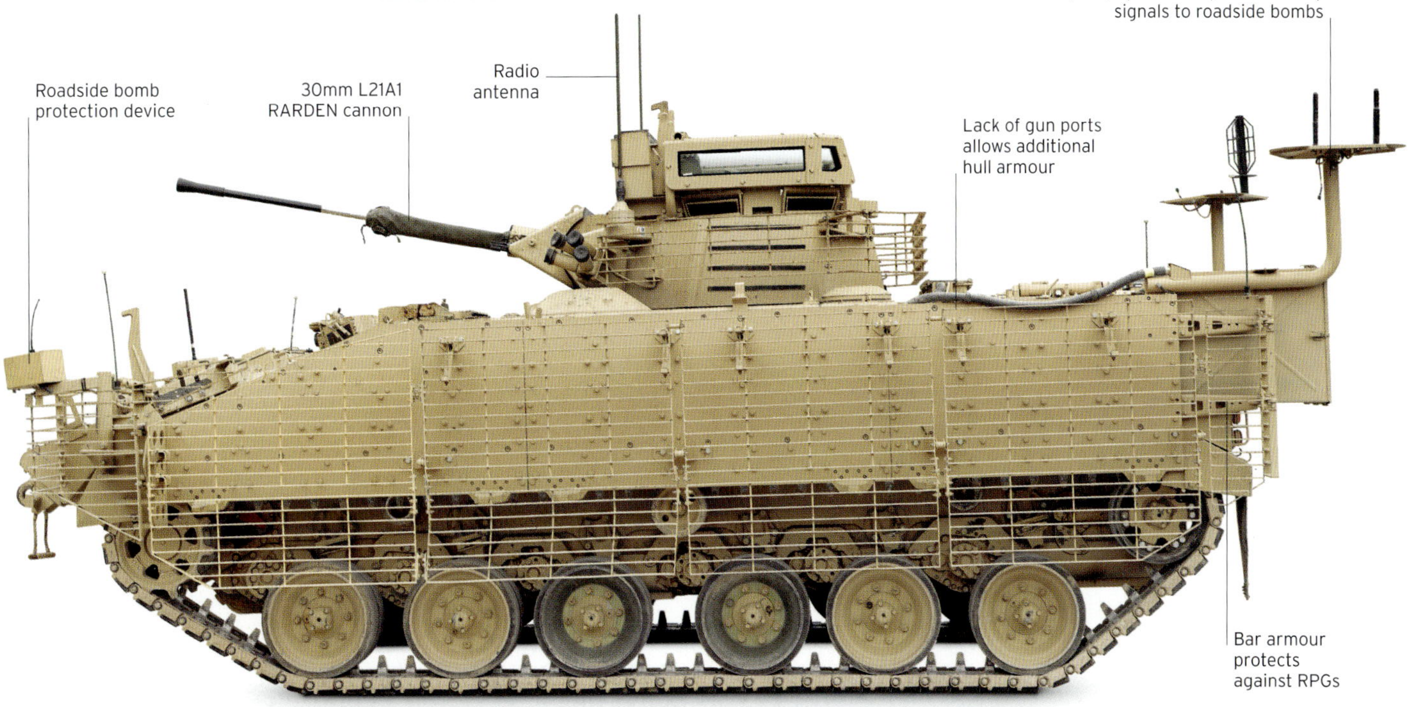

△ **Warrior**	
Date 1986	**Origin** UK
Weight 28 tonnes (30.9 tons)	
Engine Perkins CV-8 TCA diesel, 550 hp	
Main armament 30 mm L21A1 RARDEN cannon	

The Warrior IFV (FV510) originally carried seven infantry. In the upgraded version seen here this was reduced to six, although the seats provided better protection against mine blasts. Suspension and crew visibility were also improved. Extra armour and electronic countermeasures were added for service in the Gulf, the Balkans, and Afghanistan. Command post, repair, and recovery variants have since been developed.

Armoured Reconnaissance Vehicles

Reconnaissance vehicles were not intended to fight, but to find enemy forces and report back. This role drove their design, which emphasized mobility over protection to the point that many were light enough to float across rivers. They were armed with machine-guns or light cannon designed for self-defence only; their main weapon was still the radio. Wheeled vehicles allowed for faster and quieter mobility, although their limitations on rough terrain led to several countries using tracked vehicles instead.

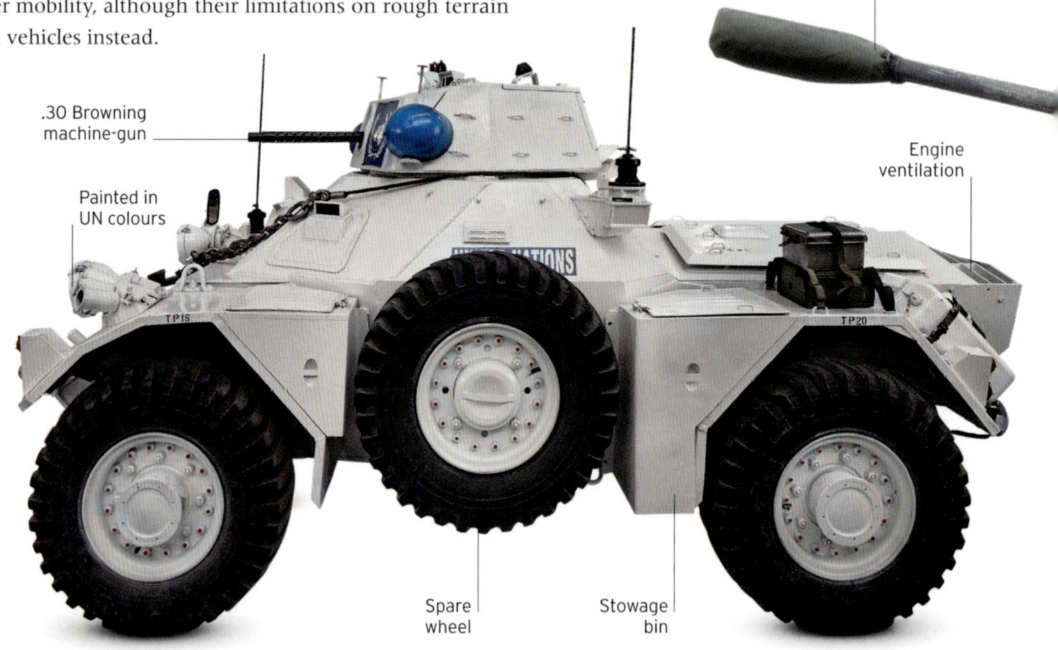

▷ FV701(E) Ferret Mark 2/5

Date 1952 **Origin** UK

Weight 4.4 tonnes (4.8 tons)

Engine Rolls-Royce B60 Mark 6A petrol, 129 hp

Main armament .30 Browning M1919 machine-gun

The development of Ferret began in 1947 as a replacement for the successful Dingo. The Mark I had an open top like the Dingo, but most had a machine-gun turret, as here. Its main roles were reconnaissance and liaison, but some variants carried antitank missiles. A total of 4,409 were built, finding service in more than 30 countries.

▽ BRDM 2

Date 1962 **Origin** Soviet Union

Weight 7 tonnes (7.7 tons)

Engine GAZ-41 V8 petrol, 140 hp

Main armament 14.5 mm KPVT machine-gun

Many limitations of the BRDM-1 were corrected in its successor, the BRDM 2. This featured an NBC protection system, better sights, and an armoured turret housing its machine-gun. It retained the BRDM-1's belly wheels and its amphibious capability.

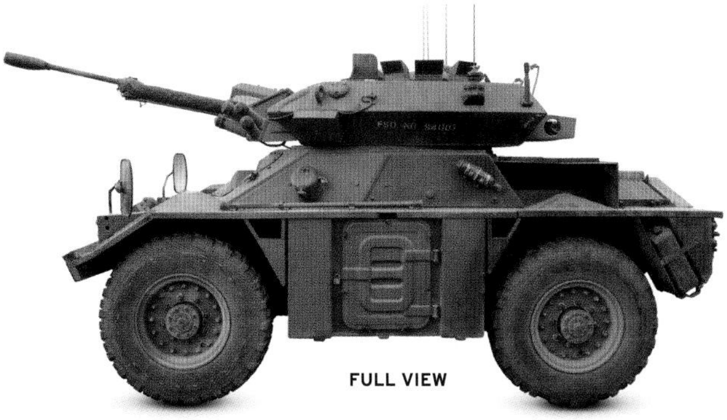

FULL VIEW

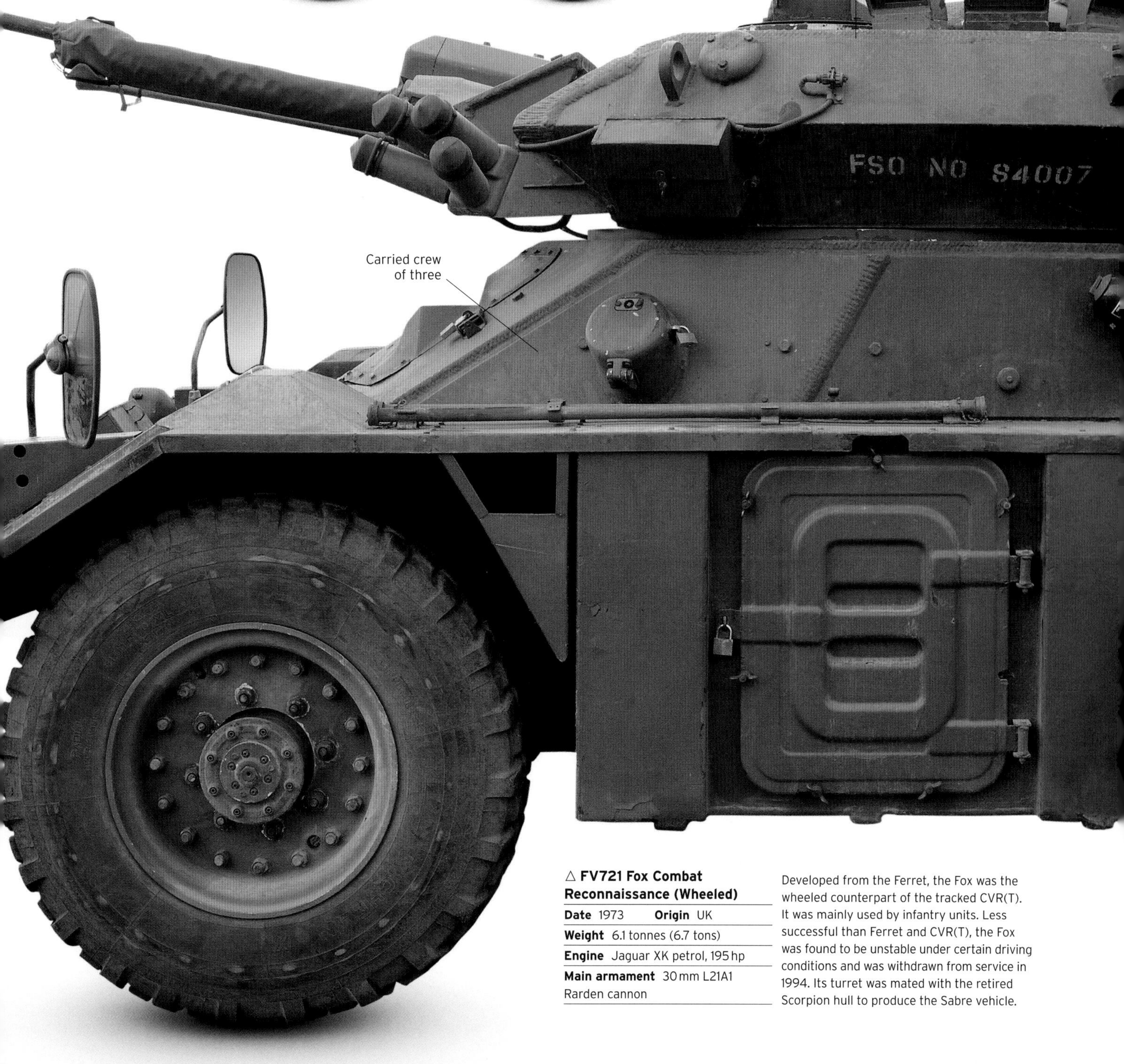

△ **FV721 Fox Combat Reconnaissance (Wheeled)**

Date 1973 **Origin** UK

Weight 6.1 tonnes (6.7 tons)

Engine Jaguar XK petrol, 195 hp

Main armament 30 mm L21A1 Rarden cannon

Developed from the Ferret, the Fox was the wheeled counterpart of the tracked CVR(T). It was mainly used by infantry units. Less successful than Ferret and CVR(T), the Fox was found to be unstable under certain driving conditions and was withdrawn from service in 1994. Its turret was mated with the retired Scorpion hull to produce the Sabre vehicle.

Tank Destroyers

Tracked tank destroyers, as used in World War II, became less common as the Cold War progressed. By the 1970s, the development of lightweight antitank missiles meant that a heavy, gun-armed vehicle was no longer needed to destroy a tank. Many countries adapted their standard Armoured Personnel Carriers (APCs) for the job. Some countries retained the gun-armed vehicles for specific conditions such as close support for infantry or airborne forces, where the ability to fire high explosive shells remained important. These new wheeled vehicles offered great speed and were lighter than tracked versions, giving them superior mobility over long distances or poor terrain.

▷ EE-9 Cascavel

Date 1974 **Origin** Brazil

Weight 13.2 tonnes (14.6 tons)

Engine Mercedes-Benz OM 352 diesel, 190 hp

Main armament 90 mm EC-90 rifled gun

The EE-9 and the EE-11 Urutu APC were developed together. Both used the unique Boomerang suspension system on the rear wheels, ensuring that both wheels remained on the ground over a larger range of motion. The Cascavel has seen combat with Libyan, Iraqi, and Zimbabwean forces.

▽ Saladin

Date 1958 **Origin** UK

Weight 11.3 tonnes (12.4 tons)

Engine Rolls-Royce B80 Mark 6A petrol, 160 hp

Main armament 76 mm L5A1 rifled gun

Designed to replace the wartime Daimler and AEC armoured cars, the Saladin had heavier firepower and six-wheel drive, giving it excellent cross-country mobility. It was developed alongside the Saracen, with which it shared many components. Highly successful, almost 1,200 Saladins were built. It was exported to more than 20 countries, and saw combat with several, including Oman and Kuwait.

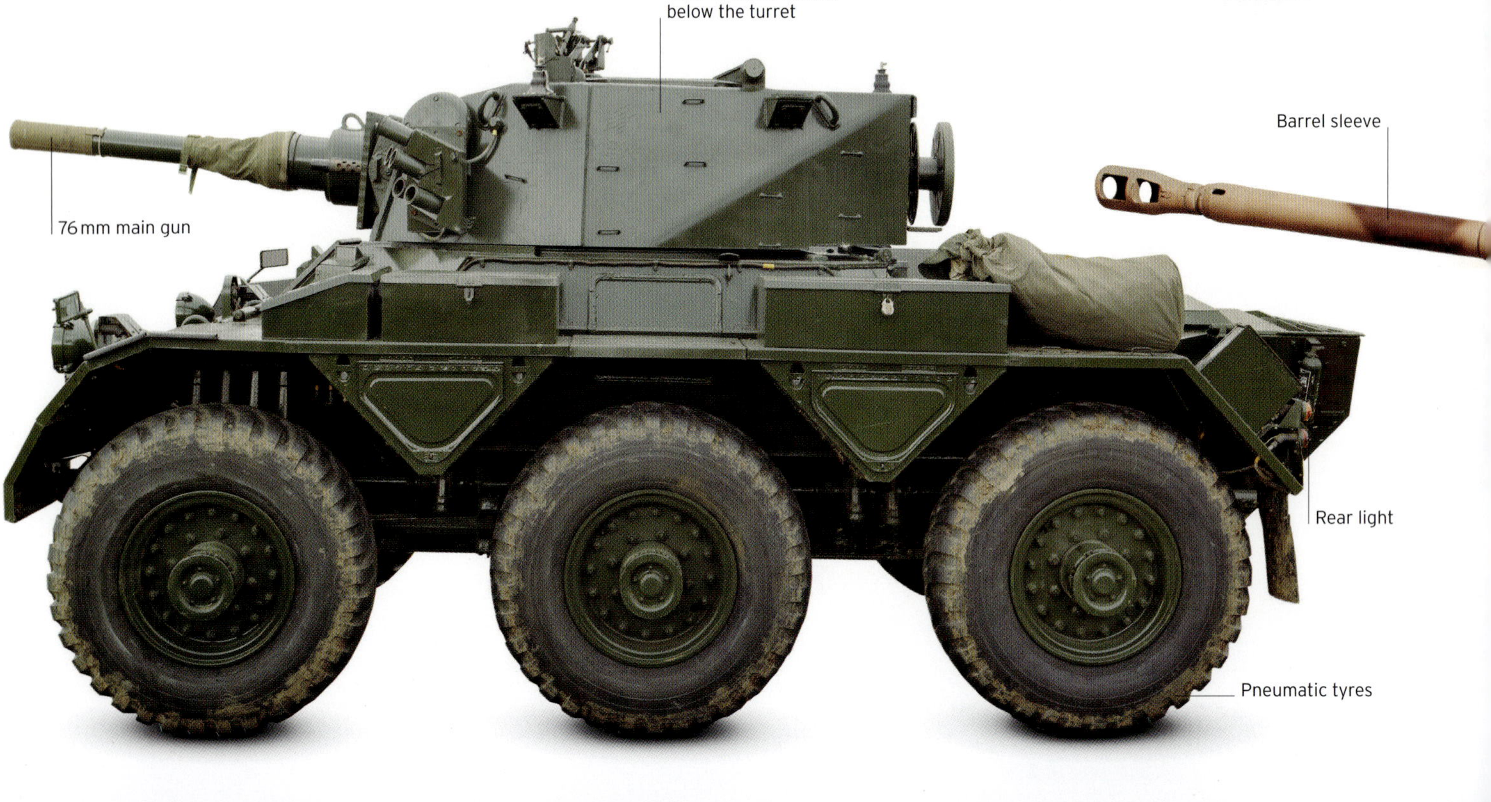

▽ AMX-10RC

Date 1981 **Origin** France

Weight 15.9 tonnes (17.5 tons)

Engine Renault HS 115 diesel, 260 hp

Main armament 105 mm F2 L/48 rifled gun

Intended for reconnaissance and fire support, the AMX-10RC has seen combat in Chad and Afghanistan. Extensive upgrades have been applied during its service, especially to the sights and fire-control systems. Unusually for a wheeled vehicle, it uses skid steering rather than a conventional mechanism.

Helicopters

The adoption of the turbine engine in the 1950s revolutionized the helicopter industry. Small, light, and powerful turbines displaced less reliable piston engines and allowed a steep change in size, speed, and lifting capacity. This new breed of helicopter had many different military uses, from transporting troops, observing enemy troops' positions, and evacuating injured troops to undertaking combat search and rescue missions and, if suitably armed, attacking ground targets. At sea, some were also used in antisubmarine warfare.

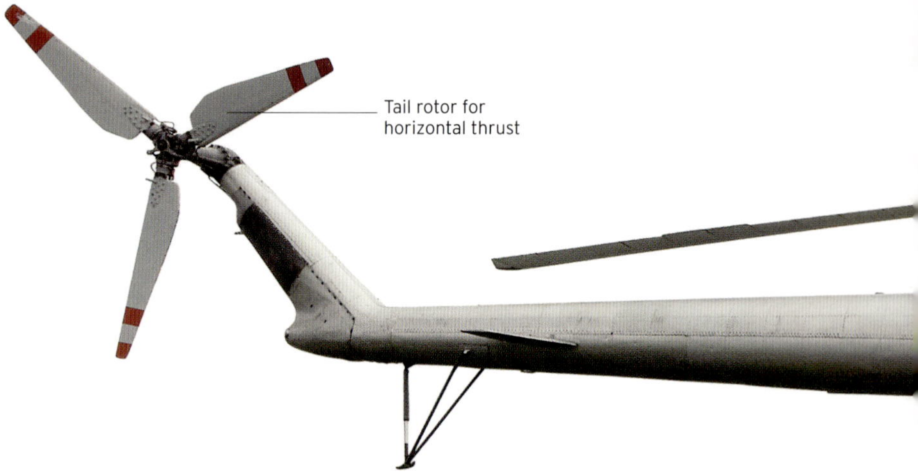

Tail rotor for horizontal thrust

△ Mil Mi-4

Date 1952	**Origin** USSR
Engine 1,675 hp Shvetsov ASh 82 14-cylinder radial	
Top speed 186 km/h (116 mph)	

Rushed out in response to the US deployment of helicopters in Korea, the Mi-4 has served in virtually every military and civil role from gunship to crop sprayer.

Main rotors help to deliver top speed of 300 km/h (186 mph)

Carries crew of five, plus seating for 65 troops or 41 stretchers

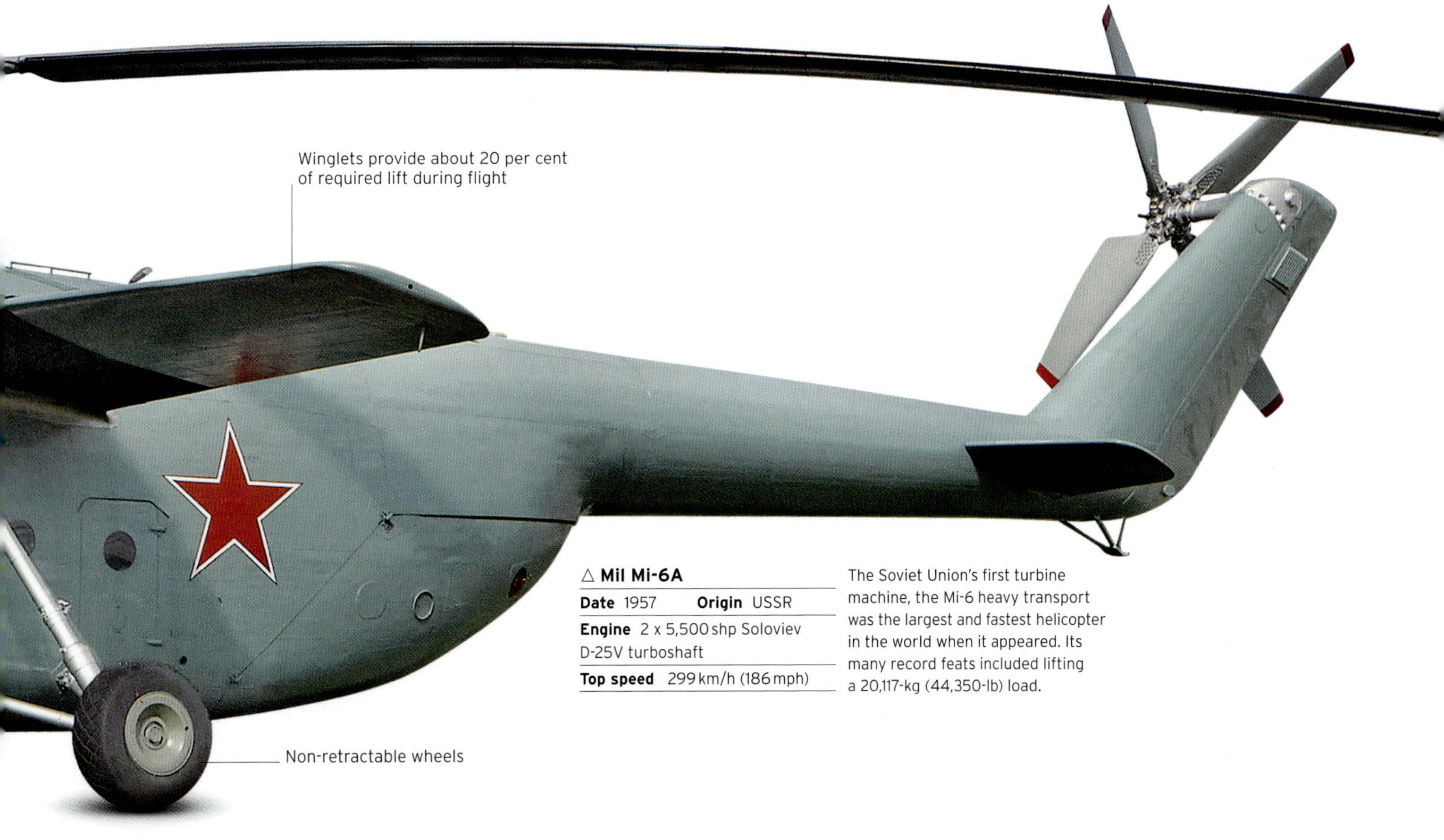

△ **Mil Mi-6A**

Date 1957 **Origin** USSR

Engine 2 x 5,500 shp Soloviev D-25V turboshaft

Top speed 299 km/h (186 mph)

The Soviet Union's first turbine machine, the Mi-6 heavy transport was the largest and fastest helicopter in the world when it appeared. Its many record feats included lifting a 20,117-kg (44,350-lb) load.

Helicopters (cont.)

▽ SA Gazelle

Date 1973 **Origin** France

Engine 590 shp Turbomeca Astazou IIIA turboshaft

Top speed 263 km/h (164 mph)

The Gazelle introduced the concept of a fenestron, or fantail – a ducted multiblade tail rotor. Entering service in 1973, it was used for observation, liaison, and pilot training roles.

▷ Boeing CH-47D Chinook

Date 1982 **Origin** US

Engine 2 x 3,750 shp Honeywell T55-L-712 turboshaft

Top speed 294 km/h (183 mph)

The long-lived CH-47 Chinook heavy-lift helicopter entered service with the US Army in 1962. The CH-47D and the CH-47F remain in service around the world.

△ **Sikorsky HH-60G Pave Hawk**

Date 1988 **Origin** US

Engine 2 x 1,630 shp GE T700-GE-701 turboshaft

Top speed 360 km/h (224 mph)

Derived from the US Army UH-60 Black Hawk, this machine was specifically developed for a US Air Force combat search and rescue role, recovering personnel by day or night in hostile environments.

Nuclear Bombers and Interceptors

For 20 years after the attacks on Hiroshima and Nagasaki in 1945, the long-range strategic bomber – which had to be fast and capable of carrying a heavy payload – remained a vital element in every nuclear power's arsenal. A new type of fighter aircraft was produced to counter this threat: the exceptionally fast "interceptor", whose role was to shoot down bombers before they could do any damage. By the mid-1960s, however, the development of Intercontinental Ballistic Missiles (ICBMs) rendered the strategic bomber obsolete and the role of the interceptor was reduced accordingly.

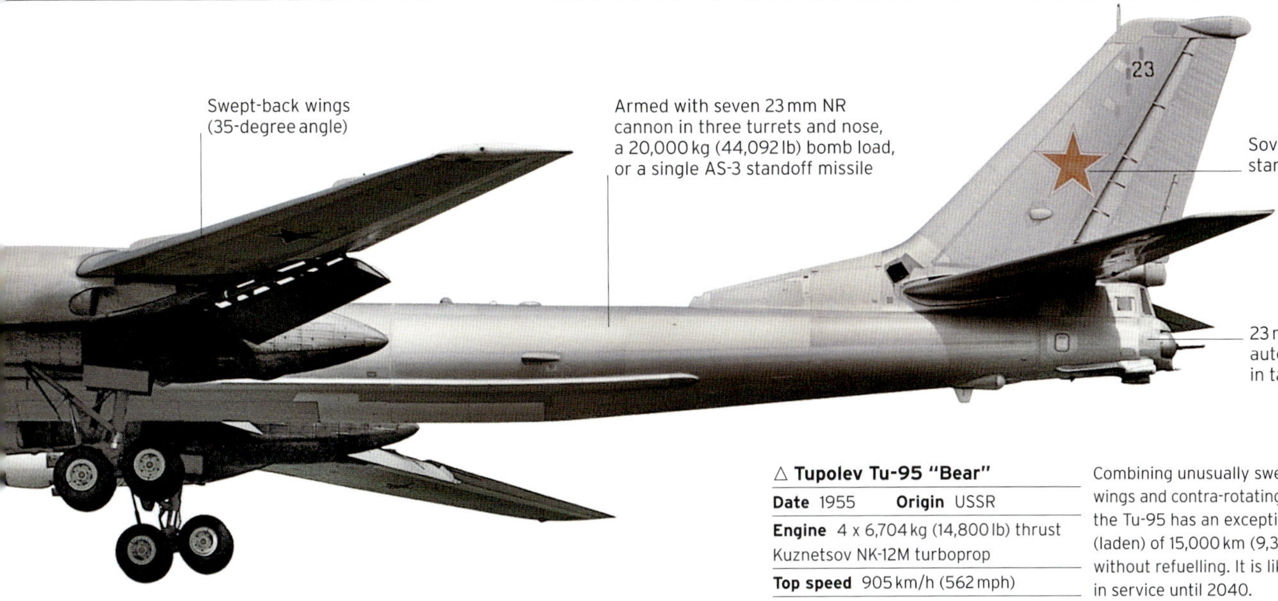

△ **Tupolev Tu-95 "Bear"**

Date 1955 **Origin** USSR

Engine 4 x 6,704 kg (14,800 lb) thrust Kuznetsov NK-12M turboprop

Top speed 905 km/h (562 mph)

Combining unusually sweptback wings and contra-rotating propellers, the Tu-95 has an exceptional range (laden) of 15,000 km (9,320 miles) without refuelling. It is likely to be in service until 2040.

△ **Boeing B-52 Stratofortress**

Date 1960 **Origin** US

Engine 8 x 5,164 kg (11,400 lb) thrust Pratt & Whitney J57 turbojet; later, 7,701 kg (17,000 lb) thrust turbofans

Top speed 1,047 km/h (650 mph)

Designed to carry nuclear warheads across continents, the huge B-52 has served with the USAF since 1955 (extensively in Vietnam) and is still in service. With current upgrades it is expected to serve into the 2040s.

△ **Dassault Mirage III**

Date 1960 **Origin** France

Engine 4,275–6,192 kg (9,436–13,668 lb) thrust SNECMA Atar 9C afterburning turbojet

Top speed 2,350 km/h (1,460 mph)

Developed in the late 1950s, the delta-wing Mirage III was a successful light interceptor that, along with this stretched IIIE fighter-bomber variant, still serves with many smaller air forces.

The Gulf War

The first Gulf War, fought in 1990–91 to evict Iraqi forces from Kuwait, involved US naval ships in the Persian Gulf. The aircraft carrier USS *Independence* was the first carrier to arrive in the Gulf, and she remained on station for 112 days. From 1992 to 1995, she undertook three further missions to the Gulf, where her aircraft enforced the no-fly zone over southern Iraq.

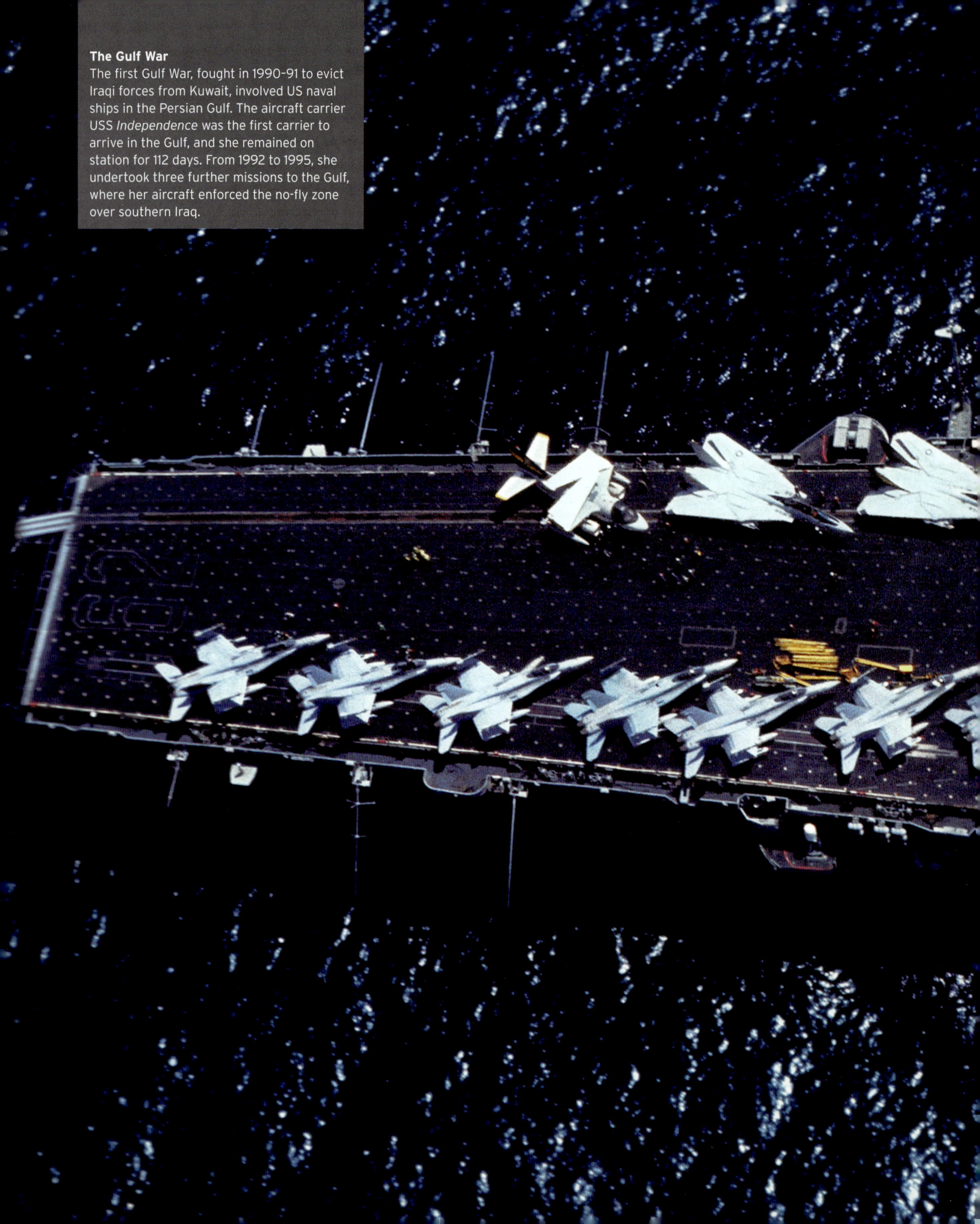

Fighter and Strike Aircraft

The legacy of World War II was a tremendous advance in jet development. Fighters now had to be jet-powered to be competitive, and able to reach supersonic speeds. The 1950s was a time of tremendous change in the fighter world. Ever more powerful engines and an increasing understanding of supersonic aerodynamics, fuelled by Cold War paranoia and big research and development budgets, saw top speeds rise from barely breaking the sound barrier in a dive, to greater than Mach 2 – twice the speed of sound – in level flight.

▷ Republic F-84C Thunderjet

Date 1946 **Origin** US

Engine 2,522 kg (5,560 lb) thrust Allison J-35 turbojet

Top speed 1,000 km/h (622 mph)

Republic's first jet fighter, this aircraft was intended as a jet-powered replacement for their P-47 Thunderbolt. After a long and troubled gestation period, it evolved into a highly capable fighter-bomber that saw extensive service in the Korean War. The Thunderjet was also the first aircraft flown by the USAF aerobatic team, the Thunderbirds.

▽ North American F-86H Sabre

Date 1953 **Origin** US

Engine 2,681 kg (5,910 lb) thrust General Electric J47-GE-27 turbojet

Top speed 1,115 km/h (693 mph)

Progressive development kept the Sabre competitive against updated MiGs. It had an uprated engine, more adaptable wings, a low-altitude bombing system, and provision to carry nuclear weapons.

▽ Mikoyan-Gurevich MiG-19

Date 1955	**Origin** USSR
Engine 2 x 3,256 kg (7,178 lb) thrust Tumansky RD-9B turbojets	
Top speed 1,455 km/h (909 mph)	

Known by NATO as the "Farmer", the MiG-19 was the first Soviet fighter to be capable of sustained supersonic flight. Although around 5,500 were produced, it was not as popular as the MiG-17, which it replaced, or the MiG-21, which superseded it.

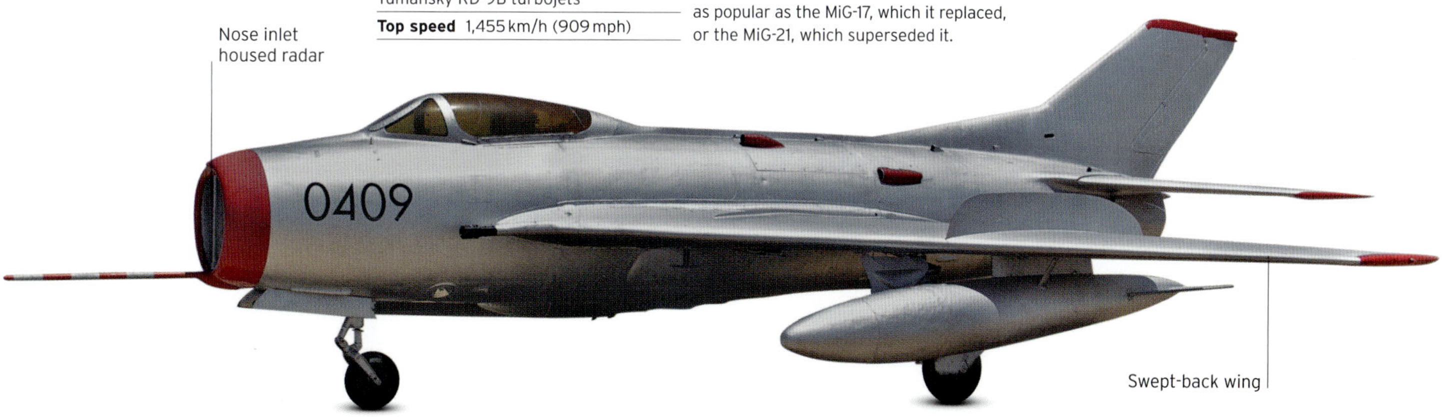

Fighter and Strike Aircraft (cont.)

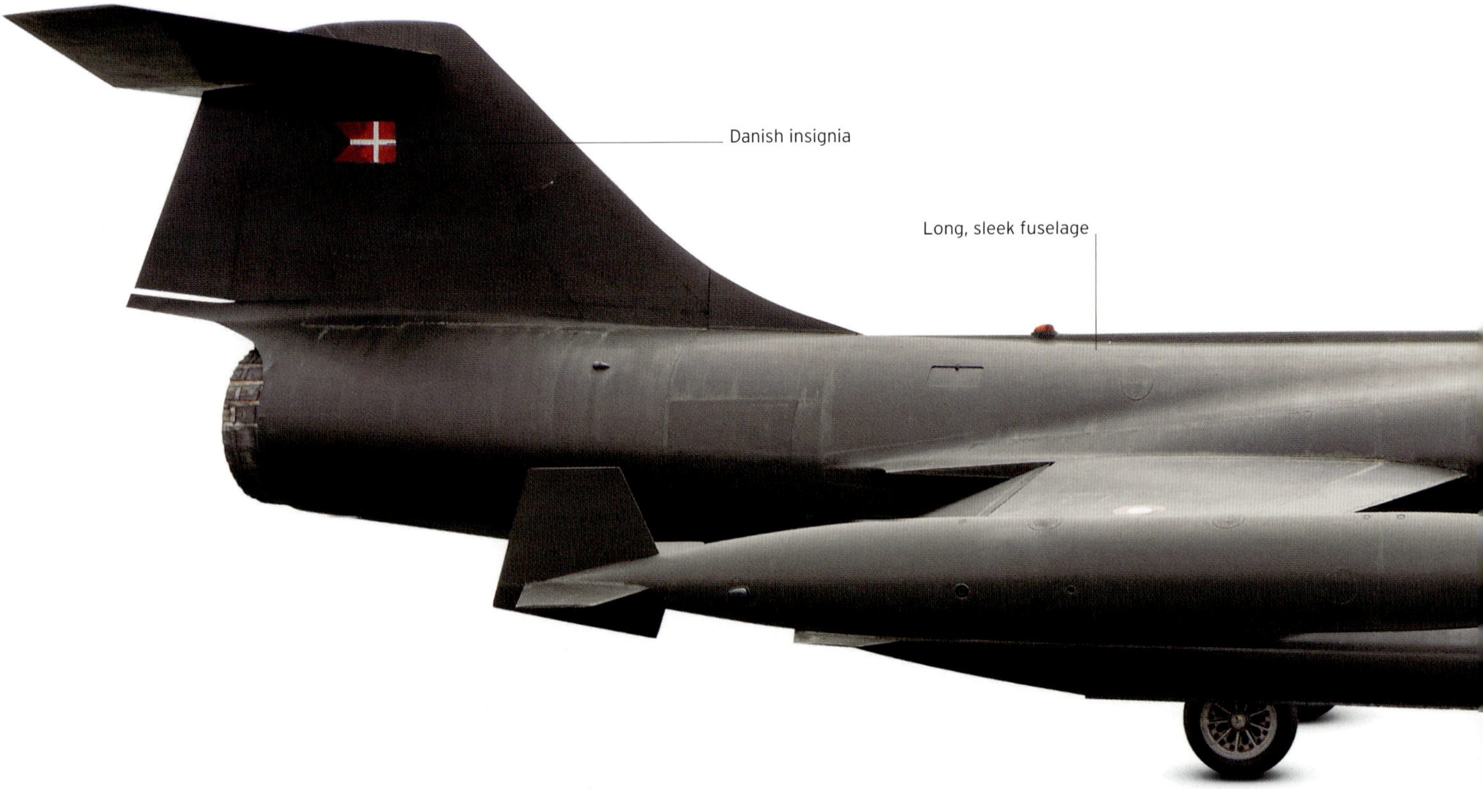

▽ **Lockheed F-104G Starfighter**

Date 1958 **Origin** US

Engine 7,484 kg (16,500 lb) thrust General Electric J-79 turbojet

Top speed 2,125 km/h (1,328 mph)

The aircraft was known as "the missile with a man in it". The Starfighter was the first fighter capable of sustained flight at speeds in excess of Mach 2.

▽ **McDonnell Douglas F-15 Eagle**

Date 1972 **Origin** US

Engine 2 x 7,915-11,340 kg (17,450-25,000 lb) thrust Pratt & Whitney F100-100/-220 afterburning turbofan

Top speed 2,660+ km/h (1,650+ mph)

The Eagle is a highly successful tactical fighter with over 100 dogfight wins and no losses, as a result of its advanced avionics with immense power and performance. Upgraded, the USAF plans to fly it until 2025.

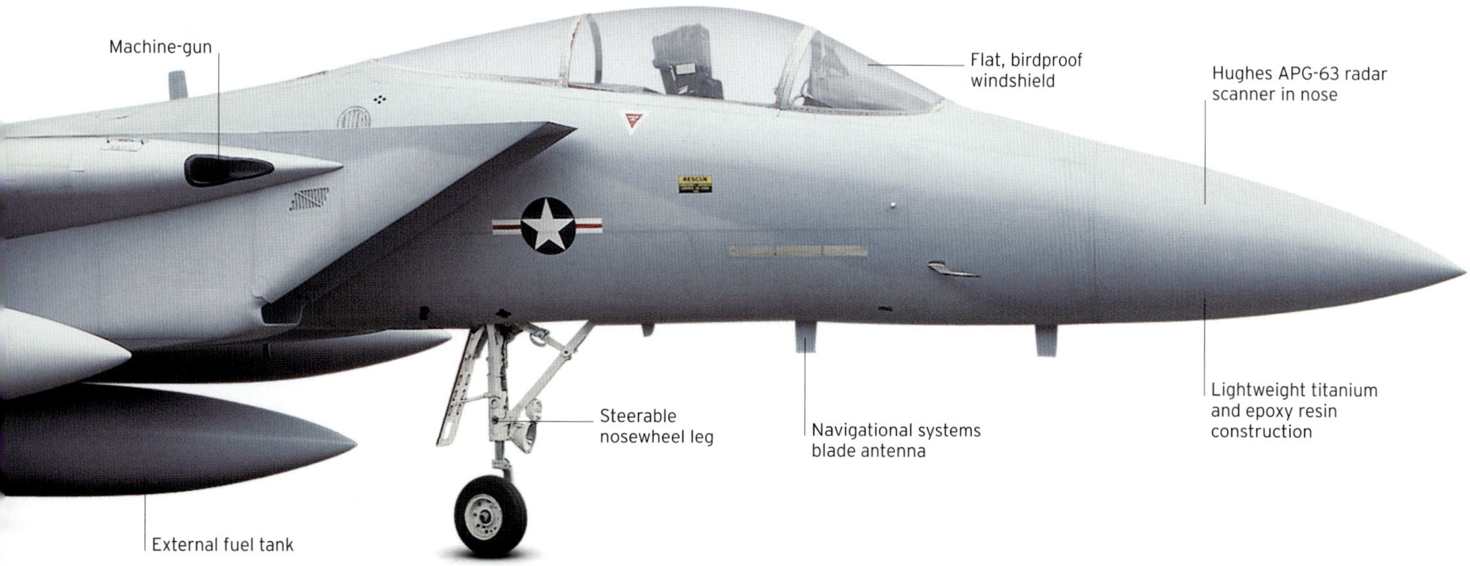

Fighter and Strike Aircraft (cont.)

▽ **Sea Harrier FRS.1**

Date 1980 **Origin** UK

Engine 9,751 kg (21,498 lb) thrust Rolls-Royce Pegasus-Mk104 turbofan

Top speed 1,200 km/h (746 mph)

The Naval version of Hawker's brilliant Harrier entered service in 1980, providing air defence for carriers - particularly effectively in the Falklands War, where it was Britain's only fixed-wing fighter.

Pronounced tail fin under fuselage

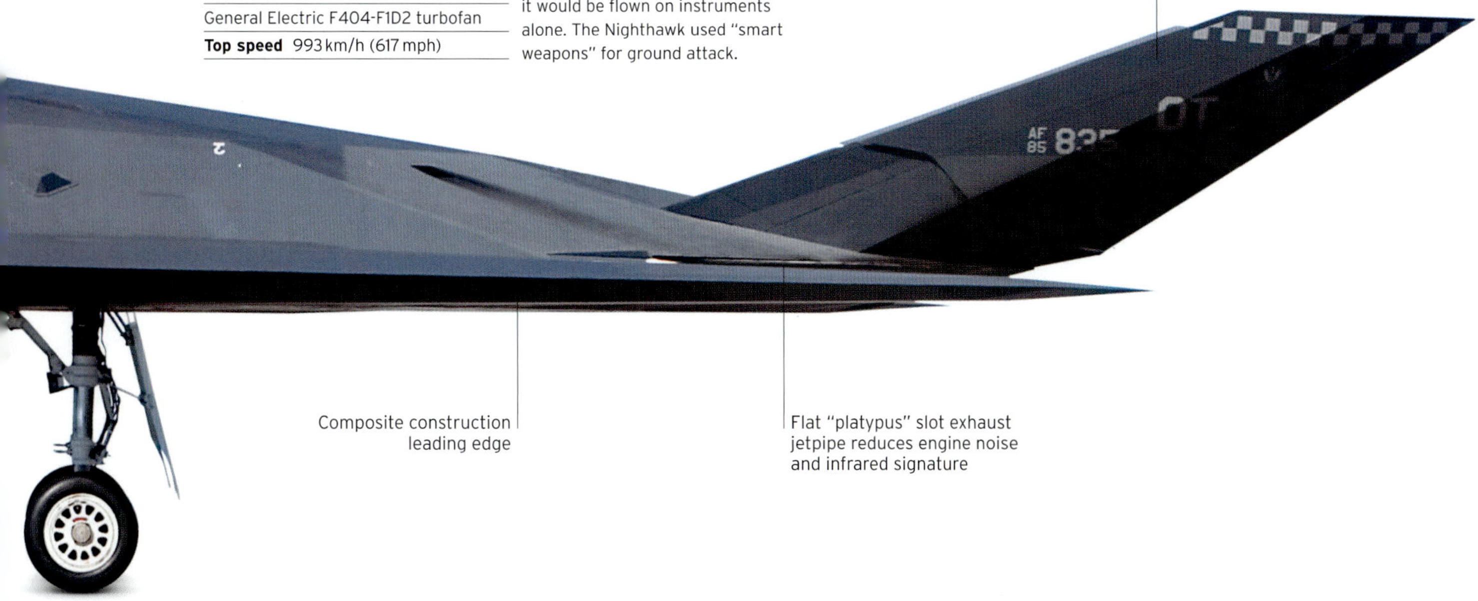

▽ **Lockheed F-117 Nighthawk**

Date 1981 **Origin** US

Engine 2 x 4,989 kg (10,800 lb) thrust General Electric F404-F1D2 turbofan

Top speed 993 km/h (617 mph)

Kept secret until 1988 the F-117 was designed to be undetectable by radar. Built solely for night attacks it would be flown on instruments alone. The Nighthawk used "smart weapons" for ground attack.

Ruddervators combine functions of rudders and elevators

Composite construction leading edge

Flat "platypus" slot exhaust jetpipe reduces engine noise and infrared signature

Mikoyan MiG-29

The Soviet MiG-29 was one of the most potent fighter-bombers of the 1980s and early 1990s. Jaw-droppingly agile and equipped with the world's best short-range missiles, tests proved it was almost impossible to defeat in a low-speed dogfight. The aircraft was tough and cheap, and spurned advanced electronics in favour of raw performance. More than 1,650 have been produced, serving with more than 40 air forces around the world.

SPECIFICATIONS	
Model	Mikoyan-Gurevich MiG-29
Date	1982
Origin	USSR
Production	1,650
Construction	Largely aluminium; some composites
Maximum weight	20,000 kg (44,100 lb)
Engines	2 x 8,300 kg (18,300 lb) thrust Klimov RD-33 afterburning turbofans
Wingspan	11.4 m (37 ft 3 in)
Length	17.37 m (57 ft)
Range	2,100 km (1,300 miles) ferry range
Top speed	2,450 km/h (1,522 mph)

DESIGNED TO COUNTER the American F-15 and F-16, the MiG-29 entered service in 1983 and replaced the MiG-23 as the main tactical fighter of the Soviet air force. The early MiG-29s lacked a fly-by-wire system – an electronic interface between pilot and flight controls – something all other agile fighters of its generation included. It was the first major fighter to feature a pilot's helmet that could be used to aim weapons, making it almost invincible in a dogfight. The most surprising operator was the United States Air Force, which flew a top secret training unit equipped with the MiG-29. Today an aircraft-carrier variant flies with the Indian Navy. The most advanced version of this aircraft is the MiG-35 (introduced in 2007), which can be fitted with thrust-vectoring control, making it the most manoeuvrable fighter in the world.

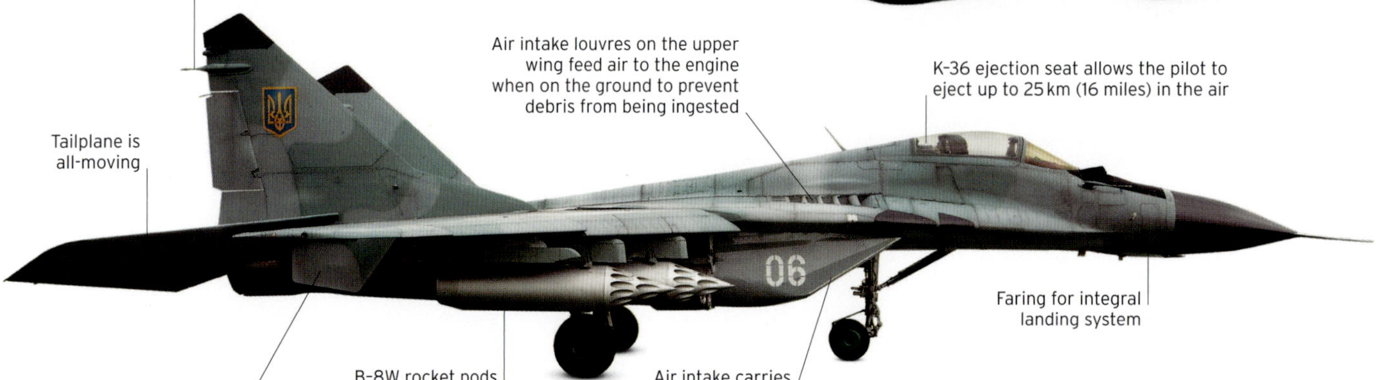

SIDE VIEW

Superb performance
The large leading-edge wing root extensions and under-slung engines both contribute to the aircraft's superb high alpha performance – the ability to control the aircraft when the nose is raised at large angles.

THE EXTERIOR

The MiG-29 (codenamed "Fulcrum" by NATO) has a mid-mounted wing with blended leading-edge root extensions (LERX). The engines are underslung and separated by a large channel. The MiG-29 is immensely strong structurally, and this is apparent in its beefy, almost "agricultural" appearance. The twin vertical tails are a feature inherited from the MiG-25, although while the earlier aircraft design emphasized speed, the MiG-29 design prioritizes agility.

1. Infrared search and track sensor/laser range finder **2.** GSh-301 30 mm cannon muzzle apertures **3.** Landing gear **4.** B-8W rocket pod for 20 rounds of 80 mm calibre **5.** Loading area for rocket pod at rear **6.** Variable area afterburner nozzle **7.** Heading setting indicator **8.** Combined oxygen panel **9.** Radar warning receiver **10.** Landing gear select and radar control panel **11.** Control stick **12.** Cockpit

1

2

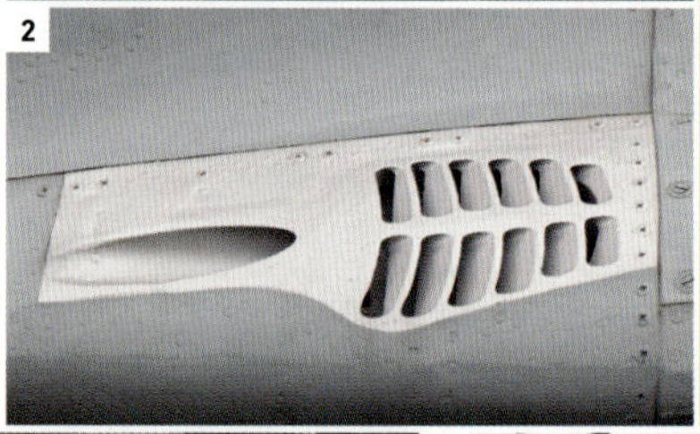

3

4

5

6

7

8

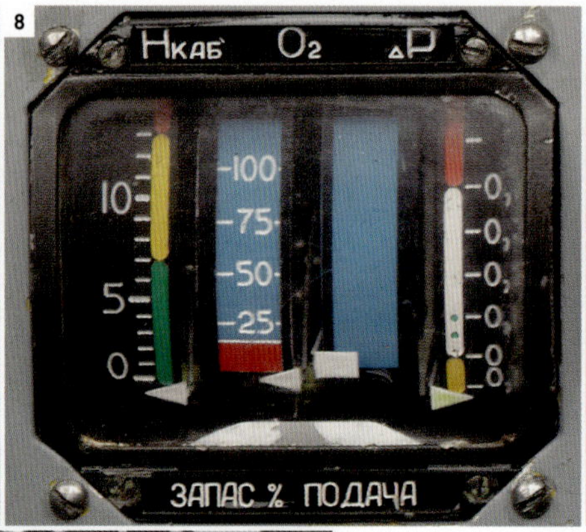

9

10

11

THE COCKPIT

The MiG-29 cockpit lacked the "glass" electronics carried by the US F/A-18 Hornet; instead, the displays were traditional analogue dials. The exception to this was the pilot's Shchel-3UM Helmet Mounted Display (HMD). The main control column was centrally mounted, and did not include Hands On Throttle-and-Stick technology. The cockpit was spacious with good visibility (by Soviet standards). This particular example is an early 9.12 model MiG-29 operated by the Ukrainian air force. The latest member of the family, the MiG-35, has replaced analogue instruments and has three large multi-functional displays (and four in the rear cockpit of the two-seat MiG-35D).

12
МЕТКА
ТАКТ.
ТРАССА
ДУБЛ
ТЕСТ
ЯРК
СЕТКА
ДЕНЬ
НОЧЬ
ГЛАВН
КОМПЛ
БАЗА
СКОРОСТЬ
ЯРК.

Frontline Aircraft

The Cold War saw tremendous advances in warplane design and armament. Building on the great progress in technology through the 1960s – notably the development of variable geometry wing and vertical take-off capacity – and utilizing the immense power of turbojet engines, combat aircraft dominated the skies in the 1970s. With appropriate weapons, engines, and technology upgrades, such aircraft are still defending major nations 50 years on.

Single pilot in bubble canopy

High ground clearance to enable bombs to be loaded

External auxiliary fuel tank

Variable geometry wing, or "swing wing"

External fuel drop tank

▽ **Douglas A-4 Skyhawk**

Date 1956 **Origin** US

Engine 3,715 kg (8,200 lb) thrust Wright J65 turbojet

Top speed 1,077 km/h (673 mph)

This was a front-line jet that achieved performance through reduced size and weight rather than sheer engine power. Ed Heinemann's design for the US Navy had such a small delta wing it had no need to fold for carrier use.

Diminutive wingspan of only 8.38 m (26½ ft)

▽ **Mikoyan-Gurevich MiG-23**

Date 1970 **Origin** USSR

Engine 9,979–12,474 kg (22,000–27,500 lb) thrust Tumansky R-29 afterburning turbojet

Top speed 2,445 km/h (1,519 mph)

This swing-wing interceptor with sophisticated radar targeting and beyond-visual-range missiles effectively fixed the weak points of the MiG-21. It was cheap compared with rivals; 5,047 were built.

Radar in nose cone

Long sweeping tail fin

FULL VIEW

Frontline Aircraft (cont.)

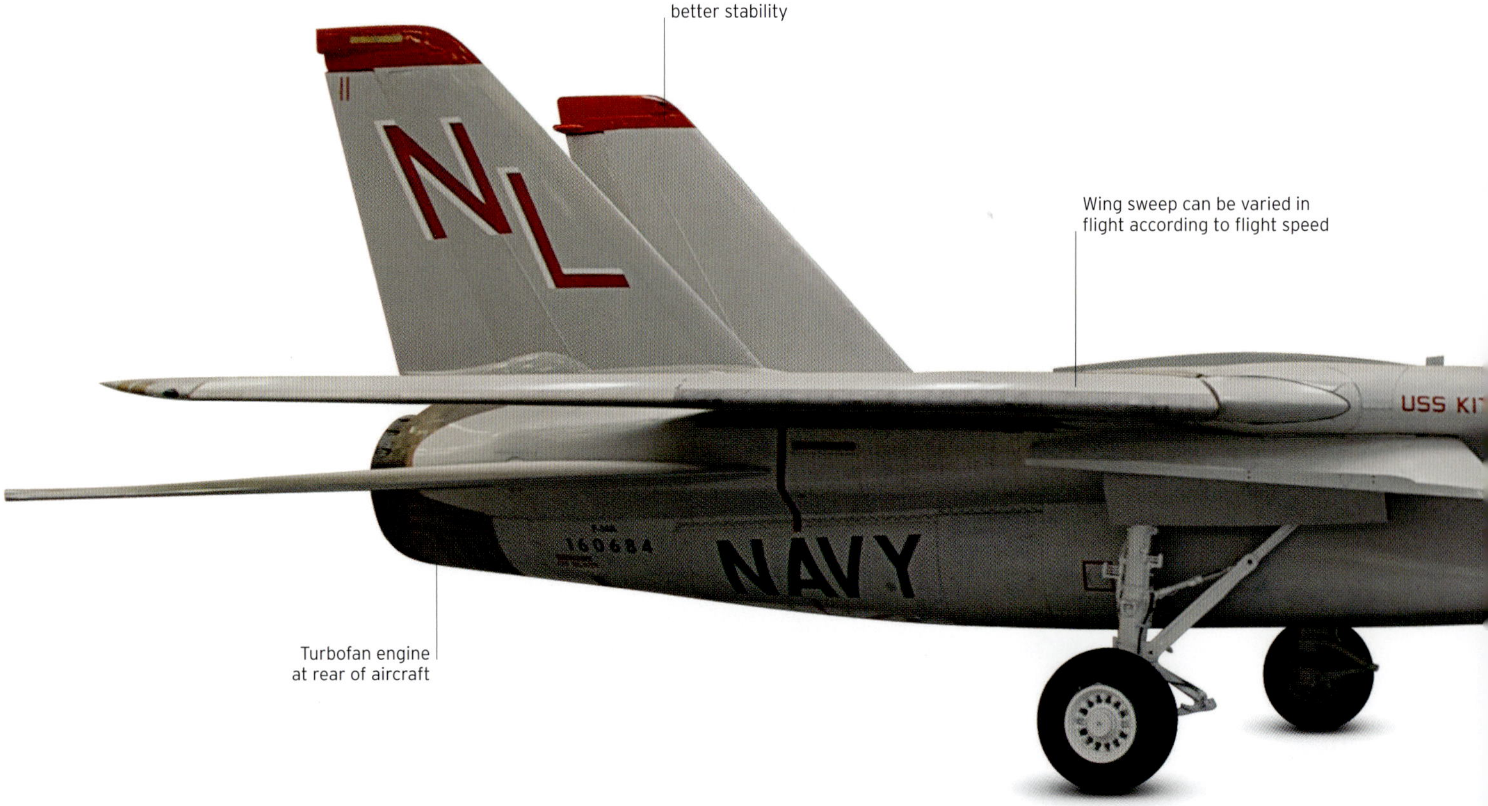

▽ Yakovlev Yak-38

Date 1971 **Origin** USSR

Engine 6,804 kg (15,000 lb) thrust Tumansky R-28 V-300 turbojet, plus 2 x 3,568 kg (7,870 lb) thrust Rybinsk RD-38 turbojet

Top speed 1,280 km/h (795 mph)

The Soviet Navy's only vertical takeoff and landing fighter, guided by its mother ship's computer to land automatically from several miles away, it used its two extra engines for takeoff, but was underpowered.

▽ Grumman F-14 Tomcat

Date 1974 **Origin** US

Engine 2 x 9,480 kg (20,900 lb) thrust Pratt & Whitney TF-30-P-414A afterburning turbofan

Top speed 2,485 km/h (1,544 mph)

Built to protect US navy ships against enemy aircraft and missiles, the swing-wing Tomcat was in service from 1974 to 2006, with numerous upgrades to its engines, weapons, and radar.

Electronic Warfare and Reconnaissance Aircraft

Aerial reconnaissance plays a vital role in intelligence gathering, whether at a tactical level via the MiG-21 and OV-1 Mohawk, or at a strategic level via the U-2 or SR-71. These "eyes in the sky" reached a new level of sophistication with the introduction of Airborne Early Warning (AEW) aircraft, which can build up an electronic picture of enemy movements from enormous distances. These in turn have evolved into Airborne Warning and Control System (AWACS) aircraft, which provide all-weather command, communications, and surveillance.

△ Lockheed U-2

Date 1957	**Origin** US
Engine 8,618 kg (19,000 lb) General Electric F118-101 turbofan	
Top speed 805 km/h (500 mph)	

A strategic reconnaissance aircraft, the U-2 – capable of cruising at heights of 21,000 m (70,000 ft) – was used by the Central Intelligence Agency (CIA) as a spy plane. It earned infamy when one was shot down in Soviet airspace in 1960.

△ **Boeing E-3 Sentry**

Date 1975	**Origin** US
Engine 4 x 9,752 kg (21,500 lb) thrust Pratt & Whitney TF33-PW-100 turbofan	
Top speed 855 km/h (530 mph)	

Operated by US, UK, French, and Saudi air forces, this aircraft uses an airborne warning and control system (AWACS). A rotating dish antenna is mounted on a converted 707 and it can detect even low-flying aircraft within 394 km (245 miles).

△ **Dassault Falcon 10MER**

Date 1975	**Origin** France
Engine 2 x 1,465 kg (3,230 lb) thrust Garrett TFE731-2 turbofan	
Top speed 912 km/h (566 mph)	

The French Navy commissioned Dassault to supply a small number of specially adapted business jets for training, electronic countermeasures, communications, and transport services, which emerged as the Falcon 10MER.

Destroyers

The primary function of a destroyer during conflict was to defend the battle fleet against attack from similar ships or torpedo-boats, although they were also used to hunt submarines. The battle fleet became an obsolete concept by 1939, but destroyers survived. Enlarged still further, up-gunned, and armed with an array of depth-charges, they were employed, along with a new generation of smaller escorts, to guard convoys of merchant ships against attack from submarines and aircraft.

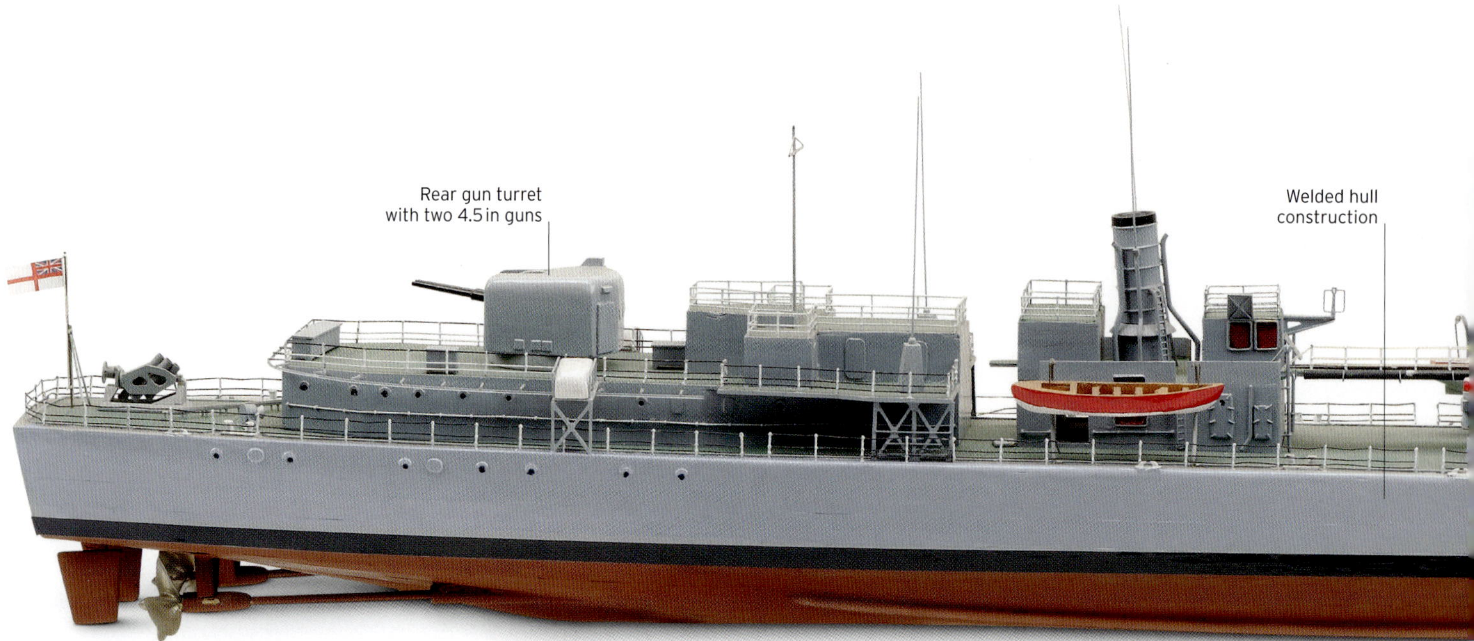

▽ HMS *Agincourt*

Commissioned	1947
Origin	UK
Displacement	3,420 tons
Length	115.5 m (379 ft)
Top speed	35.5 knots

HMS *Agincourt* was the first of the second group of *Battle*-class destroyers built for the British Royal Navy for operations in the Pacific. These had an extra dual-purpose 4.5 in gun, because the earlier ships proved to be under-armed. None of the second group was completed before the war's end.

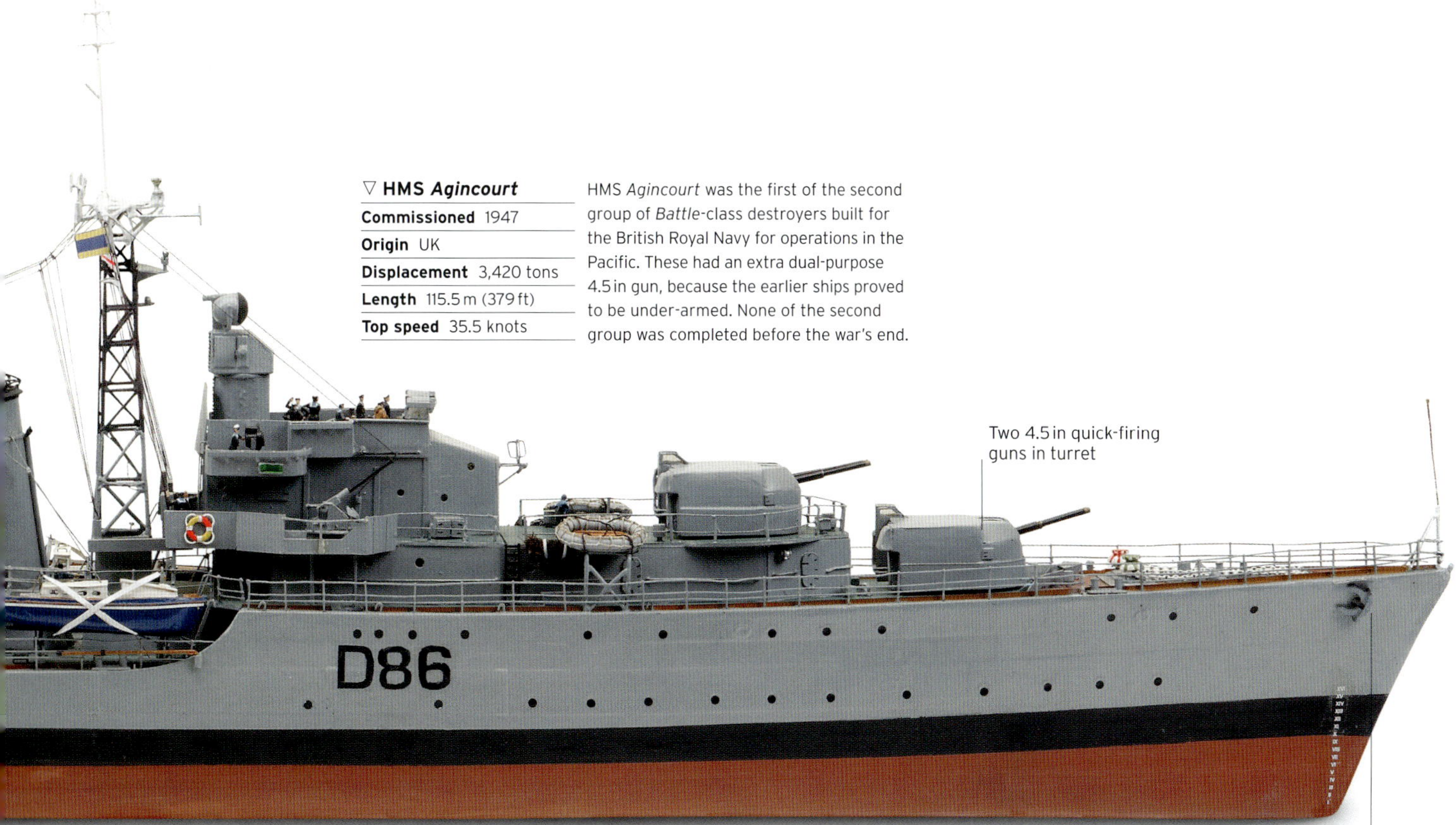

▽ HMS *Diamond*

Commissioned	1952
Origin	UK
Displacement	3,580 tons
Length	119 m (390 ft)
Top speed	30 knots

As a *Daring*-class destroyer, *Diamond* was the last such vessel in the British Royal Navy to be fitted with guns as its main armament before the widespread introduction of guided missiles.

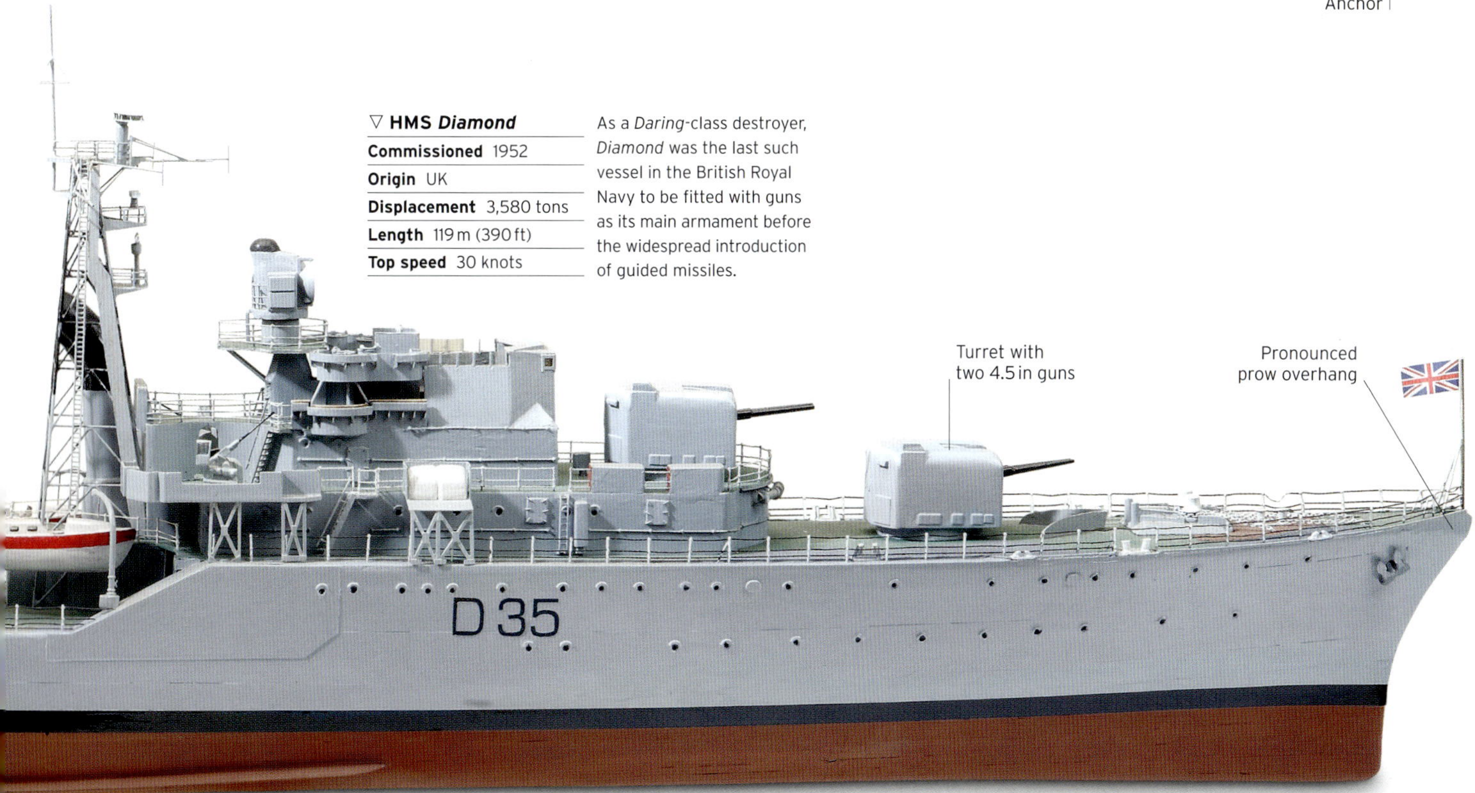

Submarines

Nuclear-powered submarines and their armament of Submarine-Launched Ballistic Missiles (SLBMs) are arguably the most potent weapon system ever developed. Hidden beneath the waves, they are able to launch their deadly missiles without warning and are virtually immune from retaliatory action by the enemy. Their high level of concealment also provides them with an invaluable second-strike capability. More conventional attack submarines, powered either by nuclear reactors or diesel-electric motors, operate against surface vessels or hunt down other submarines.

▷ **USS *Nautilus* (SSN-571)**

Commissioned 1954

Origin US

Displacement 3,535 tons (4,090 tons submerged)

Length 98.8 m (324 ft)

Top speed 22 knots (25 knots submerged)

A ground-breaking vessel, the *Nautilus* was the world's first operational nuclear-powered submarine and, in 1958, the first to complete an underwater transit of the North Pole.

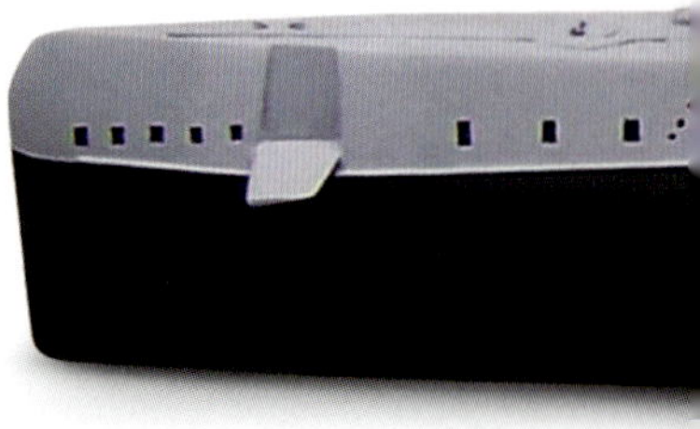

▷ ***Akula* Class**

Commissioned 1981

Origin Soviet Union

Displacement 18,500 tons (25,000 tons submerged)

Length 175 m (574 ft)

Top speed 22 knots (27 knots submerged)

Originally named the *Shchuka-B* ("pike" in Russian) class submarine, the West named it the *Akula* ("shark" in Russian) class after its lead ship. These submarines were the largest undersea vessels ever built. They were designed to fire SLBMs while hidden under the Arctic ice.

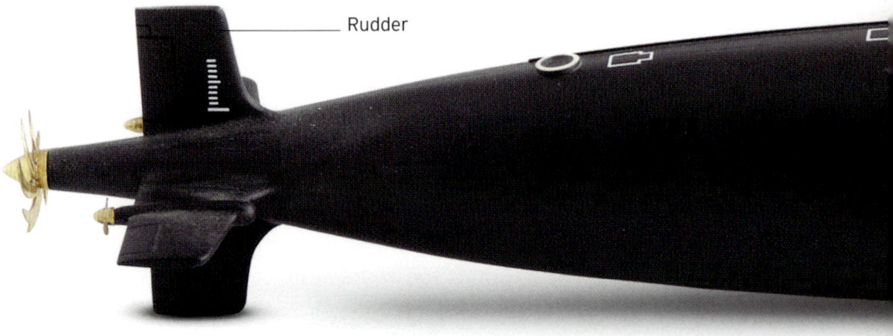

▽ ***Novosibirsk* (B-401)**

Commissioned 1984

Origin Soviet Union

Displacement 2,325 tons (3,075 tons submerged)

Length 67 m (220 ft)

Top speed 15 knots (24 knots submerged)

A diesel-electric attack submarine of the *Kilo* class, *Novosibirsk* was armed with minelaying equipment and conventional torpedoes, as well as antiship and antiaircraft missiles. Crewed by 57 men, it operated at depths of 240 m (787 ft).

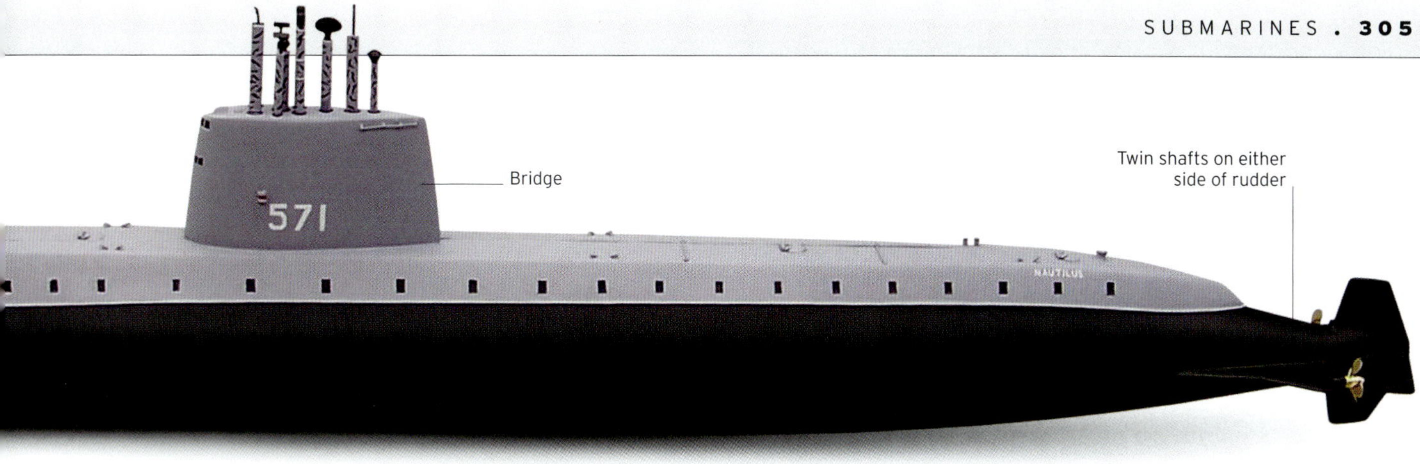
571
Bridge
Twin shafts on either side of rudder

Ballistic missile deck
Double-hull construction for extra buoyancy
Forward hydroplane

Total length of 73.8 m (242 ft)
Bow fitted with six torpedo tubes

1991–present THE MODERN WORLD

The 1991 Gulf War – the first major post-Cold War conflict – revealed the true scale of recent technological progress, showcasing such wonders as smart bombs, stealth aircraft, and cruise missiles. At the same time, guerrilla warfare and terrorism proved resistant to the most advanced military arsenals. Although they may lack access to advanced weaponry, guerrillas have benefitted from modern infantry weapons and explosives. Low-level conflicts have been aided by a ready supply of automatic arms and ammunition.

FIRE ACCESS

Modern Long Guns

Many modern firearms utilize modular designs, so that they can be swiftly converted and perform a variety of different roles. The Belgian-made FN SCAR, for example, can function as a designated sharpshooter rifle, an assault rifle, or a personal-defence carbine. Other innovations include Corner Shot, installed here on an Israeli M16, which allows a soldier to both look and shoot around corners.

▽ M16 with Corner Shot

Date 2003	**Origin** Israel
Weight 3.86 kg (8½ lb)	
Barrel 82 cm (32½ in)	
Calibre 5.56 mm x 45 NATO	

Developed for antiinsurgency operations, Corner Shot can pivot a clamped-on weapon (a pistol or M16) up to 90 degrees. A forward camera sends a visual feed to an LCD screen, allowing the operator to fire at targets without being exposed.

△ FN SCAR-L CQC Assault Rifle

Date 2009	**Origin** Belgium
Weight 3.04 kg (6½ lb)	
Barrel 25.4 cm (10 in)	
Calibre 5.56 mm x 45 NATO	

The Special operations forces Combat Assault Rifle (SCAR) is one of the most versatile modular rifle sytems, shown here with a 40 mm Underslung Grenade Launcher (UGL), which can fire high-explosive, smoke, and tear gas rounds.

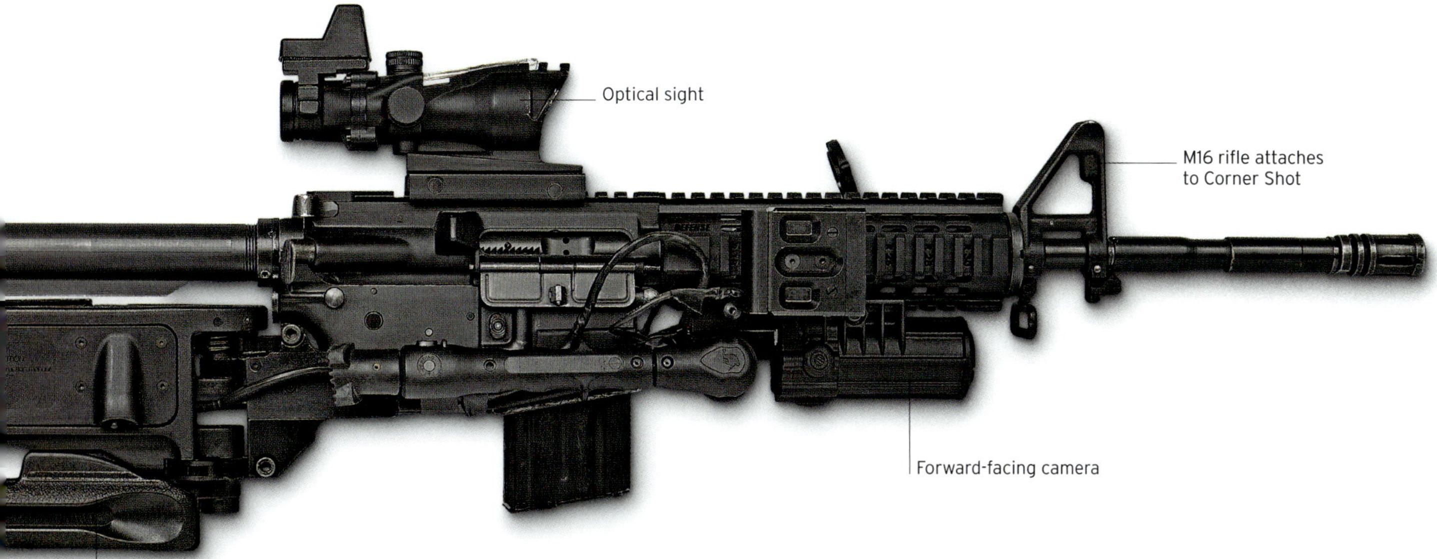

FN SCAR WITHOUT UNDERSLUNG GRENADE LAUNCHER

△ Heckler & Koch USP

Date 1993
Origin Germany
Weight 0.75 kg (1 lb)
Barrel 10.7 cm (4¼ in)
Calibre 9 mm Parabellum

The Universal Service pistol (USP) was Heckler & Koch's answer to the Glock 17, and it, too, was largely made of plastic and employed the tried-and-tested Browning locking system. The USP could be configured in nine different ways – for instance, the trigger assemblies and magazines could be changed quickly.

△ Glock 19 Gen 4 9 mm

Date 2000s
Origin Austria
Weight 0.67 kg (1½ lb)
Barrel 10.2 cm (4 in)
Calibre 9 mm Parabellum

The fourth generation series of Glock pistols is identifiable by the thumb rest on the upper part of the grip, the finger grooves on the forward edge of the grip strap, and the pattern of roughening cast into the grip plates themselves. The most distinctive feature, however, is the accessory rail forward of the trigger guard for installing a laser sight.

Modern Pistols

Modern self-loading pistols differ little from their predecessors visually. However, their construction now involves an increased use of carbon composites, plastics, and lightweight metal alloys. Another key development is that their grips are designed to allow the use of high-capacity magazines capable of holding up to 20 rounds. The profile of the forward trigger guard bow has also become more vertical and grooved, a configuration that allows shooters to hold a pistol securely with both hands.

△ Smith & Wesson M&P9 Pistol

Date	2005
Origin	US
Weight	0.67 kg (1½ lb)
Barrel	10.8 cm (4¼ in)
Calibre	9 mm

One of Smith & Wesson's M&P (Military and Police) range, this striker-fire weapon has been developed for law enforcement agencies. Combining modern plastics and metals, it features a 17-round magazine and ambidextrous controls.

△ Skorpion VZ83

Date 1990s	**Origin** Czechoslovakia
Weight 1.34 kg (3 lb)	
Barrel 11.5 cm (4½ in)	
Calibre 9 mm Kurz	

The Skorpion VZ61 was modified following its introduction to accept larger cartridges, including 9 mm Kurz and 9 mm Parabellum, but did not go into production. In the 1990s, the rechambered versions were introduced officially. The version using the 9 mm Kurz cartridge was called the VZ83.

Special Forces Weapons

Modern Special Forces units require a range of specialized weapons for their often secret operations. Complete reliability is a precondition for any such selection, as well as a high level of firepower. At other times, stealth weapons are needed. The most notable recent development has been the introduction of the Personal Defense Weapon (PDW), such as the Heckler & Koch MP7, that fires a powerful round that can penetrate body armour.

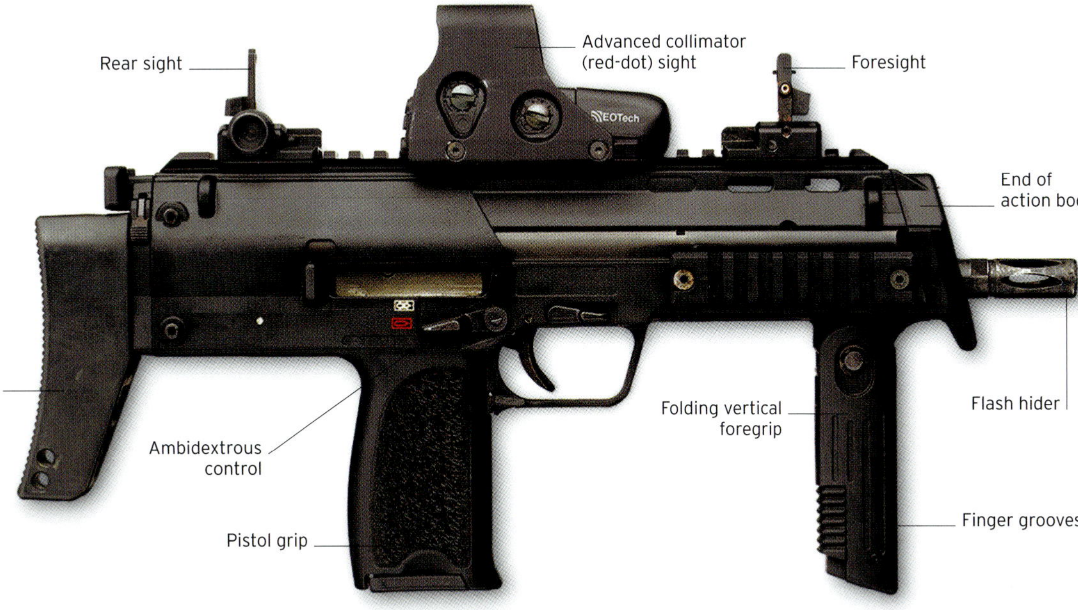

△ Heckler & Koch MP7

Date 2001	**Origin** Germany
Weight 1.9 kg (4¼ lb)	
Barrel 18 cm (7 in)	
Calibre 4.6 x 30 mm	

Similar in concept to the FN P90, the MP7 is a "personal defence weapon" that fires one of the new-generation reduced calibre, high-velocity rounds, in this case the 4.6 x 30 mm cartridge, which it can fire 950 times a minute. It has a fully ambidextrous design - having controls, such as the safety switch and decocking device, on both sides, accommodating both left- and right-handed operators.

△ Heckler & Koch 416 Assault Rifle

Date 2013	**Origin** Germany
Weight 3.12 kg (6¾ lb)	
Barrel 27.9 cm (11 in)	
Calibre 5.56 mm x 45 NATO	

Taking elements from the classic AR15 (M16) assault rifle, this short-barelled H&K 416 A5 utilizes a short-stroke piston and is popular with Special Forces' units - it was used by US Navy SEALs to kill Osama bin Laden in 2011.

Elevation adjustment
Bolt handle
Five-round removable box magazine

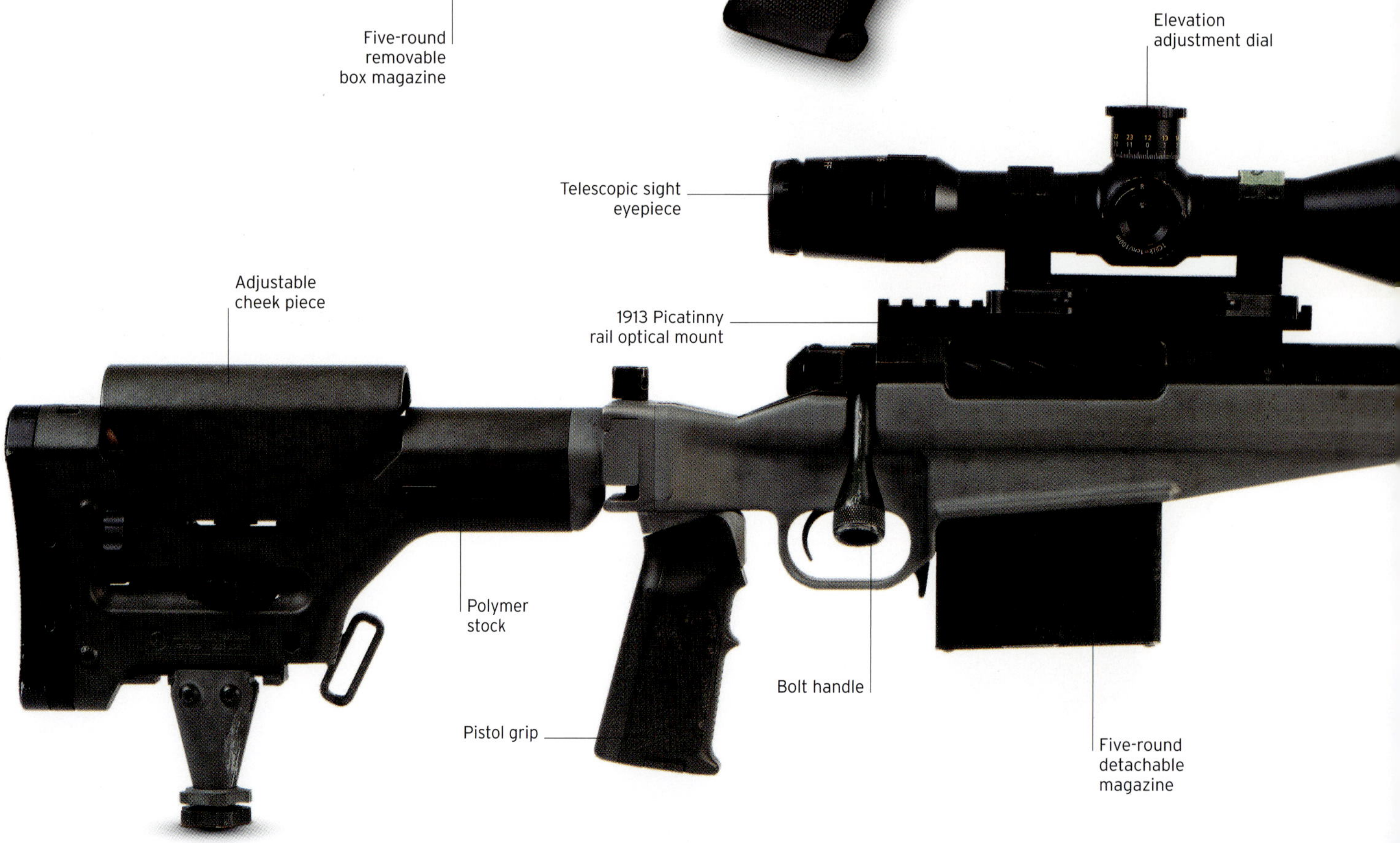

Elevation adjustment dial
Telescopic sight eyepiece
Adjustable cheek piece
1913 Picatinny rail optical mount
Polymer stock
Bolt handle
Pistol grip
Five-round detachable magazine

Heavy Sniper Rifles

Since the mid-1980s, sniper rifles have become increasingly specialized, incorporating new materials and manufacturing techniques, a far cry from the adapted service rifles and sporting arms that were standard for most of the 20th century. The optical quality of telescopic sights and magnification has improved, and 10x variable-power scopes are now common. The most important advance, however, has been in the development of more powerful ammunition.

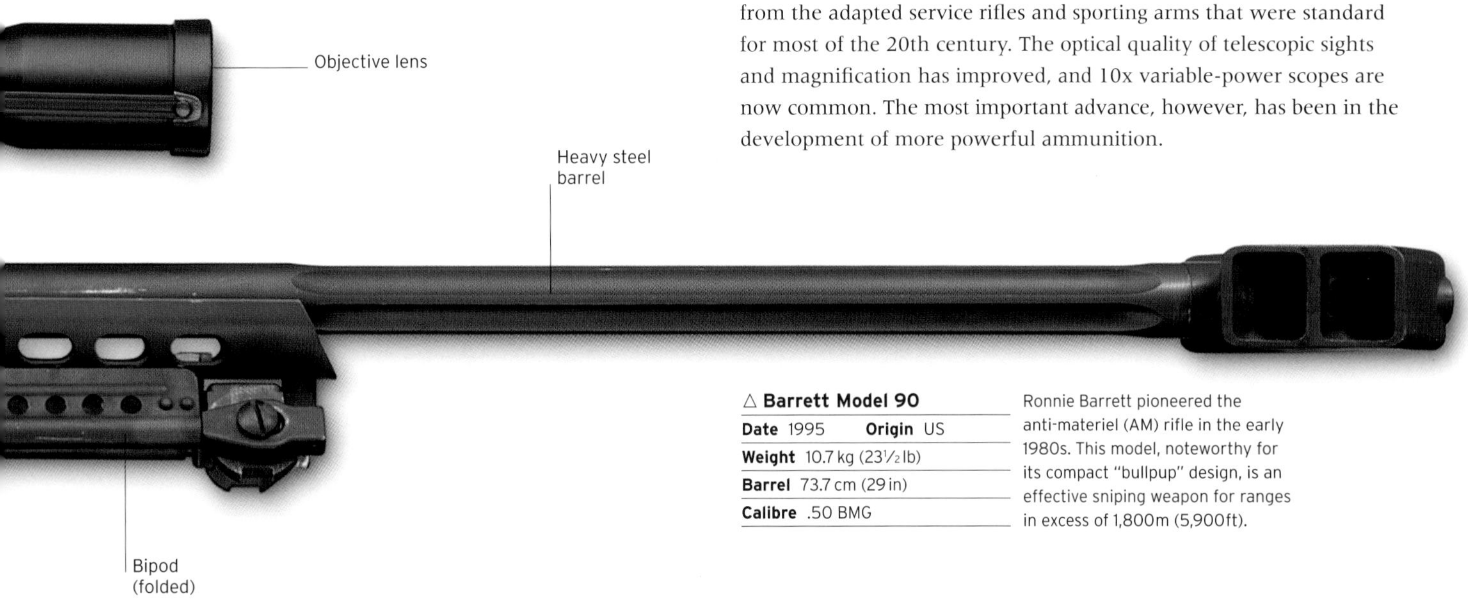

△ **Barrett Model 90**

Date 1995	**Origin** US
Weight 10.7 kg (23½ lb)	
Barrel 73.7 cm (29 in)	
Calibre .50 BMG	

Ronnie Barrett pioneered the anti-materiel (AM) rifle in the early 1980s. This model, noteworthy for its compact "bullpup" design, is an effective sniping weapon for ranges in excess of 1,800m (5,900ft).

△ **C14 Timberwolf Sniper Rifle**

Date 2005	**Origin** Canada
Weight 6.8 kg (15 lb)	
Barrel 66 cm (26 in)	
Calibre .338 in Lapua Magnum	

Following recent trends in antipersonnel sniper-rifle design, the Timberwolf has been chambered for the powerful .338 in Lapua Magnum round, which extends a rifle's effective range to over 1,200 m (3,940 ft).

In memory
Russian T-72B3 tanks roll across Dvortsovaya, or Palace Square in St Petersburg, on 5 May 2015 during a rehearsal for the Victory Day parade of 9 May, during which Russia celebrated the 70th anniversary of the defeat of Nazi Germany in 1945.

Post-Cold War Tanks

The end of the Cold War slowed down the development of tanks, but by no means ended it. Former adversaries reduced the size of their armed forces, and subsequently sold or scrapped many vehicles as they were no longer needed. The majority of vehicles that were under development during the late 1980s were brought into service slowly and in small numbers. However, some existing tanks continued to receive upgrades, such as the introduction of the L/55 120mm gun mounted on the German Leopard 2A6.

▽ Leclerc

Date 1992 **Origin** France

Weight 56.5 tonnes (62.3 tons)

Engine Wartsila V8X T9 diesel, 1,500 hp

Main armament 120 mm CN120-26 L/52 smoothbore gun

The Leclerc replaced the much lighter AMX-30. A total of 406 were built for France and 388 for the United Arab Emirates (UAE). An autoloader has reduced its crew to three. The electronics and armour have been steadily improved across production batches. French Leclercs have been used for peacekeeping in Kosovo and Lebanon, and the UAE's tanks have seen service in Yemen.

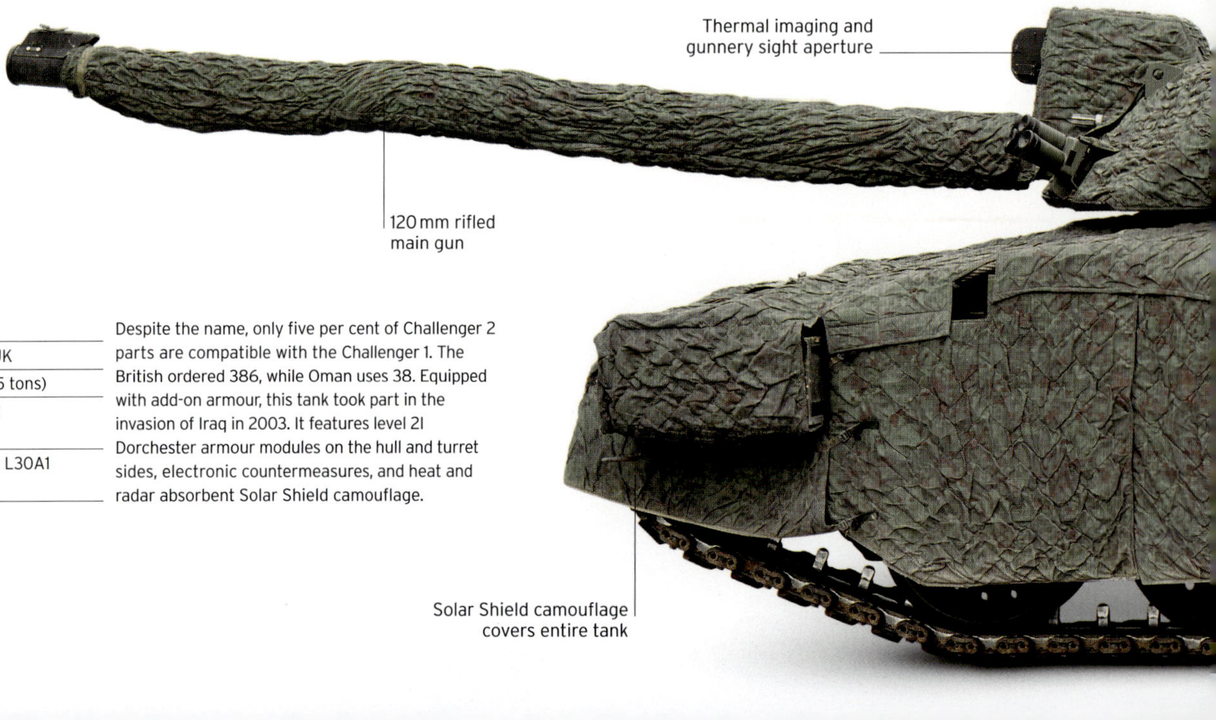

▷ Challenger 2

Date 1994 **Origin** UK

Weight 74.9 tonnes (82.5 tons)

Engine Perkins CV12 V12 diesel, 1,200 hp

Main armament 120 mm L30A1 L/55 rifled gun

Despite the name, only five per cent of Challenger 2 parts are compatible with the Challenger 1. The British ordered 386, while Oman uses 38. Equipped with add-on armour, this tank took part in the invasion of Iraq in 2003. It features level 2I Dorchester armour modules on the hull and turret sides, electronic countermeasures, and heat and radar absorbent Solar Shield camouflage.

△ Leopard 2A6

Date 2001 **Origin** Germany

Weight 62.4 tonnes (68.8 tons)

Engine MTU MB 873 Ka-501 diesel, 1,500 hp

Main armament 120 mm Rheinmetall 120 L/55 smoothbore gun

A significant upgrade to the 2A4 from the Cold War era, the 2A6 incorporates distinctive wedge-shaped spaced armour on the turret and the more powerful L/55 gun. The gunner's sight has moved to the turret roof, and the turret is now electrically powered rather than being hydraulically driven.

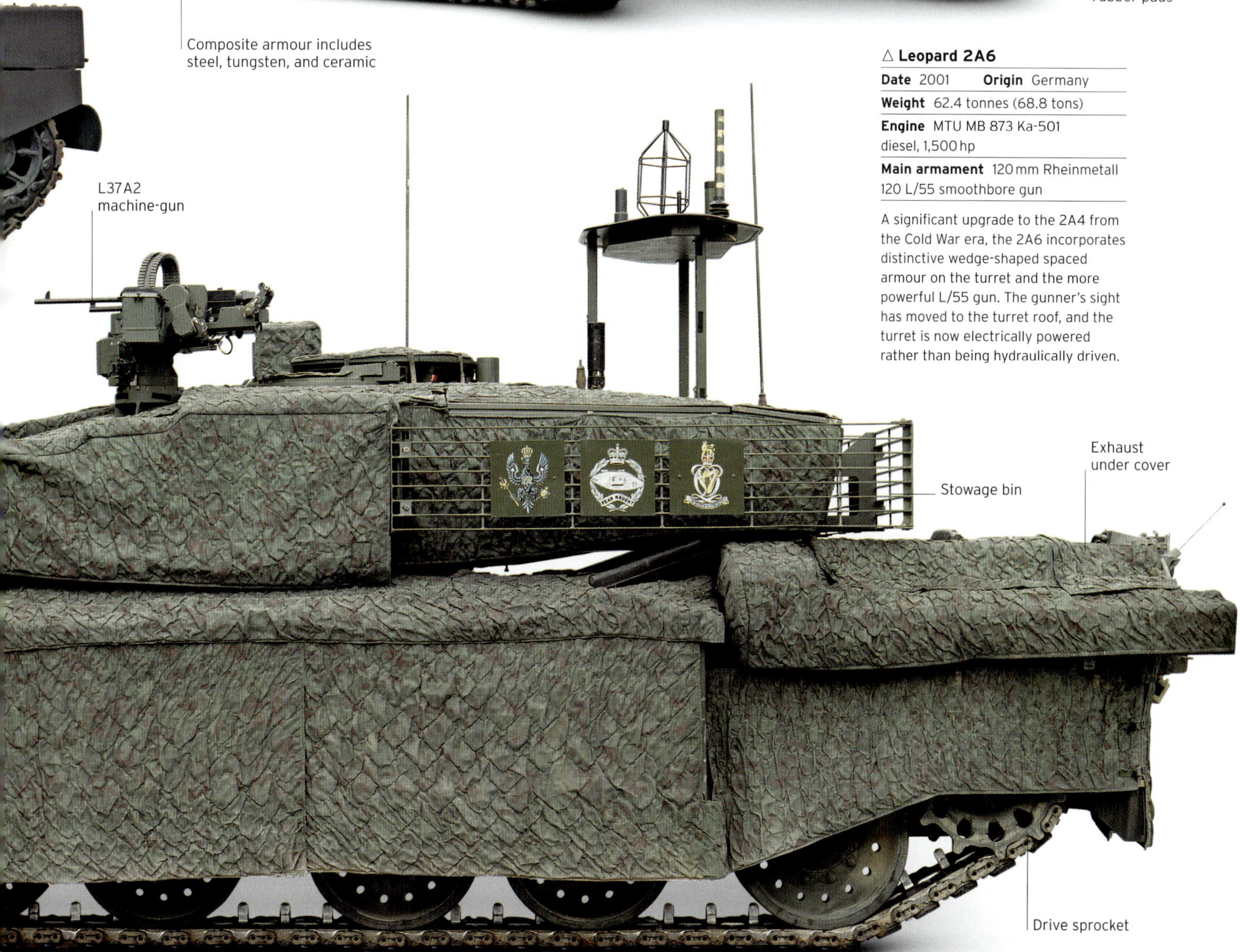

M1A2 Abrams

The American Abrams has been made in large numbers (some 11,000) and now equips seven national armies. Nevertheless, it has been subject to the West's ambivalent attitude to tanks - the dilemma of potentially needing them and seeing others still developing them versus the pressure on factory capacity amid tightening military budgets.

SPECIFICATIONS	
Name	M1A2 Abrams
Date	1992
Origin	US
Production	Approx 1,500
Engine	Textron Lycoming AGT1500 gas turbine, 1,500 hp
Weight	63 tonnes (69.4 tons)
Main armament	120 mm M256 smoothbore
Secondary armament	.50 Browning M2HB, 2 x 7.62 mm M240 MGs
Crew	4
Armour thickness	Unknown

THE ABRAMS WAS DESIGNED as a replacement for the M60 at a time when Soviet Bloc tanks were considered the most likely enemy. The first model was equipped with a version of the L7 105 mm gun from the UK, separate ammunition storage in a blow-out compartment to protect the crew, and a gas turbine engine that was small and incredibly powerful but twice as thirsty as an equivalent diesel engine. During a visit to the UK in 1973, an American team was shown the latest developments in Chobham armour, and this led to a redesign of the tank to incorporate the new protection system. Later, a new version of the laminate armour incorporating depleted uranium was fitted to the M1A1 model of the tank, doubling protection levels. The M1A1 was also equipped with the 120 mm German smoothbore gun, which gave it a tremendous advantage in the 1991 Gulf War.

Further upgrades, such as a new Fire Control System, Commander's Independent Thermal Viewer, and improved digital systems, led to the M1A2 model. City fighting in the Iraq War led to the development of the Tank Urban Survival Kit (TUSK) in 2006. These were fitted to tanks in theatre to improve protection in built-up areas.

Time and again the Abrams has proved itself in battle, and it will undoubtedly continue to be a potent weapon for decades to come.

Mobile powerhouse
The latest version of the Abrams is the M1A2 SEPv2 (System Enhancement Package). This has added an Auxiliary Power Unit, a Thermal Management System, and upgrades to electronic systems such as communications, display screens, and sights.

FRONT VIEW

REAR VIEW

Depleted uranium armour on front of turret

120 mm smoothbore gun

Rubber pads on tracks

EXTERIOR

The M1A2 is one of the heaviest main battle tanks in the world – partly due to its formidable composite armour, which has been further improved by the addition of depleted uranium mesh at the front of the hull and turret. This extraordinary armour offers protection against all known antitank weapons.

1. Commander's (left) and loader's hatches **2.** Commander's cupola **3.** Loader's 7.62 mm M240 machine-gun **4.** Nuclear, Biological, and Chemical protection system vent **5.** Infantry phone **6.** Drive sprocket **7.** Commander's station, looking right **8.** Gunner's station **9.** Gunner's Primary Sight eyepiece **10.** Driver's station, looking forward **11.** Gunner's control handles

1

2

3

4

5

6

7

9
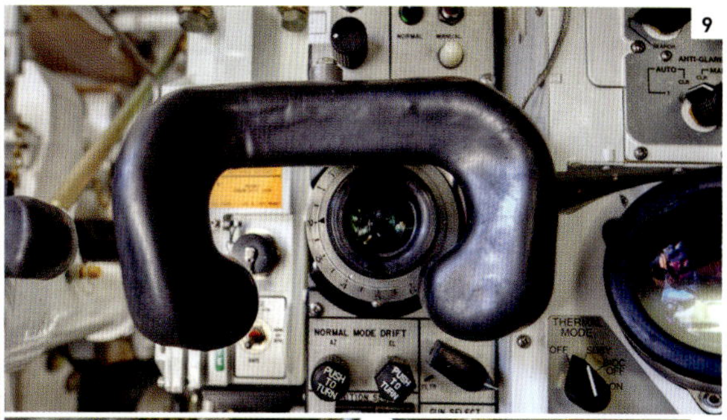

10
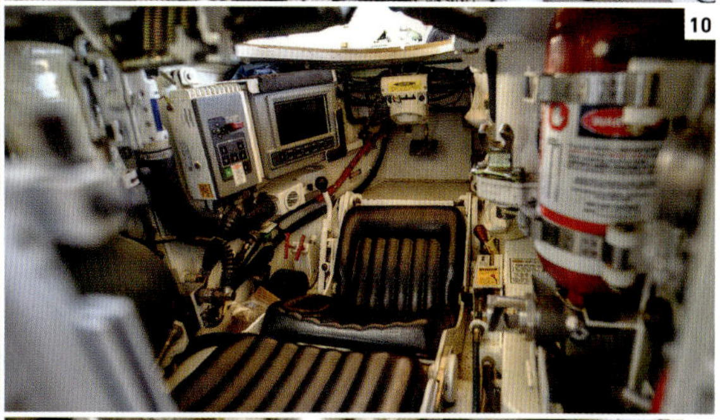

8

11

INTERIOR

The M1A2's interior is lined with Kevlar, which protects the crew against spalling (splinters caused by the explosion of enemy projectiles). Ammunition is kept in armoured compartments, which feature blow-out panels. These minimize the damage caused by ammunition "cooking off" in the heat of an explosion by ensuring the force of the blast is directed away from the crew compartment.

Counterinsurgency Vehicles

Political considerations often restricted the types of vehicles that could be used in counterinsurgency operations to lighter-wheeled vehicles, which were often equipped with extra armour. The South African Border War of the 1980s saw the development of vehicles that protected against both mines and direct fire. When the Improvised Explosive Device (IED) threat began to arise in Iraq and Afghanistan during the 21st century, these designs formed the starting point for the American Mine-Resistant Ambush Protected (MRAP) vehicle programme.

▽ Buffalo

Date 2002	**Origin** US
Weight 34.5 tonnes (38.1 tons)	
Engine Caterpillar C13 Diesel, 440 hp	
Main armament None	

Designed to carry EOD personnel, the Buffalo is significantly longer and taller than other MRAPs. It is equipped with a 10 m (33 ft) articulated manipulator arm that can be used to uncover and disable IEDs. The Buffalo is also used by British, Canadian, French, Italian, and Pakistani forces.

◁ **Mastiff**

Date 2002 **Origin** UK

Weight 23.6 tonnes (26 tons)

Engine Caterpillar C7 diesel, 330 hp

Main armament 40 mm automatic grenade launcher

The Mastiff is the British Army's version of the Force Protection Cougar MRAP, which saved thousands of lives in Iraq and Afghanistan. Unlike Cougar, the Mastiff has armour plate instead of armoured side windows, and is equipped with bar armour.

◁ **MaxxPro**

Date 2007 **Origin** US

Weight 13.4 tonnes (14.8 tons)

Engine MaxxForce D9.316 diesel, 330 hp

Main armament Varies

Navistar International manufactured a range of MaxxPro MRAPS for US forces in Afghanistan and Iraq. They are the most widely used MRAP design with over 7,000 built to date. Although the MaxxPro affords its crew of seven excellent protection, concerns have been raised about its poor off-road performance and its tendency to roll over.

Fighter and Strike Planes

Fighter aircraft have been transformed since the first subsonic jets fought in the Korean War. Today, they have the capacity to travel at more than twice the speed of sound and are capable of carrying an enormous weight of missiles and rockets. The most recent advances, however, have been in the field of aviation electronics. The latest fly-by-wire (computerized) control systems allow a manoeuvrability that would be impossible using conventional means, while weapons can be guided toward their target with pinpoint accuracy.

△ Dassault Mirage 2000D

Date 1991 **Origin** France

Engine 6,486-9,707 kg (14,300-21,400 lb) thrust SNECMA M53-P2 afterburning turbofan

Top speed 2,338 km/h (1,453 mph)

France's nuclear strike Mirage 2000N was developed into the 2000D for long-range strikes with conventional weapons, being equipped with improved controls, navigation, and defences.

△ Panavia Tornado GR4

Date 1997 **Origin** UK

Engine 2 x 4,468-7,833 kg (9,850-17,270 lb) thrust Turbo Union RB199-34R Mk103 afterburning turbofan

Top speed 2,431 km/h (1,511 mph)

The GR4 was a midlife update of the Tornado, vastly improving the navigation systems, avionics, and weapons capability following lessons learned in Gulf War use, particularly at medium altitude.

Sleek fuselage for
aerodynamic efficiency
Variable
exhaust
nozzle
375
MIRAGE
2000
ARMEE DE L'AIR
AMD_BA

Swept-back
tail fin
Variable sweep-wing
that can be moved
during flight
Missiles and bombs
hung below wings

Fighter and Strike Helicopters

Initially, wars in Iraq and Afghanistan involved large numbers of military helicopters, while the offshore oil industry kept civilian producers in profit. However, the recession of 2008 hit the helicopter industry hard, as their private buyers vanished and defence budgets were cut. However, military forces continue to need modern fighter and strike helicopters, as their manoeuvrability and ability to land and take off in restricted conditions make them an essential weapon in today's military arsenal.

△ **AgustaWestland AW101 Merlin**

Date 2000	**Origin** Italy/UK
Engine 3 x 2,100 shp Rolls-Royce Turbomeca RTM322-01 turboshaft	
Top speed 309 km/h (192 mph)	

Few aircraft have had a gestation period as long as the quarter-century of the AW101; nine prototypes were built while Westland went through three owners and a merger.

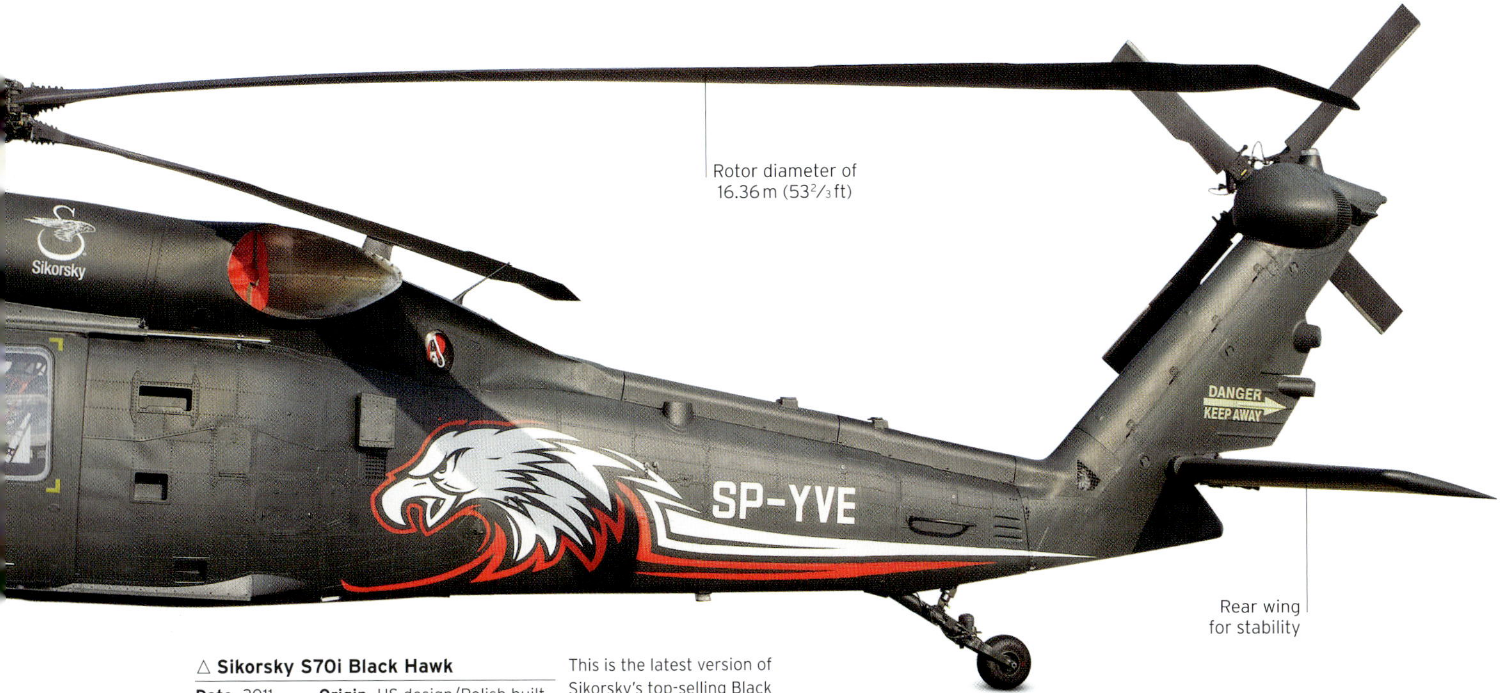

△ **Sikorsky S70i Black Hawk**

Date 2011	**Origin** US design/Polish built
Engine 2 x 2,000 shp General Electric T700-GE-701D turbine	
Top speed 294 km/h (183 mph)	

This is the latest version of Sikorsky's top-selling Black Hawk built in Poland by PZL Mielec, a company acquired by Sikorsky in 2007, and offered on international markets.

High-tech Fighter Aircraft

Fast, agile, and well-equipped with sensors and weapons, the European-made Typhoon is an advanced tactical fighter and one of the world's leading combat aircraft. Its excellent manoeuvrability, acceleration, and climb rate make it a formidable foe in air-to-air battles. In training exercises, it has proved itself superior to most existing aircraft. Its main rival is the American-designed-and-built Lockheed Martin F-35 Lightning II, a stealth, multi-role fighter designed for both ground attack and air defence.

▽ Lockheed Martin F-35A Lightning II

Date 2006	**Origin** US
Engine 12,700-19,500 kg (28,000-43,000 lb) thrust Pratt & Whitney F135 afterburning turbofan	
Top speed 1,930 km/h (1,200 mph)	

The advanced-stealth-technology F-35 has three forms: F-35A conventional takeoff and landing; F-35B short takeoff, vertical landing; F-35C carrier-based. It will equip most of the western world.

FULL VIEW

△ Eurofighter Typhoon FGR4

Date 2007

Origin UK, Germany, Italy, and Spain

Engines 2 x 9,060 kg (20,000 lb) thrust EJ200 turboFAN

Top speed 2,475 km/h (1,538 mph)

The FGR4 – Fighter, Ground attack, and Reconnaissance, Mk4 – was introduced in 2007 when the RAF's Typhoon fighters were upgraded to these two new roles. Some were modified and some newly built.

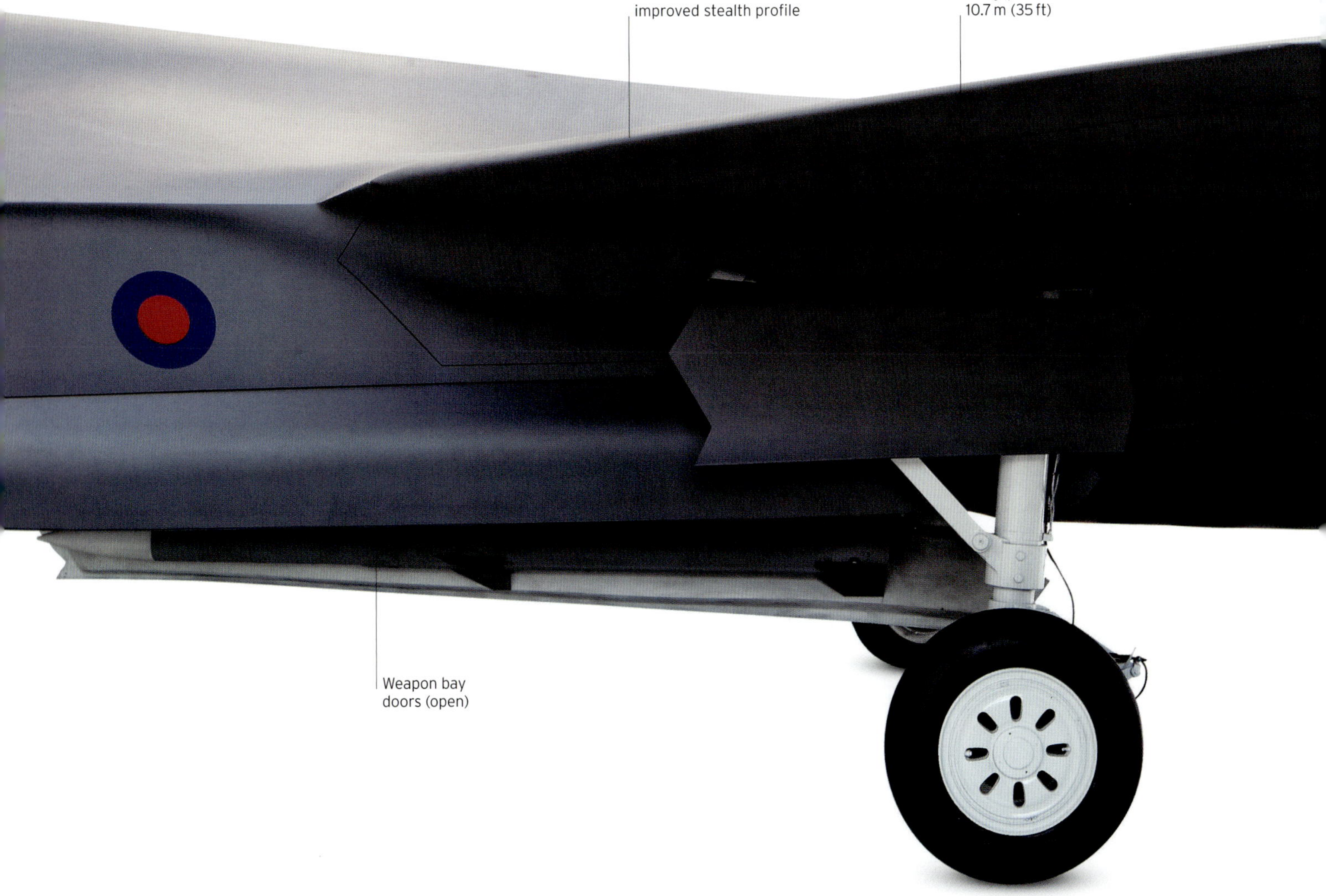

Modern Utility Planes

The utility planes of the 1990s were the result of a long period of development and improvement. Existing models had been updated and upgraded, using the latest technology and materials to increase their efficiency and range and improve their navigation systems. The Boeing C-17 Globemaster carried forward the name of two Douglas Globemaster predecessors, while the Hercules now boasts more than 40 different variants and versions.

Total wingspan of 52 m (170 ft)

△ **McDonnell Douglas/ Boeing C-17 Globemaster III**

Date 1991 **Origin** US

Engine 4 x 18,325 kg (40,400 lb) thrust Pratt & Whitney F117-PW-100 turbofan

Top speed 830 km/h (515 mph)

Designed to replace the Starlifter, this large military transport aircraft began development in the 1980s. It proved to be capable and adaptable, carrying military equipment and troops to and from the battlefield.

Newer versions have four-bladed propellers

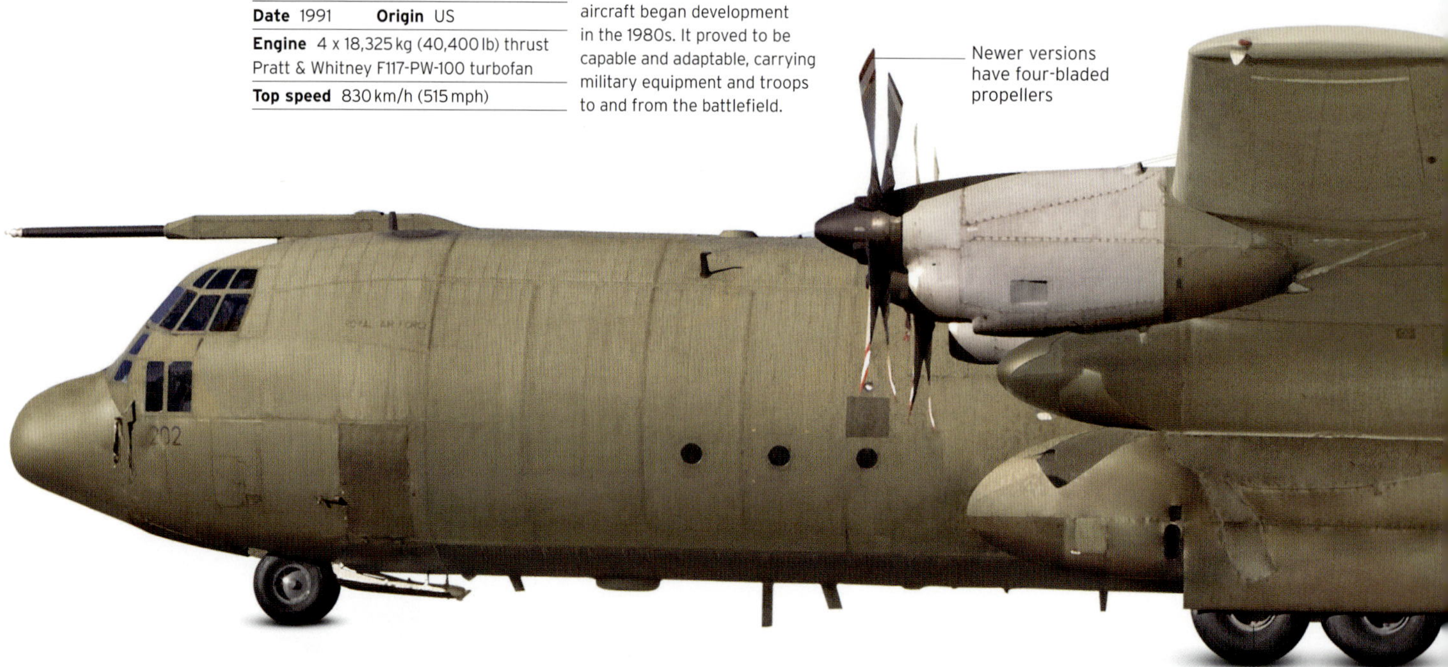

△ **Lockheed Hercules C-130K Mk3**

Date 1992 **Origin** US

Engine 4 x 4,590 hp Allison T56-A-15 turboprop

Top speed 589 km/h (366 mph)

First flown in 1954, the rugged and versatile Hercules has fulfilled vital roles in every major conflict since and is still being updated for the future. This 1990s K-spec is in RAF Gulf War camouflage.

Powerful landing gear to support plane on runway

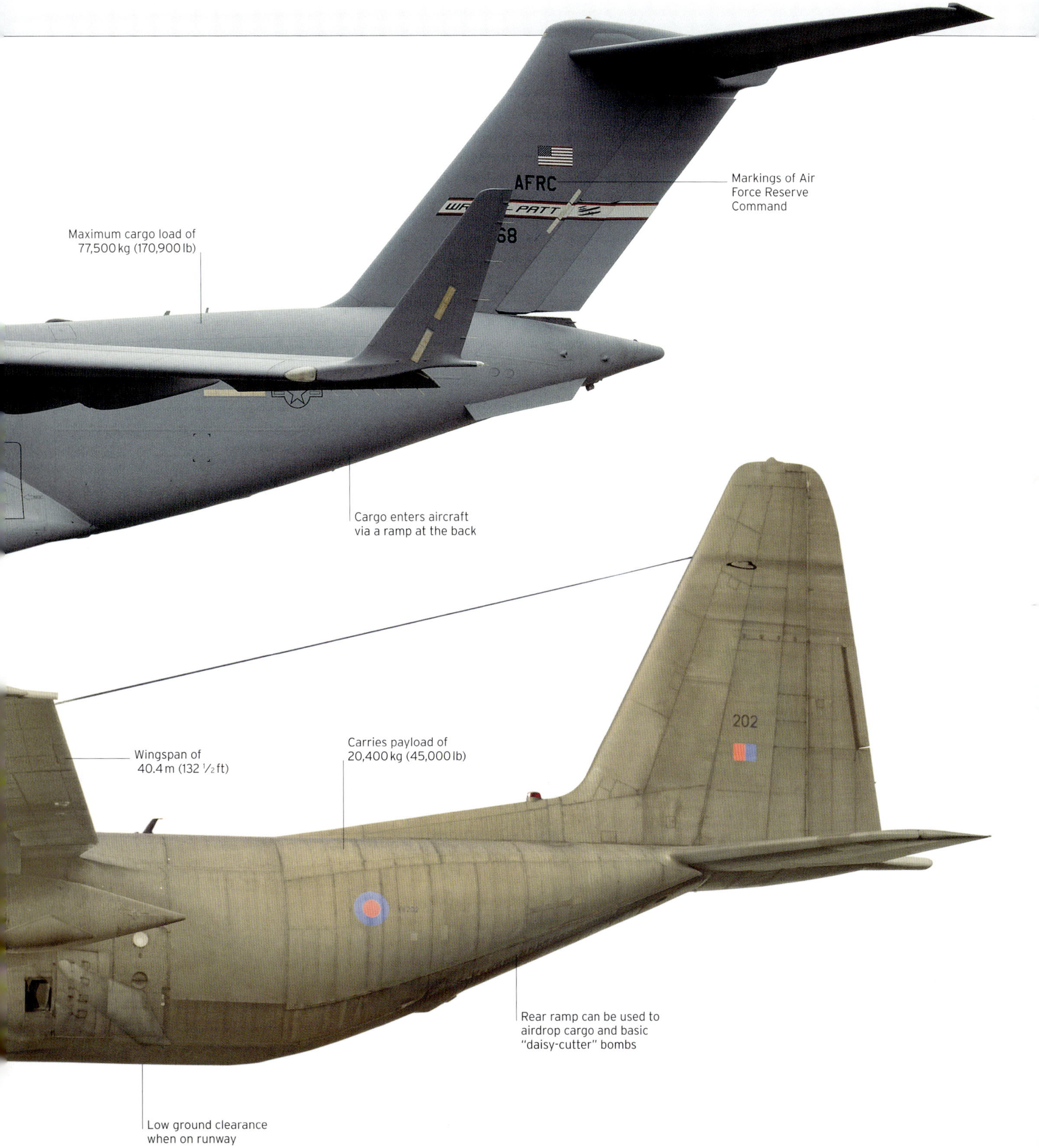
AFRC
Markings of Air Force Reserve Command
Maximum cargo load of 77,500 kg (170,900 lb)
Cargo enters aircraft via a ramp at the back
202
Wingspan of 40.4 m (132 ½ ft)
Carries payload of 20,400 kg (45,000 lb)
Rear ramp can be used to airdrop cargo and basic "daisy-cutter" bombs
Low ground clearance when on runway

△ AS 555 Fennec

Date 1992 **Origin** France

Engine 2 x 456 shp Turbomeca TM319 Arrius 1M turboshaft

Top speed 287 km/h (178 mph)

This aircraft was a twin-engined military version of the venerable and globally popular Ecuriel (Squirrel) line. The 1990s upgrades included navigation, radar, autopilot, and weapons systems.

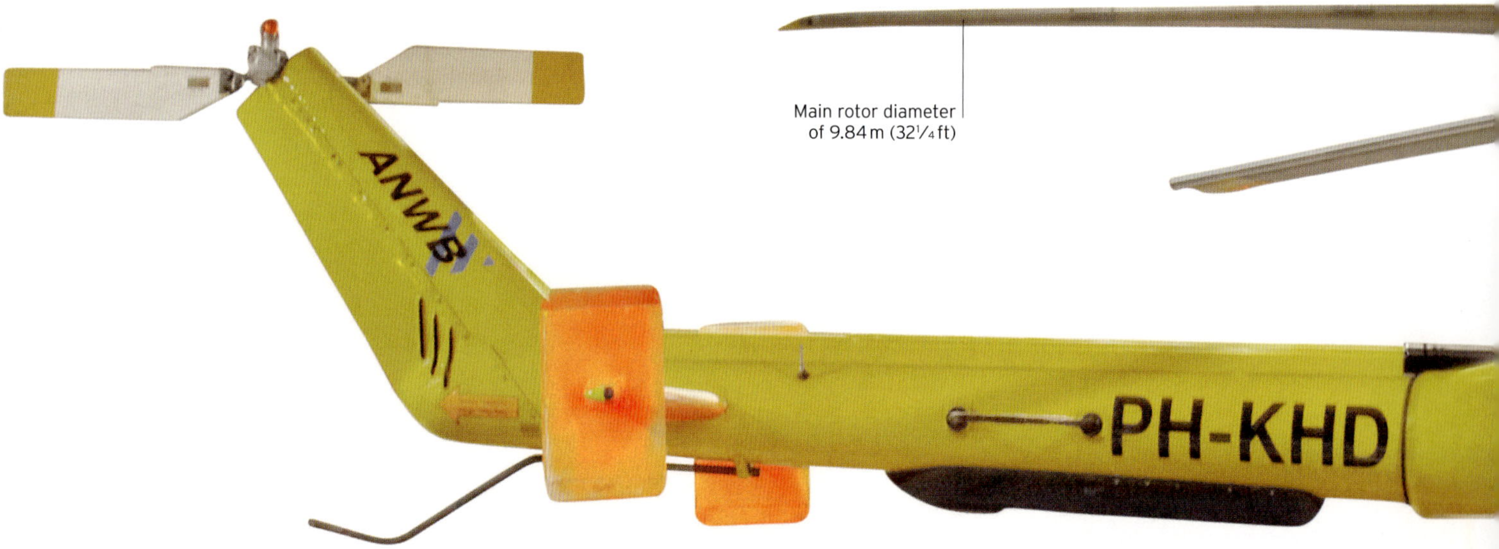

△ Messerschmitt-Boelkow-Blohm MBB Bo 105LS A3 Superlifter

Date 1995 **Origin** Germany

Engine 2 x 650 shp Rolls-Royce 250-C30 turboshaft

Top speed 241 km/h (150 mph)

Forerunner of the EC135, the 105 was the smallest and least expensive twin-turbine helicopter. The 1995 variant included more powerful engines and improved rotor blades.

Modern Utility Helicopters

The decade-long hiatus between the end of the Cold War and the start of the War on Terror caused a fallow period for military helicopter development and sales, especially for Soviet and Eastern Bloc manufacturers. The wars in both Afghanistan and Iraq, however, involved increasing numbers of military helicopters, specifically the utility helicopters used to transport troops and equipment, evacuate casualties, and provide reconnaissance and reconnoitre capabilities.

Main rotor diameter of 11 m (36 ft)

Crew of one or two pilots

△ **Eurocopter UH-72 Lakota**

Date 2004	**Origin** France
Engine 2 x 738 shp Turbomeca Arriel 1E2 turboshaft	
Top speed 268 km/h (167 mph)	

Eurocopter beat the American manufacturers on their own turf by winning a US Army light utility helicopter competition with this military variant of the EC145.

Solid titanium rotor head with hingeless blades

Crew of one or two pilots, plus four passengers

Training exercises
Troops must train regularly to ensure that they are battle-ready. Here US and Japanese Forces training together in Japan board a Boeing CH-47 Chinook in December 2014.

USS George Washington

Aircraft carriers are the ultimate symbol of naval power. The *George Washington* is one of 10 *Nimitz*-class supercarriers in the US Navy – the largest military vessels ever to take to the seas.

SPECIFICATIONS	
Class	*Nimitz*-class aircraft carrier
Commissioned	1992
Origin	US
Displacement	104,200 tons
Length	332.8 m (1,092 ft)
Beam	76.8 m (252 ft)
Engines	2 x Westinghouse A4W nuclear reactors, 4 x steam turbines
Top Speed	56+ km/h (30+ knots)
Range	Unlimited
Complement	6,102
Armament	2 x Mk 57 Mod3 Sea Sparrow surface-to-air missiles; 2 x RIM-116 Rolling Airframe infrared surface-to-air missiles; 3 x Phalanx CIWS missile defence system
Armour	Unknown

COMMISSIONED IN 1992, the *George Washington* can accommodate 85 aircraft, including fighter, strike, and transport planes, airborne early warning (AEW) aircraft, and helicopters. It is also a floating home for around 6,000 service men and women. Although designed primarily to offer an offensive strike capability, the ship is equipped with its own defences, such as antiaircraft and antimissile weapon systems, and rapid-fire 20 mm guns.

On the starboard side and overlooking the deck is the island superstructure – the ship's command-and-control centre, which houses the bridge and primary flight-control area. From here, officers keep a careful watch on the massive flight deck, which covers 1.8 hectares (4.5 acres) – about the size of two-and-a-half football fields.

During flying operations, the deck is a hive of activity, with aircraft taking off and landing, and being manoeuvred, refuelled, and armed. Aircraft are launched by four catapults, two at the forward end of the angled deck and two in the bows. The landing deck is angled to the port side to allow other activities to take place as aircraft return to the ship. When touching down, a pilot must ensure that the plane's tailhook catches one of four high-tensile steel arrestor wires that run across the flight deck. These decelerate the aircraft rapidly and bring it to a halt within two seconds.

When not in use, most aircraft are stored beneath the flight deck in the vast hangar, which stretches for much of the ship's length. On the decks below are living quarters for the ship's personnel.

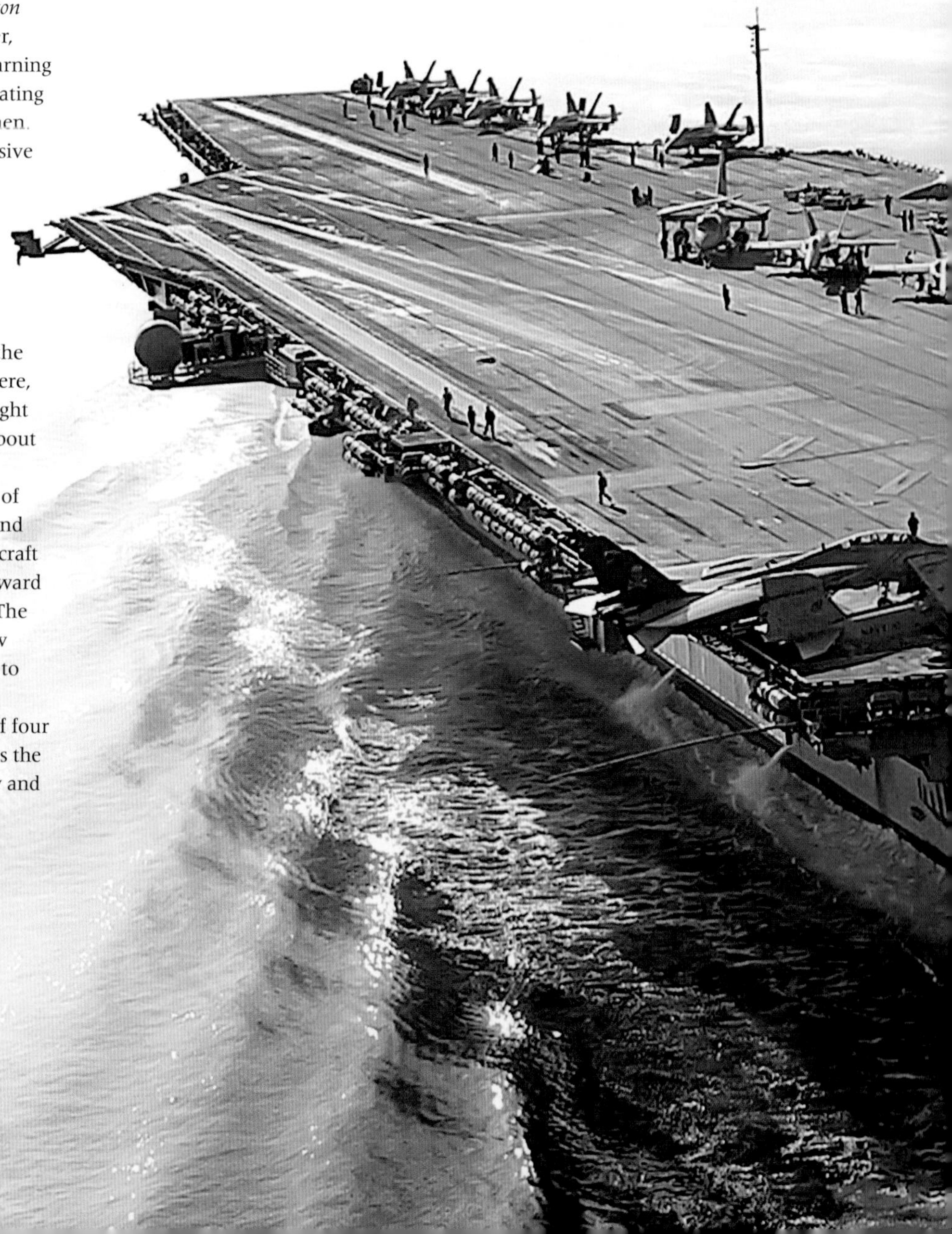

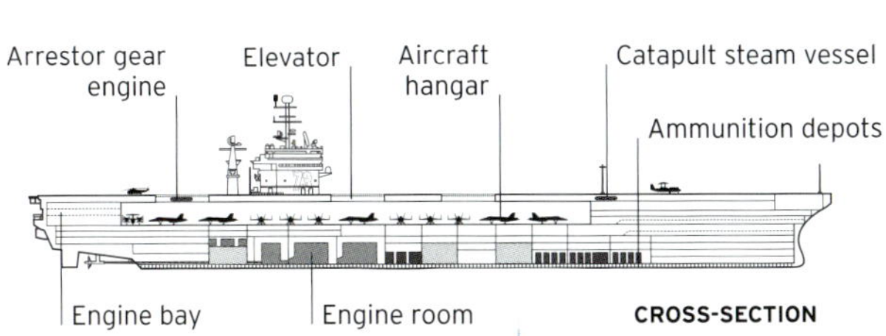

CROSS-SECTION

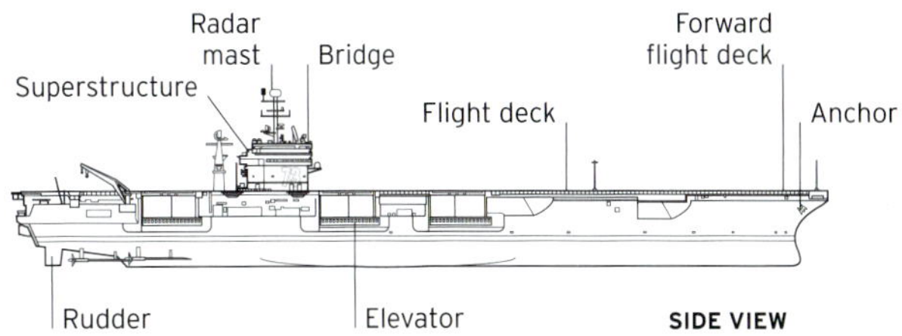

SIDE VIEW

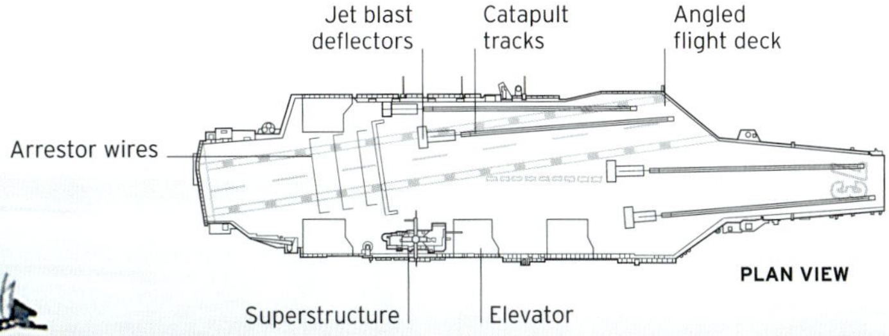

PLAN VIEW

Floating airstrip
Carriers such as the *George Washington* provide the strategic benefit of a mobile strike platform that can operate from anywhere in international waters.

ON DECK

The observation pod, which retracts below the flight-deck, enables the crew controlling aircraft catapult launches to see what is happening while remaining safe from moving aircraft and their exhausts. For a catapult launch, a shuttle is attached to the aircraft's undercarriage and propelled along a track set into the surface of the ship's flight deck by a steam-powered piston.

1

4

1. Catapult control pod **2.** Preparing for take-off **3.** Shuttle track **4.** Jet-blast deflector **5.** Grumman F-14 Tomcat landing **6.** Elevator **7.** Aircraft weaponry **8.** Operations room **9.** Bridge **10.** Instrument panel **11.** Engine bay **12.** Primary flight control

8

2

3

7

5

6

9

11

10

12

INSIDE AND DOWN BELOW

The control rooms are based in the island superstructure up above and elsewhere below deck. In addition to the aircraft hangar, the lower-deck areas include the catapult and arrestor gear machinery, 44 magazines, and the power plant and engine room. Facilities for the thousands of crew and air wing include messes, medical facilities, and a gym.

△ USS *Maryland* (SSBN-738)

Commissioned 1992 **Origin** US

Displacement 16,000 tons (18,700 tons submerged)

Length 171 m (561 ft)

Top speed 20 knots (25 knots submerged)

An *Ohio*-class ballistic missile submarine, *Maryland* is at the forefront of America's nuclear deterrent. Its 24 Trident missiles are capable of delivering up to 12 warheads per missile to a range of 11,300 km (7,021 miles).

△ USS *Virginia* (SSN-74)

Commissioned 2004 **Origin** US

Displacement 6,455 tons (7,101 tons submerged)

Length 115 m (377 ft)

Top speed 25 knots (32 knots submerged)

The *Virginia* - lead vessel in its class - is a nuclear-powered attack submarine, armed with Mark 48 guided torpedoes and Tomahawk cruise missiles. It features a pressure chamber that can release SEAL divers while submerged.

Submarines

The submarines of the modern era are all developments of their predecessors. All of these sleek, powerful, almost invisible war machines are armed to the teeth with Trident, cruise, and other missiles, as well as guided torpedoes. Most modern submarines are nuclear powered, although auxiliary diesel engines are also used. The latest of these vessels – the Russian *Yuri Dolgoruki* – showed signs of a rushed development, although it was successfully commissioned in 2012.

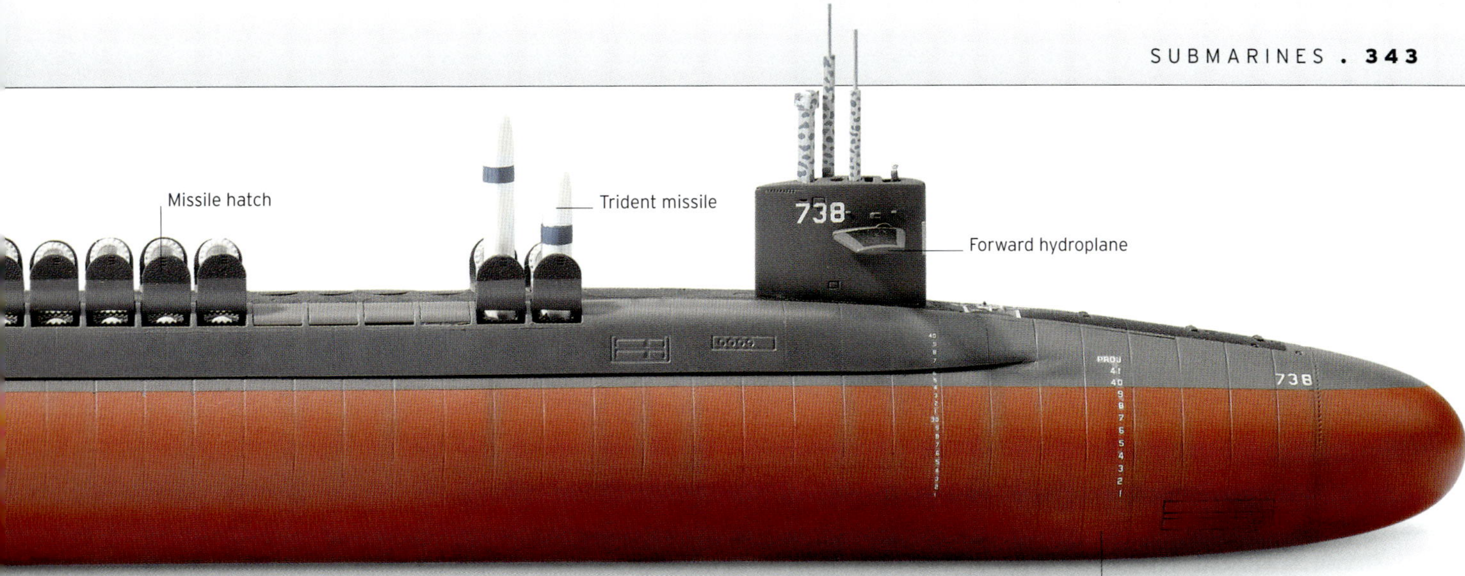

▽ *Yuri Dolgoruki*

Commissioned 2012 **Origin** Russia

Displacement 14,490 tons (23,620 tons submerged)

Length 170 m (558 ft)

Top speed 15 knots (29 knots submerged)

One of the latest *Borey*-class nuclear-powered submarines, the *Yuri Dolgoruki* is armed with 16 RSM-56 Bulava SLBMs, each missile containing six warheads with a range of up to 10,000 km (6,214 miles).

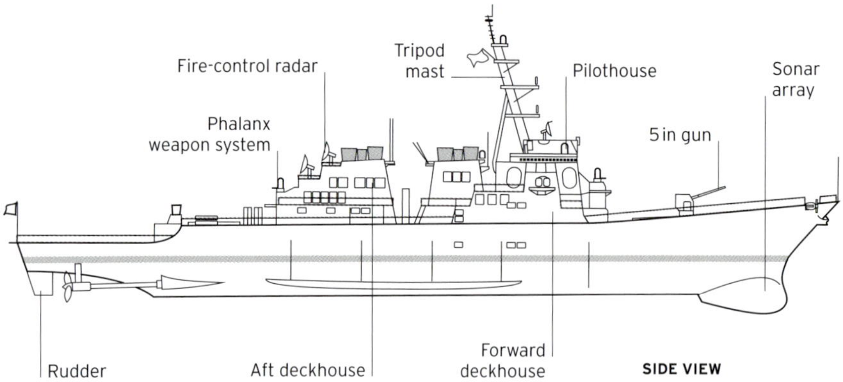
Fire-control radar
Tripod mast
Pilothouse
Sonar array
Phalanx weapon system
5 in gun
Rudder
Aft deckhouse
Forward deckhouse
SIDE VIEW

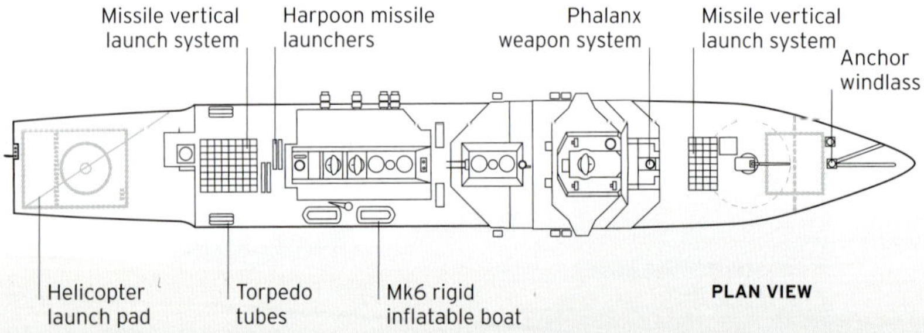
Missile vertical launch system
Harpoon missile launchers
Phalanx weapon system
Missile vertical launch system
Anchor windlass
Helicopter launch pad
Torpedo tubes
Mk6 rigid inflatable boat
PLAN VIEW

USS Donald Cook

The US Navy's guided-missile destroyer *Donald Cook* saw action in the Iraq War. Deployed in Operation Iraqi Freedom in March 2003, it was among the first ships to launch strikes against Iraqi targets.

SPECIFICATIONS	
Class	*Arleigh Burke*-class guided missile destroyer
Commissioned	1998
Origin	US
Displacement	8,900 tons
Length	154 m (505 ft)
Beam	20 m (66 ft)
Engines	4 x General Electric LM2500-30 gas turbines
Top Speed	56 km/h (30 knots)
Range	8,100 km (4,374 nautical miles)
Complement	330
Armament	1 x 29 cell and 1 x 61 cell Mk 41 vertical missile launchers; 2 x Mk 141 Harpoon missile launchers; 7 guns; 2 x 20 mm Phalanx CIWS missile defence system; 2 x Mk 32 triple torpedo tubes
Armour	Unknown

THE *DONALD COOK* and her fellow *Arleigh Burke*-class destroyers are among the most advanced surface warships in service today. Launched in 1997 and the 25th ship in the class, the *Donald Cook* belongs to Flight II, which embodies significant advances in armaments and electronics on earlier versions. The ship is packed with diverse weaponry, giving her what the US Navy calls "multi-mission offensive and defensive capabilities". The heart of the destroyer's offensive capabilities are the two Mk41 Vertical Launch Systems (VLS). These can fire antiaircraft missiles, antisubmarine missiles, missiles for destroying other surface ships, and cruise missiles for strike operations against land targets. The ship also has a launch pad from which an attack helicopter can operate. The destroyer's design is intended to maximize its chances of surviving. The *Arleigh Burke* class were among the first ships to incorporate "stealth" technology, with buried funnels and angled shapes that reduce their radar profile, as well as features to suppress infrared emissions. They were also the first all-steel American warships. Using steel rather than aluminium for the destroyer's superstructure reduces damage in the event of a missile hit. The *Donald Cook* has a crew of 30 officers and over 300 enlisted personnel.

USS *DONALD COOK*
Despite being classed as a destroyer, *Donald Cook* is over 150 m (500 ft) long and displaces 8,900 tons, making her similar in size to many World War II cruisers.

ABOVE DECK

The deck of USS *Donald Cook* has a bare profile, as the compact weaponry is mostly concealed. A Super Rapid Bloom Offboard Chaff system launches chaff and infrared decoys to confuse enemy missiles and fire-control systems. The ship can embark and refuel a Sikorsky SH-60 Seahawk helicopter for search and attack missions or for transporting personnel and cargo.

1

2

1. Chaff and decoy launcher **2.** Helicopter landing pad **3.** Ship's bridge **4.** Gas turbine **5.** Main engine room **6.** Main passageway **7.** Battle room **8.** CIC screen **9.** Tactical coordinator **10.** Ammunition loading system **11.** 5 in gun magazine **12.** Propellant store

3

4

5

6

7

10

11

8

12

9

INSIDE AND BELOW DECK

Battle operations are coordinated by the Combat Information Center (CIC). This is dominated by the computer-based AEGIS combat system, which can simultaneously engage in air, surface, and subsurface warfare. Steel bulkheads are located throughout the ship in case a hit is suffered, and vital equipment is also protected by Kevlar shields. An air filtration system helps guard against nuclear, biological, and chemical attack.

Drone warfare
The use of unmanned aerial vehicles (UAVs) for both airstrikes and reconnaissance has revolutionized modern warfare. Here, a US Air Force MQ-1B Predator drone, carrying a Hellfire air-to-surface missile, lands at a secret base in the Persian Gulf in January 2016. Predators have been used to launch airstrikes against ISIS in both Iraq and Syria.

NO PUSH

▷ **Northrop Grumman RQ-4 Global Hawk**

Date 2000 **Origin** US

Engine 3,198 kg (7,050 lb) thrust Allison Rolls-Royce AE3007H turbofan

Top speed 650 km/h (404 mph)

This unmanned surveillance aircraft has state-of-the-art radar and camera gear. Able to survey through sandstorm and cloud, the Global Hawk was extensively used in Iran and Afghanistan.

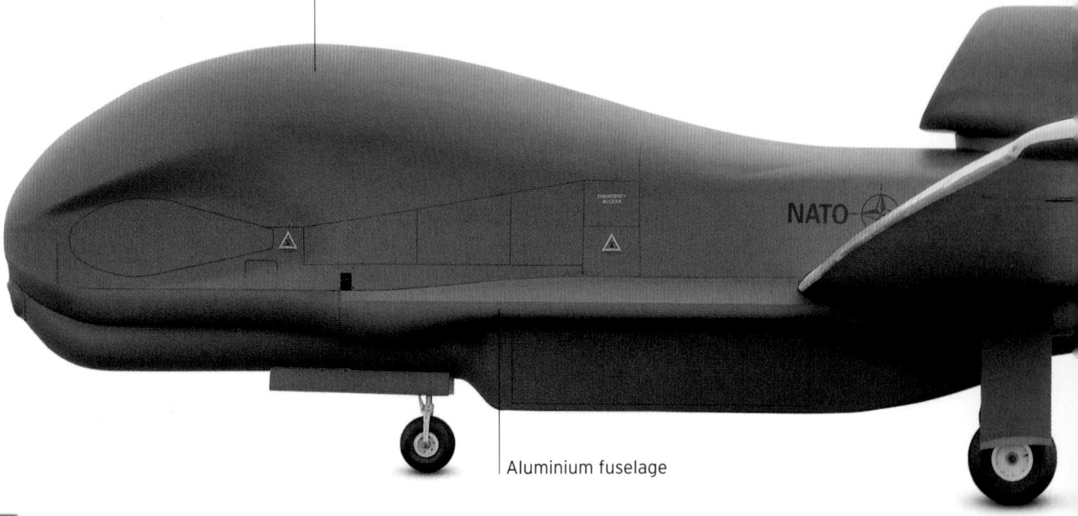

Uses synthetic aperture radar to create two- or three-dimensional images of objects

Aluminium fuselage

Propeller for forward thrust

Twin tail fins

▽ **BAE Systems Mantis**

Date 2009 **Origin** UK

Engine 2 x 380 hp Rolls-Royce M250B-17 turboshaft

Top speed 555 km/h (345 mph)

Built to demonstrate and test Unmanned Autonomous Systems, Mantis has 24-hour endurance, flies itself, and plots its own route. It relays observations to its base station via satellites.

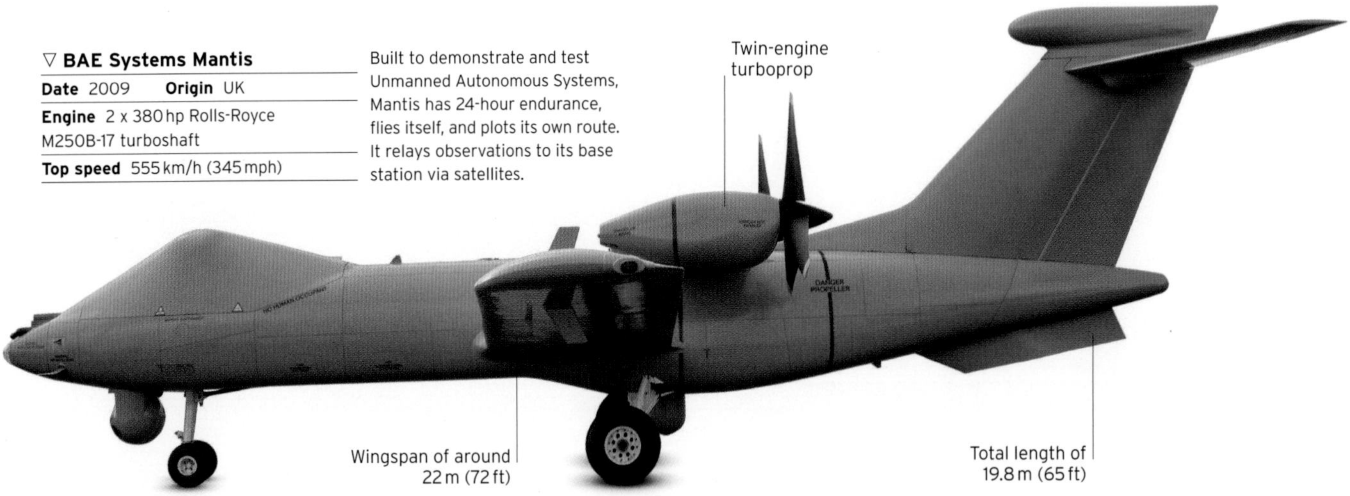

Twin-engine turboprop

Wingspan of around 22 m (72 ft)

Total length of 19.8 m (65 ft)

Unmanned Warfare

Are Unmanned Aerial Vehicles (UAVs), or drones, the future of aerial warfare? Will they slug it out in dogfights, rescue lost troops, or shoot down enemy bombers? Their use for the purposes of observation started in the 1990s with the Predator, and as technology has advanced, some can now carry, and fire, missiles. It is possible for troops and supplies to be carried to the frontline in craft flown only by computers. However, there is still a long way to go before the fighter ace is relegated to the history books.

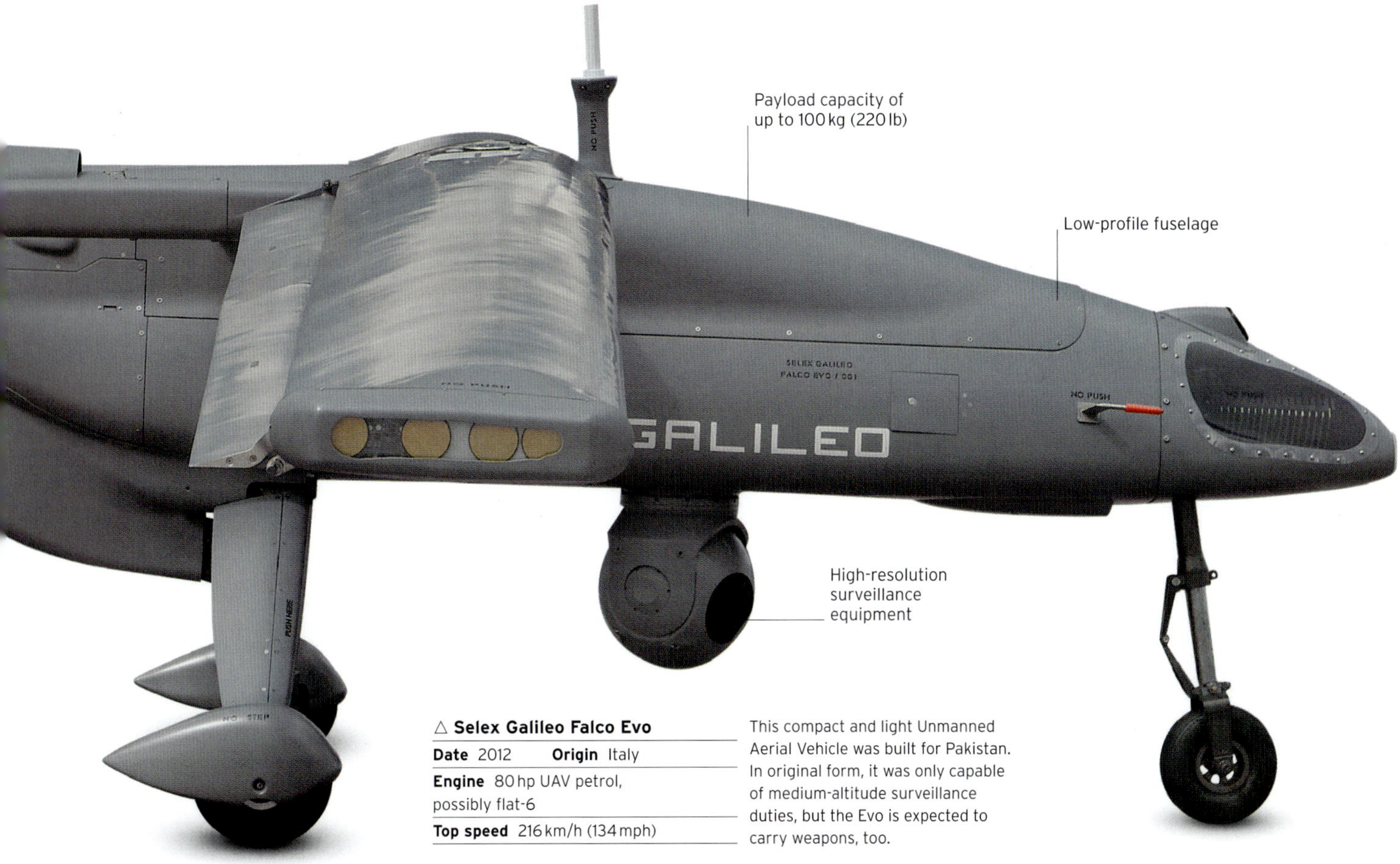

△ Selex Galileo Falco Evo

Date 2012	**Origin** Italy
Engine 80 hp UAV petrol, possibly flat-6	
Top speed 216 km/h (134 mph)	

This compact and light Unmanned Aerial Vehicle was built for Pakistan. In original form, it was only capable of medium-altitude surveillance duties, but the Evo is expected to carry weapons, too.

Index

Note: page numbers in **bold** refer to virtual tours

L

M

NO

P

R

U

V

W

YZ

Acknowledgements

The publisher would like to thank Bharti Bedi, Antara Raghavan, Rupa Rao, Juliet Stanley, and Vatsal Verma for editorial assistance; Gillian Andrews for design assistance; and Jayati Sood for picture research assistance.

Picture credits
The publisher would like to thank the following for their kind permission to reproduce their photographs:

(Key: a-above; b-below/bottom; c-centre; f-far; l-left; r-right; t-top)

2 Dorling Kindersley: Brian Piper / Tanks, Trucks and Firepower Show (t). **2-3 Dorling Kindersley:** Royal International Air Tattoo 2011 (b). **4 Dorling Kindersley:** Fort Nelson (br). **5 Dorling Kindersley:** Shuttleworth Collection (bl); The Tank Museum, Bovington (br). **6 Dorling Kindersley. 7 Dorling Kindersley:** Ukraine State Aviation Museum (bl). **8 Dorling Kindersley:** Paul Rackham (br). **9 Dorling Kindersley:** Ukraine State Aviation Museum (bl). **EAA:** (br). **10-11 Dorling Kindersley:** Board of Trustees of the Royal Armouries. **12 Dorling Kindersley:** Museum of London (ca). **12-13 Dorling Kindersley:** Board of Trustees of the Royal Armouries (b). **13 Dorling Kindersley:** Board of Trustees of the Royal Armouries (cr); Board of Trustees of the Royal Armouries (r). **14 Dorling Kindersley:** Ermine Street Guard (l). **14-15 Dorling Kindersley:** Ermine Street Guard (t). **16 Dorling Kindersley:** Board of Trustees of the Royal Armouries (c). **16-17 Dorling Kindersley:** Board of Trustees of the Royal Armouries (t). **18-19 Dorling Kindersley:** Wallace Collection, London. **18 Dorling Kindersley:** Board of Trustees of the Royal Armouries (bl); Wallace Collection, London (c). **19 Dorling Kindersley:** The Tank Museum (cb); Wallace Collection, London (cl, bl). **20-21 Getty Images:** DEA / A. Dagli Orti. **22-23 Dorling Kindersley:** Board of Trustees of the Royal Armouries (t, c); Royal Armouries, Leeds (b). **23 Dorling Kindersley:** Royal Armouries, Leeds (b). **24-25 Dorling Kindersley:** Fort Nelson. **26 Dorling Kindersley:** Board of Trustees of the Royal Armouries (cb, bc, br, bl); Fort Nelson (ca). **26-27 Dorling Kindersley:** Fort Nelson. **30-31 Dorling Kindersley:** Board of Trustees of the Royal Armouries (t); Board of Trustees of the Royal Armouries (c); Board of Trustees of the Royal Armouries (cb). **30 Dorling Kindersley:** Board of Trustees of the Royal Armouries (b). **31 Dorling Kindersley:** 95th Rifles and Re-enactment Living History (cra). **32-33 Dorling Kindersley:** Board of Trustees of the Royal Armouries. **34-35 Dorling Kindersley:** Board of Trustees of the Royal Armouries. **36-37 Dorling Kindersley:** Board of Trustees of the Royal Armouries. **38-39 Dorling Kindersley:** Board of Trustees of the Royal Armouries. **40-41 Dorling Kindersley:** Board of Trustees of the Royal Armouries (c); The Combined Military Services Museum (CMSM) (t). **41 Dorling Kindersley:** Tank Museum (cb). **42-43 Alamy Stock Photo:** Derek Bayes / Lebrecht Music and Arts Photo Library. **44-45 Dorling Kindersley:** Board of Trustees of the Royal Armouries. **46-47 Dorling Kindersley:** Board of Trustees of the Royal Armouries. **48-49 Dorling Kindersley:** Board of Trustees of the Royal Armouries. **50-51 Dorling Kindersley:** Board of Trustees of the Royal Armouries. **52-53 Dorling Kindersley:** Board of Trustees of the Royal Armouries. **54-55 Dorling Kindersley:** Board of Trustees of the Royal Armouries. **56 Dorling Kindersley:** Fort Nelson. **56-57 Dorling Kindersley:** Tank Museum. **57 Dorling Kindersley:** Fort Nelson (br). **58-59 Dorling Kindersley:** Fort Nelson (b); Royal Artillery, Woolwich (t). **59 Dorling Kindersley:** Fort Nelson. **60-61 Dorling Kindersley:** Fort Nelson. **63 Dorling Kindersley. 66-67 Dorling Kindersley:** Springfield Armory (c). **67 Dorling Kindersley:** Board of Trustees of the Royal Armouries (t); Combined Military Services Museum (CMSM) (b). **68-69 Alamy Stock Photo:** Granger Historical Picture Archive. **70-71 Dorling Kindersley:** Mikasa Preservation Society. **72-73 Dorling Kindersley:** Mikasa Preservation Society. **74-75 Dorling Kindersley:** Musée des blindés, Saumur, France. **76-77 Dorling Kindersley:** Board of Trustees of the Royal Armouries. **78-79 Dorling Kindersley:** Board of Trustees of the Royal Armouries (c); Tank Museum (t). **78 Dorling Kindersley:** Tank Museum (b). **79 Dorling Kindersley:** Board of Trustees of the Royal Armouries (br). **80-81 Dorling Kindersley:** Board of Trustees of the Royal Armouries. **82-83 Dorling Kindersley:** Jean-Pierre Verney (cb). **82 Dorling Kindersley:** Jean-Pierre Verney (t). **84-85 Dorling Kindersley:** Fort Nelson. **84 Dorling Kindersley:** Royal Museum of the Armed Forces and of Military History, Brussels, Belgium. **86-87 Alamy Stock Photo:** Trinity Mirror / Mirrorpix. **88-89 Alamy Stock Photo:** Sunpix Travel (t). **88 Bovington Tank Museum:** (bl). **89 Bovington Tank Museum. 90-91 Dorling Kindersley:** The Tank Museum, Bovington. **92-93 Dorling Kindersley:** The Tank Museum, Bovington. **94-95 Dorling Kindersley:** Tank Museum. **94 Dorling Kindersley:** Tank Museum. **95 Dorling Kindersley:** Musée des blindés, Saumur, France. **96-97 Dorling Kindersley:** Tank Museum. **98-99 Dorling Kindersley:** Musée des blindés, Saumur, France. **100-101 Dorling Kindersley:** Musée des blindés, Saumur, France. **102 Dorling Kindersley:** Royal Airforce Museum, London (b). **102-103 Dorling Kindersley:** Matthew Boddington. **103 Dorling Kindersley:** Royal Airforce Museum, London (b). **104-105 Dorling Kindersley:** Shuttleworth Collection. **105 Dorling Kindersley:** Ukraine State Aviation Museum. **106-107 Dorling Kindersley:** Royal Airforce Museum, London (Hendon). **106 Dorling Kindersley:** Shuttleworth Collection, Bedfordshire (b). **107 Dorling Kindersley:** Brooklands Museum (b). **108-109 Dorling Kindersley:** Shuttleworth Collection. **110-111 Dorling Kindersley:** Shuttleworth Collection. **112-113 Getty Images:** IWM / Contributor. **118-119 Dorling Kindersley:** The Tank Museum, Bovington. **120-121 Dorling Kindersley:** Board of Trustees of the Royal Armouries (t, cb); Combined Military Services Museum (CMSM) (c). **122-123 Dorling Kindersley:** Board of Trustees of the Royal Armouries. **122 Dorling Kindersley:** Board of Trustees of the Royal Armouries (cb). **123 Dorling Kindersley:** Combined Military Services Museum (CMSM). **124-125 Dorling Kindersley:** Board of Trustees of the Royal Armouries. **126-127 Getty Images:** Keystone-France / Contributor. **128-129 Dorling Kindersley:** Combined Military Services Museum (CMSM). **130-131 Dorling Kindersley:** Tank Museum (t); Tank Museum (c). **131 Dorling Kindersley:** Board of Trustees of the Royal Armouries (t); Tank

Museum (b). **132-133 Dorling Kindersley:** Tank Museum. **134-135 Dorling Kindersley:** The Tank Museum. **136 Dorling Kindersley:** The Tank Museum, Bovington. **136-137 Dorling Kindersley:** Tank Museum. **137 Dorling Kindersley:** The Tank Museum, Bovington. **138-139 Dorling Kindersley:** The Tank Museum, Bovington. **140-141 Dorling Kindersley:** The Tank Museum, Bovington. **142-143 Dorling Kindersley:** Gary Ombler / Sarl Salis Aviation. **142 Dorling Kindersley:** Shuttleworth Collection. **144-145 Dorling Kindersley:** Royal Airforce Museum, London (b); Shuttleworth Collection (t). **145 Dorling Kindersley:** Fleet Air Arm Museum. **146 Dorling Kindersley:** Royal Airforce Museum, London. **146-147 Dorling Kindersley:** Gatwick Aviation Museum. **147 Dorling Kindersley:** Yorkshire Air Museum. **148-149 Getty Images:** Walter Bellamy / Stringer. **150-151 Dorling Kindersley:** RAF Museum, Cosford. **150 Dorling Kindersley:** Gatwick Aviation Museum (b). **151 Dorling Kindersley:** Fleet Air Arm Museum. **152-153 Dorling Kindersley:** Paul Rackham. **154-155 Dorling Kindersley:** Sarl Salis Aviation. **156-157 Dorling Kindersley:** Board of Trustees of the Royal Armouries (c); Tank Museum (b); Tank Museum (t). **157 Dorling Kindersley:** Tank Museum (bc). **158-159 Dorling Kindersley:** Combined Military Services Museum (CMSM). **160-161 Dorling Kindersley:** Musée des blindés, Saumur, France. **160 Dorling Kindersley:** Tank Museum. **161 Dorling Kindersley:** Tank Museum. **162 Dorling Kindersley:** Tank Museum (c). **163 123RF.com:** Vitali Burlakou / mrvitkin. **164-165 Dorling Kindersley:** Tank Museum. **166-167 Dorling Kindersley:** The Tank Museum, Bovington. **168-169 Dorling Kindersley:** The Tank Museum, Bovington. **170-171 Dorling Kindersley:** Board of Trustees of the Royal Armouries (c, cb, bl); Combined Military Services Museum (CMSM) (t). **172-173 Rex Shutterstock:** AP. **174-175 Dorling Kindersley:** Gordon McKenna (b); Tank Museum. **174 Dorling Kindersley:** Tank Museum (b). **176-177 Dorling Kindersley:** Tank Museum. **176 Dorling Kindersley:** Tank Museum (cra). **177 Dorling Kindersley:** Musée des blindés, Saumur, France (b); Tank Museum (ca). **178 Dorling Kindersley:** Combined Military Services Museum (CMSM) (b); Fort Nelson (cr). **178-179 Dorling Kindersley:** Fort Nelson. **180 Dorling Kindersley:** Tank Museum (cra). **180-181 Dorling Kindersley:** Tank Museum. **180-182 Dorling Kindersley:** Royal International Air Tattoo 2011 (b). **181 Dorling Kindersley:** Ted Bear / The War and Peace Show (t). **182 Dorling Kindersley:** Tony Corbin / The War and Peace Show (b). **182-183 Dorling Kindersley:** Neill Bruce and Peter Roberts. **183 Dorling Kindersley:** Tank Museum, Bovington (b). **184-185 Dorling Kindersley:** Aces High Ltd, Hangar 6 (c); Gatwick Aviation Museum (b). **186-187 Dorling Kindersley:** Royal Airforce Museum, London (b); Shuttleworth Collection (c). **188-189 Dorling Kindersley:** RAF Battle of Britain Memorial Flight. **190-191 Dorling Kindersley:** RAF Battle of Britain Memorial Flight. **192-193 Dorling Kindersley:** Royal Airforce Museum, London (Hendon) (t); Royal Airforce Museum, London (b). **193 Dorling Kindersley:** Scale Model World, Steve Abbey (ca). **194-195 Dorling Kindersley:** Royal Airforce Museum, London. **196-197 Dorling Kindersley:** Gatwick Aviation Museum. **198 Dorling Kindersley:** Gatwick Aviation Museum. **198-199 Dorling Kindersley:** Lincolnshire Aviation Heritage Centre (t). **199 Dorling Kindersley:** B17 Preservation (cb). **200-201 Dorling Kindersley:** B17 Preservation. **202-203 Dorling Kindersley:** B17 Preservation. **202 Dorling Kindersley. EAA:** (crb). **204-205 Dorling Kindersley:** RAF Museum, Cosford. **206-207 Getty Images:** Hulton Archive / Stringer. **208-209 Dorling Kindersley:** Fleet Air Arm Museum (b); Model Exhibition, Telford (ca). **210-211 Dorling Kindersley:** Fleet Air Arm Museum (ca); Model Exhibition, Telford (b). **212-213 Dorling Kindersley:** Fleet Air Arm Museum (t); Scale Model World (c); Scale Model World, Allan Toyne (b). **214 Dorling Kindersley:** Combined Military Services Museum (CMSM) (tc); Victory Show 2015, Foxlands Farm (b). **214-215 Dorling Kindersley:** Combined Military Services Museum (CMSM) (t). **215 Dorling Kindersley:** Bicycle Museum Of America (b). **216-217 Dorling Kindersley:** Motorcycle Heritage Museum, Westerville, Ohio. **218-219 Dorling Kindersley:** National Motor Museum, Beaulieu. **220-221 Dorling Kindersley:** National Motor Museum, Beaulieu. **222-223 Dorling Kindersley:** Paul Rackham (c). **223 Dorling Kindersley:** Ken Barber (t); Paul Rackham (b). **224-225 Dorling Kindersley:** The Tank Museum, Bovington. **226-227 Dorling Kindersley:** Fleet Air Arm Museum. **228-229 Dorling Kindersley:** Board of Trustees of the Royal Armouries (t); Tank Museum (cb). **229 Dorling Kindersley:** Board of Trustees of the Royal Armouries (ca); Tank Museum (bc). **230-231 Dorling Kindersley:** Tank Museum (t, cb). **231 Dorling Kindersley:** Board of Trustees of the Royal Armouries (b). **232-233 Dorling Kindersley:** Board of Trustees of the Royal Armouries (t); Tank Museum (c). **233 Dorling Kindersley:** Board of Trustees of the Royal Armouries (t). **234-235 Dorling Kindersley:** Board of Trustees of the Royal Armouries (t, b). **234 Dorling Kindersley:** Tank Museum (ca). **236-237 Dorling Kindersley:** Board of Trustees of the Royal Armouries. **238-239 Dorling Kindersley:** Board of Trustees of the Royal Armouries. **240-241 Dorling Kindersley:** Board of Trustees of the Royal Armouries. **242-243 Getty Images:** Bettmann / Contributor. **244-245 Dorling Kindersley:** Board of Trustees of the Royal Armouries. **246-247 Dorling Kindersley:** © The Board of Trustees of the Armouries. **248-249 Dorling Kindersley:** Board of Trustees of the Royal Armouries. **250-251 Dorling Kindersley:** Board of Trustees of the Royal Armouries. **252-253 Dorling Kindersley:** Board of Trustees of the Royal Armouries. **254-255 Dorling Kindersley:** Tank Museum (t). **254 Dorling Kindersley:** The Tank Museum, Bovington. **255 Dorling Kindersley:** Norfolk Tank Museum (b). **256-257 Dorling Kindersley:** The Tank Museum, Bovington. **258-259 Dorling Kindersley:** The Tank Museum, Bovington. **260-261 Dorling Kindersley:** Musée des blindés, Saumur, France (b); Tank Museum (t). **262-263 Dorling Kindersley:** The Tank Museum. **264-265 Dorling Kindersley:** The Tank Museum. **266 Dorling Kindersley:** Musée des blindés, Saumur, France (bc). **266-267 Paul Appleyard:** (t). **Dorling Kindersley:** Musée des blindés, Saumur, France (b). **268-269 Dorling Kindersley:** Brian Piper / Tanks, Trucks and Firepower Show (b); Tanks, Trucks and Firepower Show (t). **269 Dorling Kindersley:** Tanks, Trucks and Firepower

Show (c). **270-271 Dorling Kindersley:** Musée des blindés, Saumur, France (b); Norfolk Tank Museum (tc). **270 Massimo Foti:** (clb). **272 Dorling Kindersley:** The Tank Museum, Bovington (cb). **272-273 Dorling Kindersley:** Musée des blindés, Saumur, France. **274-275 Dorling Kindersley:** Richard Morris / Tanks, Trucks and Firepower Show. **274 Dorling Kindersley:** Tank Museum (cra). **275 Dorling Kindersley:** Richard Morris / Tanks, Trucks and Firepower Show (tc). **276 Dorling Kindersley:** Nick Hurt / Tanks, Trucks and Firepower Show (b). **276-277 Dorling Kindersley:** Musée des blindés, Saumur, France (t); Musée des blindés, Saumur, France (b). **278-279 Dorling Kindersley:** Flugausstellung (t); Ukraine State Aviation Museum (b). **280 Dorling Kindersley:** Royal International Air Tattoo 2011 (c). **282-283 aviationpictures.com:** (t). **Dorling Kindersley:** Pima Air and Space Museum, Tuscon, Arizona (c); Yorkshire Air Museum (b). **284-285 Getty Images:** Eric Bouvet / Contributor. **286-287 Dorling Kindersley:** March Field Air Museum, California. **288-289 Dorling Kindersley:** Imperial War Museum, Duxford (b); Midlands Air Museum (t). **290-291 Alamy Stock Photo:** Stocktrek Images, Inc (b). **Dorling Kindersley:** Fleet Air Arm Museum (t). **292-293 Dorling Kindersley:** Ukraine State Aviation Museum. **294-295 Dorling Kindersley:** Ukraine State Aviation Museum. **296-297 Dorling Kindersley:** Flugausstellung (b); Intrepid Sea, Air and Space Museum, New York (t). **297 Dorling Kindersley:** Flugausstellung (bc). **298-299 Dorling Kindersley:** Pima Air and Space Museum, Tuscon, Arizona (b); Ukraine State Aviation Museum (t). **300-301 Alamy Stock Photo:** Kevin Maskell (t). **Dorling Kindersley:** Model Exhibition, Telford (c). **302-303 Dorling Kindersley:** Fleet Air Arm Museum (c); Fleet Air Arm Museum, Eric Dyke (b). **304-305 Dorling Kindersley:** Fleet Air Arm Museum (b). **SD Model Makers:** (t). **306-307 Dorling Kindersley:** Fleet Air Arm Museum. **310 Dorling Kindersley:** Board of Trustees of the Royal Armouries (t); Royal Armouries, Leeds (b). **312 Dorling Kindersley:** Board of Trustees of the Royal Armouries (t). **313 Dorling Kindersley:** Board of Trustees of the Royal Armouries (t). **314-315 Dorling Kindersley:** Board of Trustees of the Royal Armouries (t); Small Arms School, Warminster (b). **316-317 Getty Images:** Olga Maltseva / Stringer. **318 Dorling Kindersley:** Musée des blindés, Saumur, France (ca). **319 Combat Camera Europe:** (t). **320-321 Image courtesy of General Dynamics Ordnance and Tactical Systems. 321 USAASC:** (tl). **322-323 Fort Benning, GA. 324 Courtesy of U.S. Army:** (bl). **325 Alamy Stock Photo:** Sueddeutsche Zeitung Photo (b). **326-327 Dorling Kindersley:** Royal International Air Tattoo 2011 (t); Yorkshire Air Museum (b). **328-329 Dorling Kindersley:** Royal International Air Tattoo 2011 (b). **330 Dorling Kindersley:** Royal Airforce Museum, London (bl). **330-331 Dorling Kindersley:** Royal International Air Tattoo 2011 (t); Royal Airforce Museum, London (c). **332-333 Dorling Kindersley:** RAF Museum, Cosford (b). **334 Dorling Kindersley:** Royal International Air Tattoo 2011 (t). **334-335 Dorling Kindersley:** Nationaal Luchtvaart Themapark Aviodome (b). **336-337 Getty Images:** The Asahi Shimbun / Contributor. **338-339 Courtesy of U.S. Navy. 342-343 Dorling Kindersley:** Fleet Air Arm Museum. **344-345 Alamy Stock Photo:** Marco McGinty. **348-349 Getty Images:** John Moore / Staff.

All other images © Dorling Kindersley
For further information see:
www.dkimages.com

ON
FLAPS MUST NOT BE
DOWN OR LOWERED
AT SPEEDS ABOVE
120 KTS. I.A.S.
ON
GEN.
WARNING
START
ISOLATE
OXYGEN REGULATOR MARK VIIIA
REF. Nº 6D/124
DELIVERY
OXYGEN
FEET. SUPPLY AVAILABLE
EMPTY
FULL
KNOTS
SAFE
FIRE
ALT
PULL DOWN FOR NIGHT USE
UP
DOWN
CHASSIS
NOSE
UP
NOSE
DOWN
SUPPLY
LB/□
BRAKES
PORT
STARBD
PORT
ON
OFF
COMPASS
ON
OFF